EVOLUTION

and

POETIC BELIEF

EVOLUTION
and
POETIC BELIEF

A Study in Some Victorian
and Modern Writers

By

GEORG ROPPEN

OSLO 1956

OSLO UNIVERSITY PRESS

OXFORD: BASIL BLACKWELL

OSLO STUDIES IN ENGLISH NO. 5

Publications of the British Institute in the University of Oslo

General editors:

Professor Paul Christophersen; Professor Kristian Smidt

Printed on a grant from

The Norwegian Research Council for Science

and the Humanities

Printed in Norway by

A. W. Brøggers Boktrykkeri A/S, Oslo

PREFACE

A CONSIDERABLE MASS of well-informed scholarship has already been devoted to the charting of evolutionary themes in English poets and writers of the last hundred years, and the influence exercised by the idea of evolution upon the literature of that period is no longer a matter of pioneer effort or learned dispute. It would indeed be superfluous to attempt another catalogue of mainly historical and ideological evidence, for such surveys have been provided in more comprehensive studies and in those dealing with individual 'poets of Evolution'.

What still remains to be done, however, is a more direct investigation of the nature and function of the evolutionary themes in writers to whom Lamarck and Darwin revealed new and significant truths about existence. There is a need to determine whether and to what extent these ideas and motifs are expressive of fundamental and coherent attitudes and beliefs. For if they are, it is obvious that they hold important clues, not only to the individual writers, but to the conditions of mind and life in their times.

Naturally, those who first explored this field have not failed to indicate the personal and poetic significance which the idea of evolution receives in the individual writers: the charging of it with religious, metaphysical and moral content; the interaction of its various direct or implicit meanings with emotional needs and impulses underlying the larger structures of their work. Yet, apart from Mr. Curtis Webster's study of Hardy, and various analyses of Meredith, and of Shaw's Life Force religion, this more intimate connexion between idea and belief has been largely ignored. Consequently, there is a tendency to neglect these themes in their contextual relations, and also the genuinely poetic or creative function of the idea itself—a function which can be studied only in the transition from idea to belief, from conceptual framework material to personal and intuitive symbol or vision, expressive of profound emotional attachments. To trace this connexion is the object of the present inquiry.

A word must be said in definition of the term 'poetic belief', since it here obviously embraces a great deal of formally incongruous subject-matter and a complex of meanings, among them some that may seem ambiguous and controversial with regard to the accepted or primary connotations of each term. I have used 'poetic' also of prose-writers like Butler, Shaw and Wells, in an extended sense as describing a process of visionary and imaginative search and creation, and I hope to make it clear, in scanning some of the main themes of this evolutionary literature, that the poets and prose-writers share not only this creative process, independently of their literary forms or techniques, but also certain fundamental impulses and visions.

'Belief' again has been used in a more general sense than that of religious faith, for though we have to deal with convictions and attachments of a predominantly religious character, belief with reference to our writers does not denote exclusively the acceptance of non-observable, sacral truth, nor is it limited to the more definite symbols of such acceptance in cultic practices and systems. The secondary meanings of the term, such as 'outlook', 'opinion' and 'persuasion' will also be relevant to our discussion.

'Poetic belief' in this wider sense denotes, therefore, both a search and its object, a process and the world it creates. Whatever direction this search may take, and whatever forms its object may assume, the psychological urges and impulses informing the writers' belief are generally of a fervent religious nature. Whether the writers draw their symbols and concepts from Christian doctrine and Idealistic cosmology, or from the Positivistic apotheosis of Life and Humanity, we find that they meet on common ground in their effort to discover a moral, and even in a certain sense, a transcendental meaning in existence, in terms of evolutionary direction and accumulated value. It is in this latter aspect that the idea of evolution, as a creative and integrative element, proves to be of such unique and compelling interest. For in their intuitive search for significance and value, which is the distinctive poetic task and recognized by them as such, our writers make of their evolutionary motifs a deeply personal confession, and in so expressing their own condition they interpret the condition of mind in their times. This poetic search is the more important as it coincides with, and to a large extent is provoked by, the anarchy and bewilderment of modern thought. A better understanding of these themes and beliefs should, therefore, not only deepen our comprehension of the individual writers and of their changing background, but of our present problems in literature and in life.

A limitation of our subject has been necessary, and I am fully aware that a selection of writers invites perils of omission and also of undue emphasis on certain aspects to the exclusion of others. There is, too, the constant risk of following what may seem a beaten track. I have chosen our writers partly according to the intrinsic value and importance of their works, partly for the reason that they offer exceptionally telling examples of the interaction of idea with belief and attitude. Moreover, the predominant interest which the idea holds to these, and the frequent recurrence of evolutionary themes in their works, have naturally given them preference over authors in whose writings the idea shows a more intermittent and incidental existence.

A clearer comprehension of these writers should, I hope, provide useful clues to other poets and their works, of such varied range and interest as the harsh and tormented *Testaments* of John Davidson and the academic, serene *Testament of Beauty* of Robert Bridges.

ACKNOWLEDGEMENTS

I wish to express my deep gratitude to Professor A. H. Winsnes, of the University of Oslo, for his generous help, advice and stimulating encouragement throughout. At times, indeed, his kind and critical support seemed a condition of 'survival' for the whole work.

I am also greatly indebted to Professor K. Smidt, of the University of Oslo, for suggesting various improvements in style, and to my friends in England for their invaluable help in checking my English while the work was in progress; in particular to Miss Eithne Parker of Instone Court, Herefordshire, Dr. R. Popperwell of Cambridge, Mrs. J. M. Yeates, and Mr. R. F. Sinclair, of Newcastle upon Tyne.

My thanks are also due to *Norges Almenvitenskapelige Forskningsråd* (The Norwegian Research Council for Science and the Humanities) for their generosity in making the publication of this book possible.

Finally, I would like to acknowledge the kind permission granted by the following publishers to quote copyright material:

Jonathan Cape, Ltd., from Samuel Butler, *The Note-Books*, 1930; *Unconscious Memory*, 1922.
Constable and Company, Ltd., from *The Works of George Meredith* (Mem. ed.), 1910.
Macmillan & Co., Ltd., from *The Works of Thomas Hardy in Prose and Verse*, 1912; *The Dynasts*, 1915; *Collected Poems*, 1928.
John Murray, Ltd., from *The Letters of Robert Browning*, 1933.

ix

Presses Universitaires de France, from Henri Bergson, *L'Evolution Créatrice*, 1948.

The Public Trustee and the Society of Authors, from Bernard Shaw, *Major Critical Essays*, 1948; *Man and Superman*, 1947; *Back to Methuselah*, 1921.

The Executors of H. G. Wells, from *The Sleeper Awakes* and *Men Like Gods*, 1921; *Experiment in Autobiography*, 1934; *Star Begotten*, 1937.

Oslo, 1956.   *G. R.*

CONTENTS

xi

CHAPTER 1

THE BACKGROUND

Evolution and Progress

THE MODERN IDEA OF EVOLUTION, in the formulation which Lamarck and Darwin gave to it, emerged in an age of intense historical preoccupation. In France, since the middle of the eighteenth century, the study of history had been dominated by the idea of Progress, and Turgot, according to Bury, was one of its pioneers: 'He conceives universal history as the progress of the human race advancing as an immense whole steadily, though slowly, through alternating periods of calm and disturbance towards greater perfection.'[1] Voltaire and the Encyclopaedists interpreted history as the triumphant advance of human reason, and Condorcet crowned this intellectual optimism with prophetic promises for the future. Towards the end of the century, the idea of Progress had established itself and penetrated into other fields of thought and research. Thus the analogy of history as a process of change, development and progress was adopted as a useful working hypothesis also by natural science. Erasmus Darwin expounded a theory of progressive organic evolution in *Zoonomia* (1794—98) which anticipated that of Lamarck in the *Philosophie Zoologique* (1808).[2]

[1] J. B. Bury, *The Idea of Progress*, p. 155.
[2] Cf. R. G. Collingwood: 'Modern cosmology could only have arisen from a widespread familiarity with historical studies, and in particular with historical studies of the kind which placed the conception of process, change, development in the centre of their picture and recognized it as the fundamental category of historical thought.' *The Idea of Nature, p. 10.)*

In England, the doctrine of Progress, as a historical and social theory, found in William Godwin its most fervent advocate. His *Political Justice* (1793) reflected the spirit of France with its anarchy and faith in human nature, and Godwin's gospel, though shortlived, fired the younger generation and made converts like Wordsworth, Coleridge and Shelley.[1]

The general propagation and acceptance of the doctrine of Progress in England was furthered, says Bury, by two important factors: the rise of socialism, and the technical and scientific advances which followed in the wake of the Industrial Revolution. Robert Owen preached and practised a gospel of meliorism derived from French revolutionary ideas and the rationalistic belief in the perfectibility of man. Moreover, technical progress was everywhere manifest, and those who reflected on man and society at a time when industrial expansion shook and transformed the social structure could not help feeling that, though the present was dark, the future seemed bright with a promise of wellbeing and happiness.

The eighteenth-century doctrines of Progress were based on abstract speculations on human nature and prevailing social conditions, with emphasis on ethical and humanitarian aspects. They assumed that man, given the right conditions, would be happy and good. The ideal state, the Millennium, might be founded through a drastic alteration of the human environment over a short period. It is this impetuous conquest of the future which characterizes the English radicals of the Godwin circle. The Utilitarians, though inspired by the same master, Condorcet, and fighting for the same ideals, were more cautious in their optimism. To them, the problem of future overpopulation, as analysed by Malthus in his *Essay on the Principle of Population* (1798), presented a serious obstacle to social harmony.

---

[1] Southey's study in moral and social progress, *Sir Thomas More*, or *Colloquies on the Progress of Society* (1829), is a Utopian prophecy in the spirit of Godwin.

Jeremy Bentham, who founded the school, did not hold out any rash promises of the Millennium, though he asserted the need and value of human effort towards a better world.

If the eighteenth century had discovered the idea of Progress, it remained for the nineteenth to give it a formula and a law. Again France headed the search. Early in the century Saint-Simon echoed the optimism of the preceding generation: 'The Golden Age is not behind us, but in front of us. It is the perfection of social order. Our fathers have not seen it; our children will arrive there one day, and it is for us to clear the way for them.' [1] Saint-Simon's law of Progress is that of alternating periods of construction and destruction ('organic' and 'critical'), determined by the advance of human intelligence and knowledge.

Auguste Comte, the pupil and collaborator of Saint-Simon, established sociology as an independent branch of research and built on the idea of Progress a major system of philosophy. His *Cours de Philosophie Positive* (1830—42) is an attempt to deduce a general law of progress from an analysis of the psychological development of man. Like Saint-Simon, he claims that human history has been determined by the growth of opinion and understanding, interacting constantly with material and social environments and modifying these. Mankind has passed through two stages of development, the theological and the metaphysical, and is now embarking on its third, the positive stage. In the positive stage, which corresponds to the Golden Age of Saint-Simon and the Millennium of Condorcet, without their definite goal of happiness, society is organized on scientific principles, and its government as well as its intellectual and moral life is directed and inspired by men of science. Its dominant feature is harmony.

Comte's Positivism was introduced in England by G. H. Lewes and John Stuart Mill. Mill found in it, if not the whole truth, at

[1] From *De la réorganisation de la société européenne* (1814); *op. cit.* Bury, p. 282.

least a stimulating social theory. While rejecting the idea of Progress as an *inevitable* movement of history towards perfection, he agreed that, in general, the course of history supported this view. Mill's *System of Logic* (1843) gave to the idea of Progress a prestige and significance which it had not achieved through lesser prophets like Godwin, Southey or Hamilton.

About mid-century, the intellectual climate in England was saturated with the idea of Progress. In the world of action, it expressed itself in the Great Exhibition of 1851, which was organized not only as a stock-taking of the industrial expansion, but as a demonstration of political and social optimism. This vast international effort pointed to a future of prosperity and peace.

Progress, as a general law of history, was again restated by two important publications in 1857. Buckle's *History of Civilization in England* (vol. 1) popularized the ideas of Comte and Mill and applied them to a familiar scene. Herbert Spencer published in the *Westminster Review* a long article on 'Progress: Its Law and Cause', in which he paralleled the growth of organisms and the development of society. Spencer's association of social progress with biological evolution shows an important interaction of ideas from two distinct fields of inquiry, which had begun with Erasmus Darwin and Lamarck in the eighteenth century and continued, through tentative efforts, to exercise a considerable influence in the nineteenth. Though Lamarck's theory of transmutation of species had been discarded by English naturalists before Charles Darwin, their own alternative, the theory of 'special Creations' and 'Progression', which recognized a perfecting principle in natural process, implied a doctrine of Progress.[1]

---

[1] A. Sedgwick speaks of the 'creative additions' in nature: 'and it is by watching these additions that we get some insight into Nature's true historical progress'. *Discourse on the Studies of the University of Cambridge;* pref. to 5th ed., 1850.

While thus the idea of evolution was stimulated by the analogy of history, it received little aid from the current cosmologies of the eighteenth century, nor was it at any time directly related to, or derived from, their theories of nature. Rather it stood over against them as an outsider and a revolutionary.[1] The philosophers had, since Leibniz, wrestled with Plato's and Aristotle's problem of cosmic process and development, and Leibniz solved it, as well as could be, in terms of the matter-mind dualism, which remained a central aspect also in the neo-Platonist theories of knowledge of the later eighteenth century. Collingwood gives him credit for reaffirming the doctrine of 'final causes' and for having a 'clear conception of development', which he sees as purposive; and moreover:

Leibniz's nature is a vast organism whose parts are lesser organisms, permeated by life and growth and effort, and forming a continuous scale from almost unmitigated mechanism at one end to the highest conscious developments of mental life at the other, with a constant drive or nisus working upwards along the scale.[2]

Yet, to Leibniz, and to the neo-Platonists, this growth is ideal —a *natura naturans*, and not a continuous development of higher life from lower life preceding it in time.

Berkeley and Kant offered in turn their theories of nature as centred in the reality of mind, the universal God-mind which makes

---

[1] R. G. Collingwood sees in the modern theory of evolution the sharp dividing line between modern cosmology and that of the Cartesian dualistic tradition, which even Hegel did not overcome. He stresses the essential difference between the *modus operandi* of development in Platonistic theories of the eighteenth century and those of natural science since Lamarck. Cf. *The Idea of Nature*. H. Fairfield Osborn comments on the curious fact that naturalists of that period same so near to a complete theory of evolution and yet maintained the fixity of species; see *From the Greeks to Darwin*. A. Lovejoy tends to find a more continuous development of the idea from the various conceptions of cosmic evolution, chiefly within the Platonic tradition in philosophy; *The Great Chain of Being*.

[2] *The Idea of Nature*, p. 110.

nature and *thinks* the development which takes place within it. Again, in Hegels cosmology, the concept of change and process is fundamental. To the question of what force drives the process, and what is the relationship between the world of mind, or the Idea, and its externalized, material world, Hegel (in Collingwood's summary) answered that

God is the self-creating and self-subsisting world or organism of pure concepts, and mind is only one, though the highest and most perfect, of the determinations which God acquires in that process of self-creation which is also the process of creating the world.[1]

The process of *becoming* in nature, arising from a necessity in the world of concepts, shows nature as a state of incompleteness which is striving to attain completeness, and hence 'nature is one phase in a real process which is leading on to the existence of mind'.[2] Hence also, nature to Hegel is a scheme of stratified existence where the higher forms of life succeed the lower; but the transition is ideal, not organic or temporal.

Obviously, such a theory of nature would be difficult to translate into terms of natural science. It would mean that Genesis still represented a true picture of Creation, though, as the geological discoveries made clear, it would have to be extended over a period longer than that in the Mosaic account. This position was in fact taken by men of science, geologists and zoologists, before Charles Darwin, with one or two exceptions.

There had been several evolutionary conjectures during the eighteenth century, and notably Maupertuis and Diderot (according to Osborn and Lovejoy) thought it possible that species had developed from a few primordial types, or even from one pair, an archetype. Locke too was conscious of the unity of life:

[1] *Op. cit.,* p. 122.
[2] *Ibid.,* p. 130.

6

In all the visible corporeal world we see no chasms or gaps. All quite down from us the descent is by easy steps, and a continued series that in each remove differ very little one from the other. . . . There are some brutes that seem to have as much reason and knowledge as some that are called men; and the animal and vegetable kingdoms are so nearly joined, that if you will take the lowest of one and the highest of the other, there will scarce be perceived any great difference between them; and so on until we come to the lowest and the most unorganical parts of matter, we shall find everywhere that the several species are linked together, and differ but in almost insensible degrees. And when we consider the infinite power and wisdom of the Maker, we have reason to think, that it is suitable to the magnificent harmony of the universe, and the great design and infinite goodness of the architect, that the species of creatures should also, by gentle degrees, ascend upwards from us towards his infinite perfection, as we see they gradually descend from us downwards.[1]

While Locke here comes very near to the idea of transmutation, it is still the conception of *natura naturans* which underlies the process of development. Yet Locke's argument points to the type of reasoning which enabled the evolutionists to find their solution, for notions like 'archetypal plan', 'chain of being' and 'scale of life' which recur constantly in the eighteenth-century natural philosophy, show an insistence both upon the unity of life and on organic progress, and this insistence on aspects which became integral to the modern theories of evolution, indirectly cleared the way for a purely historical account of biological development. In the same direction pointed Kant's theories of cosmic evolution, and the formulation by Laplace of the Nebular Hypothesis.

Natural science in the eighteenth century, having inherited and elaborated the Renaissance view of the organism as a machine, or automaton, was even more indifferent to the idea of evolution than

---

[1] *Essay Concerning Human Understanding,* ed. A. C. Fraser (1894), vol. ii, p. 67—68).

philosophy. The followers of Newton show in various atomist theories an increasing tendency towards materialism, which, when allied to the mechanical determinism of the Cartesian tradition, produced such ideas about man as those expressed in de la Mettrie's *L'Homme Machine* (1748). The study of plants and animals had, since the days of Linnaeus, become a sterile exercise in description and classification into 'system' and 'order', with emphasis on distinguishing characters, and with little interest in the unity of life as bearing on practical research.[1]

The Testimony of the Rocks

The task with which Lamarck wrestled in his *Philosophie Zoologique* was that of explaining why species, whether plants or animals, in one geological stratum differed from those in the preceding, while showing distinct features of affinity. Had these species not produced identical offspring but actually changed, and if so, what had caused this change? Was nature experimenting like a cattle-breeder to produce new and better types? Had life, like history, progressed in time to realize some distant ideal or to embody some idea? Was this development imposed on life by Divine action, by some aspect in the natural environment, or by an innate tendency or urge in the organism itself?

In answer to these questions Lamarck formulated the first modern theory of evolution, which he later, in the *Histoire Naturelle*,

---

[1] Canon Raven, like Collingwood, stresses the materialist approach of eighteenth-century science, which, 'dominated ... by the categories of physics and chemistry and by inanimate and mechanistic analogies, went far towards destroying all consciousness of the wholeness of nature and of the integrative life of the organism'; *Natural Religion and Christian Theology*, p. 163. In agreement with these authors, D. Dampier-Whetham sees in the evolutionary view of nature a radical departure from materialist science as well as from the cosmologies of Leibniz, Kant, Hegel; *The History of Science*, p. 293.

condensed into his four famous laws: 1) Life by its internal forces tends continually to increase the volume of every body that possesses it, as well as to increase the size of all the parts of the body up to a limit which it brings about. 2) The production of a new organ or part results from a need or want, which continues to be felt, and from the new movement which this need initiates and causes to continue. 3) The development of organs and their force or power of action are always in direct relation to the employment of these organs. 4) All that has been acquired or altered in the organization of individuals during their life is preserved by generation and transmitted to new individuals which proceed from those which have undergone these changes.

To Lamarck, says Haeckel, is due the 'immortal glory of having for the first time worked out the Theory of Descent as an independent scientific theory of the first order, and as the philosophical foundation of a whole science of biology'.[1] Yet recognition came late to him, and his pioneer effort in the cause of evolution soon turned to that of the martyr. His theory might have provided the inspiring working hypothesis the age needed, co-ordinating the rapid advances in all fields of natural science, but for the hostile opposition from his contemporary, Georges Cuvier. The powerful Head of the École des Faits, a protégé of Napoleon, who had founded comparative anatomy and palaeontology, had his own doctrine to defend. Cuvier's 'Catastrophism' explained the changes in fauna and flora from one geological age to another in terms of cataclysmic destructions succeeded by creations of new species.

In England, Lamarck's theory had been in part anticipated by Erasmus Darwin who asserted, in *Zoonomia* (1794), that animals are transformed, through constant exercise, according to their

[1] For this reference I am indebted to H. Fairfield Osborn, *From the Greeks to Darwin*. Osborn sees Lamarck as the most prominent figure in natural science between Aristotle and Darwin.

needs, and the changes thus produced are inherited in the offspring.

Neither Lamarck's ideas, nor those of Erasmus Darwin, made any noticeable impact upon contemporary science or philosophy. In both France and England, Cuvier was the main influence, and decided on the type of work to be carried out for nearly half a century. Geologists, anatomists and palaeontologists accepted Catastrophism and Special Creations and followed Cuvier's advice, moreover, to pursue their patient collection of material and their studies without embarking on hazardous speculation. In England, research in these branches of science was not co-ordinated as in France, and to posterity it appears indeed as a period of trial and error. Criticisms were forthcoming even at the time, such as the article on 'Decline of the State of Science in England', (*The Edinburgh Review,* 1830) directed against the Royal Society. One might blame this 'decline' on individualism and lack of co-operation, but it was chiefly due to the unyielding working hypothesis of Special Creations.[1]

The leading naturalists in England, most of them Cambridge scholars, continued, with few modifications, Cuvier's line of research. They include names like Whewell, Herschel and Henslow. Sedgwick, of Trinity, stated in his address to the Geological Society of London in 1830 that the occurrence and distribution of organic types through the successive strata of the earth 'prove most conclusively the theory of a gradual progressive development of life'. Later he defined his standpoint more in detail:

The elevation of the *Fauna* of successive periods was not therefore made by transmutation, but by creative additions; and it is by watching these additions that we get some insight into Nature's true historical progress .... there was a time when *Cephalopoda* were the

---

[1] Th. Merz, in his apologetic *History of European Thought in the Nineteenth Century,* vol. i, p. 277, adopts the former argument.

highest types of animal life ... the *Primates* of the world ... Fishes next took the lead ... Reptiles next ... Mammals were added next ... and she [Nature] became what she now is, by the addition of Man.[1]

This doctrine of 'Progression' was shared by other Cambridge dons, thus the anatomist Owen. There is in Nature, he maintained, a precognitive organizing principle, which, as in the case of man, 'planned the archetype' and 'foreknew all its modifications'. The history of the globe tells us that

nature has advanced with slow and stately steps, guided by the archetypal light, amidst the wreck of worlds, from the first embodiment of the vertebrate idea under its old ichthyc vestment until it became arrayed in the glorious garb of the human form.[2]

Hugh Miller, the amateur geologist, argued against the idea of mutability of species and invented the term 'Geological Prophecies' to describe the affinity in organic types: fossil forms of one geological age foretell the appearance of higher forms in the next.[3]

These men of science, who ranked as the greatest scholars of their time in England, agreed that in the organic world a unity was present—a chain of being—which could only be described as an architectural plan, upon which the Creator had built the profusion of forms and species, the higher succeeding the lower, so varied and yet conforming to one basic pattern. This plan could be traced back through the 'testimony of the rocks'; it could be observed

[1] *Discourse on the Studies of the University of Cambridge,* pref. to 5th ed., 1850, pp. ccvi—vii.

[2] *On the Nature of Limbs* (1849), p. 85—6. H. Fairfield Osborn, to whom I am indebted for these references, points out that Owen expresses the Aristotelian idea of *nisus* or inner perfecting principle in nature.

[3] *The Testimony of the Rocks,* (1857).

n the phases of growth in the human embryo, each one reflecting corresponding stages in the biological ascent. Charles Lyell, the eminent geologist, states in his great and representative survey of research, *The Geological Evidence of the Antiquity of Man* (1863), that the doctrine of 'Progression' was 'embraced with eagerness' from the close of the eighteenth century up to the time when he wrote *Principles of Geology* (1830).[1] Most of the progressionists worked out their theories in conscious opposition to the idea of evolution: Lamarck's formidable ghost haunted them yet.[2] Lyell in his *Principles of Geology* gave a damaging critique of Lamarck's ideas, as well as of Cuvier's Catastrophism, so that, from 1830, the days of Cuvier's authority in England were numbered. The theory of Uniformity, or continuous geological process, which Lyell offered as an alternative, had been pioneered in England by Hutton (*Theories of the Earth,* 1785) and by William Smith some thirty years earlier. Now Lyell placed it on a broader basis of fossil evidence and observation of physical changes slowly but continually taking place on the surface of the earth. This process of change was sufficient, Lyell maintained, to explain fossil distribution, though the extinction of species and the emergence of new ones would remain a mystery, due to a causation 'quite beyond our comprehension'. And ultimately he too, like Cuvier, upholds special creation against evolution; how otherwise should one account for the appearance of man:

We may easily conceive that there was a considerable departure from the succession of phenomena previously exhibited in the

[1] *Op. cit.,* p. 445.

[2] Herschel, in *On the Study of Natural Philosophy* (1831), shows a tendency to prefer natural law or 'secondary causes' to the direct intervention of the Creator (p. 37), though in his comment on the geological strata and changing species (p. 283), and the 'fossil remains of a former state of creation' (p. 344), he is in complete agreement with his contemporaries. His caution concerning the Catastrophe theory (p. 285) shows that Cuvier was losing his hold in England.

organic world, when so new and extraordinary a circumstance arose, as the union for the first time, of moral and intellectual faculties capable of indefinite improvement, with the animal nature.[1]

While in France Lamarck's theory was gradually eclipsed by Cuvier, and shows a steady decline through the subsequent efforts of Geoffroy St. Hilaire and of his son Isidore, there was none among the outstanding English scholars who attempted to give it a justification. They remained, for about half a century, faithful to their specific formula of compromise, 'Special Creations' and 'Progression', and adapted it well to the intellectual climate of the country. Their refusal to strike out on a more radical line of inquiry was partly due to orthodox scruples, partly to a dislike of deductive speculation. In fact, their attitude is, to begin with at least, agnostic rather than apologetic. Meanwhile, their patient research constantly added new detail to the records of geology, palaeontology, comparative anatomy and histology. It was an age of scientific exploration of fauna and flora in far-off regions, which often produced striking evidence against the fixed systems and natural orders established by Linnaeus and his school. Gradually, the time-perspective receded, and revealed a planet older than anyone had thought possible. Gradually, too, it became evident that man had lived on earth, not six thousand years, nor four thousand and four, as one divine had calculated, but probably for more than a hundred thousand years.[2]

[1] *Principles of Geology* (10th ed.), vol. i, p. 157.
[2] The paleolithic flint implements found near Amiens in 1847, and similar discoveries of the same period, brought about a revision of theories concerning the age of the human race. Lartet thought it possible that man had existed in Tertiary times; his find in 1845 of the fossil remains of an anthropoid ape conduced to unsettle the traditional calculations.

The *Origin of Species*

The frozen motion of nature began to dissolve, almost imperceptibly at first, then slowly gathering speed, until the static world of Cuvier had been swept away by the rush and surge of Darwin's theory. From several directions converged the ideas which, directly or indirectly, pointed to this event. Thus Lyell's *Principles of Geology* revealed a panorama of slow change. In Germany, one of the founders of modern embryology, Meckel, stated the theory of 'Recapitulation', which described the development of the human foetus as a repetition of all organic growth, from the lowest to the highest organisms, reflecting, at each stage, some main type or species, (1811). Von Baer continued this line of argument and approached even closer to a general theory of evolution:

Only in a very childish view of Nature could species be regarded as permanent and unchangeable types, (and that, in fact,) they can be only passing series of generations, which have developed by transmission from the common original form.[1]

In England, the theory of evolution broke to the surface only once during the first half-century. The anonymous publication, in 1844, of the *Vestiges of the Natural History of Creation* had a *succés de scandale,* and the author, later known to be Robert Chambers, ˋnever acknowledged the authorship. Since it was a survey of research and of various evolutionary theories, compiled by an amateur, few scholars condescended to take it seriously, and most of those who did, rallied to the aid of theologians who gave free vent to their indignation. It was thus characterized in the *North British Review:* 'Prophetic of infidel times, and indicating

---

[1] Lecture on 'The Most General Laws of Nature in all Development', 1834. Quoted from Osborn, *From the Greeks to Darwin.* According to Osborn, Von Baer's work became known in England through T. H. Huxley's translation. Spencer was familiar with it.

14

the unsoundness of our general education, the *Vestiges* has started into public favour with a fair chance of poisoning the fountains of science, and sapping the foundations of religion'. The public favour was such that ten editions were called for during the ensuing nine years. For the work appealed to the popular imagination, and with its simple treatment and persuasive tone it offered an attractive heresy which might be toyed with where intellectuals met. The author had done his utmost, however, to blunt its inherent challenge to orthodoxy, notably in his insistence upon a Divine creative principle:

We have seen powerful evidence that the construction of this globe and its associates ... was the result, not of any immediate or personal exertion on the part of the Deity, but of natural laws which are the expressions of His will. What is to hinder our supposing that the organic creation is also a result of natural laws, which are in like manner an expression of His will?[1]

In his apologetic effort to show that the transmutation of species does not reduce the dignity of man, the author refers to the recapitulation theory in embryology:

The very faintest notion of there being anything ridiculous or degrading in the theory . . . how absurd does it appear, when we remember that every individual amongst us, actually passes through the stages of the insect, the fish, the reptile (to speak nothing of others) before he is permitted to breathe the breath of life.[2]

Of the various evolutionary theories, the author prefers the argument of the direct action of environment, which Buffon had indicated, to Lamarck's factor of need and striving. Later, in the tenth edition, he combines Buffon's idea with the Aristotelian perfecting principle, or *nisus*, in a teleological outlook.

[1] *Op. cit.*, 1844 ed., ch. 12. [2] *Ibid.*, p. 233.

To the scholars, *Vestiges* contained nothing more than theories already known and rejected. Yet Lyell liked it for its 'clear attractive style', and considered, years later, that it had paved the way, along with his own *Principles of Geology*, for Darwin's epoch-making work of 1859.[1] Darwin himself pays tribute to the book in his *Historical Sketch*, for having done 'excellent service in this country in calling attention to the subject, in removing prejudice, and in thus preparing the ground for the reception of analogous views'. T. H. Huxley mentions it only casually in his contribution to Darwin's *Life and Letters*.[2] Huxley's attitude at that time concerning evolution was, as he claims, generally shared:

I imagine that most of those of my contemporaries who thought seriously about the matter were very much in my own state of mind—inclined to say to both Mosaists and Evolutionists: "A plague on both your houses!" and disposed to turn aside from an interminable and apparently fruitless discussion to labour in the fertile fields of ascertainable fact'.

Of Huxley's contemporaries there was only one evolutionist whose 'knowledge and capacity compelled respect'—Herbert Spencer, who at the time when Huxley first met him (1852), published his eloquent defence of evolution, 'The Development Hypothesis' in *The Leader*. One more expert voice came out in vindication of the idea before 1859; this was Alfred Russel Wallace, the zoologist, in an article: 'On the Law which has regulated the Introduction of New Species' (1855), which, however, passed unnoticed.

To the scholarly *élite*, indifferent if not hostile, and to the educated public recently stirred to interest in the problem of creation or evolution?—came the publication in 1859 of Darwin's *Origin of Species*. The work had been anticipated in the previous year by two papers to the Linnaean Society, (printed in the *Journal of the*

---

[1] Cf. *The Antiquity of Man*, 4th ed., p. 454.
[2] 'On the Reception of the *Origin of Species.*'

16

Linnaean Society, June 30th), the one by Darwin, the other by Wallace.[1] Both dealt with transmutation of species and showed a surprisingly analogous line of thought.

In Darwin's *Autobiography* (1876) there is a chapter on the development of his views concerning transmutation. Up to 1831, when he set out on the cruise in the 'Beagle', he was convinced of the permanence of species, and the reading of Lyell's *Principles of Geology* on the voyage confirmed his opinion. On the other hand, Lyell's world was one of natural causes and forces constantly changing the geographical environment, a world very different from that described by Cuvier. Now Darwin allowed his discoveries to speak their own impartial language:

During the voyage of the *Beagle* I had been deeply impressed by discovering in the Pampean formation great fossil animals covered with armour like that on the existing armadillos; secondly, by the manner in which closely allied animals replace one another in proceeding southwards over the Continent; and thirdly, by the South American character of most of the productions of the Galapagos archipelago, and more especially by the manner in which they differ slightly on each island of the group; none of the islands appearing to be very ancient in a geological sense.

It was evident that such facts as these, as well as many others, could only be explained on the supposition that species gradually become modified; and the subject haunted me. But it was equally evident that neither the action of the surrounding conditions, nor the will of the organisms (especially in the case of plants) could account for the innumerable cases in which organisms of every kind are beautifully adapted to their habits of life—for instance, a woodpecker or a tree-frog to climb trees, or a seed for dispersal by hooks or plumes. I had always been much struck by such adaptations, and until these could be explained it seemed to me almost useless to endeavour to prove by indirect evidence that species have been modified.[2]

[1] See Osborn's account of the strange coincidence of the discovery of the principle of natural selection by Darwin and Wallace.

[2] *Autobiography*, ch. II.

2

Back in England, Darwin continued his research with a patience and thoroughness that have become legendary, and he accumulated, 'on true Baconian principles', a wealth of material in botany, zoology, and concerning the selective breeding of domestic animals. But he still lacked the working hypothesis, the shaft of light, which he needed to arrange this vast mass of fragments into a significant whole. Then, in 1838, he read by pure chance Malthus' *Essay on Population,* and was struck by its doctrine of overcrowding: organisms tend to multiply in a geometrical ratio, while their means of subsistence increases only in a mathematical ratio, which produces the 'struggle for existence'. In this struggle the most enduring —the fittest type—will necessarily survive. Here was the formula which, when applied to nature as a whole, would explain the survival, or natural selection, of certain new species and variations, and the extinction of others. To Darwin, who had been acutely aware of this struggle in nature, the idea came indeed as a shaft of light. And twenty years later, by a curious coincidence, the same work by Malthus suggested to Wallace his almost identical theory of evolution.

The new working hypothesis proved a useful instrument. Gradually, it brought order and structure to the many data of observation, and by 1844 the substance of *Origin of Species* was complete. In that year Darwin writes to Hooker: 'I am almost convinced (quite contrary to the opinion I started with) that species are not (it is like confessing a murder) immutable.'[1] His forebodings were great: almost against his own will he found himself a defender of the lost cause of evolution, an intellectual heir of his grandfather, perhaps an outcast like Lamarck. In this uneasy situation he began reading widely in evolutionary literature—Buffon, Lamarck, St. Hilaire, De Candolle, and others, to see how far he agreed with or differed from the pioneers in this field.

[1] Quoted from *Life of Charles Darwin,* by Francis Darwin, (1902 ed.), p. 174.

Unlike Aristotle among the ancients, and Lamarck among the moderns, Darwin maintained a strictly agnostic attitude to the ultimate *causes* of variations. He equally rejected Aristotle's 'inner perfecting principle' and Lamarck's second law, viz. the tendency in organisms to vary according to need or want: 'Heaven forfend me from Lamarck nonsense of a 'tendency to progression', 'adaptations from the slow willing of animals', etc!'[1] Yet he admits that his conclusions are not very different from those of Lamarck, 'though the means of change are wholly so'. The problem of teleology or pure chance in organic development continued to haunt his mind, both before the publication of *Origin* and after. The world as a whole, he reflected, cannot conceivably be the outcome of chance, yet it seemed equally impossible to explain individual beings or types as products of planning or design.[2] He ventures the conclusion that 'designed laws' have been at work shaping the larger aspects of the world, while the details have been left to chance. It is with greater confidence that Darwin defines his own views on the factors which have been important in the preservation of species. The competitive drama of life was to him the final reality, and in this drama there was no place for the weak. The fittest would triumph, be the advantage it possessed only a minor variation from the type. Nature's own choice was an ineluctable law in the organic world: 'I believe', Darwin wrote to Lyell in 1859, 'Natural Selection will account for the production of every vertebrate animal'. In the *Origin,* however, the tone is less dogmatic[3]. Gradually, his theory grew more comprehensive and flexible, and by 1862 it included also the direct action of environment, which Buffon had considered the most important force. Again, in the light of new discoveries, Darwin accepted Lamarck's factor (4th law) of the inheritance of characters

---

[1] Letter to Hooker, *ibid.*
[2] Cf. letter to Asa Gray, *Ibid.,* p. 63; cf. also p. 57.
[3] Cf. Conclusion (1860 ed.) p. 490: 'These laws ....'

acquired through use or disuse. Thus, after a remarkably cautious and honest growth of opinion, Darwin arrived in 1872 at the final formulation of his evolutionary theory. He writes on the transmutation of species:

This has been effected chiefly through the natural selection of numerous successive slight, favourable variations; aided in an important manner by the inherited effects of the use and disuse of parts; and in an unimportant manner, that is in relation to adaptive structures, whether past or present, by the direct action of external conditions, and by variations which seem to us in our ignorance to arise spontaneously.[1]

Origin of Species had been writing since 1844, but Darwin did not commit the manuscript to publication till 1859. It sold to the last copy the day it appeared on the counters.[2] For some time Darwin had tried to forestall the shock of adverse critique, which he was certain would come, by appealing to the judgement of his friends. Lyell had already encouraged him to publish, and though he hesitated to make a final statement, his admiration for Darwin's work was great. Even before the first reviews were out, T. H. Huxley declared his allegiance:

I trust you will not allow yourself to be in any way disgusted or annoyed by the considerable abuse and misrepresentation which, unless I greatly mistake, is in store for you. Depend upon it you have earned the lasting gratitude of all thoughtful men. And as to the curs which will bark and yelp, you must recollect that some of your friends, at any rate, are endowed with an amount of combativeness which...may stand you in good stead.

I am sharpening up my claws and beak in readiness.[3]

From the beginning, Huxley was by far the most enthusiastic convert, and when he years later wrote 'On the Reception of the *Origin*

[1] *Origin*, corr. copyright ed. (1910), p. 395.
[2] 24th Nov., 1250 copies. Second ed. Jan. 1860, 3000 copies.
[3] *Life*, p. 214.

of Species', he characterized the effect of the work as a 'flash of light' and its theory so self-evident that he said to himself: 'How extremely stupid not to have thought of that.' Huxley's letter came as a fiery encouragement on the eve of the battle, and Darwin, who dreaded public controversy and knew himself to be ill-equipped for it, replied: 'I am now contented, and can sing my "nunc dimittis."'[1]

A few days later Sedgwick wrote to him from Cambridge:

I have read your book with more pain than pleasure. Parts of it I admired greatly, parts I laughed at till my sides were almost sore; other parts I read with absolute sorrow, because I think them utterly false and grievously mischievous. You have *deserted*...the true method of induction... As to your grand principle—*natural selection*—what is it but a secondary consequence of supposed, or known, primary facts? Development is a better word, because more close to the cause of the fact? For you do not deny causation. I call (in the abstract) causation the will of God; and I can prove that He acts for the good of His creatures. He also acts by laws which we can study and comprehend. Acting by law, and under what is called final causes, comprehends, I think, your whole principle.[2]

This outspoken criticism from an old friend of Darwin epitomized the general tone and argument of the press reviews. Except for Huxley's eulogy in the *Times*, the treatment of the book was unsparing. Sedgwick came out in open polemic in the *Spectator*, according to Darwin 'savagely and unfairly'.[3] The most fierce onslaught appeared in the *Edinburgh Review* (April 1860), yet Darwin, though he was grieved at its spite and feared it would do great harm, decided to hold his peace. The author was the Cambridge anatomist Owen, and his hostility irritated Darwin's circle both because of his face-to-face evasiveness, and because he had held views very close to a theory of evolution.[4] Apart from Henslow, Darwin's old tutor, Cambridge was unanimous in its condemnation.

---

[1] *Ibid.*, p. 214. [2] *Ibid.*, pp. 216—17. [3] *Ibid.*, p. 231.
[4] Cf. *supra*, p. 11.

The Philosophical Society found no excuse for it, and when Darwin heard of the stormy meeting provoked by his work, he wrote to Hooker: 'I am got case-hardened. As for the old fogies in Cambridge, it really signifies nothing. I look at their attacks as a proof that our work is worth the doing.'[1]

Late in 1860, after a year of polemic and ridicule, Darwin's theory was still a challenge, though its weak points had been revealed *ad nauseam*. And the battle continued, in its desultory fashion —a battle between 'ignorant armies'—since the crucial problem, that of causation, could be solved by neither. If any strategic gains were made, they were on Darwin's side, for a modest number of naturalists had been won over.[2] Besides, Darwin's European fame was spreading quickly in that year: already the first translations were called for in Germany and Holland, to be followed, in 1861, by one in French.

The Missing Link[3]

In *Fraser's Magazine* for July 1860 a Cambridge-man, Hopkins, reviewed the *Origin* in terms which expressed the perplexities of a generation to come. If we assume, he says, that there has been a

continuous variation of all organic forms from the lowest to the highest, including man as the last link in the chain of being, there must have been a transition from the instincts of the brute to the noble mind of Man; and in that case, where are the missing links, and at what point of his progressive improvement did man acquire the spiritual part of his being and become endowed with the awful attribute of immortality?

[1] *Ibid.*, p. 234.
[2] Darwin's memorandum to Hooker, March 1860, gives as converts, Lyell, Huxley, Hooker, Ramsay, H. D. Rogers, H. C. Watson and some more—16 in all. Cf. *Life*, p. 230.
[3] Darwin had played this objection: the imperfection of the geological record, into the hands of his critics in *Origin*, 1st ed., p. 463.

The missing link became the dominant theme of evolutionary discussion and a stumbling block to shatter Darwin's theory. The author of *Origin* had committed himself on this issue since, in the earlier formulations of his views, he maintained the dogma *Natura non facit saltum.*[1] With fossil material still fragmentary and ambiguous, the mutability theory had not yet passed its hypothetical phase.

On the controversial scene which opened on this topic it is interesting to watch the movements of Lyell who, though he had not yet accepted transmutation in so many words, vividly reflects the process of intellectual readjustment of his younger contemporaries. In the *Antiquity of Man* he maintains that the 'doctrine of Progression is not gainsaid', despite the new situation in the biological field: it is an 'indispensable hypothesis' which may see great modifications in the future, but 'will never be overthrown'.[2] Yet Lyell does not quarrel with Darwin's principle of 'natural selection', nor is he dismayed by the gaps in fossil evidence. These, he says, were inevitable, considering the many forces of destruction operating in successive geological ages. Besides, there is a steady accumulation of proofs, and with the growing co-operation in the natural sciences in many countries Lyell feels confident that the discoveries of missing links will become more frequent.[3] It is when dealing with the enigma of ultimate *cause* in the progression (or evolution) of species that Lyell, a figure of transition and compromise, points to a solution so widely shared by people from both camps in the future: The process in Nature is governed by secondary causes which it has pleased the Author of Nature to establish. Factors like 'variation' and 'natural selection' are merely 'subordinate agencies' to that higher creational law which is the Divine Principle.[4] This was a conviction which Lyell never abandoned, and on which there was no infringement

[1] Abandoned in the 6th ed. (1872).   [2] *Op. cit.,* 4th ed., p. 451.
[3] *Ibid.,* p. 486.   [4] *Ibid.,* p. 470.

when he, in the tenth edition of *Principles of Geology* (1867—68), made public his acceptance of Darwin's theory. Lyell's intellectual integrity and his open mind made a profound impression on his contemporaries, and with his enormous prestige he bridged two phases of biological thought, by assimilating to his doctrine of Progression that of transmutation of species in a teleological concept of evolution. Moreover, he demonstrated that, in the metaphysical implications of the clash between theories old and new, it was possible to match Darwin's cautious agnosticism with an attitude of a strongly theistic cast.

The crux of the scholarly debate remained, at heart, the position of man in the chain of being, involving the complex problem of his descent and his relationship to the animal orders, and, ultimately, the reality of his soul and immortality. Under the advance of palaeontology and comparative anatomy the traditional systems of classification were breaking down, and archeological finds added greatly to the supposed age of the human race. Darwin's theory drew strength from these discoveries, since it needed vast periods of time, and a more complete fossil record for its sanction.

Still, there remained the argument of the structural difference of the human brain, and its superiority over that of anthropoid apes. Owen declared that the brain of the gorilla was more akin to that of the lower Quadrumana than to the brain of man.[1] Huxley rose with his habitual vigour to this challenge, and dealt with it in a series of lectures which he later published as *Man's Place in Nature* (1863). Here he examined in detail the various controversial aspects of the missing link and tried to clarify the meaning and importance of gaps found in the development of species. These gaps appear everywhere, between various animal species, and between apes and

---

[1] *Athenæum*, July 1860. Owen argued the absence of the 'Hippocampus minor' in the brain of the ape in support of his thesis, but was disproved on this point by Huxley, *Natural History Review* (1861).

monkeys, no less than between ape and man. Yet, Huxley claimed, it would be absurd to conclude against evolution on this purely negative evidence. In cerebral structure, man is more closely related to the gorilla than this is to the lower types of monkeys, hence the argument against mental continuity from animal to man is as futile as that against physical continuity.

Both these works — the strictly objective *Antiquity of Man* and the aggressive *Man's Place in Nature*—added greatly to the *odium theologicum* between the two opposed parties. Lyell's 'object', said the reviewers, was to make man old, that of Huxley to degrade him.[1] Yet on the issue of man there was a split in the evolutionist camp, too. Both Lyell and Wallace maintained for man a principle of double causation: Natural Selection accounted only for his physical nature, while his spiritual being could only have its origin 'in the unseen universe of Spirit'. This was the position held by a younger evolutionist, Mivart, who stood forth as the first important representative of a neo-Lamarckian reaction to the theory of Natural Selection. Mivart's *Genesis of Species* (1871) was planned both as a refutation of Darwin's law as the chief cause of transmutation, and as an argument in the discussion of man and the missing link, launched from a very definite religious (Catholic) angle. Mivart's controversial skill was hailed by the supporters of Special Creations, and Darwin, who was tired and ill, wrote to Wallace: 'I feel very doubtful how far I shall succeed in answering Mivart, it is so difficult to answer objections to doubtful points, and make the discussion readable'.[2]

Since 1867 Darwin had been at work on his own contribution to the discussion of man's place in Nature—the *Descent of Man*—which, owing to ill health and his usual caution, he did not publish

---

[1] *Athenæum*, March 1863.

[2] *Life*, p. 276.

till 1871. It is stamped by a more explicit agnosticism than his
previous work, and, as expected, his conclusion came as a corollary
to the theory of *Origin:*

The great principle of Evolution stands up clear and firm . . . We
are forced to admit that the close resemblance of the embryo of
man to that, for instance, of a dog—the construction of his skull,
limbs and whole frame—all point in the plainest manner to the
conclusion that man is the co-descendant with other mammals of a
common progenitor.[1]

The *Descent of Man* was, on the whole, better received than its
precursor. Darwin was grateful that there was so little abuse in the
press, and many reviews were even highly favourable.[2] In the
Saturday Review, the critic pointed to the increased 'phalanx of
names full of distinction and promise' which now supported
Darwin's theory. Huxley made a similar comment in *Contemporary
Review,* stating that

'in a dozen years the *Origin of Species* has worked as complete a
revolution in Biological Science as the *Principia* did in Astronomy
. . . The mixture of ignorance and insolence which at first
characterized a large proportion of the attacks with which he was
assailed, is no longer the sad distinction of anti-Darwinian criticism'.

It was obvious, after these twelve years of embittered controversy,
that Darwin's theory, in some form or other, had come to stay.
Among the younger generation the turn of tide was felt most
strongly, and already in 1863 Charles Kingsley wrote to his friend
F. D. Maurice: 'Darwin is conquering everywhere, and rushing in
like a flood, by the mere force of truth and fact'.[3]

---

[1] *Op. cit.,* vol. II, p. 385.
[2] The *Edinburgh Review* commented: 'On every side it is raising a
storm of mingled wrath, wonder and admiration'.—There were adverse
critiques in the *Athenæum* and the *Times.*
[3] *Op. cit., Life of Darwin,* p. 253.

Yet, the discussion of man's place in Nature and the missing link continued, in terms that revealed, at times very acutely, an emotional aversion or a religious concern. Ultimately, for the naturalists, as for the layman and the clergy, it was a battle for man's soul: man as a spiritual being and immortal.

Ape or Angel?

The terminology of Natural Science in England during the first half of the nineteenth century is a language of compromise, in which the tenets of Christian dogma are respected and a harmony between revelation and scientific fact is maintained in spite of the contradictions inherent in the growth of knowledge. Such theories of organic development as 'Catastrophism', 'Special Creations' and 'Progression' represent a process of adjustment and demarcation between two bodies of doctrine, of which the one remained static while the other grew and altered day by day. Occasionally, as when Lyell expounded his Uniformitarian theory in *Principles of Geology*, there was a cry of heresy, yet Lyell acknowledged a Divine principle as the primary cause in Creation, and halted reverently on the border of the unknown. Again, the vigilance of orthodoxy made itself felt on the publication of *Vestiges of Creation*, since here, in spite of many concessions to dogma, there was a wide departure from the biblical Genesis. On the whole, however, peace reigned between religion and science. In organic development, which all naturalists agreed had taken place, 'Creation' continued to denote the mysterious and supranatural emergence of higher forms of life.[1] Hugh Miller wrote a work on *Footprints of the Creator* (1847); J. Herschel spoke of the 'Divine Author of the Universe'; Whewell

---

[1] Cf. letter from Sedgwick to Darwin, Nov. 1859: 'We all admit development as a fact of history: but how came it about?' Above he declared: 'I call . . . causation the will of God'; *Life of Darwin*, p. 217.

of God as the 'Author and Governor of the Universe'; and Lyell of the 'Author of Nature'.

The *Origin of Species* shattered this harmony. It was perhaps inevitable since the thesis it erected on its solid mass of facts differed so widely from established scientific doctrine and implicitly contradicted the principle of Divine Providence in Creation. Not since Copernicus displaced the earth from the centre of the universe had scientific theory so threatened the convictions and beliefs through which man saw himself, the Universe, and God. The Cartesian dualistic doctrine of mind and matter was yielding to a theory of life as a force or impulse, linking matter and mind in a mysterious union and yet different from both. This reorientation was of little consequence to the remoter moral and metaphysical implications as long as the various forms of life, the orders or species, were conceived as fixed and invariable, reproducing the same type as far back as their pedigree could be traced. To accept the mutability of species was to endow the life-impulse with an autonomous creative power, working through the medium of matter and adapting itself incessantly to prevailing conditions, and producing, at the summit of its achievement, the self-conscious human mind, in the same manner as it had once produced the horse's hoof or the ape's finger. If Darwin's theory was sound, there appeared to be no inevitable link between the process of evolving nature and the immortal soul of man, unless it could be established that man had a double origin, a material as well as spiritual. This, clearly, would remain a matter of belief, and to adopt such an explanation would mean to transfer the discussion from the field of biology altogether, and the supporters of Christian dogma were not prepared to do so as long as they thought the challenge could be met in open contest. From the very beginning the Church leaders decided that on this issue there could be no truce or compromise. It was not a question of defending dogma for the sake of Church prestige, but a struggle of life and death for the central truths on which Christian faith rested: Sin, Redemption and Immortality. Behind the seemingly pedantic and inquisitional antagonism there is a very real horror of an absurd, mechanical universe emerging with logical force from the new theory, and governed by the meaningless law of Natural Selection.

Darwin anticipated this reaction when he wrote to Lyell before the publication of *Origin:* 'Would you advise me to tell Murray that my book is not more *un*-orthodox than the subject makes inevitable. That I do not discuss the origin of man. That I do not bring in any discussion about Genesis, & c.'.[1] More than the scholarly controversy, Darwin dreaded the repercussions in orthodox circles. It was different with Huxley, who rejoiced in the intellectual drama which was being played out against the background of evolution:

The general mind is seething strangely, and to those who watch the signs of the times it seems plain that this nineteenth century will see revolutions of thought and practice as great as those which the sixteenth witnessed.[2]

Instead of biding their time while the naturalists contested the various technical and scientific aspects of transmutation by natural selection, and hoping that Darwin might be defeated on his own ground, Church leaders and the clergy in general began their crusade. From the outset, Bishop Wilberforce was an active combatant, and still undaunted after his unfortunate effort at the legendary 'battle of Oxford' in June 1860, he brought a more damaging critique of *Origin* in the *Quarterly Review* for July. The article, according to Darwin, was 'uncommonly clever . . . it picks out with skill all the conjectural parts, and brings forward well all

[1] *Life,* p. 197.
[2] Lecture to the Royal Institution, Febr. 1860.

the difficulties'.[1] The author appealed to Lyell to help in bringing Darwin back to reason, so that this 'flimsy speculation may be as completely put down as was what in spite of all denials we must call its twin though less instructed brother, the *Vestiges of Creation*'.

Though the Bishop of Oxford had considerable influence on public opinion, it is plain that the evolutionists considered him mainly as the spokesman of somebody who would not openly engage in the controversy, and who was yet keen to inform and stimulate the courageous bishop. Behind Wilberforce they discerned the evasive shadow of the anonymous critic from the *Edinburgh Review*.

In her effort to stem the tide of Darwinism, as Germany had dubbed the new theory, the Church not only reasserted the dogma of Genesis, but wielded every argument that had been established in support of the doctrine of Special Creations. As yet, the greater number of eminent scholars were still on her side, and there was aid forthcoming in the learned debate on the missing link. Meantime, the uncompromising and often arrogant attitude of leaders on both sides widened the cleavage. Wilberforce branded mutability as 'incompatible with the word of God'; to Cardinal Manning it was a 'brutal philosophy'. In the opposing camp Huxley matched this crusading spirit:

In addition to the truth of the doctrine of evolution, indeed, one of its greatest merits in my eyes, is the fact that it occupies a position of complete and irreconcilable antagonism to that vigorous and consistent enemy of the highest intellectual, moral and social life of mankind—the Catholic Church.[2]

And again:

[1] *Life,* p. 242.
[2] Article on 'Mr. Darwin's Critics', *Collected Essays* (1894), vol. II, p. 146.

The antagonism of science is not to religion, but to the heathen survivals and the bad philosophy under which religion herself is often well-nigh crushed. And, for my part, I trust that this antagonism will never cease; but that, to the end of time, true science will continue to fulfil one of her most beneficent functions, that of relieving men from the burden of false science which is imposed upon them in the name of religion.[1]

Darwin remained silent, though to his friends he often expressed dismay at the upheaval caused by his work.[2] And he was grateful to the few liberal theologians who did not follow Wilberforce and Cardinal Manning, but pointed to a compromise. F. D. Maurice admired Darwin and regarded his theory as part of God's advancing revelation of truth; he had, which was rare among his contemporaries, 'reached a position where he could defend freedom of enquiry in the study of both history and nature and where he could welcome the results of such enquiry'.[3] Charles Kingsley, the vicar of Winchfield, to whom Darwin had sent a copy of the *Origin,* said in reply that the book had *awed* him, and that it would affect his beliefs profoundly if the theory was sound. He declared himself free from two 'common superstitions', namely that species were immutable, and that God supplied the *lacunas* in Nature by new creations. To Kingsley, who was himself a naturalist, it was equally legitimate to believe that the Deity had created primal forms capable of self-development.[4]

A more uneasy reaction, and undoubtedly more typical, is found in James Maurice Wilson, who was science master at Rugby School

---

[1] 'The Interpreters of Genesis and the Interpreters of Nature', *The Nineteenth Century,* Dec. 1885.

[2] 'With respect to the theological view of the question. This is always painful to me. I am bewildered. I had no intention to write atheistically'. Letter, quoted from *Life,* p. 236.

[3] H. G. Wood, *Frederick Denison Maurice,* p. 16.

[4] *Life of Darwin,* p. 228.

in 1859. Wilson saw that for him and his generation, Darwin had filled the vacuum left by Catastrophism and Lyell's Uniformity while creating a new, more frightening and permanent. It marked a new epoch in their lives, and it seemed unanswerable. A blind natural law had relegated the loving Creator to some precarious, mystical realm of conjecture, and the struggle for life had lost its transcendent justification and its moral significance. Wilson, like so many others, was cut adrift from orthodoxy. When he eventually returned to his faith, it was to find in evolution 'God's purpose in Creation', or 'the method of the Creative Mind.'[1] Many years later, in 1896, when Canon Wilson addressed a church congress at Shrewsbury, he stated that 'The bearing of Evolution on Christian doctrine is, therefore, in a word, to modify, not the doctrine, but the form in which it is expressed.'[2]

The solution arrived at by Wilson offered itself to an increasing number of theologians and laymen whom Darwin's theory had plunged into spiritual crisis, and it points the *via media*—the constructive effort of intellectual readjustment—which Lyell had indicated in the *Antiquity,* and which, in the years to come, both members of the Church and more independent thinkers tried to work out in precise theological terms.[3]

Among the naturalists too, there were some inspired by a wish to end the state of perplexity, and to unite the seemingly conflicting truths. Already in 1860, Asa Gray had written a series of articles in the *Atlantic Monthly* which, on Darwin's initiative, were published in England as a pamphlet entitled: 'Natural Selection not inconsistent

[1] See 'The Religious Effect of the Idea of Evolution', *Evolution in the Light of Modern Knowledge,* pp. 490 ff.

[2] Quoted from E. Clodd, *Pioneers of Evolution,* p. 149.

[3] Bishop Colenso was an early spokesman for a reconciliation between religion and science in his *Commentary on the Pentateuch;* vol. I, (1862).

with Natural Theology.'[1] To the fretful minds of the time, it held out the hope of finding, over the anathema of Wilberforce and the challenge of Huxley, a truth which satisfied faith and reason alike. Natural Selection remained, however, a serious obstacle to the many, and it was not until other, less mechanical causes of evolution had been more fully recognized that peace was made between orthodoxy and evolution. The most important step in this direction was taken by Mivart in his *Genesis of Species,* for Mivart argued well his two dominant themes: that Natural Selection could only be a relatively minor cause in the development of species, and that evolution is 'perfectly consistent with the strictest and most orthodox Christian theology'.[2] This theme is amplified in the last chapter, 'Theology and Evolution', where the Schoolmen and Christian philosophers are shown to have interpreted Creation in a derivative sense: God gave matter the power to evolve, and only in man do we find direct intervention or 'absolute creation'. According to the Scriptures, 'God made man from the dust of the earth' (by the normal course of Evolution), but he also 'breathed into him the breath of life'—his soul. In this dualistic interpretation of the descent of man, which, we remember, was shared by Wallace and Lyell, Mivart finds a 'true reconciliation of science and religion, in which each gains and neither loses, one being complementary to the other.'[3] Mivart reintroduces the active principle of intelligence—the Lamarckian factor—as the most important agent in the evolutionary process, and this emphasis on teleology (in fact a revival of the Aristotelian concept of *nisus*) did much to break down the emotional and religious aversion to the theory of evolution.

From time to time, the gloom of the controversy was shot through with flashes of humour, as when Disraeli in 1864 took part in another 'battle of Oxford', at a diocesan conference with Bishop

---

[1] Reprinted in Gray's *Darwiniana,* p. 87.
[2] *Op. cit.,* p. 5.   [3] *Ibid.,* p. 287.

Wilberforce in the chair. In the course of his speech Disraeli commented on the recent biological theories, and asked: 'What is the question now placed before society with a glib assurance the most astounding? The question is this: Is man an ape or an angel? I, my Lord, I am on the side of the angels. I repudiate with indignation and abhorrence the contrary view, which I believe foreign to the conscience of humanity.'[1]

Ten years after the publication of the *Origin,* in 1869, James Knowles, the editor of *The Nineteenth Century*, took the initiative to found *The Metaphysical Society,* with the purpose, originally, to combat the growing materialistic scepticism. This one-sided plan was criticized by Christians as well as agnostics, and finally prominent men from both sides were invited to join as members. It was the first attempt to meet in a friendly non-sectarian atmosphere and in mutual respect, to discuss the controversial problems which had received such belligerent treatment in the press. As such, during the short period the Society lasted (until 1881), it had an important function and made for increasing understanding and tolerance. Among its members were Tennyson, Browning, Gladstone, Dean Stanley, F. D. Maurice, T. H. Huxley—who coined the word 'agnostic' to define his position before joining—and Tyndall, Leslie Stephen, J. A. Froude, Ruskin and R. H. Hutton.

Spencer and the Synthetic Philosophy

In the meantime, over and above the clamour of polemics, an ambitious mind was at work to transform the theory of evolution into a universal philosophical doctrine. It took Herbert Spencer thirty-six years to complete his *Synthetic Philosophy,* and, like Lyell, he spanned the whole first evolutionary epoch. Long before Darwin's publication of *Origin* he had challenged the special crea-

[1] *Op. cit.* J. A. Froude, *Life of the Earl of Beaconsfield* (Everyman ed.), p. 176.

tionists,[1] and in 1862 appeared the first volume, *First Principles,* of the enormous work to which he added in 1896 the last—*Principles of Sociology.*

Spencer owed none of his basic conceptions to Darwin, though he often called in his evidence. Single-minded, caught in a life-long obsessive preoccupation, he officiated with priestlike pomp at the altar of Evolution, always with an absolute trust in his own ideas, and always with high hopes for mankind. His deism turned to agnosticism—a movement congenial to his age. It left him with the expanding wonderland of the 'Knowable' to explore, and for what might be beyond, in the 'Unknowable', he had little curiosity.

Spencer's philosophy of Evolution is a doctrine of cosmic process and change, anticipated as far back in time as Anaximander, and with distinct positivistic features. The *First Principles* serves as an introduction, with a preliminary discussion of the 'Knowable' and 'Unknowable' which reconciles Religion and Science in the statement that, ultimately, every phenomenon must be seen as a manifestation of an unlimited and incomprehensible power. The task of philosophy is to formulate the transition from the 'Unknowable' to the 'Knowable', from the imperceptible to the perceptible, and then back to the imperceptible. The human intellect moves within these cognitive limits, and the curtain of the 'Unknowable' falls at either end.

To Spencer nothing *is*: everything *becomes,* and, consequently, he sees the phenomenal world as history, change, evolution. He claims to have found the universal law of this process in

the integration of matter and concomitant dissipation of motion; during which the matter passes from an indefinite. incoherent homogeneity to a definite, coherent heterogeneity; and during which the retained motion undergoes a parallel transformation.[2]

[1] 'The Development Hypothesis', *Leader,* 1852.
[2] *An Epitome of the Synthetic Philosophy,* p. 145.

35

Cosmic Evolution furnishes the starting point for this formula: the Solar system has changed from the diffused, incoherent state of the gaseous nebula to a state of coherence and consolidation. Simultaneously there has been a progressive differentiation of matter; its forms and structures have developed in many directions, and produced an increasingly heterogeneous state. In flora and fauna, in man, in society, in all products of civilization this growing complexity is manifest.

The evolution from the homogeneous state to the heterogeneous might, if unchecked or undirected, lead to chaos. A principle is needed to explain how order is maintained; how, instead of disintegration and conflicting processes, there is an essential harmony throughout the Universe. Spencer finds this law in the tendency in matter to change from an indefinite to a definite arrangement. Thus an approximate balance or equilibrium is maintained between the two essential aspects of Evolution: Force and Matter.

The cognitive distinction of the 'Unknowable' forbids Spencer to seek for the noumenal cause of evolution. Within the orb of the 'Knowable', we merely perceive one original persistent force working through matter and splitting up into a vast number of forces, each producing a multiplicity of effects. Hence the evolution from the homogeneous to the heterogeneous state. Harmony is maintained owing to the constant equilibration taking place between the force and the matter on which it acts. When a state of complete equilibrium has been attained throughout the Universe, Evolution will come to an end. Then the reverse process, dissolution, will operate, followed by yet another phase of Evolution—*ad infinitum.*

Spencer's cosmology appears to repeat the cyclic systems of the Greeks. It is not, however, a Penelope's web, weaving and unweaving, but always a new adventure. And for our moral attitude to existence, Spencer claims, it is sufficient to know that Evolution progresses towards balance and harmony: We are inevitably led to the conviction that Evolution will end in the establishment of the greatest perfection and the most complete happiness.[1]

This argument epitomizes the essential meaning which Evolution, already at an early stage, acquired in Spencer's thought. It is synonymous with Progress. And since he conceives this aspect as an urge or tendency: a *nisus*, he shows himself an heir of Lamarck rather than a colleague of Darwin.[2] Yet Spencer never accepted Lamarck's concept of the 'innate desire' in the organism to evolve; he sees it, in his early work, as a fundamental necessity—a law established by the Divine Ruler,[3] and in later years, by the 'Unknowable'.

Already in the first sketches of his evolutionary theory Spencer applies it as a general law to society and human history. *Social Statics* (1851) and 'Progress: Its Law and Cause'[4] anticipate the argument of *Principles of Ethics* and *Principles of Sociology*. The essence of human nature, according to this argument, is change: it follows the universal pattern of Evolution in its progress towards a complete adjustment between internal and external relations. Man undergoes an incessant adaptation to his surroundings which is due mainly to the pressure of population. The struggle for life, with Spencer as with Malthus and Darwin, is an important creative aspect. Yet to him it is a necessary urge which spurs man to higher achievement, to more intense thought and thus to mental growth. This intellectual and emotional evolution is accompanied by social progress, and Spencer calls the interaction of these processes the 'super-organic evolution'.[5] He distinguishes between two main phases of development in human society: the 'militant' and the

---

[1] *First Principles,* ch. xxii.

[2] Bury has noted that Spencer's theory of evolution depends on Lamarck's contention that acquired characters are inherited. *The Idea of Progress,* p. 342.

[3] 'Development Hypothesis', and *Social Statics* (1851).

[4] *Westminster Review,* 1857.

[5] *Principles of Sociology,* ch. i.

'industrial' phase. In the earliest and most primitive type, the 'militant society', all institutions and functions are so many forms of 'regimentation', and it tends to consolidate its system at all costs, suppressing fruitful competition and individual freedom.[1]

Though the militant type is still in a majority, there are unmistakeable signs that the more highly civilized industrial type is about to supersede it. In the future, a voluntary co-operative effort will take the place of the older compulsory system. The industrial society is democratic, flexible and cosmopolitan; it offers freedom and justice, a wider scope for individuality and more opportunity for individuals to improve their status in life. Thus the industrial society represents the true progress of civilization, and its crowning achievement, according to Spencer, is that it has brought forth humanism. In countries like England, which Spencer no doubt uses as pattern, the industrial type is well advanced. Yet its complete realization does not depend on the condition in individual countries, but on international peace: war is the greatest obstacle with which civilization has to cope, as it inevitably prevents or neutralizes social and moral improvement. Permanent peace, Spencer assumes, would necessarily produce amelioration in all fields of life.

Social progress, as Spencer sees it, does not imply advances in material comfort and wellbeing—not a purely utilitarian ideal—but development in the social system owing to an increased interdependence and mutual sympathy among individuals. The greater the complexity of social functions and relations, the finer the individual awareness and adjustment.[2]

Since Spencer equates Evolution with Progress, he is convinced that the industrial society, though never quite perfect, at some future time will approach very near to an ideal state, a state in which happiness individual and general is the normal condition. The moral

[1] *Ibid.*, 'Political Institutions', ch. xvii, xviii.
[2] 'Progress: Its Law and Cause'.

progress in man which alone can further such a state is, according to Spencer, a process of evolution analogous to that which adapts an organism to its environment. In *Social Statics* Spencer expounds the theory that evil and unhappiness are products of maladaptation, or lack of fitness in the individual human condition. Evil is outgrown and civilization advances with a more perfect adjustment of the individual to his surroundings, and Spencer describes this process of adaptation as an evolution of moral consciousness which will result in the reconciliation of egoism and altruism. Sympathy, which he recognizes has a spontaneous, and not only utilitarian quality, will grow where unhappiness has been removed, and man and his society will be moulded and remoulded into mutual fitness through the interaction of sympathy and pleasure. In time, through constant social discipline, man will practise altruism spontaneously and seek contentment in the general happiness of his fellow beings.[1]

Spencer's ethics thus rests upon two main assumptions—A: The ultimate moral object is a state of life that might be defined as gratification, enjoyment, happiness. B: Human nature, subject to the universal law of Evolution, will inevitably progress towards such moral conduct as will make for happiness general and individual.

This ethical doctrine is fatalistic only in appearance. Its facile optimism as to the perfectibility of human nature does not exempt man from unceasing moral effort. On the contrary, the fact that such a progress is possible, and depends on conscious adaptation, should encourage man to do his utmost for the general good: the happiness of society is a condition of individual happiness.

John Locke had first formulated the moral doctrine which later inspired the Utilitarians, and many of its leading ideas recur in naturalistic ethics throughout the nineteenth century: 'Things are good or evil only in relation to pleasure and pain. That we call "good" which is apt to cause or increase pleasure, or diminish pain

---

[1] Cf. *Principles of Ethics*, ch. xi—xiv.

in us.' Jeremy Bentham, by extending this argument, concluded that what gives pleasure and happiness is necessarily good. Spencer too accepts this ethical relativism, and denies the existence of absolute ethical standards.[1] Yet in moral conduct he allows greater scope to spontaneous sympathy, and he criticizes the Utilitarian school for their crude pragmatism, testing means by ends and acts by results, which blinds them to the fact that it is possible to deduce from fundamental principles what conduct is good or beneficial.[2] Bentham, and all recent schools of ethics have failed, Spencer claims, because they have neglected ultimate causal connexions and the fact that moral phenomena are phenomena of Evolution.

Spencer's contribution to the theory of evolution has been variously assessed, and his work soon fell into desuetude. Yet at the time his idea of universal evolution, and its application to nature, psychology, ethics and sociology met a real intellectual need and inspired an age that was anxious to force the world of phenomena into one unifying conception. Many of his ideas, and notably those concerned with mental and social evolution, became integral parts of the hopes and ideals of the humanitarians and the utopian dreamers of the century. For his optimism was congenial to and indeed epitomizes the attitude of an epoch that had not yet begun to doubt in the historical law of progress.[3]

---

[1] *Principles of Ethics*, ch. xv.   [2] *Ibid.*, ch. iii.

[3] Spencer's evolutionary philosophy has not only suffered neglect during the last generation, but has also been exposed to severe criticism. Bergson stated that *'l'artifice ordinaire de la méthode de Spencer consiste à reconstituer l'évolution avec des fragments de l'évolué'; L'Évolution Créatrice,* p. 363. James Ward has played havoc with the metaphysical distinction of the 'Knowable' and the 'Unknowable', in *Naturalism and Agnosticism.* Spencer's universal application of the evolutionary concept was, according to R. G. Collingwood, so 'amateurish and inconclusive' that it discouraged further philosophical inquiry; *The Idea of Nature*, p. 11. Edw. Caird in *Evolution and Religion,* and Julian Huxley in *Evolution and Ethics* have discussed the 'fallacy' of Spencer's ethics. J. B. Bury, on the other hand,

The Ethical Process

Spencer's ethics offers the most striking early example of the way in which Humanitarianism and the theory of Evolution fused to create something new in the speculation about moral value and conduct, and the process through which their determinative or formative concepts emerge. The moral challenge of evolution was, from the beginning, unavoidable, and it remained closely related to the metaphysical issues of the evolutionary controversy.

Broadly speaking, three currents of thought conflued visibly in the English panorama: Bentham's doctrine of Utility, Comte's Positivism and Darwin's as well as Lamarck's theories of Evolution. Utilitarianism, the fruit of a long rationalist tradition, had its earliest spokesmen in Locke and Helvetius, from whom Bentham and Stuart Mill indirectly drew their inspiration. With Mill, the narrow doctrine of Bentham was caught into the wider perspective of nineteenth-century Humanitarianism and positivist philosophy.[1]

From the middle of the century, natural science invaded ethical thought with greater force, and it coincided with the powerful current of scepticism and the spread of the new cult—Humanitarianism. The finds in geology and palaeontology revealed a history of mankind more ancient than anyone had ever dreamed, and with

claims that 'The ablest and most influential development of the argument from evolution to Progress was the work of Spencer'; *The Idea of Progress,* p. 336.

[1] See Mill's essay on 'Utilitarianism' in *Fraser's Magazine* (1861), in which he contends that 'pleasure' should not be judged quantitatively only, but by quality; that conscience does not depend exclusively on 'external sanction' or public opinion, but on 'internal sanction'; and that sympathetic fellowship is the foundation of happiness and therefore of moral consciousness. This attitude shows a compromise between the pragmatic outlook of the Utilitarians and the intuitionist ethics of the Idealist school. Spencer probably learned from this expansion of the Utilitarian doctrine—at least there is agreement in his criticism of its narrow pragmatism; see *Principles of Ethics,* ch. iii.

41

terrifying evidence of all the changes, accidents and vicissitudes to which it had been subject. Archeology added its own story of the instability and flux of civilizations. Then, in 1859, Man was dethroned from his unique position and had to find a place closer to his animal ancestry. With evolution, the innate moral instinct, Kant's Categorical Imperative, as well as the Ten Commandments seemed no longer founded in psychological or historical fact.

To the evolutionists of the nineteenth century it was urgent to reassess, in the light of these discoveries, the meaning and nature of moral conduct and standards, of conscience and obligation. From this revaluation the ethical relativism of Locke and the Positivist school emerged with, as it seemed, a new force of factual persuasion. Thus, in their definition of criteria like 'good' and 'bad' and of moral obligation the evolutionists merely paraphrased, with biological reference, the pleasure- and contentment-doctrine of Utilitarian ethics. The main interest produced by their effort to place ethics upon a naturalistic basis was a growing insight into the development of conscience and conduct.

Very soon, evolution, in the progressive sense which Spencer and many more gave to it, offered support to the rationalist claim for the perfectibility of human nature. Lamarck's principle of the inheritance of acquired characters, in its insistence on cumulative process, became the most stimulating argument in a historical account of moral development. Darwin's Natural Selection, on the other hand, offered an argument of survival value of such moral instincts and habits as tended to protect and preserve the community. As for human perfectibility, Darwin even had concluded his *Origin* with prophetic optimism: 'And as natural selection works solely by and for the good of each being, all corporeal and mental endowments will tend to progress towards perfection.' Thus, within the perspective of evolutionary progress, the goal of the greatest happiness for the greatest number seemed to draw closer and to stand out as a real, not a Utopian, promise.

42

The Utilitarians had failed to solve the fundamental problem of moral conduct: how to reconcile man's egoistic inclinations with his duty to others, since they relied on a purely pragmatic code of conduct. Mill, as we have seen, developed their views by affirming the need of 'internal sanction' and of sympathy. Darwin too, in his *Descent of Man,* maintains that the foundation of moral qualities 'lies in the social instincts, including in this term the family ties... the more important elements for us are love, and the distinct emotion of sympathy.'[1] The sympathetic instincts integrated through habit will become more stable and permanent and overrule the fluctuating individual inclinations. For the happiness of man, Darwin agrees with Spencer and Mill, is dependent upon the emotional satisfaction he finds in the social environment, and 'happiness is an essential part of the general good'.[2] Moreover, the constant interaction of public judgement and individual judgement will give a steady and progressive direction to moral conduct. This interaction has always been important in the growth of moral consciousness in man:

The moral nature of man has reached the highest standard as yet attained, partly through the advancement of the reasoning powers and consequently of a just public opinion, but especially through the sympathies being rendered more tender and widely diffused through the effects of habit, example, instruction, and reflection.[3]

The most important feature in evolutionary ethics, as expounded by Darwin and Spencer, is the derivation of moral instincts from impulses which are not specifically human, but present in varying degree among the higher orders of the animal world: sympathy, need of happiness and protection. Here, clearly, man does not exist in the spiritual relationship of Christian and Idealist ethics, with its

[1] *Op. cit.,* p. 391, (1871 ed.).
[2] *Ibid.,* p. 393.
[3] *Ibid.,* p. 391.

transcendent sanction and absolute standards and values. Yet the moral meaning of existence is no less clear, they maintain, than it was according to these traditional creeds. For the steady progressive trend of evolution, and the emotional needs and qualities with which man is endowed provide a sound rational basis for value as well as conduct.

Not all rationalists agreed upon the moral, progressive tendency in natural process. Already before Darwin's *Origin* appeared, Stuart Mill had written his essay on 'Nature' in which he anticipates some of the leading ideas of T. H. Huxley.[1] Mill finds in Nature a pretext for an attack upon the Creator God of Christian revelation: 'If the maker of the world *can* all that he will, he wills misery, and there is no escape from the conclusion.'[2] To those who explain the imperfection of nature and the evil of the world as a purpose on the part of the Creator, to encourage good, Mill replies: 'If there are any marks at all of special design in creation, one of the things most evidently designed is that a large proportion of all animals should pass their existence in tormenting and devouring other animals . .'.[3] Obviously then, nature offers no guidance for moral conduct, no more than it bears witness to a loving God: 'Conformity to nature, has no connection whatever with right or wrong', and therefore man must look elsewhere for the laws on which he should act. These can only be found through reason, and reason tells man that 'all human action whatever, consists in altering, and all useful action in improving, the spontaneous course of nature.'[4]

Of the prominent naturalists of the later nineteenth century, none was more deeply concerned with the bearing of evolution on ethics than T. H. Huxley. His Romanes Lecture from 1893 on 'Evolution

[1] 'Nature' was published in 1874 as the first of *Three Essays on Religion 1850—1870*.
[2] *Three Essays*, (1874), p. 37.
[3] *Ibid.*, p. 58.
[4] *Ibid.*, p. 64.

and Ethics' and the 'Prolegomena' to his *Essays* of the following year contain the essence of his outlook.

Huxley's attitude to evolution is related to the teaching of Darwin as well as to that of Spencer. He sees in the unstable nature of the Universe a fundamental principle of development:

In every part, at every moment, the state of the cosmos is the expression of a transitory adjustment of contending forces; a scene of strife, in which all the combatants fall in turn. It assumes the aspect not so much of a permanent entity as of a changeful process, in which naught endures save the flow of energy and the rational order which pervades it.[1]

On this scene of strife, living beings take part in the cosmic process and develop according to their fitness in the struggle for existence. And the best endowed creature—the animal that has evolved the physical abilities of the ape along with the cunning and ferocity of the tiger: man—has come out of this cosmic process as the fittest of all beings.

Yet man too, for all his superiority, is compelled to live in societies for purposes of security, and it is as an organizer of social units that man has shown himself less competent. For in this effort he is called upon to do something utterly alien to his nature: to curb his desire for self-gratification to the common need. And the common need, according to Huxley, is at the heart of another evolutionary process, not only different from the cosmic process, but working against it: This is the ethical process.

In the 'Prolegomena' Huxley goes in quest for a formula that might describe this process of ethical development. His analysis proceeds from two analogies in which he observes the behaviour of artificial units, or 'states of art', in their competitive struggle with 'states of nature'. A wild, uncultivated area offers an example of

---

[1] 'Evolution and Ethics'.

how the cosmic process has adapted plants and produced a selection of fit specimens, while the weaker have been ousted. If man decides to make part of this area into a garden by fencing it off and clearing the wild plants to make room for domestic ones of his own choice, he works against the normal course of nature in so far as he does not select the plants fittest in the struggle for life, but those fittest for his purpose; not plants adapted to local conditions, but plants for which the environment has been adapted. Thus the garden is an artificial arrangement created by a process opposed to that of nature, and if abandoned by the gardener, would again be reclaimed by nature and changed into a scene of strife.

The same antagonistic processes could be observed in a colony of civilized men established in a barbarous and hostile country, surrounded by tribes eager to invade their land and seize their food. The success of the colony would depend on its internal strength: on law, order and loyal co-operation. If these bonds were broken by ruthless self-assertion, the days of the community would soon be numbered.

Having thus sketched the two processes in their fundamental polar relationship, Huxley goes on to elucidate the nature and growth of ethical, or social, instincts. In the animal world they have developed naturally from the need for protection and security, of which the communities of bees and ants offer striking examples. Human society grew from the same basic necessity, yet its co-operation and social instincts have emotional sources different from anything in the animal world. Family affections and sympathetic response to the feelings, sufferings and opinions in other individuals are the strongest agents in the evolution of an ordered community. The higher the level of civilization, the subtler the interplay of sympathy and empathy, until social relationship has produced and refined that sensitive instrument of control, conscience, on which a system of moral conduct can be based. Thus the ethical process is an evolution of feeling.

46

Yet, when the struggle for existence in society has ceased through the counteraction of the ethical process, and all members have been secured adequate means of subsistence, another danger will increasingly threaten its peaceful state, namely the unchecked growth of population. Within the 'garden'-scheme, surplus plants, and notably the poorer specimens, could be easily weeded out. Not so in society, where all, fit and unfit alike must be protected against starvation and violence and where, in consequence, their number will multiply regardless of a limited production of food. Of this Malthusian problem Huxley offers no solution. He rejects emphatically the gardener's 'weeding method', or eugenics—perhaps with Nietzsche in mind—and he has nothing but contempt for the 'Pigeon-Fanciers' polity', or selective breeding of the ideal citizen, which already haunted the Utopian speculations of the later nineteenth century.[1]

Spencer saw in evolution something of absolute ethical value, since it was a process in which moral consciousness emerged and was perfected, and thus would lead to a qualitative as well as quantitative expansion of existence: Health and long life would result from a state of harmony and happiness.

Huxley's attitude to ethical value is less explicit, and he does not venture a definition of concepts like 'good' and 'evil'. Evolution, as he sees it, cannot explain or produce moral values, if by evolution we mean cosmic or biological process. Moral sentiments have, no doubt, emerged in the course of evolution, but so have the immoral ones, and both find sanction within the cosmic scheme: Values cannot be referred to a universal plan or to any absolute principles. When Huxley uses terms like 'good' and 'evil', it is in a common sense manner, and they appear as fixed, irreducible concepts. The behaviour of these words in Huxley's usage shows that they draw

---

[1] *Francis Galton*, Darwin's cousin, coined the word 'eugenics' in his work *Hereditary Genius* (1869).

significance mainly from his practical and pragmatic value-judgements. 'Good' is what conduces to self-restraint, generosity, tolerance, and 'bad' is the untamed instinct of self-assertion.[1] Pain and suffering tend to be equated with 'evil'; pain—'This baleful product of evolution increases in quantity, and in intensity, with advancing grades of animal organization, until it attains its highest level in man'.[2] Modern man has brought with him the ape and tiger from his past, and 'the unwelcome intrusion of these boon companions of his hot youth into the ranged existence of civil life adds pains and griefs, innumerable and immeasurably great, to those which the cosmic process necessarily brings on the mere animal.'[3] For us, however, it is possible, in the light of evolution, to relate the evil in man to the instincts he has inherited from his animal past, and to adopt an active stoicism which endures inevitable pain, while doing our utmost to reduce it.

The goal of ethical evolution was to Spencer a state of happiness; to Huxley it appears to be rather the absence of pain. Between them there are several points of agreement as to the conduct and direction leading to these goals. Where Spencer reconciles altruism and egoism through better adaptation and self-discipline, Huxley finds a juster balance between the cosmic and ethical propensities. They have both a marked humanitarian perspective, focused on values like 'pleasure' and 'enjoyment', though Huxley rejects scornfully, as he rejected the idea of selective breeding, the apocalypse of Utopia or the Golden Age recurrent in evolutionary speculations about the future:[4]

[1] In this context Huxley's interpretation of 'original sin' as 'ape and tiger'-instincts is significant.

[2] 'Evolution and Ethics'.

[3] *Ibid.*

[4] Among Utopian works dealing with evolutionary aspects might be mentioned Lytton Bulwer's *The Coming Race* (1871); Edw. Maitland, *By and By, a historical Romance of the Future,* (1873); *A Thousand Years Hence,* anon., (1882).

48

The prospect of attaining untroubled happiness, or a state which can, even remotely, deserve the title of perfection, appears to me as misleading an illusion as ever was dangled before the eyes of poor humanity.[1]

Human life may, however, see great and noble changes in the future, as long as the ethical process continues to prevail against the cosmic forces; for man, in virtue of his energy and intelligence, 'bends the Titan to his will'.

Huxley's ethics is, essentially, a stoical doctrine of self-restraint and courage. It recognizes moral instinct and obligation, not as inherent impulse or categorical imperative, but as an emotional product of life in society. Huxley is well aware of the logical difficulty involved in his dualistic approach; yet, he claims, even if we shall be 'sorry for logic' the reality of the cosmic-ethical conflict must be accepted. It is a curious fact that Huxley, when attempting to give an account of the moral evolution of man, instead of integrating man completely with the scheme of nature, merely restates in other terms the Flesh-Spirit conflict of Christian and Idealistic ethics. His difficulty is that which has ever flawed naturalistic ethics, and Huxley is more aware of it than Spencer. It is the difficulty of how to fabricate altruism out of egoism with nothing but 'utility' and 'pleasure'.

There is considerable divergence in attitude among the evolutionists towards the part played by 'the struggle for existence' in moral development. Darwin and Spencer considered it a necessary and beneficial factor, without which moral and intellectual growth would stagnate. Mill, writing before 'natural selection' had entered the discussion, and Huxley, who had learnt both from Malthus and Mill, insisted on the cruel and often tragic quality of the struggle, and saw in it a merely negative process to be checked and overcome. The fittest, they repeat, is rarely the best. And in the end all of

---

[1] 'Evolution and Ethics'.

them, after their long search through the history of life, return to
the fundamental virtues of Christian ethics: selflessness, charity and
love, but with their hopes fixed on an immanent, historical goal, the
happiness of mankind in the future.

In the preceding sections, an attempt has been made to trace the
growth of some main ideas in biological speculation and inquiry in
England up to the last decades of the nineteenth century. Before
raising the curtain on its wider intellectual setting, and its continued
interaction with the central ideological impulses of the time, it
might be useful, here, to recapitulate one or two salient features of
the development.

In the centre of biological thought stands the problem of the
origin of species, and, according to the solutions arrived at before
1859 and after, the progress of opinion falls into two distinct
phases. In England before Darwin, naturalists had thought of life
as growth and development, but as a creative act—in the hand of
God—with new and higher species added to the lower already
existing or replacing those that had become extinct. The geological
record, which was accumulating so rapidly, was still a Book of
Genesis in which the imprints of the Creator could be contemplated
in their advance towards his highest and latest achievement, man.
Lyell's doctrine of Uniformity superseded Cuvier's Catastrophism,
yet Lyell retained the general belief in the fixity of species. His
insistence on natural causes slowly and constantly operating on the
surface of the earth cleared the way for Darwin whose main task
was to explain the gradual, formative action on organism by environment. If the period before 1859 might be equally divided between
Cuvier and Lyell, the second phase, in spite of the overwhelming
impact made by Natural Selection, shows an increasing balance
between the theories of Darwin and Lamarck. After their first
enthusiasm, the evolutionists realized that natural selection was only

one of several causes in the process which had given birth to species, that it could not—despite extremist claims—account for all the most important features of the *opus perfectum;* and that life, as a force or impulse, was capable of a more purposive and intelligent growth than the casual stamp of environment warranted. A teleological theory of evolution, represented by Mivart, looked back to Lamarck, the martyr of Evolution, whose ingenius hypothesis had been prematurely advanced and untimely destroyed.

Next an outline was given of the controversy which swept the intellectual *milieu* from 1859 for about twenty years onwards, and which split the scholars and the educated public into two hostile factions. Undue emphasis on purely mechanical and environmental causes of evolution on the one side and an equally fanatic rejection of the fact of evolution on the other, created from the beginning an atmosphere of crusade which made it difficult to combine beliefs old and new in a harmonious conception. Evolution, to the orthodox camp, was antichrist, a sum and symbol of all the godless, destructive and materialistic tendencies of the infidel century. Yet, there were peacemakers on both sides, and a compromise was gradually worked out by naturalists like Lyell and Mivart, and theologians such as Charles Kingsley, F. D. Maurice and Canon Wilson. To all these, evolution was the creative method of God.

In Herbert Spencer's *Synthetic Philosophy* we found the first attempt in England to expand the concept of biological evolution into a general system of philosophy, based on the idea of progress and inspired by the conviction that mankind is moving towards a state of universal happiness: the 'Industrial state'.

Finally, the ethical theory of T. H. Huxley was outlined, as an example of the early efforts to analyse moral obligation and standards in the light of evolution. The conflict of 'cosmic' contra 'ethical' process through which he explored social integration past, present and future, revealed the dualism of Christian ethics in secular disguise.

51

This brief outline of the first phases of evolutionary theory and discussion has, for convenience, been sketched in a pattern too simple to include all the essential features of the scene on which it took place. In one aspect only—the religious controversy—has the relationship between the new theory and the intellectual climate been traced in more detail. It is important to remember, however, that the conflict between theology and evolution was never a two-force grapple about a scientific theory and a dogma, but part of an intense quest and reorientation in thought and practice. Huxley was right in his comment upon the disturbance of the general mind: it had indeed for some time been caught in a revolution. German biblical criticism and Comte's philosophy had thrown their seed of unrest into the quiet world of early nineteenth-century England. Since the *Origin of Species,* in its philosophical corollaries, was such another seed of rationalistic scepticism, it was adopted as a principal argument of radical thought. Finally, therefore, it would seem pertinent to examine the significance which the evolutionary theory gradually achieves within the wider intellectual panorama.

Evolution—A New Faith

'A general revolt against authority, even in matters of opinion, is a childish or anile superstition, not to be excused by the pretext that it is only due to the love of freedom cherished in excess'.[1] In those words W. E. Gladstone preached creed and conversion to an age that had loved authority so fervently that in the end it had lost it. None, perhaps, could speak for his time more knowingly and with deeper concern than Gladstone, the Liberal leader who had translated the faith in change and progress into his politics; who had felt, from his Oxford days, the stir of religious revival as well as the tide of scepticism press upon his mind, and who, after having

[1] 'Authority in Matters of Opinion'; *The Nineteenth Century,* March 1877.

seen the crumbling of Christian dogma, could still write *The Impregnable Rock of Holy Scriptures*.

Authority was an obsession of the nineteenth century, because it had inherited so much in political and intellectual anarchy, and continued to add to this eighteenth-century legacy. After the Romantic storm and stress, the Victorians craved order and certainty more and more strongly as their faith grew weak. Anarchy was, to Gladstone as to Disraeli, to Darwin as to Wilberforce, a hideous state—the ultimate worst thing. And so, in spite of the earthquakes that shook this bewildered age, the Victorians by and large persisted in their ordered way of life and thought, as if nothing had happened, and cultivated the dignity and cheerful disposition so essential to their human ideal. For this age tradition had built a temple to the common cult of dogma, reason and good manners in which practically all worshipped, and tradition, building the indestructible moral fibre which is the chief distinction of the Victorians, preserved this place of worship even while science and the higher criticism corroded it and it seemed to decay under their very eyes.

In the universities, in vicarages and schools, there were minds ill at ease as they watched the fading light of Christian doctrine. But the many, the respectable middle class core of society, had few moments of perplexity. The Tullivers and the Dodsons lived by authority, in 1877 when Gladstone wrote, as in 1830:

The religion of the Dodsons consisted in revering whatever was customary and respectable: it was necessary to be baptized, else one could not be buried in the churchyard, and to take the sacrament before death as a security against more dimly understood perils; but it was of equal necessity to have the proper pall-bearers and well-cured hams at one's funeral, and to leave an unimpeachable will. A Dodson would not be taxed with the omission of anything that was becoming, or that belonged to that eternal fitness of things which was plainly indicated in the practice of the most substantial parishioners, and in the family traditions ...[1]

---

[1] George Eliot, *The Mill on the Floss*, Book fourth, ch. 1.

This was an important area: the most extensive of nineteenth-century England. Its theory of life had, as George Eliot tells us, a 'core of soundness ... but it had the very slightest tincture of theology'.

Outside the Dodsons world, there was that quickly spreading slum-area with its ugliness and lurid forms of misery, crime and social abuse—the London Dickens knew. There was the threat of social revolt in the North and in the Midlands—the 'hungry Forties' —and the unpleasant fact that, though industrial and mercantile progress was manifest everywhere, it was marred by the sight of 'poverty, hunger and dirt'.

Under the surface of the secure middle class cosmos, minds of greater awareness saw already by 1830 a frightening process of spiritual disintegration and chaos. To Carlyle it was a nightmare world, a Twilight of the Gods:

A world all rocking and plunging, like that old Roman one when the measure of its iniquities was full; the abysses, and subterranean and supernal deluges, plainly broken loose; in the wild, dim-lighted chaos all stars of Heaven gone out ... in the leaden air, are only sudden glares of revolutionary lightning; then mere darkness, with philanthropistic phosphorescences, empty meteoric lights; here and there an ecclesiastical luminary still hovering, hanging on to its old quaking fixtures, pretending still to be a Moon or Sun... Surely as mad a world as you could wish.[1]

Already then, according to Carlyle, atheism was rampant, and the sage to which the young minds looked for guidance, Coleridge, 'sat on the brow of Highgate Hill, ... looking down on London' and the tumult and aimless wanderings of the souls, and could do little more than assert the reality of spirit in the teeth of materialism. And with Coleridge, Carlyle laments the 'sunk condition of the world'; the mechanical science now practised: 'the science not of

[1] *Life of John Sterling* (1897), p. 39.

men but of a kind of human beavers'; and the churches which had 'died away into a godless mechanical condition'.[1]

A more sober observer, Cardinal Newman, when looking 'into the world of men', saw a sight that filled him with 'unspeakable distress'. He saw

the defeat of good, the sucess of evil, physical pain, mental anguish, the prevalence and intensity of sin, the pervading idolatries, the corruptions, the dreary hopeless irreligion, that condition of the whole race, so fearfully yet exactly described in the Apostle's words, "having no hope and without God in the world"—[2]

Newman's arch-enemy, the evil spirit of the times, was, Matthew Arnold tells us, 'Liberalism'—'the great middle-class liberalism' which expressed itself in the Reform Bill of 1832, in free-trade, and in a non-conformism that was 'the Dissidence of Dissent and the Protestantism of the Protestant religion'.[3] And in this powerful liberalism of the 'Philistines' Arnold too found the spiritual anarchy so destructive to his high ideals of humanity, of 'sweetness and light', of Culture. He found an excessive materialism, which estimated coal as 'the real basis of our national greatness'; he deplored the religious intolerance of Puritanism which, though it had fostered a strong moral fibre, now was equally devoid of sweetness and light.

In all these visions of chaos and spiritual anarchy there is a common feeling of loss, a grief at the destruction and betrayal of high truths and values, and there is both fear and indignation. They represent the attitudes of the young Christian intelligentsia of the first half of the century, who felt the 'cursed spite' of Hamlet, and yet, after their denunciation of the rotten state, looked ahead and tried to find ways and means. The solutions they arrived at varied. There was the course of action taken by Arthur Coningsby, the hero

[1] *Ibid.*, p. 58.
[2] *Apologia Pro Vita Sua*, (1913 ed.), p. 334.
[3] *Culture and Anarchy*, (1909 ed.), p. 111.

of John Sterling's obscure novel, (1833), a course which Carlyle found so false and pathetic and yet described with unusual sympathy, since, like the hero, he had been an 'ardent youth' suffering in the anarchy of the time with its 'radical, utilitarian, or mutinous heathen theory', and had himself been through the 'shipwreck' crisis which called for the great decision. Here, however, their ways separate, for Coningsby 'clutches desperately towards some new method (recognisable as Coleridge's) of laying hand again on the old Church'.[1] This to Carlyle was the worst possible form of self-deceit.

Disraeli, on the other hand, approved greatly of Arthur Coningsby and his conservative religious bent, and decided to reward his virtues in the social sphere. The starting point is much the same:

Coningsby found that he was born in an age of infidelity in all things, and his heart assured him that a want of faith was a want of nature...He asked himself why governments were hated, and religions despised? Why Loyalty was dead and Reverence only a galvanised corpse? ... Some thought that systems would last their time; others, that something would turn up. His deep and pious spirit recoiled with disgust and horror from such lax, chance-medley maxims, that would reduce, in their consequences, men to the level of the brutes.[2]

In the same year as Sterling published his novel, a group of Oxford men too decided to go back to the old Church, and began publishing *Tracts for the Times*, which produced the Oxford Movement, the most significant religious revival of the century. Newman was, from the beginning, a central figure, for this was his great effort to 'withstand the liberalism of the day'. The anarchy of Liberalism, these men thought, could only be met with a return to the spiritual sources of the Church: to scriptural authority.

To Carlyle, this solution was impossible and foolish. Dogmatic religion, the 'Church-Clothes', had become 'mere hollow Shapes,

[1] *Life of John Sterling*, p. 94.
[2] *Coningsby or the New Generation*, (1849 ed.), pp. 123—24.

or Masks, under which no living Figure or Spirit any longer dwells
... ghastly affectation of life.'[1] Yet it was a form of religious truth
Carlyle too found after his wanderings through 'Our Wilderness'
of an 'Atheistic Century'. Like Bunyan he fought Giant Despair,
and then:

to me also was given, if not Victory, yet the consciousness of Battle,
and the resolve to persevere therein while life or faculty is left. To
me also, entangled in the enchanted forests, demon-peopled, doleful
of sight and of sound, it was given, after weariest wanderings, to
work out my way into the higher sunlit slopes—of that Mountain
which has no summit, or whose summit is in Heaven only![2]

As Newman returned to the Church of Rome, Carlyle reached the
extreme of Protestantism, with no dogmas left, but, instead, an un-
shakeable conviction that the 'old Eternal Powers do live forever'.
It was, from now on, the 'Everlasting Yea'; the crusade against the
dishonesty and godlessness of his time; and the incessant challenge
of: 'Conviction, were it never so excellent, is worthless till it convert
itself into Conduct.'[3]

Carlyle's answer to the spiritual problem, says Professor Basil
Willey, is similar to that of Arnold: 'It is a position common to
liberal Victorians with a religious temper; the old certainties stand
firm even when the dogmatic supports are removed.'[4] It was
Coleridge who, according to F. D. Maurice, taught his century that
'the highest truths are those which lie beyond the limits of experience', and in his brilliant essay on Coleridge, Basil Willey comments
on the significance of this claim:

Moreover, he taught this before the main attacks of the higher criticism and of science were launched, so that when the crisis came

---

[1] *Sartor Resartus,* Everyman ed., p. 163.
[2] *Ibid.,* p. 139.
[3] *Ibid.,* p. 147.
[4] *Nineteenth Century Studies,* p. 113.

(in the middle of the century in England) the defensive positions were already laid down. If, throughout the century of biblical criticism and scientific agnosticism, Christianity held its ground, contrary to the expectations of many; if it did this by discarding its pseudo-foundations in historical, prophetic, natural or miraculous 'evidences', and by discovering a firmer foundation in the specific religious experience, in man's need for a God who comes to meet and to redeem him; if this is so (and I believe that it is), then the debt of modern theology to Coleridge is very considerable.[1]

These men, Coleridge, Newman, Carlyle and Arnold write an important part of the spiritual history of the age. Newman's way was that of the exasperated intellectual who despaired of the Protestant church. Against the prevailing tendency to interpret dogma as poetic symbol and myth, which was the heritage of eighteenth-century rationalism as well as of Romantic philosophy, he asserted the absolute verbal truth of Christian revelation. Carlyle's and Arnold's way was the *via media* of intuitional religion which found its sanction in inner experience, independent of the historical vestment of dogma. They found, in contrast to Newman, a solution which satisfied the two deepest intellectual needs of the century, the desire for certainty and order, and the craving for freedom. The tension between these needs makes drama of their thought, and they reflect in a heightened light the general predicament of the age. Authority was essential to the spiritual, and especially to the moral orientation of the Victorians; freedom, or liberalism, a condition of their material and intellectual quest. Their moral fibre, rooted in religious and social tradition, formed and maintained their human ideal. Liberalism, on the other hand, was their great original adventure, their unique historical task, in which Humanitarianism joined science and material progress in a splendid onward rush towards a happy future. Yet liberalism claimed its right in all fields of activity and experience, and soon the Victorians, like the Sorcerer's

[1] *Ibid.*, pp. 31—32.

apprentice, found themselves tossed on the currents of scepticism and disillusionment. Liberalism, Arnold comments, was 'the appointed force to do the work of the hour; it was necessary, it was inevitable that it should prevail', but its outcome was anarchy.[1]

This conflict between authority and freedom penetrated also deep into the Anglican Church—the stronghold of tradition—and expressed itself in frequent theological controversies, such as those between Newman and Kingsley, F. D. Maurice and Mansel. In its attitude to scepticism and orthodoxy the Church revealed a lack of direction which made it difficult to uphold its dignity and position. Thus matters of belief were more strictly supervised in the universities than in the Church itself. Shelley had been sent down from Oxford early in the century, and in 1849 J. A. Froude made a hardly less remarkable exit with his *Nemesis of Faith*. Four years later F. D. Maurice was dismissed from his chair of Divinity at King's College, London, for his views of Eternal Punishment. Yet Maurice continued in his chaplaincy at Lincoln's Inn, and the Bishop of London never interfered with his work. Only rarely did the Church assert its authority as a body, and then as a rule against open blasphemy, in the manner of Holyoake and Bradlaugh, or against aggressive criticism such as the contributions of Williams and Wilson to the *Essays and Reviews*, (1860). On the whole, the Church remained open to a wide range of opinion, and Dean Stanley of Westminster described it rightly as neither High nor Low, but *Broad.* And the Broad Church Party, symptomatic of this attitude, was founded with the blessings of the Church and represented a systematic effort on the part of younger intellectuals to build bridges between orthodoxy and the new ideas in science and philosophy. It was Liberalism in a new disguise, and as such Disraeli, still on the side of the angels, denounced it at Oxford in 1864, when he predicted that if the Church allowed such laxity and did not assert its 'title-deeds of truth...

---

[1] *Culture and Anarchy*, p. 111.

Before long we shall be living in a flitting scene of spiritual phantasmagoria'.[1] Of a scope similar to that of the Broad Church Party were the *Bridgewater Treatises,* founded in 1829 with the purpose of approaching scientific fact to revelation, and to show 'The Goodness of God as manifested in the Creation'.

Yet, from the point of view of the Church, these efforts could only delay the more destructive flood of scepticism which had already swept the Continent. From France, the positive philosophy of Comte was making its way into England through the translations of G. H. Lewes and the works of Stuart Mill, and swelled the stagnant waters of traditional rationalism. From Germany, more fatal still, came Strauss and Feuerbach, translated by George Eliot.[2] Even before these, Hennel's *Inquiry Concerning the Origin of Christianity* (1838) indicated the type of historical criticism which was to challenge orthodoxy with greater force in the Germans, and yet, as George Eliot testified, was capable of throwing darkness, or a flash of unwelcome light, into the young minds. Oxford, the birth-place of Tractarianism and of the Broad Church Party, received Strauss too, as Comte was being received, and saw the spirit of scepticism quietly spreading among its dons and students. Meanwhile, the growing body of English positivists found a public platform in *The Westminster Review,* and here Froude, the exile from Oxford, George Eliot, G. H. Lewes and the evolutionist Herbert Spencer made their contributions. Theirs was indeed a revolt against authority, and their pretext was not so much love of freedom as love of truth. It was not a clamorous appeal to the masses, not a theatrical crusade in the manner of Voltaire, but a quiet and often painful search. Professor Willey has aptly pointed out the more damaging nature of nineteenth-century attack compared with that of the Enlightenment: more destructive

---

[1] *Op. cit.,* J. A. Froude, *The Life of the Earl of Beaconsfield,* p. 175.
[2] Strauss, *Life of Jesus,* 1846; Feuerbach, *Essence of Christianity,* 1854.

because it was based on a much wider and deeper understanding of history and of human nature: because, in a sense, it was not a direct attack at all, but undercut religion by the more subtle corrosive of a profounder comprehension. The distinctive nineteenth century phenomenon is the devout sceptic, the sage who rejects traditional religion not because he is shallow or immoral, but because he is too earnest to accept it—because he understands and tolerates all forms of religion too well to adopt any one of them.[1]

These 'devout sceptics' to whom Newman's way and Carlyle's way were equally erroneous, had yet to discover their own solution. It was not sufficient for them to learn to 'do *without opium,* and live through all our pain with conscious, clear-eyed endurance',[2] they still needed a meaning and direction for their thought and action. To some the answer was Comte: the prophet of the new era did not only offer a new way of thought and life, he gave them the positive religion, and mankind as a high and noble object of worship. Without the opium of transcendent religion, without the hopes of Heaven, their stoical, active cult of man and of human progress gathered singularly in force. For in mankind there was hope, and as the searchlight of science penetrated deeper into its savage past, and traced its glorious advance to the present, the road ahead pointed clearly to a better world, perhaps some day a perfect world. Drastic changes and improvements in the human condition were needed, better education was urgently called for, and Science would do the rest. As the positivists appreciated the importance of religion in social and moral development, they also knew the meaning and force of chiliastic aspiration: the promise of Heaven, the dream of the Golden Age, had, like all religious concretion, their core of truth, since they embodied psychological urges and attracted to them generous instincts and emotional energy. In its transcendent pro-

---

[1] *Nineteenth Century Studies,* p. 221.
[2] Letter from George Eliot, quoted from Cross, *Life of George Eliot,* vol. ii, p. 283.

jection this energy had lost a great deal of its creative force, but now that man alone was responsible for the fate of mankind, it would be directed to a great and happy future. Now his most noble instincts, his love and sympathy, his need for veneration, had found a real and worthy object, Humanity; and, at the same time, a much more compelling moral obligation was imposed upon man now that the burden of God was shifted to his shoulders. Of this new Humanitarian religion Stuart Mill wrote the apology:

The essence of religion is the strong and earnest direction of the emotions and desires towards an ideal object, recognized as one of the highest excellence, and as rightfully paramount over all selfish objects of desire. This condition is fulfilled by the Religion of Humanity in as eminent a degree, and in as high a sense, as by the supernatural religions even in their best manifestations, and far more so than in any of their others... the sense of unity with mankind, and a deep feeling for the general good, may be cultivated into a sentiment and a principle capable of fulfilling every important function of religion and itself justly entitled to the name.[1]

To the early positivists in England, Darwin's theory did not come in the nature of a momentous revelation, and to begin with left no deep traces in their thoughts about the future. It offered, no doubt, a sound explanation of biological development, and filled a gap in Comte's doctrine. It caught the process of life into the universal process of advance towards harmony and perfection. Mostly through Spencer, the group around the *Westminster Review* had been prepared for *Origin,* and thus it made little impression on George Eliot.[2] Stuart Mill, curiously enough, pointed out that Darwin's theory, which might be a plausible explanation, was not 'inconsistent with Creation'. It seemed to him, however, that teleology rather than 'natural selection' was the answer, for 'the adaptations in Nature

[1] 'Theism', *Three Essays on Religion* (1874), pp. 109—10.
[2] Cf. B. Willey, *Nineteenth Century Studies,* p. 238.

afford a large balance of probability in favour of creation by intelligence'.[1]

Yet, unquestionably, *Origin of Species* was a new ally to the positivists and it pointed in the direction of their whole intellectual effort. It meant at least two things; first, a triumph of science over ignorance and myth, to prove once more the general truth of the positivist doctrine; secondly, it was an important argument in the further advance of knowledge.

If Carlyle's temperamental vision saw a world rocking and plunging in the thirties, it was a calm scene compared to the disturbance which Darwin's work spread far and wide in the Victorian mind. In the first perplexed decades, truth was either with the Church or with Science. Science in those days was acquiring the dogmatism and fervour which orthodoxy had gradually lost, and a persuasive confidence in its ability to explain, in due course, the most unyielding enigmas of existence. Where religion ended, in the metaphysical stage, Science had taken over. In vain did Carlyle heap scorn on the ambition of science and warn against its fatal *hubris,* to the agnostics there was nothing left but 'the fertile fields of ascertainable fact'.

As scepticism swept the minds fast and far from the orthodox faith, they drifted in increasing numbers into the main stream of radical intellectualism. And this intellectualism was not bent on destruction only or mainly, but haunted by dreams and apocalyptic visions of the future. Instead of a transcendent state of bliss there appeared the outlines of an earthly paradise from which evil, pain and conflict had vanished. And it was here that the idea of evolution acquired a deeper meaning to those who had found in the religion of Humanity a new faith. Evolution became, in its natural union with the idea of progress, the very scientific foundation of this new worship. The promise of evolution was a promise of redemption, and redemption the human race needed, to expiate the ape and

---

[1] 'Theism', *Three Essays,* p. 174.

tiger trespasses which even now were perpetrated as original sin upon man. And the new saviour, the creative and perfecting impulse of life, would not fail to deliver man from evil. Sometime, if not soon, the lion would lie down with the lamb.

Yet the moral aspect of evolutionary belief was not the only one. In the poets' imagination as well as in the popular mind strange dreams of human greatness and power were beginning to arrange themselves into the portrait of the ideal future human being, the 'perfect man' or the 'superman'. It was a dream congenial to an age that still admired the great individual and leader, practised the virtues of the 'gentleman' and even occasionally worshipped the hero. If man had no hope of immortality and heavenly perfection, then this would be his compensation: a kingship on earth, an unlimited mastery of his mind over Nature and his own destiny.

Thus the idea of evolution nourished important aspects of humanitarian and Utopian speculation in the later half of the century. Even before Darwin, the *Vestiges of Creation* forecast the evolution of a superior race, and this topic became popular in literary and intellectual circles. As Disraeli demonstrated in his novel *Tancred* (1847), such evolutionary fantasies were easily exposed to ridicule. Here Lady Constance explains 'Revelations of Chaos' (alias *Vestiges*) to young Tancred:

'To judge from the title, the subject is rather obscure', said Tancred.
'No longer so', said Lady Constance. 'It is treated scientifically; everything is explained by geology and astronomy, and in that way. It shows you exactly how a star is formed; nothing can be so pretty! A cluster of vapour, the cream of the milky way, a sort of celestial cheese, churned into light, you must read it, 'tis charming.'
'Nobody ever saw a star formed', said Tancred.
'Perhaps not. You must read the 'Revelations'; it is all explained. But what is most interesting, is the way in which man has been developed. You know, all is development. The principle is perpetually going on. First, there was nothing, then there was something; then, I forget the next, I think there were shells, then fishes; then

we came, let me see, did we come next? Never mind that; we came
at last. And the next change there will be something very superior
to us, something with wings. Ah! that's it: We were fishes, and
I believe we shall be crows. But you must read it'.

'I do not believe I ever was a fish', said Tancred.

'Oh! but it is all proved; ... Everything is proved: by geology,
you know. You see exactly how everything is made; how many
worlds there have been; how long they lasted; what went before,
what comes next. We are a link in the chain, as inferior animals
were that preceded us: we in turn shall be inferior; all that will
remain of us will be some relics in a new red sandstone. This is
development. We had fins; we may have wings.'[1]

And Tancred, who had 'almost dreamed of kneeling with her at
the Holy Sepulchre', leaves this deplorable 'spiritual mistress' and
begins his new crusade alone.

However, despite controversy and ridicule, the evolutionary faith
continued to spread, and the idea of creative and ascending life became an inspiration not only to scientists, philosophers and humanitarian reformers, but also to those whom Shelley called the 'un-
acknowledged legislators of the world'. The poets and authors caught
it, as a theme of fresh imaginative value and unlimited scope, to be
worked out in fantasy or made into teaching. In the light of this
new vision of life, they tried to read the fortune of mankind.

[1] *Tancred;* (1871 ed.), pp. 109—10.

CHAPTER II

EVOLUTION IN THE PLATONIC TRADITION

1. *Alfred Tennyson*

WHEN CARLYLE SKETCHED his dramatic portrait of
Tennyson in 1842, he stressed features particularly congenial to
his own:

A man solitary and sad, as certain men are, dwelling in an element
of gloom, carrying a bit of Chaos about him, in short, which he is
manufacturing into a Cosmos.[1]

It is a person altogether different from the cheerful, serene patriarch
and Poet Laureate we meet in his son's *Memoir,* which remains to
the student of Tennyson the richest source of information available.
On the whole, though Tennyson's contemporaries felt the conflict
to which Carlyle refers, they preferred to explore the Cosmos of his
poetry, since it indicated a goal for their own spiritual pilgrimage.
In his wise words about the faith that lives in honest doubt Tennyson had drawn the *formula concordiæ* so urgently needed by their age.

It was not until the new century had begun reviewing the conduct
and beliefs of the 'Eminent Victorians' that Carlyle's portrait was
rediscovered, and further dramatized with a growing insistence upon
the 'Chaos', so that Tennyson became to some an 'unhappy mystic',
to others a 'master of melancholia'. And increasingly, this Chaos, or
spiritual tension, has gained in interest as an integral and creative
aspect in Tennyson's poetry. It is agreed now that if Tennyson is

---

[1] *Letter to Emerson.*

66

a poet of mental conflict, of faith and doubt, it is not because his age expected him to reflect its predicament in a heightened light and achieve some final synthesis of contradictions, but because he himself was profoundly disturbed by the same predicament. As it happened, he came to face this at a time when he was indeed solitary and sad, and he never quite recovered from the experience.

The history of Tennyson's intellectual background and development has been told often and in detail, and for our present purpose only a few main features will be recapitulated.[1]

In later years Tennyson regretted the reproachful *Lines on Cambridge* which, as an undergraduate in 1830, he wrote against the University

> that do profess to teach
> And teach us nothing, feeding not the heart.[1]

At Cambridge he acquired the experience which made him the poet of *The Two Voices* and *In Memoriam*. It was there, too, that he found the 'Apostles', and had the thought of Coleridge expounded by such gifted and fervent disciples as F. D. Maurice and John Sterling.[3] Coleridge's *Aids to Reflection*, with its doctrine of 'Understanding' and 'Reason', was essentially a message for the heart. 'To Coleridge', Sterling wrote to Julius Hare a few years later, 'I owe *education*. He taught me to believe that an empirical philosophy is none, that Faith is the highest Reason'. The same teaching came to Tennyson

---

[1] Apart from Th. Lounsbury's *Life and Times of Tennyson*, important as a general study of the early Tennyson, three papers have been useful for the elucidation of possible sources of Tennyson's evolutionary ideas: G. R. Potter, 'Tennyson and the Biological Theory of Mutability of Species', *Philological Quarterly*, 1937; W. Rutland, 'Tennyson and the Theory of Evolution', *Essays and Studies*, 1940, vol. xxvi; G. Hough, 'The Natural Theology of *In Memoriam*', *Review of English Studies*, 1947—48.

[2] *A Memoir*, I, p. 67.

[3] Cf. *A Memoir*, I, p. 36: 'The German School, with Coleridge, ...'; also p. 42.

[4] Sterling, *Essays and Tales*, (1848), vol. i, p. xiv.

through his enthusiastic Cambridge set, and Coleridge gave him, no doubt, a way of thinking about life and the universe which suited his inclination to mysticism, and his temperament.

Tennyson matriculated in 1828 at Trinity, and if that College failed in feeding his heart, it had for compensation some of the leading naturalists of the time. Tennyson's tutor was Whewell, professor of Mineralogy, an eminent spokesman of Cuvier's ideas, as was A. Sedgwick, the geologist. Another Trinity man, Peacock, was professor of Astronomy. Thus Tennyson, whose keen interest in astronomy and geology is early recorded, moved into a milieu that had a great deal to offer his intellectual curiosity.[1] It was during his Cambridge years that he wrote *The Palace of Art* (in the 1833 volume) to which belonged originally these stanzas, describing his soul in contemplation of the stars:

> Hither, when all the deep unsounded skies
> Shudder'd with silent stars, she clomb,
> And as with optic glasses her keen eyes
> Pierced thro' the mystic dome,
>
> Regions of lucid matter taking forms,
> Brushes of fire, hazy gleams,
> Clusters and beds of worlds, and bee-like swarms
> Of suns, and starry streams.[2]

If Tennyson at Cambridge, as we know, discarded some of his early notions about God and the universe, without breaking with Christianity, it was in part due to Coleridge's thought, in part to the attitude in the Cambridge scholars. Tennyson's faith changed into the religion of intuition which Carlyle, Matthew Arnold, F. D.

---

[1] For an account of Tennyson's preoccupation with natural history and astronomy, see *A Memoir*, I, p. 20.

[2] *A Memoir*, I, p. 120.

Maurice, and the Broad Churchmen in various formulations adapted to their own need and those of their time. Cambridge was a milieu in which such a transition might take place without spiritual crisis. In the writings of the Cambridge scholars there is an emphasis on the limitations of human knowledge not uncongenial to Coleridge's views, and in their unanimous adherence to the doctrine of 'Special Creations' they maintained a compromise between religion and science which did not even tolerate the radical advance of Lyell's theory of Uniformity. Whewell made his contribution to this compromise in writing one of the *Bridgewater Treatises* on the subject of *Astronomy and General Physics Considered with Reference to Natural Theology* (1833).

The 'Chaos' which persists in Tennyson's poetry from *The Two Voices* onwards has, therefore, no direct roots in the Cambridge background, nor can it be related to the general disturbance caused by science and the Higher Criticism.[1] Its cause, as Sir Harold Nicolson has convincingly argued, was a horror of death which the sudden loss of his friend Arthur Hallam made singularly poignant and lasting. Death and annihilation are the 'Chaos' which Tennyson, as Carlyle saw him, tried to overcome and manufacture into a Cosmos, or a vision of life—life imperishable and abundant.

Dust and Ashes

The universe that gradually emerges to the young poet has frequent references to contemporary science. It is possible to identify some of these with individual theories; others derive from a vaguer and more general background. Tennyson delights in the grand vistas of cosmic creation and development contained in Laplace's

---

[1] G. Hough sees in Lyell's *Principles of Geology*, which Tennyson read in 1837, a source of this conflict in *In Memoriam*; cf. *op. cit.* It occurs, however, earlier than this.

Nebular Hypothesis. In the early *Supposed Confessions of a Second-rate Sensitive Mind* it illustrates the growth of truth, to perfection:

> as from the storm
> Of running fires and fluid range
> Of lawless airs, at last stood out
> This excellence and solid form
> Of constant beauty.

In the omitted stanzas from *The Palace of Art* quoted above, there is a dense, jewelled star-imagery tracing the cosmic process from its 'regions of lucid matter' into the 'clusters and beds of worlds'. Again, in *The Princess* it appears in Lady Psyche's lecture:

> This world was once a fluid haze of light,
> Till toward the centre set the starry tides,
> And eddied into suns, that wheeling cast
> The planets: then the monster, then the man ...[1]

The statement, in its context, does not express a personal conviction that the world has thus evolved—it is a purely imaginative theme of splendid visual scope and majestic movement.[2] When the idea next occurs, in *In Memoriam* (cxviii), it is still referred to as a hypothesis, though an acceptance is here implicit in the deeper significance which cosmic evolution lends to existence as a whole:

> They say
> The solid earth whereon we tread

[1] Part II.

[2] Similar treatments exist prior to Kant's and Laplace's theories, thus in Young's *Night Thoughts* 1742—5: 'All the stars . . From darkness and confusion took their birth . . . from fluid dregs/Tartarean, first they rose to masses rude . .'; *Night the Ninth.)*

> In tracts of fluent heat began,
> And grew to seeming-random forms,
> The seeming prey of cyclic storms,
> Till at the last arose the man;

> Who throve and branch'd from clime to clime,
> The herald of a higher race,

> . . . . . .

> If so he type this work of time . . .

Cuvier's Catastrophism may be the source of the 'cyclic storms'. The predominant concept is, however, the process of change and transformation. It is conceived of, sometimes, as a drama through which this globe has passed, with 'fires and floods and earthquakes of the planet's dawning years'—like the emotional turmoils of youth.[1] Tennyson is strongly conscious of the forces which have acted out this drama over vast periods of time:

> the Giant Ages heave the hill
> And break the shore, and evermore
> Make and break, and work their will ...[2]

Lyonesse, Arthur's country, is 'A land of old upheaven from the abyss/By fire, to sink into the abyss again . .'.[3] Beside these ravages, other forces have been at work to change the face of the earth:

> Contemplate all this work of Time,
> The giant labouring in his youth ...[4]

[1] *Locksley Hall Sixty Years After.*
[2] *Ode on the Death of the Duke of Wellington.*
[3] *The Passing of Arthur.*
[4] *In Memoriam,* cxviii.

The poet's world is everywhere permeated by historical process, often reflected in his favourite time-image, the *Æon*.[1] He nourishes his youthful mind 'with the fairy tales of science, and the long result of Time . .'[2] He contemplates the seas of history 'that daily gain upon the shore'—'leading up the golden year'.[3] For mankind —yes; but for the individual?

> The moanings of the homeless sea,
>   The sound of streams that swift or slow
>   Draw down Æonian hills, and sow
> The dust of continents to be;
>
> And Love would answer with a sigh,
>   "The sound of that forgetful shore
>   Will change my sweetness more and more,
> Half-dead to know that I shall die."[4]

The process of change is also a *memento mori*—it reminds Tennyson of the transience of love and life; it is a working out of chaos and destruction: "Men dies: nor is there hope in dust . .". And since this is the truth science offers him, we see at this juncture how Tennyson's fear of death is interlinked with a horror of blind, mechanical forces operating without heed or plan throughout the universe.

Again and again this horror of death and meaningless existence invades Tennyson's vision of the world and leaves it a chaos. The pattern is visible already in the immature *Supposed Confessions of a Second-rate Sensitive Mind,* which contains this significant statement:

[1] 'Æon' recurs in relevant contexts in *In Memoriam,* xxxv, xcv; *De Profundis; Locksley Hall, Sixty Years After; The Making of Man; The Ring.*
[2] *Locksley Hall.*
[3] *The Golden Year.*
[4] *In Memoriam,* xxxv.

> I am too forlorn,
> Too shaken: my own weakness fools
> My judgment, and my spirit whirls,
> Moved from beneath with doubt and fear.

Arthur Hallam, Tennyson's Cambridge friend, died in 1833, and *The Two Voices,* we read in the *Memoir,* 'was begun under the cloud of this overwhelming sorrow, . . . which for a while blotted out all joy from his life, and made him long for death . . .'[1] In its astringent verse and controlled manner the poem expresses the more poignantly its experience of suicide despair. Here Tennyson for the first time is facing the reality of death as a personal and universal disaster for which nothing can compensate. Night has descended on his world, and—'the world is wide': Man, who is so 'wonderfully made' is but an insignificant atom within it, and—

> 'in a boundless universe
> Is boundless better, boundless worse.'

Measured against the vastness of a 'hundred million spheres' the individual life shrinks to nothing: 'there is plenty of the kind', and many more have been wasted. How, then, could the human being exist as part of a universal purpose? This is the acid test applied to all the various alloys of hope and faith in which the poet seeks refuge: Knowledge is useless, since it gives no certainty and no real insight, and the curse of time is upon everything. Time makes 'A dust of systems and of creeds', and man and memory perish, like all else in this

> 'life of nothings, nothing-worth,
> From that first nothing ere his birth,
> To that last nothing under earth!'

[1] I, p. 109.

The disintegration spreads outwards from this suicide trance with its repetitive 'Were it not better not to be?' to all aspects of existence.

In Memoriam provides a more comprehensive vision of the same process of decay. Here sorrow, 'Priestess in the vaults of Death', repeats the message of despair:

> "The stars," she whispers, "blindly run;
>   A web is wov'n across the sky;
>   From out waste places comes a cry,
> And murmurs from the dying sun:

> "And all the phantom, Nature, stands—
>   With all the music in her tone,
>   A hollow echo of my own,—
> A hollow form with empty hands."[1]

The ancient myth of the sun-death is caught into the vision of a meaningless cosmic process and the running-down universe. From the horror of this vision there is only one escape:

> My own dim life should teach me this,
>   That life shall live for evermore,
>   Else earth is darkness at the core,
> And dust and ashes all that is;[2]

The stanza balances the two fatal possibilities, but the death-theme gains and pursues its exploration of chaos:

> This round of green, this orb of flame,
>   Fantastic beauty, such as lurks
>   In some wild Poet, when he works
> Without a conscience or an aim.

[1] iii.   [2] xxxiv.

Perhaps the most intense experience of chaos is visualized in section 1, where agony and fear are projected into a myth, of

> Time, a maniac scattering dust,
> And Life, a Fury slinging flame.

While man dwindles and is seen, insect-size, vicious, to live for a brief moment and vanish. Evil adds its bitter ingredient to the poet's universal spleen.

The enigma of purpose is bound up, in this poem as in *The Two Voices*, with the thought of profusion and waste of life. It is a far cry from the eighteenth-century Theodicy to the tragedy of meaningless existence which Tennyson faces in the three successive groups, liv, lv, lvi. There are several themes of grief: the transience of all beings, relationships, and things; the cruel, unthinking waste of life in Nature; the indifference of fate to the individual and his values, which appears to belie the providence of God; the reality of evil. All these converge on the question: shall man

> Who loved, who suffer'd countless ills,
>> Who battled for the True, the Just,
>> Be blown about the desert dust,
> Or seal'd within the iron hills?
>
> No more? A monster then, a dream,
>> A discord ...[1]

Maud (1855) Tennyson described as a 'little Hamlet', and indeed the chief feature in the hero is death-thought and a withering sadness. He, too, is tormented by the vision of evil, of meaningless existence—a 'game' in which men are merely puppets, with no will of their own and no power to shape their destinies: puppets that are wantonly

---

[1] lvi.

75

'pushed off from the board' by an 'unseen hand'. The stars are 'pitiless, passionless eyes'—'cold fires', that 'burn and brand/His nothingness into man'.[1] The revenge of God is called down on mankind—'the whole weak race of venomous worms,/That sting each other here in the dust'[2].

In *Maud* the treatment of the death-theme is becoming more detached; it bears the stamp of an emotional after-math and of torments that no longer stand in the centre of the poet's creative experience. This is true also of *Lucretius*, which looks back to *Maud* and, remotely, to *The Two Voices*, and blends the suicide-theme with that of madness. To Lucretius, the universe is in a hideous state of disintegration:

> I saw the flaring atom-streams
> And torrents of her myriad universe,
> Ruining along the illimitable inane,
> Fly on to clash together again, and make
> Another and another frame of things
> For ever . . .

The poem develops the usual structure of painful thought, with doubt in 'the Gods', and insistence upon this 'poor little life' and its 'blind beginnings', with a vision of the ultimate break-down of the cosmic order, when all shall vanish, 'atom and void, atom and void,/Into the unseen for ever'.

The chaos-theme persists also in some of Tennyson's later poems. In *Despair* the 'limitless Universe' crushes man with terror: there is 'no soul in the heaven above', and man, 'born of a brainless Nature' is but a 'worm in the dust' and will 'die for ever'. Death awaits the whole universe:

> And the homeless planet at length will be wheel'd thro'
> the silence of space . . .

[1] XVIII, iv.   [2] XXIII, ii.

In this poem the insistence upon 'Chaos' through a repetitive, almost Baudelairean death-imagery is an effort calculated to visualize spiritual decay. A similar effort runs through much of the contentious meditation of the old man in *Locksley Hall Sixty Years After*:

Chaos, Cosmos! Cosmos, Chaos! who can tell how all will end?

Death is the common lot, and 'the sun himself will pass'. Has existence a meaning? Has God created man to any purpose?—'What are men that He should heed us?'

Insects of an hour, that hourly work their brother insect wrong . . .

Once more the human being is measured against the vastness of the 'silent Heavens' and dwindles into nothing, a mere insect. Here, as in *In Memoriam* and *Maud*, the insect-symbol blends the meaning of evil, littleness and transience. It reappears in *Vastness* in conjunction with the perennial question of the meaning of life:

What is it all but a trouble of ants in the gleam of a million million of suns?

Vastness, evil and death—these are the three weird sisters in the poet's vision of the world, and they continue to haunt him to the end. After the serene middle period of Tennyson's life, in which the cosmic enigmas were treated as mainly imaginative themes, the poet in his old age wanders again among the perplexities of his youth. Chaos spreads from his 'doubt and fear' and unfolds in *Vastness* and *The Dawn* nightmare visions of death, hatred and cruelty not less real to him for being texts on which he preaches frank moral sermons. Behind the strained prophetic fury there is all the time the still, small voice:

Will my tiny spark of being wholly vanish in your deeps and heights?[1]

[1] *God and the Universe.*

More Life, and Fuller

Tennyson's spiritual quest is like a metabolism continually breaking down and building up imaginative structures in a process that seems repetitive rather than progressive. The beliefs which inform his later poetry are more universal in orientation than the personal confessions of *The Two Voices* and *In Memoriam,* yet they have not changed essentially in character. It is convenient, therefore, to analyse his constructive effort—his Cosmos—without strict reference to a chronological scheme.

As the darkness of death closes in upon the poet in *The Two Voices,* he escapes its horror by appealing to life:

> " 'Tis life, whereof our nerves are scant,
> Oh life, not death, for which we pant:
> More life, and fuller, that I want."

'Life piled on life/Were all too little', says the old Ulysses.[1] Since bodily death, however, is inevitable, the true, the full life must lie beyond, in eternity. A large part of the poet's task is dedicated to an exploration of everlasting life, by means of intuition, unconscious memory, or feeling. He strives to follow the 'mystic gleams', the 'dim life' and 'hints' through which the soul still communicates with the world of spirit whence it came. Thus, like Coleridge, against the 'Godless deep' of unbelief, and of science, he pits the 'heat of inward evidence'. This insight, *The Ancient Sage* asserts, is more reliable than the thoughts of our 'thin minds', and the assurance it offers of life eternal is the basis on which Tennyson's Cosmos—a world of love and purpose—is seen rising, like a Phoenix, from the 'dust and ashes'.

[1] *Ulysses.*—The same idea occurs in the unpublished poem *Life, A Memoir,* I, p. 59.

Tennyson's obsessive preoccupation with death is the negative aspect of an insatiable life-zest which informs a considerable part of his poetry and seeks expansion in various directions. His craving for immortality, as Bradley first and T. S. Eliot more recently have stressed, is not an aspiration to beatitude, but to continued, happy life. His 'concern is for the loss of man rather than for the gain of God'.[1] Thus, in *In Memoriam,* Tennyson claims that his dead friend Arthur is living a 'full new life', and breathing 'an ampler day'. Our short life is merely a 'state' in the 'eternal process moving on'.[2]

To overcome the chaos which doubt and death work in his universe, Tennyson seeks a principle of Divine plan and purpose, and once he has learned to 'trust' the evidence of his 'mystic gleams', or faith, he finds this in universal Love. When, finally, the death-consciousness of *The Two Voices* is dispelled by a 'hidden hope', the poet feels that over and above the discords, his world is governed by Divine Love, and the purpose, hitherto concealed behind 'thick veils', is revealed: 'I see the end and know the good'.

In the purgatory of *In Memoriam* the Divine principle of Love is, for a long time, lost out of sight. Man seems betrayed; man

> Who trusted God was love indeed,
> And love Creation's final law—[3]

The spiritual quest throughout the poem is directed towards a reconciliation of cosmic conflict, and of Doubt and Death, with Divine love. However tentatively this is achieved, Tennyson gradually gains a deeper understanding of the love that links him with his dead

---

[1] T. S. Eliot, 'Tennyson's *In Memoriam', Selected Prose* (Penguin), p. 181. Bradley in his *Commentary on In Memoriam* (p. 51) states that Tennyson sees this life as the first. The soul does not attain final bliss in death but retains its individuality, and the new life implies generally a new embodiment in a spiritual growth towards perfection.

[2] lxxxii.   [3] lvi.

friend, and which must, he claims, derive from a universal reality. Henceforth love, as a 'final law' of Creation, not only harmonizes the discords of existence, but bridges life and eternity. And again, as in *The Two Voices*, love discloses the Divine plan in Creation:

> I see in part
> That all, as in some piece of art,
> Is toil cö-operant to an end.[1]

Throughout Tennyson's poetry, love remains the principle of order and harmony, invoked at times explicitly to dispel chaos. The old man in *Locksley Hall Sixty Years After* reaches out, over the turmoils of his world, for the promise that 'Love will conquer at the last.' *Vastness* ends on a peremptory dismissal of death-thoughts:

> Peace, let it be! for I loved him, and love him for ever:
> the dead are not dead but alive.

In *Akbar's Dream* the time is foreshadowed

> when creed and race
> Shall bear false witness, each of each, no more,
> But find their limits by that larger light,
> And overstep them, moving easily
> Thro' after-ages in the love of Truth.
> The truth of Love ...

An important effect of love upon the poet's 'Cosmos' is the basis and justification it provides for universal *law*. In *De Profundis* Tennyson, contemplating 'this changing world of changeless law', expresses a scientific and philosophical commonplace particularly dear to his age. Even through the despair of *In Memoriam* he clings

[1] cxxviii.

80

to the hope that 'nothing is that errs from law'.[1] Yet this assurance is valid only on the assumption that law is identical with the will of a loving God. *The Higher Pantheism* works out such an equation: 'God is Law' ... 'Law is God' ... The concluding stanza of *In Memoriam* contains Tennyson's 'Cosmos' in a dense, solid structure:

> That God, which ever lives and loves,
>   One God, one law, one element,
>   And one far-off divine event,
> To which the whole creation moves.

To defend this Cosmos against doubt and death became, especially in his later years, a conscious and sometimes a prophetic task. Intuition is throughout the main support in this effort, and only once, in *The Ancient Sage*, does he look beyond Coleridge to the eighteenth-century argument of design:

> But some in yonder city hold, my son,
>   That none but Gods could build this house of ours,
>   So beautiful, vast, various, so beyond
> All work of man ...

Tennyson ends his quest in the two short poems, *Faith* and *God and the Universe*, of which the first provides a symmetrical first part of the thought-structure completed in the second. It is a retrospect of the chaos he has lived through, with all that 'saddens Nature', with things ill and evil, and the burden of doubt that weighs on the human pilgrimage. Now, near the goal,

> Thro' the gates that bar the distance comes a gleam
>   of what is higher.

---

[1] lxxiii.

In the latter poem, this is the answer given to the enigma of human destiny:

'Spirit, nearing yon dark portal at the limit of thy
human state,
Fear not thou the hidden purpose of that Power
which alone is great,
Nor the myriad world, His shadow, nor the silent
Opener of the Gate.

Tennyson's 'Cosmos' is not a facile structure of belief, even though, in T. S. Eliot's opinion, it is poor theology. As Poet Laureate, Tennyson may have been 'the surface flatterer of his own time', and thus rightly deserved the post-Victorian critical spite. Yet Tennyson had worked out his 'Cosmos' already in *In Memoriam,* the most deeply personal of all his poems. It bears, and legitimately, the stamp of his time, and of the predicament which Coleridge and Newman, as well as Carlyle and Matthew Arnold faced. Newman's *Apologia* unfolds a world of spiritual disintegration, and his task is to create an order which may resist the attacks of the 'wild living intellect of man'. Arnold shared this task, though his solution was different, and he rescued from his 'honest doubt' an indestructible core of faith. Compared with these, Tennyson's intellectual formulation of his belief is vague and inconclusive, but to ignore the reality of this faith in *In Memoriam* is to disregard the development of spiritual experience to which the poem so powerfully bears witness.

The Cosmos Tennyson evolved from his faith has the intellectual weaknesses of this faith. It is a faith of hope, not unlike the trust in the existence of 'things hoped for' which to Coleridge was such an important criterion. But as a mystical, idealistic belief, Tennyson's Cosmos has nevertheless an active element of prophetic fervour and aspiration. It expresses an effort to fulfil his life-zest through a two-

82

fold spiritual ascent, on an immanent as well as on a transcendent plane, in which he feels all life is taking part, moving towards a state of ultimate harmony.

The Crowning Race

To his contemporaries, Tennyson early became 'the poet of Evolution', and it was taken for granted that certain passages of *In Memoriam* anticipated both *Vestiges of Creation* and Darwin's work of 1859.[1] Tennyson himself stated that he had written 'many a poem' about the subject of *Vestiges of Creation* when he wrote to Moxon for it in 1844.[2] At that time, however, it seems improbable that evolution meant to him what it meant to Chambers and to Darwin, i. e. transmutation of species; at least there is some agreement among scholars at present that it is evolution in the idealistic, Hegelian sense which is reflected in the early poetry of Tennyson, as in that of Browning.[3] The doctrine of 'Progression' which they found in contemporary science described an ascent of organic existence in terms of intelligent, purposive creation, and the *modus operandi* in this process was to them unimportant compared with its moral meaning and the chiliastic promise it held out to humanity. Because their interest is focused on the underlying Divine power manifested in life, and on its future goal, there is an easy transition from this belief in *natura naturans* to their later acceptance of a teleological theory of transmutation. The visions of progressive, aspiring life in *In Memoriam,* in Browning's *Paracelsus* (1835) and

[1] 'In *In Memoriam* Tennyson noted the fact, and a few years later Darwin supplied the explanation'; Romanes, *Darwin and After Darwin; op. cit. A Memoir,* I, p. 223.

[2] *Ibid.,* I, p. 223.—His son notes that Tennyson had read the 'sections about Evolution' in *In Memoriam* some time before 1844.

[3] Cf. J. Warren Beach, *The Concept of Nature in Nineteenth Century English Poetry,* p. 330; G. R. Potter, 'Tennyson and the Biological Theory of Mutability of Species', *Philological Quarterly,* 1937.

in Hugh Clough's *Natura Naturans* (1849) might, in their general descriptive terminology, express either theory, and this accounts for the favour which their 'evolutionary' poetry enjoyed on both sides.[1] In the following, therefore, the terms 'evolution' and 'evolutionary' will be used also of Tennyson's poetry before 1859.

In the early poems there are no certain traces of ideas referring to biological progress.[2] At Cambridge Tennyson is said to have toyed with the notion that 'the development of the human body might possibly be traced from the radiated, vermicular, molluscous and vertebrate organisms'.[3] This suggestion appears to reflect the current doctrine of 'Archetypal plan', in which the idea of progress was a central aspect. Two rejected stanzas from *The Palace of Art* (included in the 1833 and 1844 volumes) have also been quoted as evidence of Tennyson's interest in foetal development, from which he may have arrived at a belief in evolution:

'From shape to shape at first within the womb,
    The brain is modelled', she began,
'And through all phases of all thought I come
    Into the perfect man.

All Nature widens upwards. Evermore
    The simpler essence lower lies:
More complex is more perfect, owning more
    Discourse, more widely wise.'

[1] On reading *The Two Voices*, Spencer sent Tennyson a copy of his *Principles of Psychology*, which, he claimed, expounded the same 'hypothesis'; cf. *A Memoir*, I, p. 411.

[2] G. R. Potter rightly, it seems, denies importance to the unpublished poem from boyhood, *The Quick-wing'd Gnat*, *A Memoir*, I, p. 44, in opposition to Lionel Stevenson's opinion in *Darwin Among the Poets*.

[3] *A Memoir*, I, p. 44.—Potter here sees an influence of Von Baer's embryology, yet it is doubtful whether Tennyson knew of this at the time.

We have seen that Tennyson's world, as it emerges from the poems, is permeated by change and natural process, from the primordial amorphous state—the 'regions of lucid matter', 'haze of light' and 'tracts of fluent heat' into the 'clusters and beds of worlds'. In *The Princess* this cosmic development is continued in a perspective reaching from 'monster' to 'man'. Similarly, *The Two Voices* outlines a historical process reminiscent of Cuvier and his theory of 'Special Creations':

> I said, "When first the world began,
> Young Nature through five cycles ran,
> And in the sixth she moulded man.

This is a reinterpretation of Genesis in terms of natural law, 'Nature' here taking the place of God. In both poems the human being is closely related to the evolving natural scheme, though he is not stated to have descended from animal species. In the eighteenth century one heard frequently of man as a 'link in being's endless chain',[1] and this idea persisted in the first half of the nineteenth as embryologists and comparative anatomists continued to reconstruct the 'archetypal plan'. And as man became more definitely fitted into the organic pattern of this plan, his dualistic nature was increasingly emphasized, by the idealists in particular, since his soul could only derive from a Divine source. In *The Two Voices* the poet clings to the assumption of man's spiritual origin as an argument of cosmic purpose, while the voice of despair cynically wields the eighteenth-century argument of plenitude: Man is too imperfect to be the last goal of creation. To Pope (and to Browning) this idea was proof of sufficient reason, but to Tennyson it implies the absurdity of human existence. Man is the central fact in Tennyson's world, and every individual matters infinitely in the cosmic scheme.

[1] Cf. Young, *Night Thoughts*, 'Night the Ninth'.

In *The Two Voices* Tennyson, in his effort to explore life as a phase of spiritual existence, surveys three possibilities: The soul might have 'lapsed from nobler place', or first have been 'naked essence'; or

> "... if through lower lives I came—
> Though all experience past became
> Consolidate in mind and frame—

The boundaries of life are expanded through a notion of unconscious memory which somehow persists from one embodiment to another.[1] This spiritual continuity is, moreover, associated with phases of organic growth suggesting, though vaguely, a physical continuity as well.

The same expansion of life through the idea of metempsychosis is, in *In Memoriam*, given a more definite direction:

> I held it truth, with him who sings
> To one clear harp in divers tones,
> That men may rise on stepping-stones
> Of their dead selves to higher things.[2]

The spirit walks from 'state to state' in an 'eternal process', leaving behind the 'shatter'd stalks' of its mortal abode.[3] Here the insistence on man's spiritual destiny excludes a closer interest in the development of physical aspects. In *The Princess*, however, we are told that 'the brain was like the hand, and grew with using', and this Lamarckian idea refers not, it would seem, to the individual, but to the human race as a whole. Physical growth here, as in the omitted stanzas from *The Palace of Art*, illustrates mental development. Lady Psyche's lecture expounds in an impersonal manner a view of

---

[1] It is probable, as Potter suggests, that this idea refers to the transmigration of souls, recurrent in Tennyson's poetry.   [2] i.   [3] lxxxii.

86

cosmic evolution such as a contemporary naturalist might have stated it without reference to final causes: Man is a link in the great chain of being, and testifies to the universal progress. Later, as the problem of man's place in Nature becomes all-important and moves into the tormented world of *In Memoriam*, this confident view dissolves into a perplexed question:

And he, shall, he,

> Man, her last work, who seem'd so fair,
>   Such splendid purpose in his eyes,
>   Who roll'd the psalm to wintry skies,
> Who built him fanes of fruitless prayer,
>
> Who trusted God was love indeed,
>   And love Creation's final law—
>   Though Nature, red in tooth and claw
> With ravine, shriek'd against his creed—
>
> Who loved, who suffer'd countless ills,
>   Who battled for the True, the Just,
>   Be blown about the desert dust,
> Or seal'd within the iron hills?[1]

Man represents a distinctly new adventure in the predatory animal world. Yet is he altogether different? Is he primarily an immortal soul? Or is he merely a being mocked by his aspirations and doomed to perish utterly like the fossils of former life? The poet turns away from this vision of 'discord' and does not face the enigma again until the purgatory of grief lies behind him. As peace comes to his mind, the vision changes.[2] Man is still seen as the work of Nature

---

[1] lvi.　　[2] In section ciii two evolutionary ideas occur, casually thrown in: that of the 'great race, which is to be', and the 'shaping of a star'.

and of Time, but his spiritual being is vindicated with a new assurance:

Contemplate all this work of Time,
    The giant labouring in his youth;
    Nor dream of human love and truth,
As dying Nature's earth and lime;

But trust that those we call the dead
    Are breathers of an ampler day
    For ever nobler ends. They say
The solid earth whereon we tread

In tracts of fluent heat began,
    And grew to seeming-random forms,
    The seeming prey of cyclic storms,
Till at the last arose the man;

Who throve and branch'd from clime to clime,
    The herald of a higher race,
    And of himself in higher place,
If so he type this work of time

Within himself, from more to more;
    Or, crown'd with attributes of woe
    Like glories, move his course, and show
That life is not as idle ore,

But iron dug from central gloom,
    And heated hot with burning fears,
    And dipt in baths of hissing tears,
And batter'd with the shocks of doom

> To shape and use. Arise, and fly
> The reeling Faun, the sensual feast;
> Move upward, working out the beast,
> And let the ape and tiger die.[1]

The idea of cosmic evolution is here implicitly accepted. It is traced, as in *The Princess*, from stellar phases of development, and emphasis is throughout on progress in Nature and in man. Though efficient and final causes are not involved, the poet sheds, in the first stanzas, an indirect light on the evolutionary process: existence is the working out of a seminal principle of spirit, manifesting itself as striving, ascent—a purposive urge towards nobler life.

The Nebular Hypothesis and the theory of Catastrophism have left traces in the third stanza, in a pattern balanced between the enigma of: chance or direction? Physical nature yields no answer. Yet as man enters the scene, this ambiguity ceases, and even the 'seeming-random forms' become part of a creative purpose. Again man is seen as the last work of Nature, though how he 'arose' is not explained, probably because to Tennyson, as to Lyell, it remained a mystery. Man, however, gives to the evolutionary perspective a clear direction: he is the crowning evidence that life has a meaning, he is the shaft of light sunk to its dim origins beyond our knowledge, and he points our race to a greater future, which will be the fulfilment of his noblest aspirations. This is a historical process; but likewise in eternity the human soul will rise to higher levels of existence in an ascent that continues and completes the progress in time. The fourth stanza builds up and connects the transcendence-structure of the second stanza with that of evolution in the third.

The attainment of this double goal depends on man's moral effort. He must 'type' or re-enact the cosmic development in himself, from 'more to more'. The poet sees him as a microcosm capable of repeating the universal and phylogenetic progress, by conscious

[1] cxviii.

89

striving, and by turning to good account the emotional purgatory of his existence.[1] The ambiguities of the fourth and fifth stanzas do not impede the general unity of tone and argument: Existence is a real, historical development, though at the same time it is but a phase in the universal ascent of spirit, and man partakes in this, body and soul. Man is the outcome of a catharsis purifying life and elevating it from its lowest levels, its 'central gloom', to the highest values that man is capable of enjoying: love and truth. The universal law, as manifested in evolution, is 'from more to more', and if man conforms to this law on earth, his effort will shape out a 'higher race' in the future, and enable him to ascend in eternity to a 'higher place'. The two goals are thus seen as different aspects of the way of the soul, one racial and one individual, interacting with one another in a mutual advance.

In the fifth stanza the distinctive 'Or' seems to break the thought-structure by implying these alternatives: *either* man should follow the course of Nature, which appears as predetermined, *or* be guided by his suffering.[2] In the context of the poem, however, no such opposition between the two courses exists, and it is reasonable to

---

[1] A. C. Bradley comments on the difficulties of this passage, beginning with 'if so he type', and suggests that 'type' means 'repeat': there are 'two possible ways by which man can repeat the work of time within himself and so advance on earth and elsewhere,—the one is steady thriving and adding more to more; . . the other painful struggle'; *Commentary on Tennyson's In Memoriam*, p. 215. J. C. Collins reads 'reproduce' for 'type', and agrees in the main with the interpretation of Bradlew; *In Memoriam, The Princess, Maud*, p. 127. G. R. Potter claims that 'type' means 'parallel': man may parallel the cosmic process, but he is not part of it, since the evolution is a *natura naturans; op. cit.*—This distinction would seem to be somewhat artificial in view of the place occupied by man in the evolutionary pattern in the third stanza, and the purgatory structure, including all life, of the three final ones.

[2] A. C. Bradley notes that 'Or' reads 'And' in the first edition, which indicates that Tennyson originally had no sharp distinction in mind; *Commentary*, p. 214.

see the function of 'Or' as an emphasis, rather than as a choice. At this point a greater awareness of human suffering forces the poet's vision in a new direction, so that the development is felt to be, above all, a purgatory of man's emotional nature. Thus with man, evil and pain receive a new significance, as instruments of working out his animal, baser self. The central experience of *In Memoriam*, here condensed into the words 'fears' and 'tears' and the imagery of plastic and purifying process, moves from the individual stance into the universal destiny of the human race, through a clearer perception of teleological development. In the final stanza, the reconciliation of man with his purpose takes the form of a direct moral exhortation, and its dynamic, vertical movement built up on 'Arise', 'fly' and 'move upward', visualizes an ultimate evolutionary liberation from the animal chain.

This poem (cxviii.) shows clearly the meaning which Tennyson reads into the idea of evolution, and how it effects his vision of the world. It does not disperse his Chaos, for only his faith, or hope, that love is Creation's final law, can reassure him of the purpose and significance of life. Yet, having achieved this certainty, as far as he is able to, evolution offers strong evidence of a Divine plan in the ordered and progressive growth of life to higher levels. It speaks, moreover, of the triumph of life over death, of the glory of human effort and endurance, of fulfilment in life and in eternity. Now that Chaos has ceased, the force of evolution in the poet's cosmos is seen as an impetus thrown out towards two great goals of human aspiration. Within the framework of this idealistic and mystical belief, the question whether the idea expressed by Tennyson in *In Memoriam* is transmutation or *natura naturans* would seem to be of minor consequence.[1]

---

[1] G. Hough suspects the influence of *Vestiges of Creation* on this poem, and points out the contrast between this section and liv—lvi, which he explains by the transition in Tennyson's reading from Lyell to Chambers; 'The Natural Theology of *In Memoriam*', *Review of English Studies*, 1947—8.

The recurrence of the evolution-theme in the Epilogue is an indication that it is beginning to assume a profounder and more vital significance in Tennyson's belief. Here the moral exhortation in the final stanza of section cxviii is developed into a prophecy of the new human life, in which the individual soul participates as a creative energy, and illumines the destiny of the race:

A soul shall draw from out the vast
And strike his being into bounds,

And, moved through life of lower phase,
Result in man, be born and think,
And act and love, a closer link
Betwixt us and the crowning race

Of those that, eye to eye, shall look
On knowledge; under whose command
Is Earth and Earth's, and in their hand
Is Nature like an open book;

No longer half-akin to brute,
For all we thought, and loved, and did,
And hoped, and suffer'd, is but seed
Of what in them is flower and fruit;

Whereof the man, that with me trod
This planet, was a noble type
Appearing ere the times were ripe,
That friend of mine who lives in God—

That God, which ever lives and loves,
One God, one law, one element,

And one far-off divine event,
To which the whole creation moves.[1]

In 'life of lower phase' there is probably a statement of Von Baer's
'Recapitulation'-theory: the ontogenesis repeats the phylogenesis.[2]
The predominant trend is, however, the Platonic idea of spirit or
soul flowing into matter and urging life upwards through various
phases of growth. Through the connective action of 'link', the word
which stands, as it were, at the centre of the thought-structure, the
universal progress of life is seen moving from its 'lower phase',
through man, towards the crowning race of the future.[3] It is a
historical, cumulative process: Man as yet is half-akin to brute, but
through his intellectual effort and emotional purgatory, he will be
freed in the future from the animal chain. The form and content of
Tennyson's 'crowning race' prophecy is dictated partly by his
emotional and intellectual aspiration, partly by the grief for his
friend, who, as he elsewhere states—'bore without abuse/The grand
old name of gentleman . .'; who was 'Seraphic intellect', and 'High
nature amorous of the good'[4]. This 'noble type' predicts a fulfil-

---

[1] W. Rutland thinks that *Vestiges of Creation* may have influenced
Tennyson here, and discusses the chronological problem; 'Tennyson and
the Theory of Evolution', *Essays and Studies*, 1940, vol. xxvi. The same
view is argued by G. Hough, who finds in these stanzas an impact stronger
even than in cxviii; *op. cit.* It would appear, however, that in supposing
Vestiges to have relieved Tennyson of the pessimism, due, it is thought, to
Lyell's *Principles of Geology*, one pays scant heed to the deeper and more
personal experience through which the poet lived while at work on *In
Memoriam*.

[2] Thus A. C. Bradley, *op. cit.*, p. 239, and G. R. Potter, on the authority
of W. North Price, *op. cit.*

[3] W. Rutland sees a striking resemblance between the 'crowning race'
and a similar prophecy in *Vestiges of Creation*, p. 276: 'Is our race but the
initial of the grand crowning type?' Yet Tennyson had used 'great race'
already in ciii, dated by Bradley to 1837, *Commentary*, p. 15.   [4] cxi, cix.

ment of the best features in man. In the final stanza, however, the prophecy points beyond this 'crowning race' to a transcendent goal in which all existence will find consummation. The idea appears to be a development of the corresponding pattern in section cxviii, in that it foreshadows not only an ascent to a 'higher place' in eternity, but an ultimate arrival.

In *De Profundis*, written in 1852 and published in the *Ballads* volume of 1880, Tennyson returns to the evolutionary theme of the Epilogue:

> Out of the deep, my child, out of the deep,
> Where all that was to be, in all that was,
> Whirl'd for a million æons thro' the vast
> Waste dawn of multitudinous-eddying light—
> Out of the deep, my child, out of the deep,
> Thro' all this changing world of changeless law,
> And every phase of ever-heightening life,
> And nine long months of antenatal gloom,
> With this last moon, this crescent—her dark orb
> Touch'd with earth's light—thou comest, darling boy;
> Our own; a babe in lineament and limb
> Perfect, and prophet of the perfect man . . .

Cosmic evolution, in a pattern composed of Platonism, modern cosmogony (Nebular Hypothesis) and biological 'Progression' again forms the background of the embryological growth of an individual which repeats this evolution through phases of 'ever-heightening life'. Both processes stem from a common source, and the passage through 'this changing world of changeless law' does not necessarily imply a historical, organic transmutation, but certainly, seen in connexion with the following line, implies progressive development. It either means that the child achieves existence in the spiritual world, the 'deep', in a process analogous to that of cosmic evolution,

94

which it merely reflects, in an ideal sense, or it may mean that the child has a double origin, the 'deep' from which the soul directly emerges, and the physical, organic process which brings forth the human body from lower forms. In this last reading Tennyson's outlook would approach to the views of organic evolution later held by Wallace and Lyell.

The poem is vague in its blending of transcendent and immanent aspects, and the general impact is that of *natura naturans*. It is probable however, that the idea of 'ever-heightening life' should be connected with the 'perfect man' anticipation in a coherent evolutionary structure, similar to that in the Epilogue. In the perspective here opened up the process of ascending life assumes a real and historical meaning. Yet, clearly, the question whether it takes place through special creations or transmutation is not involved.

Tennyson's treatment of the theme of cosmic evolution in *The Two Voices, The Princess, In Memoriam* and *De Profundis* shows that to him it contains less of directive metaphysical thought than of spiritual aspiration and quest for life. If it confirms his belief in purposive and providential creation, and a universal principle of love, it is largely because the development reveals an increasing presence of mind and moral consciousness in the world. In these realities, too, he sees the strongest proof of the immortality of the soul: of the 'ever nobler ends' for which man is bound. Conversely, these are also evidence against the 'cunning casts in clay' that materialistic science makes of human beings. Hence his exhortation to moral effort; for the working out of the beast, the attainment to the perfect man and finally to the 'full new life', whether in time or in eternity, depends in no small degree on human striving. This tendency to charge the evolutionary theme with a moral content is explicit already in *In Memoriam,* and is next woven into the meditation of the young man in *Maud:*

A monstrous eft was of old the Lord and Master of Earth,
For him did his high sun flame, and his river billowing ran,
And he felt himself in his force to be Nature's crowning race.
As nine months go to the shaping an infant ripe for his birth,
So many a million of ages have gone to the making of man:
He now is first, but is he the last? is he not too base?[1]

In this poem Tennyson finds more precise use for the Recapitulation theory: it now works as an analogy defining and limiting the concept of growth as applied directly to the evolution of the human race. Possibly by this year (1855) he had come to adopt the ideas expounded in *Vestiges of Creation*, and at the same time Spencer's bold defence of the 'Development Hypothesis' in *The Leader* (1852) might have been known to him and helped to clarify his own belief.[2] Man is seen as the outcome of a slow and continuous process; the ontogenesis repeats the phylogenesis in a millionth fraction of time, and testifies clearly to the progressive direction in organic development. In *Maud* the ambiguity which still remains is due to the uncertain meaning of the 'eft'-image. If 'monstrous eft' means literally a prehistoric animal, then the poet implies that man has actually developed from such a creature, and the pre-natal growth of the foetus illustrates in a real sense the various stages of his evolution. In that case, Tennyson's outlook has become more 'naturalistic' since he wrote in *The Princess* of the successive appearances of 'then the monster, then the man'. If, on the other hand, 'eft' is merely a symbol of the brutish amoral nature of primitive man, the development is one of emotional and intellectual faculties within the human species. This reading, however, would

[1] IV, vi.

[2] W. Rutland finds in *Maud* a direct influence from *Vestiges* in the idea of the 'crowning race'; *op. cit.*—*Vestiges of Creation*, it will be remembered, used the Recapitulation theory as a defence of transmutation and as an argument to overcome emotional prejudice. Cf. *supra* p. 15.

surrender the analogy of foetal growth, which is here the very clue to the creative mystery, and it is reasonable to think that in *Maud* Tennyson for the first time has consciously expressed a belief in the transmutation of species. Yet his main interest, here as in the earlier poems, is focused on the moral nature of man capable of improvement. While *In Memoriam* derives from cosmic evolution, from the increasing presence of soul in the world, and from the effects of emotional purgatory, a promise of the 'higher race', *Maud* is a negative approach, and its tone and feeling lend to the argument an aspect of nausea with existing things, and a contempt for man: Man is too *base* to remain the crowning achievement in Nature. The same idea emerged as a theme of despair in *The Two Voices*, rooted in a different emotional experience. Here the young soliloquist in his universal spleen judges man by eighteenth-century principles of sufficient reason and plenitude: If the human being is bound to develop, it is not only because he has, in fact, greatly changed in the past, but because he falls short of an ideal of perfection inherent in the cosmic scheme. This ideal, seen through the word 'base', is essentially a moral destination. As a corollary, an important directive principle in evolution is ethical necessity.[1]

After *Origin of Species* had appeared, and Tennyson got the reassuring answer from its author to his question: 'Your theory of Evolution does not make against Christianity?', it was still this moral and spiritual significance of the evolutionary process which held his interest.[2] He remained, on the whole, undisturbed by the

---

[1] Cf. *A Memoir*, I, p. 324: 'The answer he would give to this query ['He now is first, but is he the last?'] was: "No, mankind is as yet on one of the lowest rungs of the ladder, although every man has and has had from everlasting his true and perfect being in the Divine Consciousness."

[2] *Loc. cit., A Memoir*, II, p. 57. It is not probable that, as G. R. Potter contends, Tennyson's question proves that he was unfamiliar with the idea before Darwin's publication. He knew of evolutionary ideas even before *Vestiges of Creation*, and his question implies merely: 'Your *specific*, or *new* theory' . . etc..

remoter philosophical implications of Darwin's thesis, and did not take part in the controversy, though in one or two of his later poems there are oblique references to it. Much in the same spirit as F. D. Maurice and Charles Kingsley, Tennyson adapted the new doctrine to his fundamental idealistic belief:

That makes no difference to me, even if the Darwinians did not, as they do, exaggerate Darwinism. To God all is present. He sees present, past, and future as one.[1]

Like Lyell, he moved naturally from a progressionist standpoint to one of teleological evolution, convinced that in cosmic and organic process works a power from which the individual soul emanates and of which it is an imperishable part. He saw

Life of Nature as a lower stage in the manifestation of a principle which is more fully manifested in the spiritual life of man, with the idea that in this process of Evolution the lower is to be regarded as a means to the higher.[2]

Tennyson's attitude to the problem of man's place in Nature is stamped by the spiritual, idealistic meaning he reads into the evolutionary process, and he states it also in negative terms similar to those of Lyell and the neo-Lamarckians:

No evolutionist is able to explain the mind of Man or how any possible physiological change of tissue can produce conscious thought.[3]

The human soul derives its existence from a non-material, supranatural source, and man thus, as the poet had vaguely indicated in De Profundis, has a double origin, which is merely two different

[1] A Memoir, I, p. 322; Cf. also: 'Darwinism, Man from Ape, would that really make any difference?', ibid. p. 514. See the striking parallelism with Browning's attitude, infra pp. 112, 125.
[2] Ibid., p. 323.   [3] Ibid., p. 323.

facets of the Divine creative power. Evolution is the gradual fulfilment of the striving of the soul after perfection and fuller life, and it takes place in time as well as in eternity.[1] On the issue of man Tennyson deplored the standpoint of the extreme Darwinians, and he voiced, in *Despair* (1881), the sad perplexity which their denial of man's immortal soul had thrust upon his age, and perhaps, sometimes, upon himself:

> O we poor orphans of nothing—alone on that lonely shore—
> Born of the brainless Nature who knew not that which
>   she bore!
>
> . . . . .
> Come from the brute, poor souls—no souls—and to die
>   with the brute————

Though the statement, one feels, has no deep personal root, it is related to the emotional tension which elsewhere makes Chaos in the poet's universe. It is again the horror of a blind, clock-work process in Nature, and this time under the impact of that principle of chance—Natural Selection. The final conclusion is reached through an in-flowing of Darwinian doctrine upon his fear of death, and tinged with the pervading pessimism of the 70's and 80's. In Thomas Hardy, as we shall see, similar visions, derived from the same sources of despair, had already from 1866 (*Hap*) formed integral parts of his consistently fatalistic belief.

The attack on Darwinism in *Despair* is levelled against the agnostic and materialistic formulation of the theory which tended to banish soul and intelligent plan from the universe. In general, however, evolution, in the sense of expansion and progress of life, remained to Tennyson a source of optimism, and a buttress to his Cosmos. It becomes a theme of life-assertive prophecy, as when

---

[1] Cf. *A Memoir*, I, p. 321: 'I can hardly understand, how any great, imaginative man, who has deeply lived, suffered, thought and wrought, can doubt of the Soul's continuous progress in the after-life'.

The Ancient Sage (Tiresias volume 1885) anticipates that the creative power—'That which knows',

> shall descend
>
> On this half-deed, and shape it at the last
> According to the Highest in the Highest.

In evolution there is a proof that the human race is bound, by law of Nature, to ascend to higher levels of life. It does not, indeed, explain evil and imperfection, but it reveals man as participator in a great cosmic enterprise, a pilgrimage upwards through the ages, and a future bright with promise. It sanctions, moreover, the belief in social and material progress so dear to the age. Tennyson wanted to share this faith, yet here too his attitude is often one of doubt and vacillation. He was, temperamentally, a troubadour of the past, of *In Memoriam,* of King Arthur and Ulysses. His delight in the gains of industrial and material progress suffered intrusion from regrets of things ancient end treasured which were, or would be, swept away. The world he loved was in danger of sinking, like Arthur's Lyonesse, into the abyss for ever.

It has been observed that Tennyson's conservative bent was not just this loyalty to the past, but a distrust in truths untried which might lead to strange gods and dead ends of anarchy. However, to dispel this threat of chaos, the idea of evolution points the movement to the 'crowning race' and reassures him that the world is 'wholly fair'. In the first *Locksley Hall* Tennyson is in search of a directive principle:

> Yet I doubt not through the ages one increasing
> purpose runs,
> And the thoughts of men are widen'd with the
> process of the suns.

In the bewilderment of the second *Locksley Hall*, as in *In Memoriam*, the principle is seen emerging despite evil and pain:

> Is there evil but on earth? or pain in every peopled
>   sphere?
> Well be grateful for the sounding watchword
>   'Evolution' here.

Yet, if the general direction is clear, human progress is often thwarted and apparently futile. It is again the drama of Cosmos and Chaos:

> Evolution ever climbing after some ideal good,
> And Reversion ever dragging Evolution in the mud.

In this poem as in *The Ancient Sage,* the Divine power is invoked to assert its purpose: 'A God must mingle with the game.' Thus Tennyson's evolutionary belief continues to interact with his religion as with his ethics. His prophetic vision ranges forward to a 'warless world, a single race, a single tongue' when man has outgrown his base nature:

> Every tiger madness muzzled, every serpent passion kill'd.

This moral message is the sole theme of *By An Evolutionist* (1888). It visualizes a conflict between man and animal, spirit and flesh:

> The Lord let the house of a brute to the soul of a man,
>   And the man said 'Am I your debtor?'
> And the Lord — 'Not yet: but make it as clean as you can,
>   And then I will let you a better.'

The stanza illustrates well Tennyson's moral reading of evolution. It is a variation on the purgatory theme of *In Memoriam* (cxviii) which marks a significant change of psychological emphasis in that it, contrary to the naturalistic doctrine, dwells on man's dualistic nature and the widening cleavage between his physical and spiritual instincts. Evolution, in Darwin's theory, implied an integration of all faculties and instincts with man's animal past and with his physical nature: man is a purely natural being. As this integration threatened to swamp the reality of his soul, it was counteracted by Christians and neo-Lamarckian scholars who offered an alternative teleological formulation of the theory. It seems to be this religious effort that makes its impact on Tennyson's frank sermon on Evolution. The second stanza of the poem adduces an argument for the pleasures of the 'brute'—a kind of Epicurean logic drawn from the possibility that the life of the flesh is the only one, so: eat and drink, for to-morrow we die!

> If my body come from brutes, my soul uncertain, or a fable,

> Why not bask amid the senses while the sun of morning shines ...

For creatures that are nothing but mechanical products of Natural Selection, nothing but 'cunning casts in clay', extreme materialism and sensualism seems indeed the rational way of life. Few of the naturalists, and least of all Darwin and Huxley had accepted this as a corollary of the biological facts, and they repeatedly asserted that the instincts of man, though 'natural', are not all of them necessarily 'good'. Yet evolutionary ideas were increasingly adopted in the utilitarian and naturalistic doctrines of ethics and furnished some of the main arguments to those who sought to establish a code of conduct, and a theory of values, on a scientific and sociological basis. This aggressive materialism, Tennyson feared, would lead to a disintegration of moral consciousness and brutalize man. In *The Promise of May* (1884) Edgar, the villain, personifies the cynical modern sophist who makes his 'natural' instincts and the new scientific theory an excuse for licentious living:

> And when the man,
> The child of evolution, flings aside
> His swaddling-bands, the morals of the tribe,
> He, following his own instincts as his God,
> Will enter on the larger golden age;
> No pleasure there taboo'd ...

To fight this vicious attitude, human experience, wisdom, Old Age in *By An Evolutionist*, assures us that the moral effort of a life-time is not futile: it is necessary to starve the 'wild beast' with which we are 'linkt' in a youth of reckless cravings, for only thus can we reach our spiritual destination, and fulfil our great task:

> If my body come from brutes, tho' somewhat finer than their own,
>   I am heir, and this my kingdom. Shall the royal voice be mute?
> No, but if the rebel subject seek to drag me from the throne,
>   Hold the sceptre, Human Soul, and rule thy Province of the brute.

This moral challenge casts back to *In Memoriam* (cxviii), but the stanza is essentially about the restoration of man to spiritual dignity and kingship. It contains an oblique attack on materialistic ethics, and reads like a belated comment on the 'Man's place in Nature'-controversy of the 1860's. The radical movement headed by Huxley had 'degraded' man—dethroned him from his sovereign place in Nature. It was imperative to reassert that man is indeed heir to something more than 'the Province of the brute', that his soul has royal command over the rebel subject of the flesh. The stanza seeks to build up, in majestic size, a portrait of the ideal man as Tennyson saw him; the man who 'bore without abuse/The grand old name of gentleman'. Human dignity and nobility, the glory and greatness

103

of moral effort—it was necessary to insist on these threatened values in the teeth of agnostic science and utilitarian ethics. The wisdom of Old Age has something to say about the meaning and rewards of the struggle:

> I have climb'd to the snows of Age, and I gaze at a field
>   in the past,
>   Where I sank with the body at times in the sloughs
>   of a low desire,
>
> But I hear no yelp of the beast, and the Man is quiet at last
>   As he stands on the heights of his life with a glimpse
>   of a height that is higher.

In two of Tennyson's last poems about Evolution, *The Dawn* and *The Making of Man* emphasis is again on this moral and spiritual progress. Though less direct in their exhortation to the good life than *By An Evolutionist,* these too are built on an obvious moral programme. Human evil is a predominant theme, and notably in *The Dawn* the baroque verbal fury and strained imagery mark, rather sadly, the change in Tennyson's treatment of the cosmic theme since *The Two Voices* and *In Memoriam.* It seeks to dramatize the role of man in his evolutionary advance through a close contemplation of evil, similar to the denunciations of *Vastness,* but with this difference that here the misery of mankind is seen as a phase that is slowly yielding to brighter prospects. The poet surveys history as a nightmare panorama of infanticide, cannibalism, holocausts, war and destruction. But, looking ahead, he finds that the oppressive darkness is lifting, to reveal an upward movement: we are reminded of the struggle of Old Age (*By An Evolutionist*) climbing to the 'snows of age' from the 'sloughs of low desire'. In a universal perspective, here too is a movement from animal to man, death to life:

> Dawn not Day!
> Is it Shame, so few should have climb'd from the dens in
> the level below,
> Men, with a heart and a soul, no slaves of a four-footed will?
> But if twenty million of summers are stored in the
> sunlight still,
> We are far from the noon of man, there is time for the
> race to grow.
>
> Red of the Dawn!
> Is it turning a fainter red? so be it, but when shall we lay
> The Ghost of the Brute that is walking and haunting
> us yet, and be free?
> In a hundred, a thousand winters? Ah, what will *our*
> children be,
> The men of a hundred thousand, a million summers away?

The underlying impulse is still a craving for abundant life, and perfect happiness, for the race as for the individual. Yet the poet is going back on his old tracks and the pattern has become stereotype: there is no imaginative growth, no chiliastic concretion, no uprush of vision or theory. His question appears to beat in vain upon the future, as it did in *Locksley Hall Sixty Years After*:

> Far away beyond her myriad coming changes earth will be
> Something other than the wildest modern guess of you and me.

The same vagueness of anticipation persists in *The Making of Man,* which repeats the pattern of the final stanza of *The Dawn*:

> Where is one that, born of woman, altogether can escape
> From the lower world within him, moods of tiger, or of ape?
> Man as yet is being made, and ere the crowning Age of ages,
> Shall not æon after æon pass and touch him into shape?

All about him shadow still, but, while the races flower and fade,
Prophet-eyes may catch a glory slowly gaining on the shade,
    Till the peoples all are one, and all their voices blend in choric
Hallelujah to the Maker 'It is finish'd. Man is made.'

The structure is lacking in inventiveness, for even the positive assertion of the second stanza is nothing but a reiteration of ideas similarly expressed in the two *Locksley Hall* poems: The goal of
evolutionary progress on earth is peace and harmony—a 'federation
of the world', and the 'crowning Age', more so than the 'crowning
race' prophecy, foreshadows a moral attainment. This feature has
not, however, gained in sharpness of definition, and it betrays a
singular lack of imaginative challenge, which may be due to Tennyson's emotional conservatism. His ideal is all the time the 'perfect
man'—a being of sweetness and light. Thus instead of preaching
the superman, Tennyson rather tends to insist that man is not yet
'man', not yet 'made' or perfected into the 'shape and use' which
he is meant to be, and which evolution seeks to realize.

The vast time-perspective which evolution always cuts into ages
past and future, is a salient feature in Tennyson's later poems, as in
those of earlier years. The process is infinitely slow, and takes *æons*
to complete its successive tasks:

Many an Æon moulded earth before her highest, man, was
born . . .[1]

And yet, the past is as nothing to the future: in this certainty Tennyson finds a paradox:

        For we are Ancients of the earth,
        And in the morning of the times.[2]

[1] *Locksley Hall Sixty Years After.*   [2] *The Golden Year.*

106

The Princess advises patience with 'this fine old world', since it is still 'a child in the go-cart'. Man is heir to much imperfection, to pain and weakness and 'tiger spasms', but, as the Ancient Sage assumes, 'this earth-narrow life' may be 'but yolk, and forming in the shell'. Similarly, the old man in *Locksley Hall Sixty Years After* anticipates future world harmony: 'for is not Earth as yet so young?' *The Dawn* explores infinite vistas of future ages, and trusts that, in the period calculated for this running down solar system to last, 'there is time for the race to gow'. Man has just begun his pilgrimage, and ahead of him there is almost unending adventure. In these prophecies Tennyson clearly, and it would seem deliberately, speaks as a representative of his age, for the idea of the perfectibility of man was one particularly dear to the Victorian, and could be shared by agnostics and Christians alike. Thus Stuart Mill made it the very basis for his religion of Humanity:

Let it be remembered that if individual life is short, the life of the human species is not short; its indefinite duration is practically equivalent to endlessness; and being combined with indefinite capability of improvement, it offers to the imagination and sympathies a large enough object to satisfy any reasonable demand for grandeur of aspiration.[1]

In *The Making of Man* the poet returns to his favourite time-image—the 'æon'. In a sense he is, in this poem and in *The Dawn*, doing for the human race what he struggled to achieve for himself in *In Memoriam*; to expand life into eternity. Since the race shall have life and evolutionary growth in 'æon after æon', then the time-process, with its tragic inevitability of transience and death loses some of its frightening aspect. Without the belief in continued life for the individual after death, this thought would have been merely a philosophical consolation, but clutching at this assurance,

---

[1] 'The Utility of Religion', *Three Essays on Religion* (1874), p. 106.

Tennyson is able to identify his own life-zest with that of mankind and glory in its future greatness. Symbolized by the 'æon', temporal existence becomes, as it were, eternalized, and the evolution of man is felt as a process that somehow will bridge the two realities, heaven and earth, in its ultimate attainment. More life, not beatitude, is his answer to the 'black negation of the bier', which even the Ancient Sage hates. Hence the fusion of immanent and transcendent existence in *In Memoriam* through the spiritual ascent by which men rise 'on stepping-stones/Of their dead selves to higher things'. This theme recurs in the late poem, *The Ring*: There is

> No sudden heaven, nor sudden hell, for man,
> But thro' the Will of One who knows and rules—
> And utter knowledge is but utter love—
> Æonian Evolution, swift or slow,
> Thro' all the Spheres—an ever opening height,
> An ever lessening earth—

And thus, with temporal and spatial boundaries opened, there is free play for the expansion of life, from this 'earth-narrow' scene (*The Ancient Sage*) to unlimited growth and fulfilment in other forms and modes of existence. *The Ring* makes a condensed and precise statement of ideas more incoherently expressed in *In Memoriam*[1] of the continuous ascent of the individual soul in eternity. Here, once more, the underlying horror of death—less obvious but still corroding at the poet's Cosmos, is translated into a vision of life everlasting and triumphant. In this victorious mood, with its attendant certainty of the direction unfailingly pursued by life, Tennyson raises the promise of Evolution at the head of the movement. In no other passage or poem has he used the concept in the same explicit way—as a focal point to organize the poetic structure into a meaningful, coherent whole.

[1] i. lxxxii, cf. also *A Memoir*, I, p. 321.

Perhaps, as T. S. Eliot claims, Tennyson never quite emerged from the torment and conflict of *In Memoriam*. It is undoubtedly true that there is no final reconciliation or resolution—no Cosmos once and for all replacing the Chaos, for Tennyson's belief is emotional, not intellectual, and his vision of the world changes with the changing fortunes of his faith and doubt—hope and fear. Yet there is an increasing certainty and a prevalence of faith, and it seems gratuitous to explain this greater serenity by a failure or refusal to confront the implications of Chaos. As theology, as dogma and doctrine, his 'Cosmos' is a shaky structure, but as effort and aspiration, it is great and valid, and it informs some of his best and most vigorous poetry.

In his own day, both scientists and the educated public gave Tennyson credit for having pioneered the idea of evolution, and few of them realized that he was the heir of a tradition as well as a representative of his time and a prophet of the future. His position, in so far as his belief might be related to any body of doctrine, is somewhere between the neo-Platonism of the eighteenth century and the biological theory of Nature advanced in the nineteenth, and his intuitive achievement is to express a synthesis of the two at a time when science, in general, was striking out on a single-minded materialist track. From eighteenth century thought, as reflected in the Idealistic systems of *natura naturans*, he received, mainly through Coleridge, a vision of Nature as the manifestation of a world of spirit—'that true world within the world we see'; and in the poets of that century he found this cosmic belief persistently focused on the growing perfection of life and the unfolding of mind upwards in the 'scale of being'.[1] These poets often gave a very precise formulation to their faith in the rational, purposive order of the universe. To them, however, this order was a static, hierarchical whole, complete and sufficient unto itself. Tennyson, moving with

[1] Thus in Pope's *Essay*, Akenside's *Pleasures of the Imagination*, Young's *Night Thoughts*.

the growing insight of his time, came to see the ideal, fixed system as development and a historical process. Even so, he retained the fundamental concept of philosophical Idealism, i. e. the world as an embodiment of spirit or mind. This implied both an insistence upon the non-material source of all being, and a teleological interpretation of the evolutionary process. For it seemed unthinkable that the increasing presence of mind in the cosmic scheme, so fully manifested in man, could be anything but the gradual attainment of a purpose—a taking possession of matter by mind to some definite end. It is true that, according to the principle of plenitude in the metaphysical speculations of the eighteenth century, man was not the crowning achievement in Creation: he was, according to Pope, placed in a 'middle state', and according to Young, 'Midway from nothing to the deity'. Yet, though other, more perfect beings were thought to exist in the universe, he was, on earth, the creature which above all others proved the excellence and purpose of the creative plan. 'If man were taken away from the world, the rest would seem to be all astray, without aim or purpose, . . . and leading to nothing'.[1] This statement by Bacon in the seventeenth century, but still as valid in the eighteenth, reads like a paraphrase of an important and recurrent theme in Tennyson's poetry. His spiritual plight, and the agony which doubt and death thrust upon him, made of the poet of *In Memoriam* a crusader for man's soul, against the heritage of Renaissance materialism, with its late fruit, the idea of the 'man machine', and against the evolutionary determinism which was to develop from Darwin's ideas of chance mutations and natural selection. Tennyson, in his search for Cosmos, sided with the neo-Lamarckians, who saw the process in nature as a penetration of matter by spirit and a growing command of mind over material aspects. This ancient idea had been given a suggestive Utopian formulation by Robinet in his *Vue philosophique de la*

[1] Bacon, *De Sapientia Veterum, Works,* vol. vi, p. 747.

gradation naturelle de l'être (1768), in that he anticipated a time when the creative force—*la force active*—might possibly become wholly independent of matter: *Enfin elle se dématérialiserait entièrement, si j'ose ainsi m'exprimer, et pour dernière métamorphose elle se transformerait en pure intelligence.* Coleridge too forecasts a 'passing away of this Earth' and the emergence of a 'state of pure intellect'.[1] Tennyson's vision of the spiritual destiny of man is rooted in this Idealistic tradition.

The idea of evolution in Tennyson's poetry expresses an attitude and a belief which lend structural coherence—within the Chaos-Cosmos pattern—to poems set widely apart in subject-matter and time. Only to a superficial view does this poetry appear as a system or method to answer the questions of the age, in the form of a sermon or 'message' worked out in dialectic designs with antiactive forces tending towards balance and harmony, in the spirit of Hegel and Spencer. If Tennyson's poetry bears the impact of a collapse of dogmatic faith, and of the fretful search for certainty of his time, it is because he lived and struggled, often fiercely, with its questions and its fears. Tennyson's poetry about the universe and the destiny of man is important and sometimes great in the way it expresses the common lot of man within the emotional intensity and drama of the individual stance. One may regret Tennyson's lack of penetrating, consistent thought and vision, the often banal formulation of his themes of doubt and faith, and their monotonous repetition. Yet they seldom lose interest and persuasive force because they are alive with a sense of the inviolable holiness of the individual soul and the universal significance of its fate. Therefore, the lasting interest of Tennyson's poetry about the pilgrimage of life lies in his tentative, incessant effort to integrate existence into a spiritual Cosmos—an effort that reaches its climax of force and expressiveness already in *The Two Voices* and *In Memoriam*. In these poems, as

[1] *Religious Musings.*

in later and minor ones, the idea of evolution is an integrative element: it helps Tennyson to escape the persecution of death by showing, in terms of historical fact, the way to a promised land of more and fuller life. This movement is the profoundest creative experience in Tennyson's poetry; and he stands therefore, not only as the 'master of melancholia', but as an ambassador of life.

2. Robert Browning

In 1881 Robert Browning wrote to his friend Furnivall:

Last, about my being 'strongly against Darwin, rejecting the truths of science and regretting its advance'—you only do as I should hope and expect in disbelieving *that*. It came, I suppose, of Hohenstiel-Schwangau's expressing the notion which was the popular one at the appearance of Darwin's book ... In reality, all that seems *proved* in Darwin's scheme was a conception familiar to me from the beginning: see in *Paracelsus* the progressive development from senseless matter to organized, until man's appearance (Part V). Also in *Cleon*, see the order of 'Life's mechanics'—and I daresay in many passages of my poetry: for how can one look at Nature as a whole and doubt that, wherever there is a gap, a 'link' must be 'missing'—through the limited power and opportunity of the looker? But go back and back as you please, *at* the back, as Mr. Sludge is made to insist, you find (*my* faith is as constant) creative intelligence, acting as matter but not resulting from it. Once set the balls rolling, and ball may hit ball and send any number in any directions over the table; but I believe in the cue pushed by a hand. When one is taunted (as I notice is often fancied an easy method with the un-Darwinized)—taunted with thinking successive acts of creation possible, metaphysics have been stopped short at, however physics may fare: time and space being purely conceptions of our own, wholly inapplicable to intelligence of another kind—with whom, as I made Luria say, there is an 'everlasting moment of creation', if one at all—past, present and future, one and the same state. This consideration does not affect Darwinism proper in any degree. But I do not consider that his case as to the changes in organization brought about by desire and will in the creature, proved. Tortoises never saw their own shells, top or bottom, nor those of their females, and are diversely variegated all over, each species after their own pattern. And the insects; this one is coloured to escape notice, this other to attract it, a third to frighten the foe—all out of one brood of caterpillars hatched in one day? No—I am incredulous.[1]

Despite its polemic twist and muddled anti-Darwinian argument, the letter might well serve as a preface to those of Browning's poems in which evolution plays a creative part. Some of their salient features are here outlined, and even if the poet looks back over a period of nearly fifty years and his retrospect is coloured by second thought, he may justly claim that the idea of evolution had been familiar to him long before Darwin. Perhaps the chief significance of this statement lies in the way he identifies his early 'conception' with mutability of species. On the other hand, the letter reveals a curious misunderstanding of Darwin's theory which partly accounts for his dislike of it. Browning reads into it a form of teleology which Darwin himself had severely criticized in Lamarck and taken great care to avoid. It would seem that the poet here joins the polemic effort of those in his time who rejected a purely naturalistic account of the transmutation of species. But in point of fact Natural Selection was a more dangerous teaching than the teleology for which Browning blames Darwin, and which is not very different in its creative process from his own finalistic belief.

However, all these indications are useful. They suggest that Browning already from his early youth had been strongly preoccupied with the idea of evolution, and continued to draw from it poetic energy. Moreover, in the 'everlasting moment of creation', there is a hint at the way in which he rescued his theistic cosmogony from the onslaught of materialistic doctrine, by reducing this doctrine to a scientific abstraction valid only within a limited field.

---

[1] *Letters of Robert Browning.* (Collected by T. J. Wise, ed. by T. L. Hood, 1933), pp. 199—200). Cf. Tennyson's outlook, *supra,* p. 98. See also Lyell on the 'missing link' and causation, *supra,* p. 23.

The Everlasting Minute of Creation

In *Paracelsus* (1835) Browning dramatizes the aspirations of his youth within a framework of Renaissance life-zest and craving for power, a framework that, as H. L. Hovelaque has pointed out, is closely related to Goethe's version of the Faust legend.[1] In the final scene of the drama Paracelsus rises from his deathbed to bequeath his philosophical testament to posterity. It is the sum of wisdom gained by a 'searching and impetuous soul' that had sought 'fit delights to stay its longings vast', and always craved 'new strifes, new triumphs'. His ambition had been, first, to obtain absolute knowledge of the world, and this, he felt, he had early achieved: 'the secret of the world was mine':

> I knew, I felt . . .
> . . . what God is, what we are,
> What life is—how God tastes an infinite joy
> In infinite ways—one everlasting bliss,
> From whom all being emanates, all power
> Proceeds; in whom is life for evermore,
> Yet whom existence in its lowest form
> Includes; where dwells enjoyment there is he:
> With still a flying point of bliss remote,
> A happiness in store afar, a sphere
> Of distant glory in full view; thus climbs
> Pleasure its heights for ever and for ever.[2]

Browning has found the prelude of his great theme, and with a thrust of energy he states it: God tastes an infinite joy in infinite ways. Here already the verbal structure which is to sustain his cosmogonic vision is completed in one swift, simple movement,

[1] Cf. *La Jeunesse de Robert Browning,* p. 256.
[2] *The Poetical Works,* (1868 ed.) Vol. I, p. 187.

114

while the vision itself continues to expand on the insistent and compact use of adjectives suggesting vast dimensions, perspectives and powerful motion.

In the idea of life as an unending movement climbing from its lowest forms to distant heights and glories, Browning expresses a neo-Platonic conception of Genesis which he further develops through the divine 'infinite joy' that flows into matter and moves the whole panorama of Creation. God's creative power objectified in this ascending movement of life is seen throughout as modes of joy—as 'bliss', 'happiness' and 'pleasure. Again, like the neo-Platonists, the poet conceives of God as both immanent and transcendent: he makes the world and he participates in it.

From this initial penetration into the mystery of the Prime Mover, Paracelsus unfolds his ecstatic vision of Nature—a scene alive with change and growth and process, shaped and reshaped by the tremendous forces surging from the 'centre-fires . . . underneath the earth', dwelling in the 'wroth sea's waves' and in seed, plant and animal through which God, in springtime, 'renews His ancient rapture'. Nature is everywhere permeated by this presence of God:

> Thus he dwells in all,
> From life's minute beginnings, up at last
> To man—the consummation of this scheme
> Of being, the completion of this sphere
> Of life: whose attributes had here and there
> Been scattered o'er the visible world before,
> Asking to be combined, dim fragments meant
> To be united in some wondrous whole,
> Imperfect qualities throughout creation,
> Suggesting some one creature yet to make,
> Some point where all those scattered rays should meet
> Convergent in the faculties of man.

The cosmogony of the poem develops on the traditional pattern of a chaos gradually organized into an ordered harmonious whole; yet the emphasis, all the time, is on life and on the idea or ideal which life is striving to realize. The passage reveals a marked and persistent trend of finalism which combines the nisus of the Platonic-Aristotelian tradition with nineteenth-century biological concepts of 'Progression'. Though there may be no direct influence from biological speculation, the 'dim fragments' and 'imperfect qualities ... suggesting some one creature yet to make' appear to echo such notions as 'Geological Prophecies' and 'Archetypal Plan'.[1] Characteristic also of nineteenth century thought is the accent on man's prerogatives in a natural scheme in which he yet has his roots: man stands forth as the focus in which the rays from lower levels of existence attain to full radiance. Man is the *Summum Bonum*— a synthesis of all that is best in inferior creatures, and life is given meaning chiefly in relation to him and in so far as it builds up to him.

The excellence of human nature depends on the triad combination of Power, Knowledge and Love. Man has got command over the realm of Nature, 'to be used at risk', guided by his knowledge, this

<blockquote>
slow
Uncertain fruit of an enhancing toil,
Strengthened by love:
</blockquote>

and guided, above all, by Love—God's greatest gift to man. To Love Paracelsus sings a hymn of praise before exploring further his vision of life's ascent. It appears first as an elaboration of the theme in the previous passage, as if the poetic energy centred in it had not yet been fully expressed or released: It is still a pæan to the glory of man, and to the aspiring, creative effort in Nature, where, he repeats, the human qualities,

[1] Cf. *supra*, p. 11.

Are strewn confusedly everywhere about
The inferior natures; and all lead up higher,
All shape out dimly the superior race,
The heir of hopes too fair to turn out false,
And man appears at last. So far the seal
Is put on life; one stage of being complete,
One scheme wound up: and from the grand result
A supplementary reflux of light,
Illustrates all the inferior grades, explains
Each back step in the circle. Not alone
For their possessor dawn those qualities,
But the new glory mixes with the heaven
And earth; man, once descried, imprints for ever
His presence on all lifeless things ...

Life is pervaded by an urge towards perfection, and in man its creative zest attains the first great goal: man is the meeting-place of heaven and earth, of God and animal. The measure of this ascent of life is visualized in the contrasts and antitheses of the poetic structure, where the movement is ever from chaos to order, from inferior to superior levels, from dimness to light.

However, man is not a static or final achievement, for his mind, his consciousness, spurs from now on to new conquest: 'to work his proper nature out'.

For these things tend still upward, progress is
The law of life, man is not Man as yet.
Nor shall I deem his object served, his end
Attained, his genuine strength put fairly forth,
While only here and there a star dispels
The darkness, here and there a towering mind
O'erlooks its prostrate fellows: when the host
Is out at once to the despair of night,

117

When all mankind alike is perfected,
Equal in full-blown powers—then, not till then,
I say, begins man's general infancy.

The poet has made another important cosmogonic discovery, or
rather he sees the full meaning of the creative process, and deduces
from it a universal principle: Progress is the law of life. And now
his vision, with a renewed energy of faith and prophetic fervour,
moves up to a point where man, for all his superior qualities, is
yet revealed as a creature that has only just begun: the human
being is realized as a type or species, but not fully developed within
the progressive scope of that type. Moreover, the high attainment
is so far only individual and uneven; it must become universal. This
is the condition for further advance, for not till human perfection
has become general is man free to move on:

Then shall his long triumphant march begin,
Thence shall his being date,—thus wholly roused,
What he achieves shall be set down to him.
When all the race is perfected alike
As man, that is; all tended to mankind,
And, man produced, all has its end thus far:
But in completed man begins anew
A tendency to God. Prognostics told
Man's near approach; so in man's self arise
August anticipations, symbols, types
Of a dim splendour ever on before
In that eternal circle life pursues.
For men begin to pass their nature's bound,
And find new hopes and cares which fast supplant
Their proper joys and griefs; they grow too great
For narrow creeds of right and wrong; which fade
Before the unmeasured thirst for good: while peace

Rises within them ever more and more.
Such men are even now upon the earth,
Serene amid the half-formed creatures round
Who should be saved by them and joined with them.

In this extending perspective, the 'tendency to God' illumines and develops the evolutionary prophecy in the previous passages. It gathers the whole movement into one continuous process, the direction of which is revealed through the 'prognostics' and 'symbols' thrown out towards man from the lowest creatures, and from man to God. Life has grown and aspired through successive forms and phases in Nature until man is made, and the human being with his superior faculties brings to an end this first stage of evolution. His physical form is perfect, but since God tastes an infinite joy in infinite ways, since progress is the law of life, the development now turns inward and pursues new glories within man's soul. God is both the Prime Mover—the efficient cause of this 'tendency', and the transcendent, final cause directing the creative energy towards its destination. In this passage the creative energy is seen moving in great waves, mounting ever higher upon the beach: life is a triumphant march. At the same time, in the notion of the 'eternal circle' of life, there appears to be an impact of Greek cosmology. To Browning, however, these are not contradictory movements, but the one contained within the other.

Browning does not explore the metaphysical perspective of this new, mental phase of growth; it is the ethical aspect which fascinates him as he contemplates the expansion of life in human nature beyond its old narrow boundaries into a new emotional and moral climate. This, by implication, is a state of unhampered good, freed from the trammels of unreason and fanaticism which crippled man in the past. Thus the 'tendency to God' is, above all, an active instinct for good in human nature.

119

The promise of this new 'splendour' lies not only in the 'august anticipations' and 'symbols' apparent in man's self, but in the actual fulfilment which makes certain individuals stand out above the 'half-formed creatures'—their fellow beings. In these great, serene men a new superior race is born, and among these, the Paracelsus of the poem claims a place. Yet he had failed, because he 'gazed on power' till he 'grew blind'. Power, he thought, was man's distinctive, supreme quality, and the surest way of progress. His own impetuous task was to 'erase' the past, this 'record of disgraces', this 'scene of degradation, ugliness and tears'; to

> Change man's condition, push each slumbering claim
> Of mastery o'er the elemental world
> At once to full maturity ...

Paracelsus warns posterity against this fatal error of ignoring the past, for it means a violation of the laws laid down for man in his condition. Paracelsus had been guilty of *hubris*, since

> The power I sought for man, seemed God's.

For this he suffered the punishment of despair, of seeing his dreams fade and his efforts everywhere thwarted and shamed. It was at this moment that Aprile, the poet dedicated to love as he himself had been to power, revealed to him 'the worth of love in man's estate'. Love must go before power: only through love is it possible to understand human beings and help them, and:

> be proud
> Of their half-reasons, faint aspirings, dim
> Struggles for truth, their poorest fallacies,
> Their prejudice and fears and cares and doubts;
> All with a touch of nobleness, despite
> Their error, upward tending all though weak,
> Like plants in mines which never saw the sun,

But dream of him, and guess where he may be,
And do their best to climb and get to him.

Through the image of the growing plant, whose nisus urges it towards the sun, Browning integrates the moral and spiritual process
of growth with all evolutionary growth whatever: all is part of the
'tendency to God'.

Though the wisdom of the old and dying Paracelsus tempers his
original youthful zest, his prophetic hope stands firm. Past, present
and future are one continuous upward struggle and effort; therefore:

> the present for thee
> Shall have distinct and trembling beauty, seen
> Beside that past's own shade when, in relief,
> Its brightness shall stand out: nor on thee yet
> Shall burst the future, as successive zones
> Of several wonder open on some spirit
> Flying secure and glad from heaven to heaven:
> But thou shalt painfully attain to joy,
> While hope and fear and love shall keep thee man!

Hope, fear and love shall keep human nature balanced within the
part set down for it, and secure against rash and onesided measures.
Paracelsus ends his great speech with the prophetic exhortation that
in the men of the future his own quest, for power, must fuse with
that of Aprile,

> and shape forth a third
> And better-tempered spirit, warned by both:
> As from the over-radiant star too mad
> To drink the life-springs, beamless thence itself—
> And the dark orb which borders the abyss,
> Ingulfed in icy night,—might have its course
> A temperate and equidistant world.

121

The fifth act of *Paracelsus* is essentially about the evolution of life as a divine and spiritual manifestation in the material world, and its central, creative experience is the joy and excitement which the poet feels at probing this mysterious growth and tracing it beyond the present to ever higher attainments in the future.

Paracelsus was published in 1835, and testifies that already then the idea of evolution was an active force in Browning's poetry and belief. But it was not the same conception which Darwin 'proved' in the *Origin of Species,* Natural Selection: It is a divine creative act, continuous and progressive; it is the way God 'dwells in all' and expresses his 'infinite joy'.[1] The evolutionary vision of the drama conforms, in its vague descriptive outline, to the biological theory of 'Progression' as well as to transmutation, and emphasis is throughout on finalistic aspects and on the cause underlying the process. Browning's teleology, like that of Tennyson, is as much a development of eighteenth-century speculations about cosmic transition and change as an anticipation of the modern evolutionary theory, which, in any case, Lamarck had clearly stated.[2] How close Browning stood to the Platonic tradition of the eighteenth century may be illustrated by a comparison with a representative work of that time — Akenside's *Pleasures of the Imagination* (1744). This is Akenside's cosmogonic vision:

> The Sovereign Spirit of the world,
> Though, self-collected from eternal time,
> Within his own deep essence he beheld
> The bounds of true felicity complete;

[1] Some scholars hold that it was the idea of *natura naturans* and not of transmutation of species which Browning expressed in *Paracelsus;* cf. J. Warren Beach, *The Concept of Nature in Nineteenth Century English Poetry.* See also *supra* p. 83 similar comments on Tennyson.

[2] H. L. Hovelaque in *La Jeunesse de Robert Browning,* and De Vane in *Browning's Parleyings. The Autobiography of a Mind,* both credit Browning with an original insight.

Yet by immense benignity inclin'd
To spread around him that primeval joy
Which fill'd himself, he raised his plastic arm
And sounded through the hollow depths of space
The strong creative mandate.[1]

And creation never ceases, for God

Not content
By one exertion of creative power
His goodness to reveal to every age,
Through every moment up the tract of time
His parent hand with ever new increase
Of happiness and virtue has adorn'd
The vast harmonious frame: his parent hand,
From the mute shell-fish gasping on the shore,
To men, to angels, to celestial minds,
Forever leads the generations on
To higher scenes of being ...
So all things which have life aspire to God,...[2]

Both poets are concerned with the divine source of all being, though Akenside's version approaches closer to biblical Genesis than that of Browning. The nineteenth century poet has a clearer perception of the development as a slow, organic growth in time accumulating and integrating in man qualities which were scattered about in 'inferior natures', and shaping out the 'superior race'. To Akenside, poet of the age of sufficient reason, all creatures existed in their own right, as parts of the universal plenitude; to Browning they are attempts at becoming man. Thus he conceives a teleological process working from 'Life's minute beginnings, ... up at last to man', animated and directed by the 'tendency to God', or the pre-

---

[1] Book ii. [2] *Ibid.*

cognitive principle, which is but another aspect of God's infinite joy in Creation. Here lies the significance of the evolutionary idea to Browning, and in this sense it engages his poetic task. No doubt this task was inspired also by the great Romantic poets who were the heroes of his youth, and his masters. In *Paracelsus* their presence is felt in more than one way. From them, more directly than from their eighteenth-century precursors, Browning received his idea of the cosmos as a growing spiritual organism—an idea to which he gave an increasing stress of immanence. It may suffice, perhaps, to recall a few lines of Shelley's *Adonais* in order to get a glimpse of the Romantic scene of Nature, in which the young Browning moved:

> Through wood and stream and field and hill and Ocean
> A quickening life from the Earth's heart has burst
> As it has ever done, with change and motion,
> From the great morning of the world when first
> God dawned on chaos; in its steam immersed,
> The lamps of heaven flash with a softer light;
> All baser things pant with life's sacred thirst;
> Diffuse themselves; and spend in love's delight,
> The beauty and the joy of their renewèd might.[1]

And, Shelley tells us, a creative Spirit is at work:

> the one Spirit's plastic stress
> Sweeps through the dull dense world, compelling there
> All new successions to the forms they wear ...[2]

With Browning, however, we enter more directly into the intellectual climate of the nineteenth century, where the idea of historical progress fused with that of organic process to formulate a new biological law. The doctrine of 'Progression' was one which, as

[1] xix. [2] xliii.

Lyell was later to argue in his *Antiquity of Man,* could be reconciled with the mutability of species in a teleological evolutionary concept. It appears to be this drift of thought which Browning grasped and worked into poetic vision in *Paracelsus.* Therefore, to say that Browning anticipated the theory of evolution is to isolate him unduly from his intellectual background. In time, *Paracelsus* is placed half way between Lamarck and Darwin, and Lamarck's theories, mainly owing to Lyell's *Principles of Geology* were again freely discussed about 1830. On the other hand, whether we base our conclusion exclusively on internal evidence and disregard Browning's letter to Furnivall in this connexion, or call in both, it would seem that his cosmogonic vision has passed beyond the fixed, stratified systems as well as the *natura naturans* of eighteenth-century philosophy. The process in Nature is to him cumulative and organic, and man emerges as the last fruit of its slow, purposive growth. Underlying this intuition there is throughout a neo-Platonic belief in God the maker of the world, whose joy and goodness permeates all being with an urge or nisus to perfection.

This neo-Platonic belief is even more articulate in *Luria,* (1846), in a short passage which resumes the main theme of Paracelsus's speech. To Paracelsus the truth was revealed through mystical insight: he 'knew' and 'felt'; Luria claims that Eastern contemplation, rather than the rational thought of the West, holds the profoundest truth, and the knowledge of God:

> We feel him, nor by painful reason know!
> The everlasting minute of creation
> Is felt there; now it is, as it was then;
> All changes at his instantaneous will,
> Not by the operation of a law
> Whose maker is elsewhere at other work.
> His hand is still engaged upon his world—

Man's praise can forward it, man's prayer suspend,
For is not God all-mighty? To recast
The world, erase old things and make them new,
What costs it him?[1]

As the most important of truths grasped in this way, the poet dwells on the creative cosmic process which is the spontaneous act of divine will and providence. There is no beginning nor end to this creative act, for in the eternity of God in which it takes place, time has no function.

The confrontation in this poem of oriental intuition with Western reason appears to stand for a more topical issue, and Browning's sympathy, speaking through Luria, is clearly enlisted. Reason is 'painful' and alienates God from man: it 'intervenes' where communication might be direct and easy. Thus, by introducing the time-concept, reason fails to see the meaning of God's creative act, for which eternity alone can serve as measure. Calculations and observations in time have produced this futile abstraction: a world governed by natural law independent of the will of God.

From this final passage in *Luria* an important trend emerges which might be woven into the larger pattern of Browning's poetry and belief. In the 'everlasting minute of creation' he has discovered a formula which defines the wonder of organic growth and change as he first came face to face with it in *Paracelsus*, and which aptly expresses his theistic and neo-Platonic attitude.[2]

Cleon, which comes second in Browning's own record of relevant evolutionary poems, belongs to the *Men and Women* volume of 1855. It is a poem about immortality and the meaning of life, in which the works of art and of kingship are rejected as a futile means of achieving eternal existence. If man is doomed to perish,

[1] *The Poetical Works*, (1868) ed.) vol. V, p. 110.
[2] Cf. Tennyson's similar belief, *supra*, p. 98, n. 1.

body and soul, there is no consolation in the permanence of his work. From this point the theme expands into a wider setting of man and Nature and the tragic role of self-consciousness and spiritual aspiration set apart for the human being. First comes a pagan version of Genesis in which the poet Cleon meditates upon Nature:

> If, in the morning of philosophy,
> Ere aught had been recorded, nay perceived,
> Thou, with the light now in thee, couldst have looked
> On all earth's tenantry, from worm to bird,
> Ere man, her last, appeared upon the stage—
> Thou wouldst have seen them perfect, and deduced
> The perfectness of others yet unseen.
> Conceding which,—had Zeus then questioned thee
> "Shall I go on a step, improve on this,
> Do more for visible creatures than is done?"
> Thou wouldst have answered, "Ay, by making each
> Grow conscious in himself—by that alone.
> All's perfect else: the shell sucks fast the rock,
> The fish strikes through the sea, the snake both swims
> And slides, the birds take flight, forth range the beasts,
> Till life's mechanics can no further go—
> And all this joy in natural life, is put,
> Like fire from off thy finger into each,
> So exquisitely perfect is the same.
> But 't is pure fire, and they mere matter are;
> It has them, not they it: and so I choose
> For man, thy last premeditated work
> (If I might add a glory to the scheme)
> That a third thing should stand apart from both,
> A quality arise within his soul,
> Which, intro-active, made to supervise
> And feel the force it has, may view itself,

127

And so be happy." Man might live at first
The animal life: but is there nothing more?
In due time, let him critically learn
How he lives; and, the more he gets to know
Of his own life's adaptabilities,
The more joy-giving will his life become.
Thus man, who hath this quality, is best.[1]

Cleon places himself at the point from which eighteenth-century exponents of the principle of plenitude and sufficient reason viewed the natural order. Every creature is perfect in his own station, and along the purely material and animal line no advance can be made. Life, the divine fire, has so entered into the material form and its function as to leave no scope for progress. And again, here as in *Paracelsus,* this fire or creative energy is seen as joy. Yet the scheme, before man, is incomplete: there is lacking that quality of self-consciousness by which man is destined to crown the order of Nature and make it a perfect whole. For in the pre-human world, as Cleon views it, there is an unresolved dualism of divine spirit and matter, and this very flaw points to a being that might integrate animal and divine nature in a new faculty which partakes of both: self-consciousness and free will. Man's distinction will be an introspective understanding playing upon the conscious experiences of his mind, which will enable him to enter more completely into possession of his soul and body, and of his environment.

In the rational order of Nature, before man, such a being would necessarily be 'premeditated' to give perfection to the scheme. Yet how is man to emerge? Cleon in answer to this question combines the idea of a static, hierarchical system with an evolutionary view of man's nature: let him grow out of the animal, let him pass through the apprenticeship of lower life until this new faculty is matured.

[1] 'Men and Women', *The Poetical Works,* (1868 ed.) vol. v, pp. 305—6.

The last lines of the passage, if one may give a moral connotation to 'best', contain an argument of ethical evolution which, under the influence of the new biological theory, was to play a central part in the thought of Spencer and Huxley. Here too, we find the idea that self-knowledge and a growing apprehension of human adaptability will guide the human species to greater satisfaction and happiness. Thus in the ideal of the 'joy-giving' life, Cleon appears to expound a utilitarian ethics, which is further amplified in the rationalistic and pragmatic notion of 'critically' learning how to live and how to adapt oneself.

The poet Cleon has spoken for the glory of Creation and the promise of this last great attainment. Now the King, whom he addresses, reveals its tragic aspect. The Browning dialectic is brought into play:

> "Let progress end at once,—man make no step
> Beyond the natural man, the better beast,
> Using his senses, not the sense of sense."

And Cleon admits that man's great privilege has not brought him content:

> In man there's failure, only since he left
> The lower and inconscious forms of life.
> We called it an advance, the rendering plain
> Man's spirit might grow conscious of man's life,
> And, by new lore so added to the old,
> Take each step higher over the brute's head.
> This grew the only life, the pleasure-house,
> Watch-tower and treasure-fortress of the soul,
> Which whole surrounding flats of natural life
> Seemed only fit to yield subsistence to;
> A tower that crowns a country. But alas,
> The soul now climbs it just to perish there!
> For thence we have discovered ('t is no dream—

We know this, which we had not else perceived)
That there 's a world of capability
For joy, spread round about us, meant for us,
Inviting us; and still the soul craves all,
And still the flesh replies, "Take no jot more
Than ere thou climbedst the tower to look abroad![1]

The passage is a lament on the perennial flesh-spirit dichotomy.
However uncongenial Schopenhauer's pessimistic philosophy was to
Browning at this period of his life, his interpretation of the specific
human tragedy, of 'man's failure', in this poem includes such a
central idea as the curse of consciousness. In man, evolution has
produced an intelligent and sensitive being torn by a conflict
between aspiration and limitation: a zest for fuller life and for
happiness cruelly and inevitably defeated by his condition. Curiously
enough, Browning, so much celebrated for his robust optimism,
foreshadows here an important feature in the sinister poetic world
of Thomas Hardy; yet, in Browning, as we shall see, the idea of
human imperfection is commonly a basis of hope and faith.

The evolutionary concept in *Cleon* shows, to begin with, diver-
gencies from that of *Paracelsus* which are mainly due to the
mythological framework. It views 'earth's tenantry' from worm to
bird and man as a perfect, fixed order directly created by Zeus,
whose fire, according to the myth, entered as life into the creatures
of the earth. Since Cleon (hypothetically) addresses Zeus, who
'premeditates' man, his vision involves a creationist pattern to
which the poem adheres where the lower orders of Nature are
concerned, but with the coming of man there is increased emphasis
on the transition from animal and on the slow, cumulative process
of mental evolution. Finally, the lamentation of man's failure
disrupts this mythological pattern and states that man has 'left/The

[1] *Ibid.*, p. 307.

130

lower and inconscious forms of life'. Therefore, *Cleon* only apparently cuts across the vision of *Paracelsus,* and expresses something like 'the everlasting minute of creation' in a pagan setting. In its panorama of nature there is movement and advance: 'forth range the beasts'; new qualities arise within the animal world; and man, though he begins by living the animal life, is able to 'take each step higher over the brute's head'.

A more serious break with the evolutionary belief of *Paracelsus* would seem to occur in *A Death in the Desert, (Dramatis Personæ,* 1864). The setting of the theme is again one of impending death—the few moments left for John the Apostle to meditate upon life and human destiny. As befits him, his mind dwells on Divine Love and its manifestation in the spiritual growth and ascent of man. In describing the nature of this ascent, John stresses the fundamental difference between body and soul:

> But see the double way wherein we are led,
> How the soul learns diversely from the flesh!
> With flesh, that hath so little time to stay,
> And yields mere basement for the soul's emprise,
> Expect prompt teaching. Helpful was the light,
> And warmth was cherishing and food was choice
> To every man's flesh, thousand years ago,
> As now to yours and mine; the body sprang
> At once to the height, and stayed: but the soul,—no![1]

Literally 'sprang' in this passage means that body attained at once to its present perfection, which may imply that the human species was created, and 'stayed' denies further physical development. It is difficult, however, to attach a precise temporal meaning to 'sprang', and the words seem to refer to the individual being growing quickly

[1] *The Poetical Works,* (1868 ed.), vol. vi, p. 119.

to maturity, and not to the human species. Here as elsewhere in Browning's poetry there is a heavy emphasis on spiritual aspects and on the destiny of the human soul, which is to ascend through arduous learning and struggle towards higher and fuller life, and to this ascent the body serves mainly as a foil.

The Apostle goes on to explain why the growth of the soul must, in contrast to that of the body, be without end. If its gains were 'safe' and 'sure to prosper', then stagnation would ensue, then 'man's probation would conclude'. Here as in *Paracelsus*, progress is the law of life:

> I say that man was made to grow, not stop;
> That help, he needed once, and needs no more,
> Having grown up but an inch by, is withdrawn:
> For he hath new needs, and new helps to these.
> This imports solely, man should mount on each
> New height in view; the help whereby he mounts,
> The ladder-rung his foot has left, may fall,
> Since all things suffer change save God the Truth.[1]

The pattern of unending quest and change set against the permanence of 'God the Truth' is neo-Platonic. Through its preoccupation with spiritual growth the poem carries on significant trends from *Paracelsus* and *Cleon,* and even repeats the warning against *hubris* of the former: If man thinks of himself as 'First, last and best of things' and forgets that love must go hand in hand with will and power, then his advance has been in vain, and his victory 'leads but to defeat'. Only in a spirit of humility can man find his right place in Nature. He will then see himself—and at this juncture the apostle John speaks like an eighteenth-century moralist—

> Lower than God who knows all and can all,
> Higher than beasts which know and can so far

[1] *Ibid.,* p. 125.

132

As each beast's limit, perfect to an end,
Nor conscious that they know, nor craving more;
While man knows partly but conceives beside,
Creeps ever on from fancies to the fact,
And in this striving, this converting air
Into a solid he may grasp and use,
Finds progress, man's distinctive mark alone,
Not God's, and not the beasts': God is, they are,
Man partly is and wholly hopes to be.
Such progress could no more attend his soul
Were all it struggles after found at first
And guesses changed to knowledge absolute,
Than motion wait his body, were all else
Than it the solid earth on every side,
Where now through space he moves from rest to rest.[1]

God and beast are invoked here as static elements to emphasize the role of spiritual quest and growth set apart for man, and to dramatize his unique place in the natural order. Browning's statement that the beasts 'are', i. e. stationary, implies fixity of species and, even more strongly than the ambiguous lines in the first passage quoted, appears to contradict his belief in evolution.

The final passage contains a telling example of the paradox that Chesterton found at the basis of Browning's optimism, and which he described as the hope which lies in the imperfection of man.[2] Browning has used the argument already in this poem: absolute attainment means stagnation—decay and death, and man's privilege, therefore, is a consciousness of his own shortcoming which makes him strive and hope and explore. Thus he learns in different ways:

[1] *Ibid.*, p. 131.
[2] *Robert Browning*, p. 177; ref. to *Old Pictures in Florence.*

Set to instruct himself by his past self:
First, like the brute, obliged by facts to learn,
Next, as man may, obliged by his own mind,
Bent, habit, nature, knowledge turned to law.
God's gift was that man should conceive of truth
And yearn to gain it, catching at mistake,
As midway help till he reach fact indeed.[1]

Cleon worked out a similar thought-structure: Man passes through a phase of animal development and then one of mental progress, which, however, meet and fuse. This fusion of animal and human experience in man's past self suggests that the contradiction involved in 'sprang' and 'stayed' is a superficial or careless verbal inconsistency, and not a change of insight. In the dialectic movement of Browning's thought there are frequent and dramatic clashes of ideas, but these do not disrupt the fundamental coherence of his belief.

When stating explicitly his faith in purposive evolution in the letter to Furnivall, Browning quoted another of his *dramatis personæ*, Mr. Sludge, whom he had made to insist that at the back of creation, there is a Prime Mover, and intelligence: Modern science has altered our understanding of Nature, and reveals to us an undreamt-of complexity in matter and organism:

grass, worm, fly grow big:
We find great things are made of little things,
And little things go lessening till at last
Comes God behind them.[2]

If we ask who caused and created this order of Nature we find, inevitably, God. 'The Name', says Mr. Sludge, 'comes close behind

[1] *Ibid.*, p. 132.   [2] *Poetical Works*, vol. vi, p. 203.

a stomach-cyst'—behind the lowest forms of life.—This common-place argument is interesting mainly because it indicates a preoccupation in Browning's mind which a few years later was expressed more completely in *Prince Hohenstiel-Schwangau* (1871). Published in the same year as Darwin's *Descent of Man* and Mivart's *Genesis of Species,* this poem is Browning's first relevant and explicit statement of the evolutionary theme to appear after *Origin of Species* and the controversies of the intervening decade, and his slowness to return to the subject, in spite of its topical importance and the problems it involved, may be evidence that, as he claimed in his letter to Furnivall, the idea contained nothing new. He does not appear to have paid much attention to the conflict before this time, but now there are signs of a greater interest.

Prince Hohenstiel-Schwangau is not a good poem, and its flaws are obvious; yet Browning's treatment of the evolutionary theme is here of considerable historical interest. In his cumbersome monologue, the Prince is trying to probe the enigma of what he regretfully calls the 'dissociation' of man. He propounds, in fact, something like Spencer's theory of differentiation: Humanity is 'born a mass', but with the advance in culture men strike out on increasingly diverging courses which lead to isolation. On lower levels of existence, at the 'base of being', he claims, there is 'absolute contact' and 'fusion', but in the 'upward progress' man 'tends to freedom and divergency'. This, then, is the conundrum of social process, and to explain it, Browning's dialectic technique seizes the theme:

> "Will you have why and wherefore, and the fact
> Made plain as pikestaff?" modern Science asks.
> "That mass man sprung from was a jelly-lump
> Once on a time; he kept an after course
> Through fish and insect, reptile, bird and beast,
> Till he attained to be an ape at last
> Or last but one. And if this doctrine shock

135

In aught the natural pride" ... Friend, banish fear,
The natural humility replies![1]

Here, with an unmistakable ring of irony, the new biological theory
is presented, and at either end of the outline loom the words which
had become so odious to Darwin's opponents — the jelly-lump or
protozoon, and the ape. In the context, however, it is not the theory
itself which is taken to task, but 'modern Science' with its arrogant
claim to know the full answer to this and other fundamental
problems.

The Prince seeks no quarrel with the new doctrine, and he is not
ashamed of his lowly origin. On the contrary: it was thus, slowly
developing, and passing from one existence to another, that he
learnt his 'trade'. Given more time, and more experience in this
development, he would have been a better and more intelligent
statesman. Individual life is too short for experiment and learning
in the manner of Nature, where the process works slowly towards
perfection:

> God takes time.
> I like the thought He should have lodged me once
> I' the hole, the cave, the hut, the tenement,
> The mansion and the palace; made me learn
> The feel o' the first, before I found myself
> Loftier i' the last, not more emancipate;
> From first to last of lodging, I was I,
> And not at all the place that harboured me.
> Do I refuse to follow farther yet
> I' the backwardness, repine if tree and flower,
> Mountain or streamlet were my dwelling-place
> Before I gained enlargement, grew mollusc?
> As well account that way for many a thrill

[1] *Op. cit. The Works of Robert Browning*, (cent. ed., 1912) vol. vii, 11.
985—993.

> Of kinship, I confess to, with the powers
> Called Nature: animate, inanimate,
> In parts or in the whole, there's something there
> Man-like that somehow meets the man in me.[1]

Despite Darwin's drastic re-formulation of the mutability-theory, Browning pursues his own track with imperturbable steadiness: God takes time, yet 'He dwells in all'; the creative process in Nature is all the time God's 'everlasting minute of creation'. Moreover, the man-idea which Paracelsus discovered as the *leit-motiv* in the advancing natural orders is again emphasized: the human mind is an integrating principle; hence the sense of oneness with the rest of Nature.

Browning's treatment of the theme in this passage, despite his claim in the Furnivall letter to express a 'popular notion', reveals an ambivalent attitude behind his acceptance of Darwin's theory, and here, perhaps, we find the main if not the only reason for the prosaic and pedestrian movement through 'cave', and 'hut' and 'tenement', compared with the energetic visions of *Paracelsus* and *Cleon*. There is a process of yielding and opposition in Browning's mind, a contest between intellectual and emotional belief which reduces the scope of his imaginative response to a mere: 'I like the thought...' An aspect of reserve and apology is being introduced into the single-minded enthusiasm of the great speech in *Paracelsus*, and the note of strain lurking in the Prince's evolutionary epic prepares us for the central metaphysical idea of this passage: 'From first to last of lodging, I was I.' What matters in the ascending metamorphoses of life is the spiritual identity persisting from one embodiment to another. With this assertion follows a renewed emphasis on finalism, more consciously formulated than in *Paracelsus* and *Cleon*: It is God who 'lodges' man—potential man— in successive tenements, and makes him 'learn' the art of living.

[1] *Ibid.* 11. 1011—1027.

From this re-enactment of the evolutionary epic the Prince goes on to illustrate his feeling of kinship with Nature through the story of Xerxes, the Persian conqueror who fell in love with a plane-tree in the desert. Then, capriciously, his thought reverts to the topical problem of the origin of species:

> O you count the links,
> Descry no bar of the unbroken man?
> Yes,—and who welds a lump of ore, suppose
> He likes to make a chain and not a bar,
> And reach by link on link, link small, link large,
> Out to the due length—why, there's forethought still
> Outside o' the series, forging at one end,
> While at the other there's—no matter what
> The kind of critical intelligence
> Believing that last link had last but one
> For parent, and no link was, first of all,
> Fitted to anvil, hammered into shape.
> Else, I accept the doctrine, and deduce
> This duty, that I recognize mankind,
> In all its height and depth and length and breadth.[1]

This sermon is, clearly, for the Darwinians, and again an often-repeated word from biological controversy is caught into the dialectic structure. The physical 'linking' is all that interests an evolutionist of the agnostic camp, and thus, Browning implies, he blinds himself to the essential continuity in organic development, which is spiritual. He blinds himself, moreover, to the underlying creative force working purposely through the links until it reaches out to the 'due length'—so far man. It is the 'unbroken man' which evolves in Nature, shaped gradually by the 'forethought' 'outside o' the series'. Ultimately, it is of no consequence what form or method the process adopts as long as it realizes its end, and thus reveals the

[1] Ll. 1042—56.

creative plan and its meaning. With this argument Browning's theistic finalism enters into the topical discussion of his time, and he seizes, incidentally, on the 'forge'-symbol which Tennyson also uses in *In Memoriam* (cxviii), in order to visualize the purposive action through which the 'links' took shape.

Browning next scrutinizes the claim of science, and the 'critical intelligence', that the first link was not directly created, as a parent for all ensuing life. This is the second point on which he cannot agree, and thus what he accepts of the new biological doctrine is indeed slight: it is chiefly an ethical implication, expressed somewhat tamely as a duty to 'recognize mankind': The variety of mankind and its uneven attainment is explained by its evolutionary background. However, this new insight fails to pursue the moral issue to any definite and satisfactory conclusion, and when the Prince attempts to apply his 'duty' to man and society, his thought wanders off into mazes of uncertainty. Perhaps one may trace this failure to the poet's own ambivalent attitude to social and political problems. He believed that progress is the law of life, yet to turn this faith into activity was no easy task, hence the half-hearted and cautionary message that there must be a 'slow and sober uprise all around', and no rash revolutionary measures.[1] Thus like Tennyson, Browning grapples with the typical Victorian dilemma of how to reconcile his own emotional conservatism with a general faith in change and progress which was growing more orthodox year by year.

Compared with *Paracelsus*, the evolutionary meditation in *Prince Hohenstiel-Schwangau* runs to a dead end, since Browning fails to translate its ethical significance into an effective vision of human relationship. In *Paracelsus* there is a glorious conquest of moral and spiritual existence, sustained throughout by poetic fervour. In this

[1] Cf. *Paracelsus, Supra* p. 120.

later poem the vision exhausts itself in conflicting loyalties and muddled thought.

As we have seen from the relevant passages in *Paracelsus, Luria, Cleon* and *A Death in the Desert*, Browning's evolutionary belief up to the time of *Prince Hohenstiel-Schwangau* was a vaguely formulated concept unrelated to any one particular theory of knowledge or of nature. It is a poet's intuition which gathers into itself eighteenth-century cosmology and nineteenth-century speculations on the historical 'Progression' in the process of nature. There is no internal evidence that Browning ever asked how this process operated, in terms of natural causes and effects. From the beginning, his vision explores the supranatural, divine power which moves and directs life towards its end, and throughout there is emphasis on plan and Providence, and on the crowning glory in Creation which is man. One might sum up this idealistic and teleological belief in the two basic tenets—the 'tendency to God', and the 'everlasting minute of creation'. Thus, the new aspect which occurs with *Prince Hohenstiel-Schwangau* is a clear demarcation between Browning's outlook, now explicitly defined with reference to the controversial issues, and that of the radical and agnostic evolutionists. Explicit, too, is his acceptance of the idea of transmutation of species.

In another poem of the same period, *Fifine at the Fair* (1872), one may observe a further development in the poet's attitude to evolution and to cosmological problems in general. It seems, at first, to take Browning to a position almost opposite to the vision of *Paracelsus*, where life is a flow and continuous ascent from inferior to superior forms: Nature is imperfect before man, and it works upwards to him through the lower creatures. *Fifine* reverses this point of view:

> Partake my confidence! No creature's made so mean
> But that, some way, it boasts, could we investigate,
> Its supreme worth ...[1]

[1] *The Works*, (Cent. ed., 1912), vol. vii, xxix.

140

In this passage Browning's intuition—his 'quick sense'—is apparently interlocked with a rational cosmic scheme, built on and derived from the eighteenth-century principle of plenitude. Yet to Browning this 'supreme worth' lies not in what the creatures are, but in what they may become. His is not a static world, but a wonder of transition and potential growth. The grain of sand, lost among myriad others on the beach, 'will leap ... to the very throne of things ...' The symbolic implication of this image is that in our world anything is possible: all being, whether animate or inanimate, is a miracle and a creative mystery, and the same metamorphosis which may operate in a grain of sand 'illustrates every man' and 'proves' the perfection of the cosmic 'plan' in its minutest detail.

This is the prelude to a theme which fills most of the metaphysical meditation in *Fifine.* The poem reveals a process of withdrawal from the exterior world of *Paracelsus, Cleon* and *Prince Hohenstiel-Schwangau* into a world of poetic and spiritual reality which stands firm amid the changing and ephemeral forms of time and space. Not, certainly, a fixed and abstract existence utterly cut off from the world of the senses, but one constantly growing from an imaginative effort of transferring the external world into the realm of spirit, where it achieves a deeper and truer meaning:

> And what a world for each
> Must somehow be i' the soul,—accept that mode
>   of speech,—
> Whether an aura gird the soul, wherein it seems
> To float and move, a belt of all the glints and
>   gleams
> It struck from out that world, its weaklier fellows
>   found
> So dead and cold; or whether these not so much
>   surround,
> As pass into the soul itself, add worth to worth,

141 .

> As wine enriches blood, and straightway send it
>   forth,
> Conquering and to conquer, through all eternity,
> That's battle without end.[1]

Thus the poet receives the world into his soul and gives it significance and a richer life. Without this spiritual conquest of reality, it would have no meaning: it would be 'inert' and mere 'stuff for transmuting'. The soul 'can absorb pure life':

>   or, rather, meeting death
> I' the shape of ugliness, by fortunate recoil
> So put on its resource, it find therein a foil
> For a new birth of life, the challenged soul's response
> To ugliness and death,—creation for the nonce.[2]

From its interaction with the external world the soul draws intenser being, for what it conceives or experiences as imperfection in that world, is transformed into beauty and truth. It would seem that Browning in this poem is approaching closer to the emotional basis of Platonism and divine discontent than he was at the time when he wrote *Cleon*, for though the manner is more restrained, there is a profounder realization that the 'inert' world in which we live is a sad condition which it is our task to overcome and 'transmute' in our soul. The movement of withdrawal from this world 'by fortunate recoil' is one of Platonic renunciation, and its cause and direction are now becoming more obvious. Confronted with death 'i' the shape of ugliness' the soul is urged to creation of a new reality; it transfers 'visible things',

> To where, secured from wrong, rest soul's
>   imaginings—[4]

[1] *Ibid.*, liv.   [2] *Ibid.*, lv.   [3] *Ibid.*, lvi.   [4] *Ibid.*, lvi.

142

These, and not external reality, are true, and significant; only these can 'do justice to the purpose' and ultimately turn 'deformity' into 'its opposite'.[1] The soul, moreover, is not closed on itself, it communes with others, and indeed derives some of its mysterious power of conquest from other souls through love. Browning goes on to interlink his soul-doctrine with a Platonic conception of love to herald a rebirth of existence:

> What joy, when each
> may supplement
> The other, changing each as changed, till, wholly
> blent,
> Our old things shall be new, and, what we both
> ignite,
> Fuse, lose the varicolor in achromatic white!
> Exemplifying law, apparent even now
> In the eternal progress,—[2]

From this inward stronghold of *soul* and *love*, Browning throughout the poem absorbs the world of phenomena into his vision. The carnival in Venice Square is the focal point of the process, since here Humanity and the architectural structures are seen changing and dissolving and reshaping themselves into new patterns. This metamorphosis recapitulates the universal condition of man, for to the poet Venice is a microcosm in which the Fair unfolds the 'state of mankind' in 'life-long permanence' and 'for all time'.[3] Gradually, the grotesque human forms and masks fade, and beneath them emerges the true human nature, still imperfect, still with a 'brute-

---

[1] The same withdrawal might be observed in Tennyson's *In Memoriam*, cxxiii, where the poet opposes the reality and permanence of his own vision to the ephemeral state of the external world: 'But in my spirit will I dwell, /And dream my dream, and hold it true;'.

[2] *Ibid.*, lix.   [3] *Ibid.*, cviii.

beast touch', and yet deserving love, for every 'variant quality' has its justification in the development of man. Thus:

> Force, guile, were
> arms which earned
> My praise, not blame at all: for we must learn
> to live,
> Case-hardened at all points, not bare and sensitive,
> — — — —
> Are we not here to learn the good of peace through
> strife,
> Of love through hate, and reach knowledge by
> ignorance?[1]

And thus, by isolating the essential and poetic vision from purely temporal and accidental elements, the new meaningful pattern emerges: there is a 'new birth' of love and understanding for mankind in his soul. All the hideous faces which previously seemed 'clawed away from God's prime purpose' now urged to 'pity rather than disgust'; and their distortions, 'which checked the man and let the beast appear' were faults in 'workmanship', not in the 'prime design'.[2] They are a 'deviation' from 'type' caused by a 'hesitancy' in the process of growth. The poet continues his exploration, and discovers

> there
> was just
> Enough and not too much of hate, love, greed
> and lust,
> Could one discerningly but hold the balance, shift
> The weight from scale to scale, do justice to the drift

[1] *Ibid.*, ci.
[2] *Ibid.*, xcix.

> Of nature, and explain the glories by the shames
> Mixed up in man, one stuff miscalled by different
>   names
> According to what stage i' the process turned his
>   rough,
> Even as I gazed, to smooth—only get close enough![1]

Browning is guided to his acceptance of mankind by the 'drift of nature', whose progress clearly shows that a transmutation is at work to create harmony from strife, good from evil. This forward-looking optimism reveals here a solid core of evolutionary faith, and *Fifine* offers recurrent evidence of the paradox—the necessary dialectic of good contra evil—on which it rests.

From the human and moral centre now established in the poetic structure Browning's vision strikes outwards in several directions to examine further this process of change:

>   Since something to
>   my mind
> Suggested soon the fancy, nay, certitude that
>   change,
> Never suspending touch, continued to derange
> What architecture, we, walled up within the cirque
> O' the world, consider fixed as fate, not fairy-work.
> For those were temples, sure, which tremblingly
>   grew blank
> From bright, then broke afresh in triumph,—ah,
>   but sank
> As soon, for liquid change through artery and vein
> O' the very marble wound its way![2]

Thus the 'stately fane' dissolves and returns to simple matter, but only to stand forth in a 'new birth', because 'something new' within

---

[1] *Ibid.*, cviii.   [2] *Ibid.*, cx.

the old structure 'pushed to gain an outlet'—and 'proved a growth of stone or brick or wood'. And this new building, if different in appearance from that which the first Builder erected, serves yet the 'prime purpose', which is to satisfy a perennial human need. Its temporal form matters little as long as it 'makes men lift their heads': Above the changing dogma and outgrown ritual, the temple of religion rises again and again, from foundations in the human soul which are permanent and stable.

Next Browning turns his eyes upon the wider panorama of human thought and activity, in which are set 'Academies', 'Domes where dwells Learning', seats and halls of 'Science' and 'Philosophy':

> do these, too, rise and
> fall,
> Based though foundations be on steadfast mother-
> earth,
> With no chimeric claim to supermundane birth,
> No boast that, dropped from cloud, they did not
> grow from ground?
> Why, these fare worst of all! these vanish and are
> found
> Nowhere, by who tasks eye some twice within his
> term
> Of threescore years and ten . . .[1]

A sudden change of tone and feeling has taken place. It is no longer the calm and confident acceptance of the temple-change, but a harsh light of irony playing upon the ephemeral scene. Like so many targets for destruction, Learning, Science and Philosophy stand exposed and ridiculed. Why? Because these have claimed (against Religion, it is implied), to base their search for truth upon a solid, factual foundation and not on the supranatural. Learning is

[1] *Ibid.*, cxi.

146

guilty of *hubris*, and the poet watches it decay with something like content. As he follows a more definite path among the ruins of 'Philosophy', he comes upon one doctrine which has known many vicissitudes, and shown a deplorable lack of permanence:

> Here gape I, all
>
> agog
> These thirty years, to learn how tadpole turns to
> frog;
> And thrice at least have gazed with mild astonish-
> ment,
> As, skyward up and up, some fire-new fabric sent
> Its challenge to mankind that, clustered underneath
> To hear the word, they straight believe, ay, in the
> teeth
> O' the Past, clap hands and hail triumphant Truth's
> outbreak—
> Tadpole-frog-theory propounded past mistake!
> In vain! A something ails the edifice, it bends,
> It bows, it buries . . .[1]

Thus Browning singles out the theory of evolution as a striking example of how scientific and philosophical truth fares. It has, during his life-time alone, crumbled and been rebuilt three times, i. e. as Progression, as Lamarckian and teleological doctrine in *Vestiges of Creation*, and finally as Natural Selection, and each time its supporters have been convinced of propounding truth 'past mistake'.

The treatment of the evolutionary theme in *Fifine*, as will become increasingly obvious from later passages, is clearly determined by an attitude very different from that of earlier poems, even from

---

[1] *Ibid.*, cxii.

Prince Hohenstiel-Schwangau. In that poem Browning still drew from the idea an optimistic and positive vision, while he rejected, without indignation, a purely naturalistic causation. Out of this rejection, however, grows the fierce irony of *Fifine,* and now the poet has a deliberate polemic task. What had happened in the meantime? Darwin's *Descent of Man*—this serious new challenge to those who believed that man was made in the image of God had appeared in 1871. Or more probably it was the aggressive propaganda of men like Tyndall and Huxley, which had been accumulating steadily since 1859. The battle around and about man's soul and his place in Nature continued and spread, and in *Fifine,* it seems, Browning too joined the fray. With this polemic task there follows a change in his attitude to the idea of evolution itself, and henceforth his treatment of the theme ceases to be visionary or prophetic except where he contemplates it as a mere aspect of the spiritual destiny of man.

In *Fifine* Browning does not recant his belief in evolution, yet he seems now more anxious to mark the distance between man and animal, and at one point he makes an oblique reference to the prevailing discussion. Elvire blames Don Juan:

> "And then" . . . .
> . . . . "you abdicate,
> With boast yet on your lip, soul's empire, and accept
> The rule of sense; the Man, from monarch's
>   throne has stept—
> Leapt, rather, at one bound, to base, and there
>   lies, Brute."[1]

These lines echo the charge brought against Huxley for his similar offence some ten years earlier, in *Man's Place in Nature,* and, both

[1] *Ibid.,* lx.

148

in phrase and intention, they point forward to Tennyson's poem *By An Evolutionist*. (Cf. *supra*, pp. 101—104.) It is from this concern for 'soul's empire' that one must work towards an understanding of the poet's changing attitude, and of his withdrawal from the external world into his 'soul's imaginings'. He is beginning to reject the 'rule of sense', and more particularly the dogmatic assumptions of empiricism. For this was the decade when the men of science, Tyndall and Huxley above all, claimed the whole field of human experience for the scientific quest. A few lines from Tyndall's famous Belfast-address in 1874 may illustrate their provocative attitude:

We claim, and we shall wrest, from theology, the entire domain of cosmological theory. All schemes and systems which thus infringe upon the domain of science, must, in so far as they do this, submit to its control, and relinquish all thought of controlling it.

A younger contemporary, the Rev. James Wilson, was distressed at the materialist determinism in these men:

All resulted from the collocations and potencies of primæval atoms, and could conceivably have been mathematically predicted. I myself have heard Tyndall and others dilate on this prospect like men inspired.[1]

To a large extent, it was this materialist challenge which gradually disenchanted the evolutionary prophet of *Paracelsus* and made him into the sarcastic dialectician of *Fifine* and later poems, so that, increasingly, the radiance of his vision became blurred by acrimonious satire. It is the intellectual fate of the Victorian theist and devout who, even when he is not clinging to dogma, watches with growing alarm the breakdown of significant relationships between the world

---

[1] 'The Religious Effect of Evolution', *Evolution in the Light of Modern Knowledge*, p. 510.

of science and the world of faith. In Matthew Arnold's *Dover Beach* this breakdown found its most poignant image: the 'darkling plain'. Ever since the 1850's, the 'ignorant armies' were abroad in greater numbers, and the necessity to take sides forced itself upon the poets—even upon those who were less afraid of anarchy than Arnold and Tennyson. At the same time, the Victorian poet, in general, has a deep desire to share the faith in progress and the advance of knowledge of his time, and this makes his choice a compromise and his fighting half-hearted. Besides, there is in many of them, as in Tennyson and Browning, a Platonic attitude to truth which leaves them open-minded to science and even enthusiastic, as to a method of discovery which could not, ultimately, conflict with the truth gained through intuition and faith. Yet, when they contemplated the nearer scene, the controversy there dismayed them, because it tended to split their world. Whether Christians or Platonists, or both, they grieved over the cleavage, for reasons which are well described by Dean Inge:

The Platonist loves Time, because it is the moving image of eternity; he loves Nature, because in Nature he perceives Spirit creating after its own likeness. As soon as the seen and unseen worlds fall apart and lose connection with each other, both are dead. Such a severance at once cuts the nerve which makes the Platonist a poet.[1]

Against such severance and death Tennyson struggles in *In Memoriam,* as Browning in *Fifine.* They have both learned from Coleridge, and their attitude and method are similar. It implies a claim that, since Truth ultimately is one, the conflict between religion and science is only temporary and apparent. Scientific discoveries have practical value, but their ambition to tell us all about the universe is the pursuit of a mirage. Science, moreover, by

[1] *The Platonic Tradition in English Religious Thought,* p. 77.

its analytical, abstract method reduces the living whole of the universe to dead entities of matter. Coleridge denounced the

philosophy of mechanism, which, in everything that is most worthy of the human intellect, strikes *Death,* and cheats itself by mistaking clear images for distinct conceptions, and which idly demands conceptions where intuitions alone are possible or adequate to the majesty of the Truth.[1]

De Vane observes that in Browning there is a marked hierarchical distinction between 'mind' and 'soul', and that the latter, overruling the authority of the former, is often invoked to verify the existence of God.[2] It is once more the influence of Coleridge's doctrine of 'Understanding' and 'Reason'. Thus in *Fifine,* through the chorus of conflicting and changing scientific truth, Browning hears the 'imperial chord' of essential Truth:

> "Truth inside, and outside, truth also; and between
> Each, falsehood that is change, as truth is permanence.
> The individual soul works through the shows of
>   sense,
> (Which, ever proving false, still promise to be true)
> Up to an outer soul as individual too;
> And, through the fleeting, lives to die into the fixed,
> And reach at length 'God, man, or both together
>   mixed,'
> Transparent through the flesh, by parts which
>   prove a whole,
> By hints which make the soul discernible by soul—
> Let only soul look up, not down, not hate but love,
> As truth successively takes shape, one grade above
> Its last presentment, . . .[3]

---

[1] *Letters,* vol. ii, p. 649.
[2] Cf. *Browning's Parleyings,* p. 275.   [3] *Ibid.,* cxxiv.

The Platonic trend in the pattern is marked, and we know it already from *A Death in the Desert*. Browning's faith in spiritual ascent here combines the evolutionary vision of *Paracelsus*—the 'tendency to God'—with the vision of soul's progress towards truth —the 'new birth'—of the earlier stanzas of *Fifine*. As before, existence is seen as a spiritual evolution, working through matter, towards God. For this reason, Browning finds it hard to forgive science for having so crudely externalized and mechanized the evolutionary process, and once more he bears down upon it, as the poem draws to a close. What science teaches is the 'False with Truth's outside' which 'plumes up his [man's] will' and 'puffs him out with pride'. The quest of the soul is of a humbler kind:

> Soul finds no triumph, here, to register like Sense
> With whom 't is ask and have,—the want, the
> evidence
> That the thing wanted, soon or late, will be supplied.
> This indeed plumes up will; this, sure, puffs out
> with pride,
> When, reading records right, man's instincts still
> attest
> Promotion comes to Sense because Sense likes it
> best;
> For bodies sprouted legs, through a desire to run:
> While hands, when fain to filch, got fingers one
> by one,
> And nature, that's ourself, accommodative brings
> To bear that, tired of legs which walk, we now
> bud wings
> Since of a mind to fly.[1]

In this satire on materialistic teleology Browning comes near, in

[1] *Ibid.*, cxxviii.

tone if not in argument, to Disraeli's ridicule of *Vestiges of Creation* in his novel *Tancred*.[1] The passage throws into relief the wide gap between this materialistic principle, quite useless, in Browning's opinion, to explain the process of growth, and, on the other hand, the teleological law which Paracelsus found in all nature. However, Browning here (as in the Furnivall letter) shows a peculiar lack of understanding for the doctrine which he set out to attack, for he hits Lamarck—or rather a distortion of Lamarck's theory—where he expected to find Darwin. Browning does not appear to have read Darwin or read him very carefully, for if he had done so, he would soon have discovered that the naturalist does not claim to know the cause of variations, (describing them often as 'spontaneous'), but only the way in which natural selection works on new varieties. Thus, by a kind of tragic irony, Browning's criticism strikes home more accurately to the neo-Lamarckian and Christian effort to reintroduce a teleological principle into the theory of nature. Or it could be that, in a flash of anticipation, Browning saw the development of the agnostic and atheistic cult of life, already pioneered by Swinburne (*Hertha*), which was soon to inform the works of Meredith, Samuel Butler and G. B. Shaw.

The polemic in *Fifine* is chiefly directed against the pride of science which claims to solve, in terms of materialistic determinism, the cosmic problems, and which fosters a desire to see purely material and utilitarian advantages as the means and ends of evolutionary progress. The poem stands at the cross-roads between Browning's earlier statements and those of his later years, and illuminates the way he has come as well as the way that lies ahead. This crucial position would seem to justify our lengthy analysis.

Seen against the background of Browning's poems before 1881, the letter which he wrote to Furnivall in that year aptly defines his attitude to evolution, and it is legitimate to regard it as his final

[1] Cf. *supra*, p. 65.

position, which one or two ambiguous lapses do not seriously shake. The first of these occurred in *A Death in the Desert*; the second appears in the *Parleyings with Bernard de Mandeville* (1887). Here, once more, Browning is firmly entrenched in the static, ideal order of Nature in eighteenth-century philosophy, and he chooses a spokesman of that age, though a very minor one, for his hero. This is Mandeville's view of Nature:

> Sun penetrates the ore, the plant—
> They feel and grow: perchance with subtler skill
> He interfuses fly, worm, brute, until
> Each favoured object pays life's ministrant
> By pressing, in obedience to his will,
> Up to completion of the task prescribed,
> So stands and stays a type.[1]

It would seem that Browning's object with such old-fashioned teaching is to insist on the creative intelligence which underlies the cosmic plan, and in this aspect Mandeville serves the poet well, for he comes back with a message of order and purposive creation from a time in which Browning now is more at ease than in his own troubled epoch. To Browning's generation chaos had ensued upon order in the world of thought, and order could only be restored by a shift of emphasis from matter to soul, phenomena to noumena, knowledge to faith. This effort, which we have studied in *Fifine at the Fair*, and which runs through a good deal of Browning's meditation in the *Parleyings*, is probably the cause of his self-contradiction in the last line here.

The polemic against the materialistic theory of evolution which Browning began in *Prince Hohenstiel-Schwangau* and continued

---

[1] *Parleyings with Certain People of Importance in their Day,* (1887 ed.), p. 45. De Vane maintains that the intention in these lines was to 'contradict the whole theory [of Evolution]'; cf. *Browning's Parleyings*, p. 199.

with greater intensity in *Fifine at the Fair,* is brought to a climax and an end in the *Parleyings with Francis Furini.* In this poem, the *mise en scène* of the theme is almost comical in its sudden and peremptory arrangement for the seventeenth century painter-priest to deliver a sermon to 'us the cultured, therefore sceptical' in 'actual London'. Indeed, even Science is made to encourage him, and 'up stands Furini':

> Evolutionists!
> At truth I glimpse from depths, you glance from heights,
> Our stations for discovery opposites,—
> How should ensue agreement? I explain:
> 'Tis the tip-top of things to which you strain
> Your vision, until atoms, protoplasm,
> And what and whence and how may be the spasm
> Which sets all going, stop you: down perforce
> Needs must your observation take its course,
> Since there's no moving upwards: link by link
> You drop to where the atoms somehow think,
> Feel, know themselves to be: the world's begun,
> Such as we recognize it. Have you done
> Descending? Here's ourself,—Man, known to-day,
> Duly evolved at last,—so far, you say,
> The sum and seal of being's progress. Good!
> Thus much at least is clearly understood—
> Of power does Man possess no particle:
> Of knowledge—just so much as shows that still
> It ends in ignorance on every side:
> But righteousness—ah, Man is deified
> Thereby, for compensation![1]

The confrontation is only apparently dramatic, for we are to watch, on Browning's own terms, the opposites wrestle in a contest where

---

[1] 1877 ed., ix.

the issue is clearly given in advance. It is a distant development of the dialectic in *Prince Hohenstiel-Schwangau* into the Platonic field of spiritual quest and withdrawal in *Fifine*. Here, too, the poet begins by stating his opponents' method, and the object of their search. This, he claims, is a recapitulation of evolutionary growth from man down to the simplest manifestation of life and energy, which, in the end, is left with three unanswerable questions about the creative 'spasm': the ultimate mystery at the root of all being. The 'Evolutionists' fail to see that the answer lies at the other end, in man, and thus they are persistently searching for truth in the wrong direction. In *Paracelsus* already, Browning had traced the development upwards, from the 'thinking atom' to man, and now, once more, he wants to make man the focal point of the discussion. Through his analysis of human nature the painter-priest Furini seeks to undercut the claims of science, and its *hubris,* by demonstrating the obvious weaknesses and limitations of the human mind. Wherever Furini turns to observe these aspects, his 'surprised reason' faces a 'double defeat'. Somewhat like Tennyson in *The Ancient Sage* Browning is at pains to show that 'nothing worthy proving can be proven', that the most important truth lies outside the cognitive range of the intellect, and, as a corollary, that science has no command in the field of the essential life, which is spirit. A similar rejection of the value of empirical knowledge, and distrust in human cognition, would commonly lead to philosophical pessimism, but in Browning it leads to the opposite, for only thus can he, like Coleridge, claim that intuition alone is 'adequate to the majesty of the Truth'.

The important thing in evolution, this first passage implies, is not the *modus operandi* or observable material aspects, but exactly those metaphysical issues which the scientists ignore, and which can only be grasped through an understanding of man. Man, it is agreed, is the 'sum and seal of being's progress'; yet he is weak and ignorant. What, then, is his title to greatness? His moral sense—his righteousness. These 'began' in man, for there were 'no signs of such before'. However, the poet hastens to limit the scope of these virtues through a renewed emphasis on the pathetic human dichotomy, in the dismal setting of 'one wide disease/Of things that are'. It is a world that mocks the 'pre-eminency' and the 'crown' awarded to man, and it will not change until his nature changes:

> But until there crown our sight
> The quite new—not the old mere infinite
> Of changings,—some fresh kind of sun and moon,—
> Then, not before, shall I expect a boon
> Of intuition just as strange, which turns
> Evil to good, and wrong to right, unlearns
> All Man's experience learned since Man was he.

Meanwhile, one must recognize in him the 'Prime Mind', 'advanced to this degree',—a high degree, no doubt, though by no means worthy of veneration. Furini continues his exposure of man in an ironical strain reminiscent of Pope's *Essay*:

> He stands
> Confessed supreme—the monarch whose commands
> Could he enforce, how bettered were the world!
> He's at the height this moment—to be hurled
> Next moment to the bottom by rebound
> Of his own peal of laughter.

Browning has indeed come a long way from *Paracelsus*, though there too the warning against human pride was already part of the theme.

Furini's demonstration of the fallacy of materialistic evolutionism harks back to the 'soul' contra 'sense' debate on truth in *Fifine*, and prepares us for the neo-Platonic method of his own approach. It is a quest in humility, and an intuitive, finalistic account of evolution which, like that of *Paracelsus,* is centred in man:

> I at the bottom, Evolutionists,
> Advise beginning, rather. I profess
> To know just one fact—my self-consciousness,—
> 'Twixt ignorance and ignorance enisled,—
> Knowledge: before me was my Cause—that's styled
> God: after, in due course succeeds the rest ...[1]

From this Cartesian position the argument moves straight into the world of Coleridge:

> Knowledge so far impinges on the Cause
> Before me, that I know—by certain laws
> Wholly unknown, whate'er I apprehend
> Within, without me, had its rise: thus blend
> I, and all things perceived, in one Effect.

This is the vantage-point of intuitive insight from which the poet may discover 'what comes after me—the universe'. He retains the subject-object distinction of the Platonic school, and rejects vehemently the pantheist's or materialist's conception of a self-moving nature:

>   'Externe
> Not inmost, is the Cause, fool!'

Not in the 'thinking atom' lies the creative force, or 'spasm', but in a power external to the universe—a transcendent cause, efficient and final. Yet, what inference should one draw from this, since the world is such a scene of strife—of 'evil and good irreconcilable'? At the core of existence Browning finds again the paradox of good from evil:

[1] *Ibid.,* x.

158

For me

...knowledge can but be
Of good by knowledge of good's opposite—
Evil,—since, to distinguish wrong from right,
Both must be known in each extreme, beside—

......

Made to know on, know ever, I must know
All to be known at any halting-stage
Of my soul's progress, such as earth, where wage
War, just for soul's instruction, pain with joy,
Folly with wisdom, all that works annoy
With all that quiets and contents,—in brief,
Good strives with evil.[1]

In his thorough analysis of the *Parleyings,* De Vane has pointed out the difficulties in which this paradox involves the poet, since he has to reconcile the idea of a loving and omnipotent God with the existence of evil and suffering, which, if only an illusory test for man, would be cruel and meaningless. Browning's solution, according to De Vane, is that 'man can have no knowledge of whether the evil is real or not, and that he must believe blindly in the goodness of God'.[2]

The faith to which *Francis Furini* bears witness, that the earth is a 'halting-stage/Of my soul's progress', connects Browning's last poem about evolution with his first, and throws into relief the coherence which underlies his poetic vision as well as his critical and polemic task: Evolution is a spiritual process. In this sense, and gradually detached from aspects of physical growth, it remains an

---

[1] In his comment on this passage De Vane agrees with Henry Jones's remark that: 'To Browning the world is a kind of moral gymnasium, crowded with phantoms, wherein by exercise man makes moral muscle'; *Browning's Parleyings*, p. 189.

[2] *Ibid.*, p. 31.

active and central concept in his poetry. One might object that, when dissociated from these aspects which are integral to the biological theory, the idea of spiritual ascent is a purely Christian and Platonic idea of purification or atonement which, at most, finds an analogy in the evolutionary doctrine, while there is no identity between the two. Yet to Browning there are not two distinct processes of development, one 'natural' and one 'spiritual', but a universal nisus, a 'tendency to God' manifest everywhere in Nature and in Man's soul, and from this tendency he deduces the first Cause, and the 'law of life', which is progress.

To explore this idealistic reading of the evolutionary process in its remoter interaction with Browning's attitudes and beliefs, it might suffice to look briefly at one characteristic poem, *Rabbi Ben Ezra* (1864), and indicate one or two others. In *Rabbi Ben Ezra*, spiritual growth and fulfilment is the main theme, and after a clear statement of this in the first stanza, the poem goes on to exult in the glory of man and his predominance over the 'low kinds' in nature. Man has a higher destination which involves doubt and struggle, yet also an existence above the earth-bound, sensuous life. 'A spark disturbs our clod' (v), and thus human life becomes a movement and a restless striving:

> For thence,—a paradox
> Which comforts while it mocks,—
> Shall life succeed in that it seems to fail:
> What I aspired to be,
> And was not, comforts me:
> A brute I might have been, but would not sink i'
> the scale.

It is once more the paradox described by Chesterton as 'the hope which lies in the imperfection of man'. Browning does not, like Tennyson, deplore the brute in man,[1] but he insists that the body,

[1] Cf. also *Fifine, supra,* p. 144.

160

man's physical nature, even 'at its best', is without power to 'project soul on its lone way'. (viii.) The 'flesh', though 'pleasant', is a 'rose-mesh' in which the soul is caught, and it longs to be completely free. As in *Fifine,* the poet laments that the soul finds no tangible 'triumphs' to 'match those manifold/Possessions of the brute',—its gains are less apparent. It would be wrong, however, to regret man's dual nature, for 'All good things/Are ours': the world is a whole, and so is human life. Yet its struggle points beyond to a new existence:

> Therefore I summon age
> To grant youth's heritage,
> Life's struggle having so far reached its term:
> Thence shall I pass, approved
> A man, for aye removed
> From the developed brute; a god though in
> the germ. (xiii.)

In individual life, as in the universal panorama spread out in *Para-celsus,* the first goal is to become man, a fulfilled being, a complete realization of the spiritual urge or 'spark' that works through matter and upwards in animal nature. When this goal is achieved through the effort of a life-time, man is free to begin a new phase of ascent and growth, from the God-seed in his soul. In the following stanza Browning states a belief in metempsychosis similar to that of Tennyson, and which corresponds to the cyclic or circular movement of all life in *Paracelsus:*

> And I shall thereupon
> Take rest, ere I be gone
> Once more on my adventure brave and new:
> Fearless and unperplexed,
> When I wage battle next,
> What weapons to select, what armour to indue.

The perspective, however, remains undeveloped, and the next stanzas are concerned with man's spiritual and moral condition. All experience, we are told, is useful, even the apparently meaningless and futile. So too, are

> All instincts immature,
> All purposes unsure,
> That weighed not as his work, yet swelled the man's
> amount:
>
> (xxiv.)

For all are part of the 'main account' of human value which God alone can appreciate. From beginning to end, man is the work of God, and to visualize His creative act, Browning develops in the concluding stanzas the metaphor of the Potter's wheel, which once more gives emphasis to his finalistic belief. It is a trope suggested either by the biblical image or the Orphic phrase 'wheel of birth', and corresponds to the forge symbolism in *Prince Hohenstiel-Schwangau,* though here it is concerned only with individual life. On this wheel the human being is shaped, body and soul, from a 'passive clay' to 'heaven's consummate cup', for the purpose of slaking the 'thirst' of God.

The faith in 'soul's progress' is strong and buoyant in *Rabbi Ben Ezra,* but at other times, as in the threnody *La Saisiaz* (1878), it dwindles to a tentative and self-persuasive hope. Sadness and bereavements left their impact on its formulation, and the ring of its message grew less triumphant with the years. Yet it achieves strength and calm again in the last poems, the *Parleyings*; and in main outline Browning's belief sustains courageously the vision of a world of love and law.

Love and law govern the 'everlasting minute of creation' and thus also the 'soul's progress'. In the *Parleyings with Gerard de Lairesse* a goal is indicated:

162

> What were life
> Did soul stand still therein, forego her strife
> Through the ambiguous present to the goal
> Of some all-reconciling future?

We are reminded of the 'far-off divine event/To which the whole Creation moves'—in *In Memoriam*: the goal is a state of absolute fulfilment and harmony.

The best and most characteristic quality in Browning's evolutionary poems is movement and energy. Despite its lack of solid, visual and metaphorical elements, this poetry is visionary—in a prophetic sense, and the term has been used in our study of the coherence which exists in a poem between the separate units of perception and thought, often purely abstract, through some link or structure of a suggestive force building a significant pattern. The absence of evocative and metaphorical language is perhaps the main weakness in Browning's poetry in general, and it accounts to a large extent for the vague and abstruse impact of his thought and emotion. In his evolutionary poetry too, the prophetic excitement tends to exhaust itself in the void of verbal abstraction, as in *Francis Furini*. At his best, however, though there may be little, apart from metre and rime, to distinguish his verse from prose, Browning's poetry about the 'everlasting minute of creation' effectively expresses his fundamental beliefs and attitudes. Gradually, his polemic task split the unity of tone and argument, and for this reason, perhaps, and because the prophetic energy here flows fresh and unhampered from a great new idea, *Paracelsus* is the most satisfactory of Browning's evolutionary pronouncements upon the destiny of life.

3. *In the Platonic Tradition*

With Tennyson and Browning the idea of evolution becomes a seminal theme in English poetry of the nineteenth century. When, in later years, they pondered the metaphysical implications of

Darwin's doctrine, they still retained their belief in evolution as a spiritual ascent, by turning their attention from Nature to Man, matter to mind. The battle of 'the ignorant armies', deplored by Matthew Arnold in *Dover Beach,* made them more strongly conscious of their Christian and Platonic heritage. This had, from the beginning, determined their search, but its force is particularly active in their later poetry, which is focused on the 'goal of some all-reconciling future'. Tennyson, more anxious to identify his quest with the aspirations and ideas of his time, continues to stare deep into the temporal vista. On the whole, however, material and historical aspects lose interest, and, increasingly, their evolutionary perspective is dominated by the 'tendency to God' and the 'far-off divine event' outside and beyond the world of space and time.

It is, of course, only in a general sense that one may describe the two poets as Platonists, for they are much else beside, and carry with them in the complexity of their heritage things old and new with equal affection. Nor are they, needless to say, consistent thinkers adhering to any one philosophical doctrine. Yet, unmistakably, they move with the main stream of Platonism, lately swelled by Coleridge and Shelley, and keep steadily to its course despite the changing intellectual scene. Platonism, it has been said, is an attitude to life rather than a philosophy, an attitude born of religious aspiration and a love of beauty, truth and perfection. In the poetry of Tennyson and Browning this main underlying impulse must be kept in sight. It was powerful in the great Romantics, and is dominant again in these two of the following generation, as a hereditary feature which links them together and decides their intellectual fate. For this reason the Platonic trends in the poetry of Tennyson and Browning acquire a historical significance, and might, if gathered into a more coherent pattern, yield some understanding of the relationship between them and their immediate forbears, and of the sources of poetic insight which they found at hand. This is the object of the ensuing brief sketch, which, though a digression from our main line of inquiry, ought to provide a useful historical context for the poets' evolutionary belief.

Dean Inge describes Platonic Christianity as a

spiritual religion, based on a firm belief in absolute and eternal values as the most real things in the universe—a confidence that these values are knowable by man—a belief that they can nevertheless be known only by whole-hearted consecration of the intellect, will, and affections to the great quest—an entirely open mind towards the discoveries of science—a reverent and receptive attitude to the beauty, sublimity, and wisdom of the creation, as a revelation of the mind and character of the Creator—a complete indifference to the current valuations of the worldling.[1]

This definition is an apt background to Coleridge, as it is to Browning, and indicates some of the basic traits in their attitude.

In the great Romantic poets it is Plato's cosmogonic vision which most frequently challenges their creative task: A divine energy flows constantly into matter, animates it and makes it grow and aspire to higher levels of existence. To Wordsworth the universe is a 'shell' that whispers to the 'ear of Faith' about 'invisible things' and 'ever-during power'.[2] All the various aspects of nature—crags, streams, clouds, darkness and light, are 'like workings of one mind .../The types and symbols of eternity ...'[3] In the wide nature panorama of Coleridge there is an 'immeasurable fount/Ebullient with creative Deity!', and spirits of 'plastic power' shaping the 'grosser and material mass'.[4] Shelley has felt the presence of this divine spirit everywhere:

> Throughout this varied and eternal world
> Soul is the only element, the block

[1] *The Platonic Tradition in English Religious Thought*, p. 33
[2] *The Excursion*, iv.
[3] *The Prelude*, vi.
[4] *Religious Musings*, Concl.

165

That for uncounted ages has remained
The moveless pillar of a mountain's weight
Is active, living spirit.[1]

It 'knows no term, cessation, or decay' (vi.); it is 'steadfast' and directs all things so that, even when to the human eye 'all seems unlinked contingency and chance', every atom 'acts but as it ought to act'. The Soul of the universe is the

> eternal spring
> Of life and death, of happiness and woe,
> Of all that chequers the phantasmal scene
> That floats before our eyes in wavering light,
> Which gleams but on the darkness of our prison,
> Whose chains and massy walls
> We feel, but cannot see.[2]

Shelley here restates the illusion of reality of Plato's 'cave'.—In Shelley's belief the 'slightest leaf' and 'meanest worm' share the 'eternal breath' of this spiritual power, and thus everything 'becomes a link/In the great chain of nature'.[3]

Shelley, moreover, is inflamed by a prophetic zest which he bequeaths directly to our two Victorian poets:

> For birth, and life, and death, and that strange state
> Before the naked soul has found its home,
> All tend to perfect happiness, and urge
> The restless wheels of being on their way,
> Whose flashing spokes, instinct with infinite life,
> Bicker and burn to gain their destined goal . . .[4]

These lines, and those already quoted from *Adonais* (*Supra*, p. 124) contain the essence of the faith which Browning received from his

---

[1] *Queen Mab*, iv.   [2] *Ibid.*, vi.   [3] *Ibid.*, ii.   [4] *Ibid.*, ix.

166

hero—the 'Sun-treader'—and channelled into the landscape of *Paracelsus,* where God dwells, as life, in all things, and all things aspire to perfection. To this spiritual doctrine Browning adds his own evolutionary prophecy, which turns the static hierarchy of life in the Platonic cosmos into a continuous flow and ascent. Yet to Browning as to Tennyson, evolution is God's 'everlasting minute of creation'. Tennyson interprets the divine creative action more directly in terms of contemporary theory of nature, with the nebular hypothesis and outlines of organic process as recurrent central trends in his cosmogonic pattern. The divine presence to him is, above all, the human soul,—something transcendent and eternal, that 'walks from state to state' in an 'eternal process', and rises to 'higher things'. Hence birth to him, as to Wordsworth, is the main creative mystery. This is the Romantic vision:

> Our birth is but a sleep and a forgetting:
> The Soul that rises with us, our life's Star,
> > Hath had elsewhere its setting,
> > > And cometh from afar:
> > Not in entire forgetfulness,
> > And not in utter nakedness,
> But trailing clouds of glory do we come
> > From God, who is our home. . . .[1]

Similarly, to Tennyson, the soul comes from the 'deep'—'that true world within the world we see', and in death, 'that which drew from out the boundless deep,/Turns again home'.

Earthly existence in the Platonic doctrine is a flux of imperfect forms aspiring to the static perfection of their eternal, transcendent models—the ideas. This flux and urge are central features in Romantic nature, and the confrontation of two worlds, one of

[1] Wordsworth, *Ode: Intimations of Immortality from Recollections of Early Childhood.*

matter and one of spirit, one changing and chaotic, the other static and harmonious, provides a congenial dramatic setting for the poets' interpretation of life. There is 'central peace, subsisting at the heart/Of endless agitation. .' in Wordsworth's nature scene.[1] Life is a 'busy dance/Of things that pass away'.[2] Browning likewise sees existence as a 'dance of plastic circumstance' in which the soul stands 'fixed'.[3] Shelley contrasts the fleeting earthly forms with a transcendent permanence:

> The One remains, the many change and pass;
> Heaven's light for ever shines, Earth's shadows fly;[4]

And Tennyson sings, more sadly:

> The hills are shadows, and they flow
> From form to form, and nothing stands ...[5]

Plato's dualistic cosmology is a drama born of a sense of imperfection which creates its opposite, the eternal beauty, harmony and peace of the world of ideas. This is how Shelley sees the difference:

> Life, like a dome of many-coloured glass,
> Stains the white radiance of Eternity ...[6]

And Browning claims that the impurity—the death and ugliness—of our earthly existence is lost in the 'achromatic white' of the world of soul. Plato thought of life as an exile from this world of soul, and its earthly abode as both a prison and a grave. It is so to the Romantics in their darker moods: Soon the 'Shades of the prison-house begin to close/Upon the growing Boy'.[7] Shelley describes birth

---

[1] *The Excursion*, iv.   [2]*Ibid.*   [3] *Rabbi Ben Ezra.*
[4] *Adonais*, lii.   [5] *In Memoriam*, cxxiii.   [6] *Adonais*, lii.
[7] Wordsworth, *Ode: Intimations of Immortality.*

as the 'eclipsing Curse',[1] and the world as a 'stern and desolate tract' to the 'stranger-soul'.[2] The soul, Tennyson agrees, is 'banished into mystery'.[3]

At the core of this dualism there is a painful realization of moral conflict, and of evil. It provides a dynamic of spiritual aspiration which often finds expression in Romantic poetry, as an unending search—for the Holy Grail, for the ultimate reconciliation and harmony when good shall triumph over evil and a state of truth and beauty be attained. In this quest the active force is love—Eros —which links the soul with its origin and guides it to its eternal home.

Coleridge, more than Wordsworth, wrestles with the human dichotomy and strives to resolve it 'into one vast harmony'. (Ode to the Departing Year.) Love and repentance, i. e. moral awakening, are at the heart of his great purgatory vision of life, with a total surrender of will and intellect to Divine Providence and Grace.[4] As in Plato, and act of recollection guides the soul to God, its essential being, so that from 'All things of terrible seeming', from 'dark passions' and 'thirsty cares' it passes to where all evils are absorbed into universal good,—'Enrobed with light and naturalised in Heaven'. For, as the poet adds in a footnote to these Religious Musings: 'Our evil Passions, under the influence of Religion, become innocent, and may be made to animate our virtue.' God—'Lord of unsleeping Love'—uses evil to discipline the soul and give it a thirst for good, as he uses 'brief wrong' to render 'Truth lovely'.[5] Shelley in his revolutionary impatience precipitates the final harmony, but is less concerned with the nature of evil than with its manifestation in political tyrants and religious demagogues. These evils are acute and will be conquered. There is crime and misery in human life, 'But the eternal world/Contains at once the

---

[1] Adonais, liv.   [2] Qeen Mab, iv.   [3] De Profundis.
[4] The Ancient Mariner.   [5] Ibid.

evil and the cure'.[1] Evil is an accidental phenomenon, not a fundamental or permanent flaw in human nature, for the heart (the
spiritual love) remains untainted. Therefore, as the poet rushes into
the future of mankind, 'soon' the 'ugly human shapes and visages'
fade, as a 'foul disguise' falling from their 'mild and lovely forms'.[2]
Through this transformation, all things ugly—'toads, snakes and
efts' grow beautiful.[3] It is the mysterious power of love, folding
itself 'round the sphered world', at work to free men from their
trammels. In this coming reign of liberty and love, 'hate, disdain
or fear' no longer sit upon the brow of men, and in their heart is
no longer the falsity and error which makes it 'deny the *yes* it
breathes'. Such free men—'gentle radiant forms'—are already on
earth:

> Speaking the wisdom once they could not think,
> Looking emotions once they feared to feel,
> And changed to all which once they dared not be,
> Yet being now, made earth like heaven . . .[4]

Within this theme Tennyson is related to Coleridge much as
Browning is to Shelley. The poet of *In Memoriam* is tormented by
the chaining of the 'soul' to 'brute', and, under the impact of the
evolutionary idea, life to him is an effort to 'work out the beast'.
In a slow purgatorial advance mankind moves up from the 'lower
world'—the 'moods of tiger and of ape'—and ultimately, he trusts,
'somehow good will be the final goal of ill'. The biological trend
thus woven into the Platonic pattern to reassure him of the historical
truth of this ascent, is a new aspect, yet fuses naturally with the

[1] *Queen Mab*, vi.
[2] *Prometheus Unbound*, III, iv.
[3] Cf. *The Ancient Mariner*.
[4] Prometheus Unbound, III, iv. In *The Cenci, Hellas* and *The Triumph
of Life* there is, however, a more complicated and sinister vision of evil.

asceticism and worldly renunciation of the Platonic attitude. Browning too, though he feels that 'all good things are ours', is an ascetic at heart, and joins Tennyson in denouncing Epicurean self-indulgence.[1] In later years, even he deplores the 'fleshly chain' weighing down 'the powers that fain/Else would soar. .'.[2] In general, however, his acceptance of the human dialectic is cheerful, and he anticipates a good-evil reconciliation so akin to Shelley's that it finds almost identical expression.[3]

Santayana contends that the Platonist's renunciation of the world is not 'radical', but 'a sort of substitution', since love means attachment and is 'based on a craving and a sense of want'.[4] Whether this is true in general of Platonism or not, it does enter into the attitudes of Tennyson and Browning. The dualism and tension that rend Tennyson's world reveal a failure to accept death, as annihilation of the self and of earthly love and beauty. Therefore, his escape into the realm of spirit is steeped in sadness and regret, and the full life to which he aspires is still an existence of the self, invulnerable by death, in eternal love and harmony. His millennial hope for mankind in time reflects the same craving for existential perfection and fulness of life. Browning also, though he is less tormented by the reality which he transforms in his soul, pursues much the same goal. In both poets the movement from mortality and limitation to an ideal, deathless world corresponds to their effort to transfer values, beauty, happiness and love, into their spiritual domain, where henceforth they may dwell—'secured from wrong'. Thus, on the one hand, they struggle to overcome the 'black negation of the bier', and on the other the 'cunning casts in clay' which science discovers in its deterministic universe. Dean Inge points out that Platonism is characterized by 'an entirely open mind to the

[1] *Rabbi Ben Ezra; By An Evolutionist.*
[2] *La Saisiaz.*
[3] *Prometheus Unbound,* III, iv; *Fifine at the Fair,* xcix.
[4] *Platonism and the Spiritual Life,* pp. 28—29.

171

discoveries of science', and the growing hostility to materialistic naturalism in Tennyson and Browning is not so much caused by these discoveries as by the spirit in which they are made. In this respect they continue Coleridge's tradition: Truth, to the Platonist, can only be intuitively and humbly grasped; it is a recollection in the soul, and is gradually unveiled with the soul's progress.[1]

Attachment to earthly values and joys is a condition of chiliastic hope, and in Romantic poetry, as in that of Tennyson and Browning, prophecies of some future paradise often appear. Both Wordsworth and Coleridge are active in this Utopian quest: There is, says the former, some truth in old tales of Elysian Fields, Atlantis and Paradises—they are poetic foreshadowings, and the poet, moved by the prophetic Spirit and 'Dreaming on things to come', anticipates justly a future harmonious state for mankind.[2] Among these things to come is a 'faery' race of new men. Coleridge has a similar hope:

> And while within myself I trace
> The greatness of some future race
> Aloof with hermit eye I scan
> The present works of present man.[3]

More explicitly formulated, Coleridge's Millennium is a state in which

I suppose that Man will continue to enjoy the highest glory of which his human nature is capable.—That all who in past ages have endeavoured to ameliorate the state of man will rise and enjoy the fruits and flowers, the imperceptible seeds of which they had sown in their former Life: and that the wicked will, during the same period, be suffering the remedies adapted to their several bad habits. I suppose that this period will be followed by the passing

[1] Cf. The Epilogue, In Memoriam; A Death in the Desert.
[2] The Recluse.
[3] Ode to Tranquillity.

away of this Earth and by our entering the state of pure intellect; when all Creation shall rest from its labours.[1]

In these reflections the Platonic trend of Divine justice is predominant. With the final prophecy, of a 'state of pure intellect' (which Robinet had dreamed of) superseding material existence as a phase of cosmic development, Coleridge points forward to Tennyson and Browning and even further, to the evolutionary Utopia of the late nineteenth and early twentieth centuries.

Shelley also, as we have seen, in his ecstatic apocalypse traces the best qualities of present man into a universal future paradise:

Happiness
And science dawn though late upon the earth;
Peace cheers the mind, health renovates the frame;
Disease and pleasure cease to mingle here,
Reason and passion cease to combat there;
Whilst each unfettered o'er the earth extend
Their all-subduing energies, and wield
The sceptre of a vast dominion there;
Whilst every shape and mode of matter lends
Its force to the omnipotence of mind,
Which from its dark mine drags the gem of truth
To decorate its paradise of peace.[2]

Most of these chiliastic and Utopian features are absorbed into the prophecies of *Paracelsus* and *In Memoriam*.

Like their Romantic forbears, Tennyson and Browning find in their human ideal 'august anticipations', and promises that 'men begin to pass their nature's bound', while 'peace rises within them ever more and more'. Knowledge and Truth will be part of their

---

[1] Footnote to *Religious Musings*.
[2] *Queen Mab*, viii.

great achievement, but above all else they will be serene and harmonious beings,—'no longer half-akin to brute',—purified in the moral and spiritual pilgrimage of the race. Coleridge's 'future race' is a cathartic outcome, and points more directly to Tennyson's 'crowning race' in *In Memoriam* than to the similar anticipations of *Paracelsus,* where the 'superior race' appears as a more naturalistic and evolutionary concept. However, to both poets the processes of organic growth and moral or spiritual ascent are closely interacting, as aspects of the same fundamental reality.

In their hope for a 'far-off divine event' and an 'all-reconciling future' Tennyson and Browning found the answer to their divine discontent and their horror of death. Yet despite this effort to overcome the persecution of earthly transience and imperfection, despite their fretful search into vistas of 'soul's progress' and 'æonian evolution', they remain lovingly attached to life on earth. For this reason, though existence is seen, at present, mainly as a purgatory and a probation ground, it tends in their vision, as in that of Coleridge, to evolve and ascend as a historical process up to a point in time where it fuses entirely with a transcendent, ideal state; the temporal blends into the eternal, and earthly values are thus transferred to security and permanence. As for what this ultimate goal—the 'divine event' or the 'all-reconciling future'—may be, both poets leave it vague and undefined, and they do so with the mystic's right. If life, this 'dome of many-coloured glass', as Shelley saw it—'Stains the white radiance of Eternity', and if the 'varicolor' of present existence is lost in the 'achromatic white' of the new life anticipated in *Fifine at the Fair,* then it would be impossible and futile indeed to describe heaven in terms of earth.

CHAPTER III

EVOLUTION AS A CULT OF LIFE AND MAN

1. *Algernon Charles Swinburne*

P O E T S O F D I V I N E D I S C O N T E N T may be banished from
a Platonic heaven, even though they scorn the temptation to
return to it, and remain for ever in heroic and voluntary exile.
Swinburne was one of these. The flame of spiritual revolt and
republican crusade which Shelley carried so far in Romantic poetry,
becomes a veritable fire in *Songs before Sunrise* (1871)—the poems
of which Swinburne said: 'Other books are books, *Songs before
Sunrise* is myself.' Because of this quality of personal confession,
because in these poems he ranges widely over the crucial problems
of human destiny and explores at the same time a cosmic panorama,
and, finally, because of the permanence of his beliefs, it is convenient
to limit one's attention to this volume and yet hope to distil from
it the essence of Swinburne's vision of life.

Just as Shelley's exploration in *Hellas* extends far beyond the
temporal and local setting of its theme, so Swinburne in *Songs
before Sunrise* pursues the cause of Italian liberty, with its champion
Mazzini, into the universal issues of existence. The nature of his
attitude and aspiration is well revealed in *Tenebrae*, through the
prayer of those 'in the grey twilight' who long for freedom and
yearn to feel its breath, its promise

> From a land whereon time hath not trod,
> Where the spirit is bondless and bare,
> And the world's rein breaks, and the rod,

175

> And the soul of a man, which is God,
> He adores without altar or prayer...

This is the ideal, spiritual world beyond our actual world of imperfection and bondage, and we know it already from a similar
quest in the Romantics. Yet here, in the equation of the human soul
with God, a new voice is heard, different even from the prophetic
iconoclasm of Shelley. In the following stanza the divine power
of the human soul is hailed as one capable of transforming existence,
and bridging the two worlds, so that the 'colours of things... And
the forms' are lost in the 'limitless white/Splendour of space without space'. And the Platonic trend persists in the life- and light-
imagery (st. 19) interweaving to create impressions of undying
spiritual life. Again the changes of earthly existence are seen as
'shadows' consumed in the pure permanence of eternity, whose 'live
light' is 'made of our lives'. Finally the poem swells to a solemn
incantation:

> O spirit of man, most holy,
> The measure of things and the root,
> In our summers and winters a lowly
> Seed, putting forth of them slowly
> Thy supreme blossom and fruit.

> In thy sacred and perfect year,
> Thy souls that were parcel of thee
> In the labour and life of us here
> Shall be rays of thy sovereign sphere,
> Springs of thy motion shall be.

> There is the fire that was man,
> The light that was love, and the breath
> That was hope ere deliverance began,
> And the wind that was life for a span,
> And the birth of new things, which is death.

The first stanza defines spirit as the ultimate reality, and as the source of all things, and in the swift figurative movement from 'seed' to 'fruit' Swinburne traces its growth and ascent to the 'sacred and perfect year', (in the next stanza), which may point a phase of human history—a future Millennium—but possibly also a transcendent 'sovereign sphere' when the individual souls shall know perfection. In the vagueness of this Platonic terminology the temporal blends with the eternal, for the poet is deliberately trying to bring heaven down to earth, and it is therefore difficult to attach any precise meaning to words like 'holy', 'sacred' and 'sovereign', through which the oracular promise is conveyed.

In stanza 23 the imagery is compacted into a structure that recurs throughout the *Songs before Sunrise* as a symbolic representation of the spiritual forces of life and of their fulfilment. These are seen as ethereal and luminous manifestations, in fire, light, breath and wind, corresponding to love, hope and life-impulse. The structure is completed in the paradox, also recurrent, that death is a birth. Whatever may be the goal of these creative, aspiring forces, the direction in which they work is unambiguous: it is towards a state (or period) when 'all chains are undone', and where 'Liberty' is 'the light' (st. 26).

With its dramatic setting, where night and light are seen contending, *Tenebrae* throws open the world of *Songs before Sunrise* in a more evocative and less programmatic manner than the *Prelude*; and it is a familiar world. It is that of Shelley in particular, yet steeped in moods of discontent and yearning that are generally Platonic. Though, as Sir Harold Nicolson thinks, the poem is about the hope of the Workers,[1] its central vision is that of spiritual endeavour, which makes of man a God. In this apotheosis of man Swinburne is seen moving away from the Platonic tradition, towards the positivistic cult of mankind.

[1] *Swinburne,* p. 128.

At the gates of the Sunrise world stands yet another poem, even more expressive of the poet's belief, and here he has seized on the greatest of subjects: *Genesis*.

> In the outer world that was before this earth,
> That was before all shape or space was born,
> Before the blind first hour of time had birth,
>   Before night knew the moonlight or the morn;
>
> Yea, before any world had any light,
>   Or anything called God or man drew breath,
> Slowly the strong sides of the heaving night
>   Moved, and brought forth the strength of life and death.
>
> And the sad shapeless horror increate
>   That was all things and one thing, without fruit,
> Limit, or law; where love was none, nor hate,
>   Where no leaf came to blossom from no root;
>
> The very darkness that time knew not of,
>   Nor God laid hand on, nor was man found there,
> Ceased, and was cloven in several shapes; above
>   Light, and night under, and fire, earth, water, and air.
>
> Sunbeams and starbeams, and all coloured things,
>   All forms and all similitudes began,
> And death, the shadow cast by life's wide wings,
>   And God, the shade cast by the soul of man.

Night is hypostatized into a transcendent power, living and creative, the mother of all things. The poem begins with a *tabula rasa* of existence in order to trace the forms and forces of life back to their ultimate origin in the unknown world beyond—'the outer world'—

178

which is not a material chaos, but a state of pre-existence containing yet the potential birth of things. Its 'shapeless horror increate' seems to imply a *horror vacui* which, in its craving for existence and order, acts as a creative urge. The whole panorama suggests something like the homogeneous state which in Spencer's cosmogony precedes the integration and differentiation of matter, though it reaches beyond it into the 'Unknowable'. In the fourth stanza this 'shapeless' pre-existential phase ceases, and differentiation begins, first in the traditional mythical division of night and day, then in the introduction of the classical elements, and finally in the regenerative process of life and in human perception.

In this mysterious genesis, the Creator God of Christianity has no part. Swinburne takes care to assert this repeatedly, in stanzas 2, 4, and 5, and in the last place God is explicitly defined as a notion created by man: a negative concomitant emerging with the human soul. Swinburne here speaks for the age of Positivism.

Hence the poem expands into a vision of the relationship between natural forces, and things, and man:

> Then between shadow and substance, night and light,
>   Then between birth and death, and deeds and days,
> The illimitable embrace and the amorous fight
>   That of itself begets, bears, rears and slays,
>
> The immortal war of mortal things, that is
>   Labour and life and growth and good and ill,
> The mild antiphonies that melt and kiss,
>   The violent symphonies that meet and kill,
>
> All nature of all things began to be.
>   But chiefliest in the spirit (beast or man,
> Planet of heaven or blossom of earth or sea)
>   The divine contraries of life began.

179

> For the great labour of growth, being many, is one;
>> One thing the white death and the ruddy birth;
> The invisible air and the all-beholden sun,
>> And barren water and many-childed earth.

Existence is a clash and grapple between opposites mysteriously attracted to one another, and from this perennial conflict everything is born and develops: it is the necessary, fundamental urge of being and becoming which interlocks life and death, good and evil, in its creative process. There is no basic split in existence, no wanton, blind battling between hostile forces, but a unity which is love. Hence, to the poet, 'the contraries' of life are 'divine'—they are merely different facets of the ultimate power immanent in the cosmic process of growth.

Notably in the first and last of these stanzas there is a passionate insistence on the monistic 'embrace' of this creative dynamic, and on the fusion of the many in the one. Swinburne's vision follows a dialectic pattern which may be inspired by the Hegelian tradition in Romantic poetry, but he organizes it very forcibly around a centre of pantheistic belief.

Man is the microcosm in which this universal law of genesis is most clearly reflected and explained:

> And these things are made manifest in men. . . (st. 10)

Thus also death, which is essential to the renewal of life:

> For if death were not, then should growth not be,
>> Change, nor the life of good nor evil things;
> Nor were there night at all nor light to see,
>> Nor water of sweet nor water of bitter springs. (st. 11)

The seed-symbolism in the following stanzas (12, 13, 14 and 15) interweaves the forces of life and death, growth and decay, in a paradoxical structure that seems to aim at a general reinterpretation of existence in terms of its 'divine contraries', and, above all, to suggest the unity and balance between its contending aspects and forces. In their fusion Swinburne perceives the creative impulse of an unending Genesis:

> And of these twain, the black seed and the white,
> All things come forth, endured of men and done;
> And still the day is great with child of night,
> And still the black night labours with the sun.

The Cosmos is a birth, mysteriously emerging from out the unknown, yet dimly understood when related to the regenerative process and fertility by which life persists.

Genesis is a curious combination of Romantic pantheism and Positivistic agnosticism, and the poet scorns not only the traditional part of the Creator God, but also whatever material natural science might place in his hands. Though Spencer would have approved of this poetic vision hovering on the verge of the unknowable, Comte might not have greatly appreciated the conflict which Swinburne sees at the root of all being. Independent of science as well as of religion, Swinburne's method of discovery is wholly mystical and intuitive, and the poem is essentially a dramatic projection, a translation into antithetical patterns of the poet's experience when facing the riddle of the many and the one, good and evil, life and death. In a real sense, and one which could be conveyed only in terms of such metaphorical flights, the whole world is to Swinburne in this poem what the elevated mind and the work of art is to Baudelaire: a flower growing from pain, struggle and suffering, even from evil. It is an idea that recurs often in the *Songs before Sunrise*, and in *Hertha*, in particular, it forms a central trend of the theme.[1]

---

[1] In the following, frequent reference will be made to E. M. W. Tillyard's brilliant analysis of *Hertha* in *Five Poems*.

Hertha is the Earth-goddess of Teutonic mythology, and the framework of the poem is determined by her presence, though it fits loosely around the thoughts and feelings which inform it, and which look to other creeds and traditions as well, such as oriental pantheism and the nineteenth-century religion of Humanity.[1] Hertha embodies the forces of growth and fertility more vaguely and generally described in *Genesis,* and she addresses man, her child, in a monologue whose didactic form and prophetic tone recalls the *Edda*-poems *Hávamál* and *Voluspá:*

> I am that which began;
> > Out of me the years roll;
> Out of me God and man;
> > I am equal and whole;
> God changes, and man, and the form of them bodily;
> I am the soul.

> Before ever land was,
> > Before ever the sea,
> Or soft hair of the grass,
> > Or fair limbs of the tree,
> Or the flesh-coloured fruit of my branches, I was,
> and thy soul was in me.

> First life on my sources
> > First drifted and swam;
> Out of me are the forces
> > That save it or damn;
> Out of me man and woman, and wild-beast and bird;
> Before God was, I am.

Hertha reveals herself as the mother of the world—a creative energy existing before space and time, a spirit which penetrates the Universe

[1] Cf. Tillyard, *op. cit.* p. 89.

and which is self-contained, always the same and always one.[1] Hertha is the essence of all things, integrating them in an organic whole, and remains undisturbed by the metamorphoses of matter. The first stanza thus expounds a doctrine of monistic permanence, mystical in its conception of an Earth or fertility-spirit giving birth to, and animating existence. Next the poet insists, as in *Genesis*, on the cosmic void before the emergence of material form and of life, to enhance the greatness and autonomy of Hertha's creative task. The notion that all things and all individual souls were contained, (potentially), within the world soul appears to be of Platonic origin.

Already in the first stanza a principle of evolution is involved, with emphasis on organic growth and change. In the third stanza evolution is directly recorded in the 'first life' or protozoa living in water, from which higher organisms have gradually developed. Hertha, the intelligent life-impulse, brings them forth and moulds them through the action of the forces and laws of nature. It would seem that the inevitable fate to which life is subject, and by which it is 'saved' or 'damned' at Hertha's will, is the deterministic principle introduced by Darwin into the theory of Nature.

In stanza 4 the distinction between creative power and its externalized manifestation, whether thing or creature, is completely removed, in a subject—object fusion common to pantheistic creeds.[2] Next this fusion is given symbolic and metaphorical expansion, and, having thus claimed the identity of spirit and matter, energy and effect, Hertha takes man to task for splitting the oneness of existence into Creator and creature, master and servant. The structure ends in a fertility-symbolism suggesting universal growth and development,

---

[1] Cf. Tillyard, who points out that st. 1—4 refer to the conservation of energy and the indestructibility of matter.

[2] Tillyard finds in st. 4—8 a description of the comprehensiveness of Hertha in terms of oriental pantheism.

while the monistic theme is still emphasized in persistently beating rhythms (st. 8). At this point Swinburne turns back to the mystery of cosmic birth:

> Hast thou known how I fashioned thee,
>   Child, underground?
> Fire that impassioned thee,
>   Iron that bound,
> Dim changes of water, what thing of all these hast
>   thou known of or found?

> Canst thou say in thine heart
>   Thou hast seen with thine eyes
> With what cunning of art
>   Thou wast wrought in what wise,
> By what force of what stuff thou wast shapen, and
>   shown on my breast to the skies?

Hertha, the Mother of life, while challenging man to admit his ignorance, lifts the veil a little from the enigma of creative process, vaguely indicating the forces and agents which have been at work to 'shape' him. 'Underground' may refer to the geological ages and strata, and successive stages of evolution, while the 'dim changes of water' cast back to stanza 3 and the idea of primordial organisms developing in water. Man—whatever the causes of development may have been, was 'wrought' with a 'cunning of art' of which Hertha alone holds the secret. The motive of this challenge is uncovered in stanzas 11, 12 and 13, where all man-made authorities are swept away. Thus the ground is cleared for one of the main themes of the poem—the iconoclasm of the following stanzas, 14 and 15. Here the man-God idea of *Tenebrae* recurs as part of the challenge, dressed in a similar light-growth imagery:

184

> A creed is a rod,
>   And a crown is of night;
> But this thing is God,
>   To be man with thy might,
> To grow straight in the strength of thy spirit, and
>   live out thy life as the light.

The opening slogans of anti-religious and republican warfare are in the true Shelleyan tradition, and so is the appeal to man to summon all his strength and courage for the Promethean task of freeing life from its chains. Swinburne here, and in stanzas 16 and 17, preaches a heroic and selfless human ideal, related to the great cause of liberty which is the *leit-motif* of *Songs before Sunrise,* and with an implicit sacrificial dedication of the individual to Humanity. It is necessary to human growth and emancipation that the lights which guided man in his infancy should fade and give way to higher truths, though courage is needed for each new departure. Once, in her compassion, Hertha gave man God for guidance, when he trod the 'dim paths of the night', (st. 19), but now that he stands fully matured in his spiritual power, he needs this help no more. Now 'the morning of manhood is risen, and the shadowless soul is in sight'. In this line there is an impact both of Shelley and Comte, and it celebrates human progress with characteristic nineteenth-century enthusiasm. Man has evolved out of the dim and distant beginnings in Mother Earth, and attained to the mental strength which makes him free and fearless. In stanza 20 Swinburne interlinks this growth with yet another Norse myth—the tree Yggdrasil —to concentrate his vision of the upward surge of life:

> The tree many-rooted
>   That swells to the sky
> With frondage red-fruited,
>   The life-tree am I;

In the buds of your lives is the sap of my leaves: ye
shall live and not die.[1]

Yggdrasil is the central integrating image of the poem, bodying
forth in an evocative form the idea of the wholeness of life and of
the forces which perpetuate its growth. From its cosmic and biological significance there follows (st. 23, 24 and 25) an expansion
into historical evolution and progress:

> Where dead ages hide under
>   The live roots of the tree,
> In my darkness the thunder
>   Makes utterance of me;
> In the clash of my boughs with each other ye hear
>   the waves sound of the sea.

> That noise is of Time,
>   As his feathers are spread
> And his feet set to climb
>   Through the boughs overhead,
> And my foliage rings round him and rustles, and
>   branches are bent with his tread.

> The storm-winds of ages
>   Blow through me and cease,
> The war-wind that rages,
>   The spring-wind of peace,
> Ere the breath of them roughen my tresses, ere one
>   of my blossoms increase.

In the antithesis of 'dead ages' and 'live roots' Swinburne reverts
to his idea of the fruitful action of death upon life: death is a prin-

---

[1] Tillyard identifies this symbol as Yggdrasil.

186

ciple of renewal. So too in history, where the process of growth is a tumultuous and noisy struggle of rival forces. In this stanza, again, darkness—the unknowable underlying energy—envelops the enigma of growth, and the sea-image, recurrent in Swinburne, is brought in to suggest cosmic vastness, and freedom, which ever beckons as an evolutionary goal. Next the historical progress is visualized by a bird-image of Time (which may be the Phoenix) releasing yet another rush of upward movement, while impressions of the growing. storm-tossed world-tree are maintained and given full force in stanza 25, with its grand, stoical survey of history and its recognition of struggle—'war-wind' and 'spring-wind'—as necessary to the perfection and increase of life. It is a biological interpretation of history, in Malthusian and Darwinian terms, based on Swinburne's intuition of the 'divine contraries' as the main stimulus of evolutionary advance. Thus in the idea that 'blossoms increase' due to the storm and struggle of existence there appears to be an impact of Darwin's survival principle and of Spencer's key-phrase.

The vision of history is completed (st. 26, 27) in a wider panorama of geological and human change, which transcends the tree-symbolism and finally issues in the hour-glass image of fatality:

> All sounds of all changes,
>   All shadows and lights
> On the world's mountain-ranges
>   And stream-riven heights,
> Whose tongue is the wind's tongue and language of
>   storm-clouds on earth-shaking nights;
>
> All forms of all faces,
>   All works of all hands
> In unsearchable places
>   Of time-stricken lands,
> All death and all life, and all reigns and all ruins,
>   drop through me as sands.

It is the flux and transience deplored by the Romantics and by
Tennyson which is here faced with stern courage: Nothing matters
except the progress of life, and Hertha is bent on it with stubborn
determination:

> Though sore be my burden
> And more than ye know,
> And my growth have no guerdon
> But only to grow,
> Yet I fail not of growing for lightnings above me or
> deathworms below.

The 'divine contraries' of existence are felt by Hertha more intensely
than by man, yet she is able to persevere and to reconcile the
antagonistic forces, because

> These too have their part in me,
> As I too in these;
> Such fire is at heart in me,
> Such sap is this tree's,
> Which hath in it all sounds and all secrets of infinite
> lands and of seas.

From this reconciliation Hertha turns to a happy retrospect of the
'spring-coloured hours'[1] when she grew 'strong blossoms with per-
fume of manhood' and gloried in their spiritual power and freedom:

> And the sound of them springing
> And smell of their shoots
> Were as warmth and sweet singing
> And strength to my roots;
> And the lives of my children made perfect with
> freedom of soul were my fruits.   (st. 31.)

[1] St. 30; identified by Tillyard as Greece of the 5th century, *op. cit.*,
p. 98.

Hertha, like *Tenebrae*, is shot through with a light-fruit symbolism interrelating spiritual force and vital process. The men of the Golden Age of Greece were 'rays' from Hertha's spirit,[1] opening their flower to life, as other men in *Tenebrae* to the 'sovereign sphere'. In that poem the 'spirit of man' is the 'measure of things and the root', here all things emerge from Hertha's soul. Again the aspiration is towards absolute freedom of soul, as a goal of perfection, once attained in the heyday of ancient Greece and still the spur of life. In *Tenebrae* this urge is directed towards the 'sacred and perfect year'—an ideal state or condition where 'liberty ... is the light'. *Hertha* has no such millennial perspective, but a more violent appeal to man to win his freedom here and now. This appeal reverts to the theme of iconoclasm in stanzas 7, 15 and 21, with a renewed attack upon the 'God that ye made you', and, finally, a positivistic anticipation of the twilight of the man-made God:

> Thought made him and breaks him,
>> Truth slays and forgives;
> But to you, as time takes him,
>> This new thing it gives,
> Even love, the beloved Republic, that feeds upon
>> freedom and lives.

As the poem draws to a close, truth and love emerge allied to freedom as the greatest values gained in the evolutionary struggle, and in a solemn hymn Hertha sings the praise of these, of man, and of life:

> For truth only is living,
>> Truth only is whole,
> And the love of his giving
>> Man's polestar and pole;
> Man, pulse of my centre, and fruit of my body, and
>> seed of my soul.

[1] Cf. *Tenebrae*, st. 21, 22.

One birth of my bosom;
    One beam of mine eye;
One topmost blossom
    That scales the sky;
Man, equal and one with me, man that is made of
    me, man that is I.

Once more, the organic unity of life is asserted through a seed-blossom-fruit imagery which culminates in the evolutionary triumph of man; and man is identical with the creative power or spirit animating this world: he represents the fulfilment of its highest aspirations.

One might now conveniently distinguish between two centres of poetic energy from which the themes and structures in *Hertha* are seen to develop, the first a passionate faith in the forces of life, the second an equally passionate craving for freedom. Vitalism and anarchy are at the root of its vision of existence.

The choice of Hertha as an interpreter of cosmic and human destiny is apt and fortunate; it shows Swinburne in search of some metaphorical framework which might carry his cult of life and give it range and significance beyond direct and doctrinal formulation. Hertha is a symbol at once precise and comprehensive, first in her original pagan connotation of Mother Earth, the source of all life; secondly as the spirit which animates nature in pantheistic cosmologies, and as such assuming the status and function of the immanent God of the Universe. Swinburne blends these meanings with great ease, and the final effect is a deeply personal heresy in which he believes with emotional as well as intellectual passion. It is an amalgam of idealistic pantheism, political anarchism and positivistic worship of humanity and of truth. To redeem the negative impact of his furious assault on authority there is his sense of the sacral greatness of life; and the danger of narcissistic self-adoration implicit in his man-God doctrine, and in the idea of a universe closed

190

on itself, is to some extent avoided through the values of truth, love and freedom.

In *Hertha*, Swinburne's vision of existence is organized around a central belief in life as vertical movement, climbing out of its origin to liberty and perfection. Organic evolution—with its various representations of growth and tree—is the doctrine on which it rests, and this provides, together with certain positivistic trends, such as the advance of truth, the pattern along which thought and imagery develop. From the outset, there is emphasis on evolutionary changes, and on the growth from the 'first life' to beasts and birds and human beings. These were 'born and not made': there was no act of creation, but a slow, formative and genetic process 'underground' and in water until life had reached its goal, in man. For evolution to Swinburne is nothing if not an intelligent, purposive and irresistible urge penetrating nature, like the Aristotelian *nisus*, and though in some aspects he approaches near to Darwin's theory of struggle and survival (the Yggdrasil structure), his general belief is fired by the conviction that life is progressive intelligence, and has a definite aim. Thus the triumph he celebrates for man at the end of the poem is intelligence victorious over bondage and error. And since evolution means progress, Swinburne has great hopes for the future. Already, the 'morning of manhood is risen'—it is now the age of Truth (and of Science), and the free, 'shadowless soul is in sight'. This prophecy of human attainment glories in a Promethean ideal of liberty and power; it is proud and defiant in a way which suggests that to Swinburne, Zeus has not, after all, faded into twilight.

In the powerful image of Yggdrasil Swinburne finds a more concrete symbol for both organic development and historical progress, which at the same time is effectively used to integrate the various facets of existence. It offers a natural setting for the fertility imagery through which the growth of life is visualized. 'Roots', 'sap', 'seed', 'shoots', 'buds' are throughout associated with the unity and

191

ascent of the whole of life, and interpret more particularly the relationship between man and his Mother, Earth. Man is the 'blossom' and the 'fruit' of evolutionary growth. Hertha claims him both as 'fruit of my body'—a fulfilment of physical process—and as 'seed of my soul'—a promise of spiritual advance. He marks a beginning as well as an end. And for man Hertha has set this great aim: the 'shadowless soul'—or the absolute power, purity and freedom of the human intellect. It is a positivistic version of the state of pure intellect of which Coleridge dreamed, here wholly immanent, since the pantheistic world in which Swinburne moves offers no transcendent goal despite the language of transcendence in which his ideal often is clothed.

Throughout the poem, and notably in the evolutionary prophecy of truth and liberty to which Hertha rises at the end, there is a significant interaction between Swinburne's faith in life and his passionate craving for freedom. This is the other centre of energy from which the poem springs, and it is volcanic indeed, with constant outbursts against 'creeds' and 'crowns' and any kind of authority, whether 'prophet' or 'poet', 'tripod' or 'throne'. Life is the only authority; it is ultimate, and it defies all categories and conventions; and as the object of life is 'only to grow' and has no other justification, so the object of the individual is to live fully and boldly—like a god in his unchallenged power. But for this creative life absolute freedom is needed; nothing must stand in its way: not the 'shadow called God', nor political tyrants and despotisms, for these are poison to the 'fair fruits' of its growth—love and truth. Hence the poet's fiery appeal to self-sacrifice in the great cause of Liberty: Give your life freely and generously, as it was given to you! (St. 17.)

It is significant that, although Swinburne is immediately concerned with the cause of Italian liberty, and makes reference to it in stanzas 16 and 38, his attack on oppression is more directly and persistently levelled at orthodoxy and dogmatic 'creeds'. Mental

192

bondage is to him the ultimate worst thing, and thus, while his political aspiration is to the 'beloved Republic', his intellect craves something like a state of anarchy. Here too his kinship with Shelley is intimate. All ways leading to the temple of Life, Liberty and Truth are good, and for this Trinity no sacrifice is too great. In *Hertha* Swinburne again officiates for an age that had discovered, or thought it had discovered, the meaning of these sacred things, and how to obtain them. It is the voice of his age which is heard in Swinburne's oracular claim that 'Truth only is living,/Truth only is whole', and 'Truth slays and forgives'; and it was a claim made not only by crusading scientists like Tyndall, but by the whole radical camp for whom Comte was the leader. 'Truth in that age', says Dr. Tillyard, 'had two great qualifications as an object of worship. She was persecuted and she demanded great sacrifices'.[1]

In *Hertha* Swinburne reached the apogee of his life-cult, and the poem is an important confession of his own spiritual plight and that of his age. It is flawed, however, by a harshness in tone and feeling, and the world it creates is an uncharitable place, with no room for the individual. Instead there is millennial hope, and the God which is Humanity, and the power and the glory of the Promethean man. In this stern, heroic world the individual is swallowed up in the mass of Humanity; here it has no soul to save, but a great deal to do for the common good and for progress towards liberty and truth: Evolution of the whole of life and a collective endeavour to speed this progress is the task for which we live. As an object of worship, Stuart Mill had just written in his essay 'Theism' (1868—70), Humanity fulfils the conditions required of the highest religions—it is 'of the highest excellence, and ... rightfully paramount over all selfish objects of desire'. The 'sense of unity with mankind, and a deep feeling for the general

[1] *Op. cit.*, p. 102.

good, may be cultivated into a sentiment ... capable of fulfilling every important function of religion ...'[1]

The sacrifice of the individual on the altar of Humanity is the point at which Swinburne breaks most decisively with his Romantic forbears and enters into alliance with the radical doctrines of his own generation, with Positivism and Evolution in particular. Except for the absence of the Superman-ideal, his cult of life, with its exaltation of vital energy and its unrestrained appeal to anarchy, anticipates Nietzsche as well as Bernard Shaw and even points, as Dr. Tillyard shows, to the remoter political and ideological doctrines based on race worship and collectivism in the modern dictatorship.

To the group of poems in which *Hertha* forms the centre and the climax belongs yet another, *Hymn of Man,* inspired by the same cult of life and the same spirit of revolt. Like *Genesis* and *Hertha* it reaches back to the cosmic 'beginning' and creates a mythological panorama around the 'new-born earth' which, as elsewhere (cf. *Mater Triumphalis*), is described as a 'maiden', and visualized through impressions of newness and morning and the young planet's volcanic surfaces: 'her maiden mouth was alight with the flame of musical speech'. This genesis-myth is not sustained or developed, however, for the poet faces directly the human condition, here seen as a blind race. He is meditating upon the heavy fate in store for this 'new-souled earth' and mankind ignorant of its future, and seeking to probe the force and intention at work in the cosmic birth. His question circles around love as a creative impulse and traces its mystery into a series of possible modes of becoming; then pauses to give one more glimpse of genesis, in which the birth of man is related to the whole cosmic process. Night, again a symbol of the unknowable creative power, is the setting:

> And her heart as a water was stirred, and its heat
>   was the firstborn man's.

[1] Cf. *supra,* p. 62.

> For the waste of the dead void air took form of
> a world at birth,
> And the waters and firmaments were, and light, and
> the life-giving earth.
> The beautiful bird unbegotten that night brought
> forth without pain
> In the fathomless years forgotten whereover the dead
> gods reign,
> Was it love, life, godhead, or fate?

The poet is coming to grips with the enigma of genesis in a new way:

> we say the spirit
>
> is one
> That moved on the dark to create out of darkness
> the stars and the sun.
> Before the growth was the grower, and the seed ere
> the plant was sown;
> But what was the seed of the sower? and the grain of
> him, whence was it grown?

Obviously, no answer can be given, and this is what the poet, in asking such futile questions, wants to emphasize: The God man has made for himself 'gives no aid'. If there is a God, he is 'the substance of men which is man'—a God wholly immanent in this world and most clearly manifested in his highest creature. From this pantheistic idea the poem now develops a vision in which 'Our lives are as pulses or pores of his manifold body and breath'; and 'all we only are he'. Existence is one: spirit and blood, body and soul are 'indivisible'. 'Man's is the glory of godhead', and he reigns in the 'kingdom of time', his spirit climbing the 'mountainous ages made hoary with snows'.[1] He is a 'soul that labours and lives, an

---

[1] Cf. Tennyson's *By An Evolutionist, supra,* p. 104.

emotion, a strenuous breath', penetrating all existence, dying with men and yet immortal in man: the individual men are 'thoughts passing through' his 'heart' and renewing it with 'spirit of sense' as 'springs fulfilling a flood'. This ecstatic vision of monistic and organic unity is not, however, wholly unaware of the painful dichotomy of 'spirit' and 'things'—our human condition—. Indeed, these 'things' are 'cruel and blind', as in the neo-Platonic doctrine, recalcitrant, and 'detain' and 'deform', so that the 'wearying wings of the mind still beat up the stream of their storms'. Here the panorama suddenly changes to a scene of strife and defeat, where man is the pathetic victim:

> As weeds or as reeds in the torrent of things are
> the wind-shaken souls.

He is now seen as a 'God sore stricken of things'—weak and vulnerable. In him he has the power to conquer these adverse things, for 'By the spirit are things overcome', yet he makes himself chains and bows to a 'master whose face is a ghost's'. Through this exposure of human weakness, misery and error Swinburne has probed beneath the symptoms and then attacks the cause, which, here as in *Hertha*, is the 'God of man's fashion'. It is a violent denunciation, issuing in this triumphant prophecy:

> Yea, man thy slave shall unmake thee, who made
> thee lord over man.
> For his face is set to the east, his feet on the past
> and its dead;
> The sun rearisen is his priest, and the heat thereof
> hallows his head.
> His eyes take part in the morning; his spirit outsounding
> the sea
> Asks no more witness or warning from temple or
> tripod or tree.

196

For the human mind, freed from its trammels of mental tyranny, there are no bounds. Man has experienced a 'death-worm fear', and the 'malice of things',—driving him to hope for blissful immortality, alienating him from the reality to which he belongs, body and soul. Now, in the dawn of his mind, however, his 'thought takes flight for the centre wherethrough it hath part in the whole', and thence will penetrate into the most unyielding enigmas of the universe. Swinburne insists on this intellectual quest and expansion through repetitive suggestions of endless space: 'Space is the soul's to inherit'; 'Space is thought's',—and his joy in man's soaring flight takes on a tone of conscious Icarian *hubris:* 'And if higher than is heaven be the reach of the soul, shall not heaven bow down?' Time is similarly related to man, in an evolutionary sense, as 'father of life',—as an active force which 'lives, thinks, and hath substance in man', and makes him share in the vast cosmic energies as well as in the endless succession of ages. With this spatial and temporal expansion (similar in its underlying motive to that in Tennyson's poetry) Swinburne declares that man has come into his own he no longer has need of 'heavenlier air' or the drugs of supernatural religion:

> He hath stirred him, and found out the flaw in his
>   fetters, and cast them behind;
> His soul to his soul is a law, and his mind is a light
>   to his mind.
> The seal of his knowledge is sure, the truth and his
>   spirit are wed;
> Men perish, but man shall endure; lives die, but
>   the life is not dead.
> He hath sight of the secrets of season, the roots of
>   the years and the fruits;
> His soul is at one with the reason of things that is
>   sap to the roots.

He can hear in their changes a sound as the conscience
    of consonant spheres;
He can see through the years flowing round him the
    law lying under the years.

This is indeed the creed of Positivism, though in the tenet that 'man
shall endure' it would appear that Swinburne adds a Platonic idea
to his cult of Humanity. Platonic terminology persists also in Swinburne's use of 'spirit', 'soul' and 'mind'. Without any precise distinction, these concepts occur as almost interchangeable synonyms am-
plifying or emphasizing the pattern of intellectual growth: Man
has now reached the stage of 'thought' and 'knowledge'—Comte's
positive stage, and 'the seal of his knowledge is sure'. In the light
of truth—scientific fact—he may explore nature and the universe
and grasp the significance of historical and biological evolution—
'the roots of the years and the fruits'. He then discovers the essential
harmony and unity between his soul and all existence. The many
have become one: even in the mutability of things there is a harmony which reveals the underlying rational order—a law and a
plan. Hence the poet's fury with those who will 'turn back times,
and the courses of stars, and the season of souls'—and exclude man
from this harmony. In a torrent of indictment and blasphemy the
poem rushes to its conclusion, with prophecies of death for the man-
made God and direct mocking appeals to this God to show his
power if he still has any. Finally, there is a cry of victory, more
ecstatic than that of *Hertha:*

Thou art smitten, thou God, thou art smitten; thy
    death is upon thee, O Lord.
And the love-song of earth as thou diest resounds
    through the wind of her wings—
Glory to Man in the highest! for Man is the master
    of things.

Hymn of Man was written 'During the Session in Rome of the Oecumenical Council' (1870), and the papal decrees of that Session were the immediate provocations of Swinburne's unholy war, but they scarcely account for the hatred and violence with which it is conducted. It would seem that the emotional source lies deeper and dates further back, to *Atalanta in Calydon* (1865) and the challenge: 'All we are against thee, against thee, O God most high.'—bound up with his warped and frustrated craving for faith. *Hymn of Man* could only have been written by a *Chrétien manqué:* it is the revolt of the fallen angel, the intellectual compensation for a paradise lost. And this tragic undercurrent saves it from being a mere charging at windmills, approaching the burlesque; though clearly, Swinburne's campaign against the Christian God, like Baudelaire's satanism, by its violent and hyperbolic language loses both in poetic communication and in intellectual thrust.

Hymn of Man shows a tendency in Swinburne to repeat and paraphrase themes which are important to him. Like *Hertha* it is a song to the birth, growth and fulfilment of life, and a cry of rebellion. The pattern also is similar: cosmic genesis surrounded by mystery (question-structure), narrowing to a perspective of history and human fate. Once more the weakness in man is blamed upon self-deceit, in the form of religion, and both poems set out to re-interpret the man-God relationship in terms of an autonomous life-force whose highest manifestation is man. They are both prophetic, celebrating the unending progress of mind and its ultimate victory over 'creeds' and 'things'.

The cult of life which informs the *Hertha*-group is present, though more intermittently, in all the *Songs before Sunrise,* and *On the Downs* contains a fully developed statement which places it close to the group. The setting is a desolate scene—a 'valley like an unsealed grave'; the sea 'blind and bare/Seems full of care', and the earth is 'discoloured and discrowned.' There is a gloom brooding over land and sea in this hour before sunrise, and life lies 'hope-

199

less'. The poet's soul wanders east and west to 'find light', but the whole world is swallowed up in darkness, and groans in pain. For in this world freedom is strangled, and to the poet it seems an absurd riddle. Until, suddenly, there is a flash of new insight:

> O fool, that for brute cries of wrong
> Heard not the grey glad mother's song
>   Ring response from the hills and waves,
> But heard harsh noises all day long
>   Of spirits that were slaves
>   And dwelt in graves.

> The wise word of the secret earth
> Who knows what life and death are worth,
>   And how no help and no control
> Can speed or stay things come to birth,
>   Nor all worlds' wheels that roll
>   Crush one born soul.

> With all her tongues of life and death,
> With all her bloom and blood and breath,
>   From all years dead and all things done,
> In the ear of man the mother saith,
>   "There is no God, O son,
>   If thou be none".

Above the man-made dejection of this world the primeval joy of earth rings out its message of hope and trust. Again, the 'grey glad mother', Earth, reveals to man her true face—that of the loving 'Mater Triumphalis' who has endowed her children with strength to work out their own destinies. And the life in which they participate is ultimate and imperishable: a spiritual force that nothing can stop and no death destroy. This, too, Earth impresses upon man, that life, through long effort and learning, in him has attained to power and glory.

With this brighter mood the whole scene changes: it comes to life. Now 'thought's soundless stream' flows through it, and now is 'answer made' to the soul's agonized question. It is

> A multitudinous monotone
> Of dust and flower and seed and stone,
> In the deep sea-rock's mid-sea sloth,
> In the live water's trembling zone,
> In all men love and loathe,
> One God at growth.
>
> One forceful nature uncreate
> That feeds itself with death and fate,
> Evil and good, and change and time,
> That within all men lies at wait
> Till the hour shall bid them climb
> And live sublime.
>
> For all things come by fate to flower
> At their unconquerable hour,
> And time brings truth, and truth makes free,
> And freedom fills time's veins with power,
> As, brooding on that sea,
> My thought filled me.

In the antithetical structure of the two first stanzas, Swinburne, here as in *Genesis* and *Hertha,* gathers the 'divine contraries' of life and every facet of existence within the all-embracing unity of a force or essence permeating the universe with growth. It is a creative energy that gains strength from the whole of life through a mysterious, intimate participation, until it is released for new tasks. Thus it lives in men, who are destined to 'climb' to a life sublime, coming

201

'by fate to flower': There is an urge and a purpose underlying the
vital process, working steadily towards truth, freedom and power.
The causal connexion between these three supreme values of evolutionary advance shows again, as in *Hertha,* to what extent Swinburne's passion for liberty inspires his cult of life.

On the Downs concludes with a jubilant pæan which, from the
colour-and-light vision of Italian liberty, widens to a universal anticipation of greater, freer life:

> And with divine triumphant awe
> My spirit moved within me saw,
>   With burning passion of stretched eyes,
> Clear as the light's own firstborn law,
>   In windless wastes of skies
>   Time's deep dawn rise.

The symbol of dawn encompasses the *Songs before Sunrise,* and
in all of them there is a 'triumphant awe' induced by the grandeur
of life and a 'burning passion' to see it conquer and expand indefinitely into the future. Swinburne's cult of life has, in these poems,
a genuine religious fervour and not a little of the bigotry and prose-
lytizing naïveté of the new convert. Thus the ritual solemnity of
his poetic medium is not a trick or an affectation, but a natural expression of his feeling for the greatness and glory of life in its
evolution. Life to him is the manifestation of some omnipotent and
providential power which can only be described in the language
of traditional worship. He retains therefore, despite his anti-Christian
challenge, words of Christian and Platonic content like 'God', 'soul',
'spirit' to indicate that inscrutable part of man and nature which
he knows to be their essence, and which, conscious of his pantheistic
heritage, he identifies as the world-soul. Once he defines it in Words-
worthian terms as

> The sense that kindles nature, and the soul that fills.[1]

[1] *A Marching Song,* st. 41.

202

It is an underived, autonomous force shaping matter and immanent in it, yet at the same time independent of it. For

> Passions and pleasures can defeat,
> Actions and agonies control,
> And life and death, but not the soul.
>
> Because man's soul is man's God still ...[1]

It leads him 'Across birth's hidden harbour-bar' to the 'Vast void of sunset hailed from far' and to the 'equal waters of the dead'.[2] On the soul depends the fate of mankind:

> Only the soul hath feet to climb,
>> Only the soul hath room to wait,
> Hath brows and eyes to hold sublime
>> Above all evil and all good,
>> All strength and all decrepitude.
>
> She only, she since earth began,
>> The many-minded soul of man,
> From one incognisable root
>> That bears such divers-coloured fruit,
> Hath ruled for blessing or for ban
>> The flight of seasons and pursuit;
> She regent, she republican,
>> With wide and equal eyes and wings
> Broods on things born and dying things.[3]

At times, such emphasis on 'soul' and 'spirit' and their implicit or attendant meanings of transcendent existence comes near to destroying the consistency of Swinburne's pantheistic and vitalist message. For there is no clear vision of the relationship between soul and its

---

[1] *Prelude.* [2] *Ibid.* [3] *Epilogue.*

manifestation in matter, except that, as with the neo-Platonists, we are made to feel that it flows into matter and animates it, and that, before this, it dwells as potential form in the night and the unknown. Such is the ambiguous scene spread out in *Genesis*; and again, in *On the Downs*, the 'One God at growth' is a 'forceful nature uncreate', or some potential energy or nisus prior to its material form. If Swinburne sees this spirit or energy as the mind-attribute of the One God, wholly immanent in this world, he yet clothes his prophetic promise in a transcendence-imagery where all earthly or material aspects tend to fade. His leaning to dualism finds, in *Tiresias*, expression in language forged in the Platonic tradition; for life, we are told, 'was given for some divine thing's sake,/To mix the bitterness of earth with heaven', and it begins to exist

> On that serenest and obscurest height
> Where dead and unborn things are one in thought
> And whence the live unconquerable springs
> Feed full of force the torrents of new things.[1]

On the other hand there are the many assertions that existence is one and indivisible, symbolized by Hertha, the Yggdrasil-tree (also in *Quia Multum Amavit*) and the man-God, or expressed in more general monistic terms recurrent throughout.

This wavering between monism and dualism in the Sunrise songs derives, undoubtedly, from a tension and an ambiguity in Swinburne's emotional condition: it is the predicament of the inadaptable genius with his craving for love, security, harmony; and his inevitable failure—seeking compensation in revolt and in negation of the territory from which he is exiled. Having once fallen from grace, he denies the existence of his paradise lost, though it continues to haunt his unconscious. And he remains at heart an idealist racked

[1] St. 26.

by the curse of earthly imperfection and misery, and straining so hard to explore a state of beatitude—a vicarious attainment to bliss through mankind—that the solid earth vanishes altogether from his eyes. This tension is at the root of his dialectic vision of the 'divine contraries' of life, which represent his intellectual effort to overcome it. For, living in an age of Hegelian dialectics and Comtean 'triad', and instructed by evolutionary doctrine, Swinburne accepts limitation and conflict as necessary to the advance of life—on intellectual terms. This involves, however, in Swinburne's predicament, a denial of the individual being as a focal point in existence, and a deliberate sacrifice of his ego and his fierce individualism on the altar of Life and Humanity. In his millennial anticipation therefore, Swinburne is content to know—intellectually—that the individual lives will fuse as 'rays' in the light of the 'sovereign sphere' of the future. Man is merely a fruit of the earth,

> And as a man before was from his birth,
> So shall a man be after among the dead.[1]

The individual is only a means to an end, and his death is of no consequence, for the race is immortal:

> Men perish, but man shall endure ...[2]

> all men born are mortal, but not man ...[3]

Yet even in these statements there is that curious blend of Platonic belief—belief in the man-idea as an imperishable seminal principle —and of positivistic man-worship which indicates Swinburne's ambiguous and conflicting loyalties.

It would seem, then, that the language of transcendence in *Songs before Sunrise* reveals an emotional predicament, while in its more

---

[1] *Genesis.*   [2] *Hymn of Man.*   [3] *The Pilgrims.*

deliberate intellectual function it expresses Swinburne's Promethean task—his stealing of the divine fire of thought and life, truth and freedom, which will pervade earthly existence and change it into the 'sovereign sphere' of the future, rich with the 'live light' of accumulated effort. This creative process, he claims, is a reward in itself: Hertha 'has no guerdon, but only to grow', and existence is for ever 'One God at growth'. The fruit of this evolutionary effort is Truth and Liberty—these are the supreme values to be realized, and without these, the *Epilogue* asserts, there would be universal death. Therefore, man must devote all his strength and courage to the aid of those forces which bring truth and make free. Like the youth in the *Prelude*, he should tread to dust 'Fear and desire, mistrust and trust'; bind Knowledge for sandals on his feet; feed his spirit on freedom; use a staff wrought of strength, and wear a cloak woven of thought. This exhortation is a *leit-motif* throughout the *Songs before Sunrise*.

Since evolution means the victory of Truth and Liberty, Swinburne insists on its destructive aspect as equally important to future fulfilment. The old and useless must be swept away to give place for the 'sacred and perfect year'. Hence his allusions to death as 'the birth of new things',[1] to the 'sunrise of death',[2] and death which comes 'to clear the sky'.[3] Hence also the violent attacks on the religious and political tyrannies of the past—the 'creeds' and 'crowns' which are now obstructions to human attainment. Against these despotisms he sets the ideal of man 'made perfect with freedom of soul', as he found him in ancient Greece. Like so many other advocates of progress, Swinburne, according to Dr. Tillyard, falls into the error of 'anthologising' history. His account is that of the 'politician in a hurry: the man who cannot allow the relevance of the past because it upsets his preconceived desire for rapid change'.[4]

[1] *The Pilgrims.*   [2] *Tenebrae.*   [3] *Mater Triumphalis.*
[4] *Op. cit.*, p. 99.

Yet,—precipitous as is this forward and backward view, it should be remembered that in his prophetic task Swinburne is moved, not only by his own emotional conflict, but by a great and generous sympathy for mankind. It is true that he sacrifices the individual to Humanity, and for this there seems to be only one excuse: that he, living in an age of utilitarian and positivistic enthusiasm believed, as Spencer believed, that general happiness must be conducive to individual happiness, and that what benefits the community is equally good for the individual. Neither had Swinburne, nor any other of the nineteenth-century prophets of Humanity seen the practical consequences—or distortions—of their Utopian and essentially idealistic dreams. His hatred of the past is due, largely, to compassion for suffering human beings—the victims of despots and errors and pain, and it is in this compassion that his love of man, his brother, reveals its tenderness:

> Ye that weep in sleep,
>   Souls and bodies bound,
> Ye that all night keep
> Watch for change, and weep
>   That no change is found;
>
> Ye that cry and die,
>   And the world goes on
> Without ear or eye,
> And the days go by
>   Till all days are gone;
>
> Man shall do for you,
>   Men the sons of man,
> What no God would do
> That they sought unto
>   While the blind years ran.

Brotherhood of good,
    Equal laws and rights,
Freedom, whose sweet food
Feeds the multitude
    All their days and nights,

With the bread full-fed
    Of her body blest
And the soul's wine shed
From her table spread
    Where the world is guest,

Mingling me and thee,
    When like light of eyes
Flashed through thee and me
Truth shall make us free,
    Liberty make wise ...[1]

This, however, is nearly all Swinburne has to say about the full
enjoyment of liberty and truth, once mankind has attained to its
happy state through struggle and sacrifice. As Dr. Tillyard comments, Swinburne is 'clearer on how to get liberty than on what
that liberty is when you have got it'.[2] In the end, the intellectual
formula of salvation which Swinburne offers in the *Songs before
Sunrise* is indeed narrow: 'Man has need of liberty and truth (scientific knowledge) only', and even more scant is his answer as to what
kind of existence this will mean for humanity. As a poetic interpretation of life, however, the *Songs* are involved in a more complex
search, before which existence is a mystery not to be approached
by any one direct track. After reading *Tenebrae* and *Tiresias* and
parts of *Genesis*, one is tempted to place Swinburne among the

[1] *Christmas Antiphones,* III.   [2] *Op. cit.,* p. 100.

208

Platonists, or somewhere close to them. But then, in the more powerful vision of *Hertha* and the embittered warfare of *Hymn of Man*, earth is the only reality, in which spirit dwells for ever and grows and gains height, until, like the tree Yggdrasil, it reaches to heaven. In this pantheistic world, too, man 'scales the sky'; but not to escape from earth with its pain and death, not to return to his true spiritual home, but because he is mind, intellect, nourished and liberated through organic evolution. He is the favourite son of earth, let loose upon the wonders of the universe, as free as a God, and as powerful.

And yet, the transcendent yearning is not wholly stifled by this passion to see existence as one and whole. In the end, Swinburne must be accepted as a citizen of two worlds, of which the one is not dead but lost and mourned, and the other about to be born in the heat and fury of his imaginative quest.

2. George Meredith

While to Swinburne Earth is 'Hertha'—the mother of man— she is to Meredith a 'Mother of all', who has an equal love for all her children, since they are

> Creatures of forest and mead, Earth's essays in being,
> all kinds
> Bound by the navel-knot to the Mother, never astray...[1]

Meredith, it has been said, was not of his time, not a Victorian; for while most other poets of the middle and later nineteenth century, like Clough and Arnold, were 'here as on a darkling plain', bewildered or saddened by spiritual conflict, or, like Hardy, obsessed by the 'Blind Will' of the universe, Meredith remained a happy pagan singing strange ritual songs to his 'fair Mother Earth'—'our Lady' of 'Gifts' and of 'Grace'.

---

[1] *Alsace-Lorraine,* ii.

In these songs, certainly, there is no painful disintegration of faith, no theological odium, no revival of moribund dogma, and no desperate search after strange gods—but a deep and spontaneous feeling of kinship with Earth, the source of life and of wisdom. Earth is all Meredith knows and needs to know, and to his loving and delighted eyes, she is Truth as well as Beauty.

Yet the Victorian era was an age of complex truth, and if Meredith's cult of 'Mother Earth' springs ultimately from the fundamental needs of his mind, it is given doctrinal sanction through the theories of Nature which, with Lamarck and Darwin, had done so much to alter the relationship—: Man—Nature.

Again, Meredith has been labelled a philosophical poet, and it would appear that his 'reading of Earth'—this exegetic and interpretative approach to Nature which is such a marked quality of his work, presents something like an epistemological problem, even if one is mainly concerned with the poetic energy and exploitation of his ideas and not with their empirical validity or 'truth'. One would have to ask: What signifies Earth to him? What does he know about her, and how does he know it? The answer to these questions can be found only on the way through his poetry, but it seems legitimate to stress at once that Meredith's conception of 'Mother Earth' is not a clue to a philosophy, nor to a mythology— though it has certain affinities with the human projection into nature through which a myth takes form. 'Mother Earth' is a metaphor already well-worn in both poetry and prose, yet Meredith has chosen it because, through the associations radiating from both words, a complex and evocative meaning emerges which might be indefinitely expanded and related to the birth, growth and fulfilment of life.

Though Meredith writes as a poet and a moralist and not as a philosopher, it is obvious that most of his work, and notably that which is concerned with his reading of Earth, is forged in the heat of intellectual passion. One should not come to him expecting to find a patiently inductive system of ideas, translated from its cool, abstract world into one of flowers and animals; but, on the other hand, one must be prepared for an unusual pressure of thought upon the imaginative structure. This quality in his work has always excited, baffled or distressed his readers, and challenged scholars and critics to find the definition through which his merit as a thinker might be more clearly seen.[1] There is wide agreement on the incisiveness and power of Meredith's intellect, but opinions are more varied as to the integration of his ideas in his poetry. From this vital point of view, his attainment is extremely uneven, but it would require a careful analysis, outside the scope of this study, to assess its formal merits. Here we are concerned with his poems as a total expression of his belief and attitude, for it is in the poems, more freely than in his novels, that Meredith confesses himself.[2]

Another aspect connected with this pressure of thought upon poetic and verbal form does, however, more directly affect our method of approach. Meredith's ideas, even if integrated in metaphorical or epigrammatic units building between them minor structures, do not generally help to unify or integrate the individual poem, as a whole. They tend rather to break up any coherent experience and split the vision into a complex, shifting pattern. For this reason one may legitimately disregard the framework of the individual poem in order to trace more conveniently the larger unity of his vision and belief.

Meredith, like Tennyson and Browning, has been called 'the poet of Evolution'. If Evolution had not been there, says Priestley, Meredith would have had to invent it. It has been claimed, moreover,

---

[1] See G. M. Trevelyan, *The Poetry and Philosophy of George Meredith*, p. 111; J. H. E. Crees, *George Meredith*, p. 85; J. B. Priestley, *George Meredith*, p. 61; B. Fehr, 'George Meredith. Der Dichter der Evolution', *Die Neueren Sprachen*, 1910, xviii, p. 69.

[2] Quotations here are from the Memorial Edition of 1910, and reference is to volume and page, where the stanzas have no number.

that while Tennyson and Browning only half-heartedly accepted the doctrine and were really scared of it, it was to Meredith a splendid and joyful revelation, congenial to his optimistic and exuberant nature.[1] Evolution no doubt means more to him, is a more important fact in life, than it is to Tennyson and Browning, and there is divergence especially in the Platonic and transcendent meaning which they read into it, as distinct from Meredith's agnostic and pantheistic worship. In common, however, they have the predominant human and moral perspective, within which Evolution is a teleological, spiritual conquest of existence, and a growing command over the animal instincts—the 'ape and tiger'—in man's nature.

Earth, the Mother of All

To the Romantics, the whole universe was an enchanted forest open to their daring exploration, and Tennyson, as well as Browning, inherited their desire to 'follow knowledge like a sinking star,/ Beyond the utmost bounds of human thought'. Meredith is content to stay on Earth, and he loves her 'too well to ask' futile questions of the beyond and the hereafter. If, as in *Meditation under Stars*, his thought takes flight for other worlds, it is only to seek in them a kinship with our 'blood-warm Earth', or to people them with earthly life:

> Implacable they shine
> To us who would of Life obtain
> An answer for the life we strain
> To nourish with one sign.
> Nor can imagination throw

[1] See B. Fehr, who describes Meredith's achievement as *eine neue, kühne Tat*, 'George Meredith. Der Dichter der Evolution'. *Die Neueren Sprachen*, 1910, xviii, p. 70; J. B. Priestley, *George Meredith*, p. 67; J. W. Cunliffe, 'Modern Thought in Meredith's Poems', *P. M. L. A.*, 1912, pp. 1—25.

The penetrative shaft: we pass
The breath of thought, who would divine
If haply they may grow
As Earth; have our desire to know;
If life comes there to grain from grass,
And flowers like ours of toil and pain...

Our senses shrink back from this mystery, but the 'spirit leaps alight', trusting to discover in the stars a universal power—'the binder of his sheaves, the sane, the right'; to find that they hold a 'great life', that 'there with toil life climbs the self-same Tree'.

Already in his *Ode to the Spirit of Earth in Autumn* Meredith is dedicated to the worship which burns through his later work:

Great Mother Nature! teach me, like thee,
To kiss the season and shun regrets.
And am I more than the mother who bore,
Mock me not with thy harmony!
Teach me to blot regrets,
Great Mother! me inspire
With faith that forward sets
But feeds the living fire,
Faith that never frets
For vagueness in the form.
In life, O keep me warm!
For, what is human grief?
And what do men desire?
Teach me to feel myself the tree,
. And not the withered leaf.
Fixed am I and await the dark to-be
And O, green bounteous Earth!
Bacchante Mother! stern to those
Who live not in thy heart of mirth;

> Death shall I shrink from, loving thee?
> Into the breast that gives the rose,
> Shall I with shuddering fall?
>
> Earth, the mother of all,
> Moves on her steadfast way,
> Gathering, flinging, sowing.
> Mortals, we live in her day,
> She in her children is growing.[1]

In this great invocation Meredith, like a true priest, passes from cultic ecstasy to moral exhortation: To live close to Earth; to be happy in her and share in her harmony; to have faith in the near solid thing as well as in the future; to be alive with Earth's warm, pulsating life and crave for no more—this is the grace for which he is praying. And, offering himself up to his Bacchante Mother, the poet-priest sheds his individuality and turns away from the 'regrets', 'griefs', desires and fear of death which sadden and distort a self-seeking human life. These vain, personal cravings lose their power when the mind is participating in the beauty and joy of Earth and in her great, generous acts which bring all life forth. If she reclaims her child, it has yet added to the glory of everlasting being, and to the progress of life.

The poet's aspiration is directed towards the beauty and holiness of a selfless mind, a mind attuned to the harmony of Earth and able to follow her when she gives wisdom and points to the good life:

> She can lead us, only she,
> Unto God's footstool, whither she reaches:
> Loved, enjoyed, her gifts must be,
> Reverenced the truths she teaches,

[1] Vol. 24, pp. 258—9.

Ere a man may hope that he
Ever can attain the glee
Of things without a destiny!

To Earth is due love, reverence and joy, for she is indeed great and beautiful, and the source of truth. If man is to attain to the highest values, he must accept her truths and her gifts; and if he is to gain happiness, he must deaden his self and his preoccupation with 'destiny'. For Earth is only concerned with the larger, more generous issues of the whole of life, and hers is a lavish, reckless enterprise, yet one fired with determination:

She knows not loss:
She feels but her need,
Who the winged seed
With the leaf doth toss.

If we allow our Mother to lead us; if we accept her magnanimous ways, will not her spirit so enter into us that we join in her 'need' and feel the 'joy of motion' and the 'rapture of being' as the supreme values of life? Once we have attained to this attitude of complete harmony with Earth, 'strong light' will radiate from us upon the rest of existence, when we are no more. And life persists:

Behold, in yon stripped Autumn, shivering grey,
Earth knows no desolation,
She smells regeneration
In the moist breath of decay.[1]

The greater part of Meredith's reading of Earth and Life will appear as a panorama spreading outwards from the devotion and insight which this Ode reveals, and if it were possible to indicate

[1] *Ibid.*, p. 260.

215

any one centre from which his vision moves, it is the faith that Earth 'in her children is growing'. To get a better grasp of the pattern, it is necessary to examine the meaning of Meredith's 'Mother Earth'-symbol, and see how this meaning is related to his evolutionary belief.

In Meredith's terminology, 'Earth' assumes a complex significance, not only through the 'Mother'-combination, but because it is synonymous with 'Nature' and 'God'.[1] More commonly, 'Mother Earth' denotes our planet, as the source of all life existing there—an organism with undying procreative power. Meredith's faith and trust in Earth is deeply rooted in this idea; for:

> Till we conceive her living we go distraught,
> ....
> Seeing she lives, and of her joy of life
> Creatively has given us blood and breath
> For endless war and never wound unhealed,
> The gloomy Wherefore of our battle-field
> Solves in the Spirit, wrought of her through strife
> To read her own and trust her down to death.[2]

Similarly Browning, in *Paracelsus,* celebrates joy as the creative life-impulse. While Browning—the Platonist—seeks and finds God, Meredith discovers a living Earth, the Mother of all beings, from whom a meaning radiates upon the most obscure regions of existence. Yet in Meredith's portrait of Mother Earth there are also Platonic features: It is not the least gift from her to her children,

> To know her a thing alive,
> Whose aspects mutably swerve,
> Whose laws immutably reign.[3]

[1] See G. M. Trevelyan, *George Meredith,* p. 124.
[2] *Sense and Spirit,* 25, p. 13.   [3] *A Faith on Trial,* 25, pp. 255—6.

216

To Meredith, as to eighteenth-century poets, and to the Romantics, the permanent laws of Earth or Nature are evidence of the rational, purposive order which underlies the mutability of things.

Meredith's conception of Earth as an organic whole is formed chiefly under the impact of the evolutionary doctrine, but it contains also an important aspect of pantheistic faith which, as we have seen in Swinburne, was a natural development of the Romantic vision of Nature into the age of agnosticism and evolutionary biology. Earth, to Meredith, is 'a thing alive' with spirit or mind, and hence, in his great Ode to Earth, he invokes her 'Spirit'. From her, again, he holds this important piece of knowledge:

> This life and her to know
> For Spirit: with awakenedness of glee
> To feel stern joy her origin: not he
> The child of woe.[1]

Life is the manifestation of a spiritual power immanent in Earth: she is 'Spirit in her clods', and through this spirit all life is united.[2]

Meredith's pantheism testifies to the persistence and vitality of philosophical Idealism in England in the latter half of the nineteenth century. To Meredith, the dilemma of Newman and Arnold had ceased to be important, yet he is for ever rooted in the tradition through which Coleridge and Carlyle, long after the Romantic Movement was dead, continued to be active. With them German Idealism swept in two great waves into England, and their claim for the Spirit, though challenged from many quarters, by

---

[1] *Earth and Man*, 25, st. xxxiii.

[2] *The Woods of Westermain*, 25, p. 43.—There is a prose comment by Meredith which elucidates the unifying action of spirit: 'Chiefly by that in my poetry which emphasizes the unity of life, the soul which breathes through the universe, do I wish to be remembered: for the spiritual is the eternal.' Quoted from E. Clodd, 'Some Recollections', *Fortnightly Review*, July 1909.

Benthamism and Science in particular, was not easily put aside. Meredith had learned not only from these, and others, like Wordsworth and Shelley, but directly from Goethe.[1] Thus, without heart-searchings and regret, he discovers his God in what is to him the most obvious divine manifestation, in Earth and Life, and he does not pause to ask why this ontological deduction is more legitimate than the transcendent object of the religious quest—the 'Whence' and 'Whither'—which he scorns as futile. His is 'no extramural God, the God within',[2] and yet, apart from this absence of transcendent and eschatological aspects, Meredith's faith in 'Mother Earth' —the 'God within'—has a similar aspiration towards the ideal, and a similar basis of mystical intuition, as all higher religious experience. It is a genuine faith, inevitable and fervent, and not, what it may seem at times, a mere hypostasis of natural law or of vital process. Nor is it tinged with the fast-fading colours of the make-shift and the substitute, which often turn the apotheoses of Truth, Humanity and Progress of the nineteenth century into such pallid ghosts.

Some attention has been given by scholars to the influence which Spinoza's pantheism exercised over Meredith through Goethe, and if one stresses this point, it is easy to forget that Meredith's vision of life is so modified by the doctrine of evolution as to make it different in essential aspects from the outlook of his masters in philosophy.[3] To Spinoza, God is the only substance, and he tries to resolve

[1] Cf. W. Zeddies, *George Merediths Naturauffassung in seinen Gedichten,* where the influence of German Idealism, and notably of Goethe, is strongly emphasized. The author contradicts Tesche's opinion, in *Das Naturgefühl bei George Meredith,* that M. refuses to see a hidden, mysterious power in Nature, and relates his attitude to that of Thomson, Akenside, Cowper and Wordsworth; p. 32.

[2] *Foresight and Patience,* 26, p. 93.

[3] W. Zeddies indicates this transition, *op. cit.,* p. 58, but agrees with Galland that Meredith's pantheism was inherited from Spinoza and Goethe; *ibid.* p. 30.

the old dualism of mind and matter by describing these as merely two attributes of the one God. And God, the Cosmos, in this doctrine, is a static, permanent whole, undisturbed and unmodified by the flux of changes in the phenomenal world. These occur, so to speak, only on the surface of reality, through the action of efficient causes, and not through any non-physical, spontaneous impulse. It is the principle of Galileo's dynamics applied as an interpretation to natural process as a whole. Modern biology destroyed this view, and developed in its place a theory of nature which unifies mind and matter in a life-process where all growth and change is organic, i. e. caused by an inherent, spontaneous impulse. As R. G. Collingwood aptly states it:

The new biology thought of life as resembling matter and unlike mind in being wholly devoid of conscious purpose, ... On the other hand, life was conceived as like mind and unlike matter in developing itself through an historic process, and orientating itself through this process not at random but in a determinate direction, towards the production of organisms more fitted to survive in the given environment .... This theory implied the philosophical conception of a life-force at once immanent and transcendent in relation to each and every living organism; immanent as existing only as embodied in these organisms, transcendent as seeking to realize itself not merely in the survival of the individual organisms, nor merely in the perpetuation of their specific type, but as always able and always trying to find for itself a more adequate realization in a new type.[1]

It is this new insight which marks the distance between Meredith and his forbears of the pantheistic (Spinozistic) tradition, for to him Nature is no longer a mechanical process, but an organism alive with spontaneous motion, and some form of 'will' and 'need'. In the end, however, Meredith parts company not only with Spinoza, and Goethe's *Dauer im Wechsel*, but also with Darwin's law of 'Natural

[1] *The Idea of Nature*, p. 135.

Selection' in its exclusive formulation.[1] On the other hand, Meredith combines in his vision of existence the pantheistic one-substance theory with the doctrine of evolution in a synthesis where the 'God within' is identical with the life-force underlying the natural process. His world, like that of Swinburne, is 'One God at growth'.[2]

As to the nature of this immanent God, Meredith remains agnostic, though once he describes him as 'The Great Unseen, nowise the Dark Unknown'.[3] 'Questions' and 'Legends' about God are futile, for Earth, who alone holds the 'mystery', gives only practical knowledge —'harsh wisdom'—and, moreover, our craving for the 'Impalpable' and the 'Invisible' is unworthy self-seeking.[4] And yet, despite this agnosticism, Meredith has his ritual of worship, through which he communes with 'the Uppermost', 'the God of Gods', and 'the Master Mind'.[5] It is a cult which seeks to participate in the greatness, beauty and goodness of the 'God within', by seizing on those aspects which —to Meredith—most clearly reveal his presence. According to G. M. Trevelyan, Meredith's

God is identified, not with all Nature, but with the good elements in her, which it is the task of man to bring to full and conscious life in himself, by the hard process of evolution, the education of blood and tears. God is immanent in Nature and in man, but at first very dimly, like the statue in the rough block of quarried marble.[6]

[1] W. Zeddies appears to disregard Meredith's organic conception of 'Mother Earth' when claiming that: *Rein geistig ist die Entwicklung gedacht bei Emerson, rein physisch ist sie bei Meredith, bis wir zum Menschen kommen.* According to this view, Earth, before man, is *Die mechanisch sich Wandelnde; op. cit.* pp. 60, 69.

[2] G. M. Trevelyan points out that in Meredith's cult of Earth 'the essence of religious feeling and the scientific idea of evolution are merged into one'; *op. cit.* p. 104.　　[3] *The Test of Manhood*, 26, p. 203.

[4] These phrases are quoted in sequence from *A Faith on Trial*, 25, p. 252; *Earth and Man*, st. xiii, viii.

[5] Quoted in sequence: *The Empty Purse*, 26, p. 52; *The Woods of Westermain*, 25, p. 43; *The Test of Manhood*, 26, p. 204.

[6] *Op. cit.* p. 119.

220

Like Tennyson and Browning, Meredith sees evolution as a mani
festation of God, gradually realizing a purpose, permeating existence
with spirit and raising it to higher levels of consciousness and a more
intense life of the soul. But it is an urge from within: the Spirit of
Earth is growing in her children, not towards any definite or final
achievement, for 'Spirit raves not for a goal', and yet it 'aspires;
dreams of a higher than it'.[1] There will not be any ultimate, divine
event in Creation, but there will be a 'blossom of Good'; and for
men Meredith has the hope, which rivals even Swinburne's, that
'To stature of the Gods will they attain'.[2]

Earth—Spirit—God: this, then, is the Trinity which stands at
the centre of Meredith's vision of existence. Through the interaction
of these three conceptions, his belief, and his attitude to life, is
wrought into imaginative structures of a unique kind. Earth is the
visible, palpable expression of the life-force which pervades our
planet, and the universe, and for which Spirit, with its composite
meanings of nisus, consciousness, intelligence and, here indirectly—
immortality, is a suggestive term. God—the 'God within'—encompasses these aspects and adds to them the divine attributes of omnipotence, love, law. Yet while these three terms interpenetrate and
are related to others, of similar connotation, like Nature, Soul, 'the
prime of Powers', it is Earth which most vividly tells Meredith about
the history and the quest of life.

At times Meredith follows this quest through the fertile world of
our 'bacchante Mother'—this 'Nurse of seed', from whom everything grows and gains strength:

> She shapes anew her dusty crops;
> Her quick in their own likeness climb.
>
> Of their own force do they create;
> They climb to light, in her their root.[3]

---

[1] *A Faith on Trial*, 25, p. 257.
[2] *Ibid.* p. 259; and *Hymn to Colour*, 25, st. xiv.
[3] *The Thrush in February*, 25, p. 224.

At times it is a deep, warm feeling of gratitude towards our generous Mother 'who bore us,/And is our only visible friend'.[1] For it is she

> Who gives us the man-loving Nazarene,
> The martyrs, the poets, the corn and the vines.[2]

She who hands to us, her 'nurslings', the 'fruitage and the cup'; who gives us the 'milk' as well as the 'spirit'.[3] And we—

> We come of earth, and rich of earth may be;[4]

Once, in a bizarre imaginative glimpse, Meredith discovers in the eyes of oxen a reflection of cosmic genesis, reaching

> Back to hours when mind was mud;
> Nigh the knot, which did untwine
> Timelessly to drowsy suns;
> Seeing Earth a slimy spine,
> Heaven a space for winging tons.[5]

On the whole, however, Meredith is not preoccupied with cosmic evolution—Laplace does not inspire him as he did Tennyson; nor is he greatly interested in the first stages of evolution here on earth. He sees it, once, as a 'first chaos'—: 'A nature of gaunt ribs, an Earth of crags',[6] but he does not dwell on it, since his heart is with the rich and varied life in Earth, with the 'many-numbered of her fold', and, above all, with man—'her great venture'.[7]

---

[1] *Ode to the Spirit of Earth in Autumn*, 24, p. 256.
[2] *The Empty Purse*, 26, p. 54.
[3] *Hard Weather*, 25, p. 212; *Earth's Secret*, 25, p. 13.
[4] *Foresight and Patience*, 26, p. 90.
[5] *The Woods of Westermain*, 25, p. 35.
[6] *The Appeasement of Demeter*, 25, st. iii.
[7] *Ode to Youth in Memory*, 26, p. 69; *Earth and Man*, 25, st. i.

In the fertility symbolism built up around his pantheistic conception of 'Mother Earth', Meredith visualizes the generative process which sustains and perpetuates life. It expresses, moreover, his faith in the love and providence of Mother Earth, much in the same way as the seed-blossom-fruit imagery in *Hertha* bears witness to Swinburne's belief. Like Swinburne, too, he extends the significance of his 'Mother Earth' symbol to interpret the laws and forces which determine the course of life. Earth not only brings forth her children, she teaches them as well. We are

> In the charge of the Mother our fate;
> Her law as the one common weal.[1]

Like Hertha, she has the power to save or damn, for 'Of Earth are we stripped or crowned'; her laws are 'immutable', her 'sentence past grace'.[2]

As a nurse, Earth is both loving and severe. At times 'she will seem/Heavenly', showing 'a kind face and sweet', while at other times

> Inconscient, insensitive, she reigns
> In iron laws, though rapturous fair her face.

Then she is like a 'Mother whom no cry can melt'. And yet, whatever face she turns upon us, 'she the laws of growth most deeply knows'.[3]

---

[1] *A Faith on Trial,* 25, p. 252.
[2] *Ibid.* pp. 253, 256, 246.
[3] Quoted in sequence: *Earth and Man,* 25, st. x; *The Woods of Westermain,* 25, p. 35; *The Test of Manhood,* 26, p. 204; *The Thrush in February,* 25, p. 224; *Modern Love,* 24, st. xiii.

The Laws of Growth

Life itself is, of course, something ultimate and unknowable—a 'Fount unresting', or 'Earth's primary heart at its active beat', and in its deepest stratum we can discern only an impulse or need—a 'first blind yearning' or 'Necessity, the primal goad to growth'. Meredith observes it in man too:

> Wearifully through forest-tracks unsown,
> He travels, urged by some internal goad.[1]

This necessity is not, then, a physical or 'efficient' cause, but a spontaneous urge, which Meredith elsewhere relates to human emotion and interprets as 'joy of life'.[2] It is an exuberance that predominates over other moods in our 'bacchante Mother', who has a 'heart of mirth'. Exuberance and joy are natural companions of love, and Earth would not be 'our Mother of Grace' if she did not love her children and conceive them in an act of love. Meredith sees it as a universal creative force:

> Love, the great volcano, flings
> Fires of lower Earth to sky;[3]

Love is the 'nerve of change', giving Earth features 'heavenly new'; it is the very 'clue' to her secret, and it explains her 'two-sexed meanings'.[4] Hatred, on the other hand, is a feeling alien to her nature—a destructive force which brings 'discord' and 'horror',[5] and throws the world 'back to first chaos'.[6]

[1] Quoted in sequence: *The Woods of Westermain*, 25, p. 41; *Alsace-Lorraine*, 26, p. 152; *The Wild Rose and the Snowdrop*, 24, st. v; *The Appeasement of Demeter*, 25, st. ii; *The Test of Manhood*, 26, p. 206.
[2] *Sense and Spirit*, 25, p. 13.
[3] *The Woods of Westermain*, 25, p. 38.
[4] *Ibid.* p. 39.   [5] *Ibid.* p. 38.
[6] *The Appeasement of Demeter*, 25, p. 227.

In identifying the creative impulse of Earth with such correlatives of human emotion as 'need', 'joy' and 'love', Meredith approaches to a faith in some directive principle in evolution, which may not be teleology in the literal sense of the word, but which excludes a purely mechanical process at any stage of growth. And he goes much further in his human analogy:

But read her thought to speed the race.[1]

Meredith's evolutionary belief was no doubt influenced in many ways by Darwin, and once he asserted that 'I back your Huxley throughout'.[2] Yet there appears to be no evidence, internal or external, that Darwin's theory came as a revelation to him and strongly modified his attitude.[3] Darwin's principle of 'natural selection', and his emphasis on environment to the exclusion of other factors, such as 'nisus', would inevitably conflict with Meredith's ethical and pantheistic reading of 'Mother Earth'. It is true that Darwin later, and notably in his final edition of *Origin of Species*[4] compromised with the neo-Lamarckians, but Meredith had already in 1862, with the *Ode to the Spirit of Earth in Autumn*, clearly stated a teleological belief.[5] Where they meet on common ground, however, and where Darwin seems most vigorously to have stimulated his vision of the evolutionary process, is the scene of strife—the battle-field of life where only the fittest survive.

Malthus, Darwin and Huxley contemplated this scene in moods of sadness and resignation, but to Meredith the struggle, far from

---

[1] *The Thrush in February*, 25, p. 224.

[2] *Letters*, vol. ii, p. 534.

[3] W. Zeddies, however, claims with B. Fehr that Darwin's influence was fundamental, and stresses the different response it evoked in Tennyson and Browning; *op. cit.* pp. 59—60.

[4] 1872; cf. *supra*, p. 20.

[5] Cf. 'Earth ... moves on her steadfast way ...'; 'feels but her need'; *supra*, pp. 214—15.

disturbing his trust in Mother Earth, is evidence of her love and care. It is a splendid tournament to which she challenges all creatures, and also her 'great venture, Man':

> For he is in the lists
> Contentious with the elements, whose dower
> First sprang him; for swift vultures to devour
> If he desists.[1]

Surrender means death; but those who have courage may live and gain strength. And thus man, Earth's 'chief Expression', is a 'creature matched with strife', though now he

> Has half transferred the battle to his brain,
> From bloody ground;[2]

Life is 'hard weather'—a tempest—a 'savage whirr', and only by plunging into it is it possible to brace oneself and grow fit.[3] We must bravely face this stormy scene of existence,

> Where Life is at her grindstone set,
> That she may give us edgeing keen,
> String us for battle, till as play
> The common strokes of fortune shower.
> Such meaning in a dagger-day
> Our wits may clasp to wax in power.[4]

---

[1] *Earth and Man*, 25, st. iii.
[2] *Ibid.*, st. xliv, iv, xvi.
[3] Cf. G. M. Trevelyan's comment on the ethical significance of storms in the novels, thus in *The Ordeal of Richard Feverel*, *op. cit.* pp. 49—50.
[4] *Hard Weather*, 25, p. 213. Cf. the 'storm-winds' in *Hertha*, *supra*, p. 186.

Like Browning, his 'brother poet', Meredith cheerfully accepts the struggle for life as a necessary urge, though with him it is not only a challenge to moral and spiritual growth, but to any kind of advance. Peace—the absence of this challenge—means stagnation, a state incompatible with the laws of growth: 'In Nature is no rearward step allowed.'[1] Therefore:

> Behold the life at ease; it drifts.
> The sharpened life commands its course.
> She winnows, winnows roughly; sifts,
> To dip her chosen in her source:
> Contention is the vital force,
> Whence pluck they brain, her prize of gifts,
> Sky of the senses![2]

Here, indeed, 'natural selection' is the central theme, and despite his buoyant tone and feeling, Meredith gives it an apologetic treatment: Contention, strife, is an ineluctable principle in all growth, necessary and beneficial; and the fittest, those who come victorious from the battle, have gained in will and intelligence. The same theme, designed in the recurrent image of Earth winnowing, or threshing the chaff from the grain, is in *The Woods of Westermain* once more associated with storms:

> So flesh
> Conjures tempest-flails to thresh
> Good from worthless.[3]

And elsewhere Attila's 'chosen warriors' are seen as 'Grain of threshing battle-dints'.[4]

---

[1] *Alsace-Lorraine*, 26, st. vi.
[2] *Hard Weather*, 25, p. 213.
[3] Vol. 25, p. 45.
[4] *The Nuptials of Attila*, 25, st. v. Cf. also *The Shaving of Shagpat*, vol. 1, p. 303.

The same law of struggle applies to all phases and spheres of growth, to 'spirit' as well as 'flesh'. Spirit is wrought of Earth through strife,[1] and, similarly

> Wisdom is won of its fight,
> The combat incessant;[2]

In man, the battle has been 'half transferred' to 'brain/From bloody ground', but it still continues to urge him on.[3]

It is obvious then, that Spencer's 'struggle for survival' and Darwin's law of Natural Selection have become integral parts of Meredith's evolutionary faith. Yet in his own vision they are modified and acquire a different meaning since they are forces operating within a teleological scheme: they reveal the purpose of Mother Earth through the biological progress, and notably in the attainment of man. Purpose and teleology in this connexion do not mean conscious thinking and planning towards a definite goal, but an Aristotelian *nisus* (like that of the seed growing into a plant) unfelt and yet creative. This impulse Meredith, again faithful to his Idealistic heritage, identifies with 'mind' or 'spirit', groping at first unconsciously after fulfilment, and finally ascending in man to consciousness and reason:

> The mastering mind in him, by tempests blown,
> By traitor inmates baited, upward burned;
> Perforce of growth, the Master mind discerned,
> The Great Unseen, nowise the Dark Unknown.
> To whom unwittingly did he aspire
> In wilderness, where bitter was his need:
> To whom in blindness, as an earthy seed

[1] *Sense and Spirit*, 25, p. 13.
[2] *A Faith on Trial*, 25, p. 254.
[3] *Earth and Man*, 25, st. xvi.

> For light and air, he struck through crimson mire.
> But not ere he upheld a forehead lamp,
> And viewed an army, once the seeming doomed,
> All choral in its fruitful garden camp,
> The spiritual the palpable illumed.[1]

The seed-analogy is significant: an urge is manifest everywhere in Nature. All the way, even in his unconscious yearning after a higher and better life, it was the same impulse—'the mastering mind'— that spurred man to the birth of consciousness and reason, which means a participation in 'the Master mind' or the 'God within'. This evolutionary attainment implies a stage of social harmony, and reason (Common sense) is, therefore, with Meredith as with Spencer the chief agent of social integration. Having reached this 'garden camp', the spiritual nature of man is liberated for its essential task of exploring existence—it may penetrate (understand) and embrace (interrelate) enigmas hitherto unnoticed or unsolved. Thus the struggle is inevitable, and fruitful, as the outcome shows:

> This gift of penetration and embrace,
> His prize from tidal battles lost or won,
> Reveals the scheme to animate his race:
> How that it is a warfare but begun;
> Unending; with no Power to interpose;[2]

The human attainment testifies to a universal purpose active throughout nature: not a *Deus ex Machina* intervening in the struggle for life, but 'the God within'—the spirit which unifies all being—participating in man's effort:

> God being there while he his fight maintains;
> Throughout his mind the Master Mind being there...[3]

---

[1] *The Test of Manhood*, 26, p. 203.   [2] *Ibid.*   [3] *Ibid.* p. 204.

In the same way as Meredith accepts the struggle for life as a law of growth, he accepts pain and suffering. Earth may seem severe, even cruel to her children,

> But read her thought to speed the race,
> And stars rush forth of blackest night: ...[1]

If, seeing her 'double visage', we doubt her loving providence, we have but to look back on human history, to realize that her ways were just and good:

> Since Pain and Pleasure on each hand
> Led our wild steps from slimy rock
> To yonder sweeps of gardenland,
> We breathe but to be sword or block.[2]

Our progress is a purgatory, and through suffering we shed our animal self-seeking aggression. Though Meredith has nothing of the puritan or ascetic idealism which so strongly informs Tennyson's and Browning's attitude, he shares their belief in the value of emotional discipline and their aspiration towards harmony. He, too, sees moral evolution as a

> conquest of the inner beast,
> Which Measure tames to movement sane,
> In harmony with what is fair.[3]

Thus, in the ode to *Youth in Memory* there is a purgatory structure closely related to that of *In Memoriam* (cxviii.), with the difference, however, that Meredith stresses the value of our animal heritage. Like Comte, he places a prize upon the sum total of human experi-

---

[1] *The Thrush in February*, 25, p. 224.   [2] *Ibid.*
[3] *Hard Weather*, 25, p. 213.

ence, and upon man's ancestry, though they may appear terrible in
retrospect:

> Accept them, them and him, though hiss thy sweat
> Off brow on breast, whose furnace flame
> Has eaten, and old Self consumes.
> Out of the purification will they leap,
> Thee renovating while new light illumes
> The dusky web of evil, known as pain,
> That heavily up healthward mounts the steep;
> Our fleshly road to beacon-fire of brain:
> Midway the tameless oceanic brute
> Below, whose heave is topped with foam for fruit,
> And the fair heaven reflecting inner peace
> On righteous warfare, that asks not to cease.
>
> Forth of such passage through black fire we win
> Clear hearing of the simple lute ...[1]

That is, we enter into the universal harmony of Earth. It is part of
the 'thought' or intention of Mother Earth to defeat our Ego, the
root of aggression and chaos, and to this end she uses adversity and
suffering. Our 'old Dragon Self' must be tamed, and on the lower
stages of life, where 'flesh' is predominant, this 'Monster' is 'Fit but
to be led by Pain'.[2] Since the laws of Earth are immutable and 'iron',
our only way is to accept them, for while the struggle for life inflicts torments innumerable, we grow by 'the spur of explicable
pains'.[3] And Earth reveals to us the underlying meaning, in which
the paradox of her 'double visage' is solved:

> and have we wept,
> And have we quailed with fears,
> Or shrunk with horrors, sure reward

[1] Vol. 26, pp. 71—72.   [2] *The Woods of Westermain*, 25, p. 45.
[3] *The Test of Manhood*, 26, p. 204.

We have whom knowledge crowns;
Who see in mould the rose unfold,
The soul through blood and tears.[1]

More directly than Swinburne even, Meredith uses Baudelaire's metaphor of *fleurs du mal* to visualize the spiritual growth of man.[2]

Facing the dichotomy of existence, Swinburne discovered in the 'divine contraries' of life a formula of reconciliation, and similarly Meredith sees the conflict between good and evil, pleasure and pain, life and death, as part of Earth's 'two-sexed meanings', which 'melt' in the thought, and acceptance, capable of reaching beyond them to the larger harmony in which they are balanced.[3] As a corollary, Meredith distils also from inevitable and final death a note of trust and optimism, with regard to the future of the human race:

By Death, as by Life, are we fed:
The two are one spring;
. . . . .
Only they can waft us in flight.[4]

Earth, which knows the laws of growth most deeply, feels no sorrow for the dying rose. In autumn, she burns under the surface with creative heat:

Quick at her wheel, while the fuel, decay,
Brightens the fire of renewal: and we?
Death is the word of a bovine day,
Know you the breast of the springing To-be.[5]

[1] *Outer and Inner*, 25, st. v.
[2] See also in *Meditation under Stars*; 'flowers like ours of toil and pain'; 25, p. 265.
[3] Cf. *The Woods of Westermain*, 25, p. 39.
[4] *A Faith on Trial*, 25, p. 253; See also *The Empty Purse*, 26, p. 40: 'as a child of the Death and the Life ...'.
[5] *Seed-Time*, 25, st. vi.

Therefore, though it may seem a paradox:

> Verily now is our season of seed,
> Now in our Autumn . . .[1]

And as in Nature, trees, flowers and fruits must fade and give way to new growth and next year's crop, so too in human life. Meredith sings the analogy in *Dirge in Woods:*

> A wind sways the pines,
>   And below
> Not a breath of wild air;
> Still as the mosses that glow
> On the flooring and over the lines
> Of the roots here and there.
> The pine-tree drops its dead;
> They are quiet, as under the sea.
> Overhead, overhead
> Rushes life in a race,
> As the clouds the clouds chase;
>   And we go,
> And we drop like the fruits of the tree,
>   Even we,
>   Even so.

In *Woodman and Echo* the analogy is expanded and given a more definite perspective: The woodman knows that something finer will grow from an earth long fertilized and sown with better seed, and therefore he clears the ground. On our attainment, and on what we bequeath to coming generations, depends the future, for as a man sows, so shall he also reap.[2]

---

[1] *Ibid.* See similar ideas of generation from decay in *Ode to the Spirit of Earth in Autumn,* 24, p. 260; *Woodland Peace,* 25, p. 235; *Youth in Memory,* 26, p. 74.

[2] See *France,* 26, pp. 140—49.

233

Meredith, then, sees no tragedy in the individual life being merely a brief flowering and season in the endless regenerative process of life. We return to Earth, we die absolutely as individuals, but in our children and in the spiritual heritage we leave there is a high and noble form of immortality. To hope for other permanence is futile self-seeking, and futile and unworthy is also our fear of death.[1] If we know and love Earth, our Mother, then her magnanimous spirit will raise us above these egoistic concerns to where we survey 'The meaning of the Pleasures, Pains/The Life, the Death ...', and then we see our personal death—'as beholds her flowers'

> Earth, from a night of frosty wreck,
> Enrobed in morning's mounted fire,
> When lowly, with a broken neck,
> The crocus lays her cheek to mire.[2]

Again, in another great poem, the *Hymn to Colour,* Meredith moves through an allegorical vision in which Life and Death meet and fuse in the action of Love, which to him, as to the Romantics, is ever the harmonizing force:

> Love took my hand when hidden stood the sun
> To fling his robe on shoulder-heights of snow.
> Then said: There lie they, Life and Death in one.
> Whichever is, the other is: but know,
> It is thy craving self that thou dost see,
>   Not in them seeing me.[3]

This stoical, self-effacing attitude to death is not, solely or mainly, derived from the pantheistic creed which regards it as a reunion of the many with the one; nor from the organic or evolutionary conception

[1] *A Faith on Trial,* 25, pp. 251—53.
[2] *The Thrush in February,* 25, p. 225.
[3] Vol. 25, st. iv.

of Earth which asserts the continuity of life. It is true that Meredith uses both these arguments whenever the craving for personal immortality occurs, yet he knows that neither of them is adequate to prove that death is not ultimate loss of existence for the individual. So he faces this loss in an act of courage and will, denying its tragedy and forcing himself to accept it as necessary and good.[1] There is, at the root of his attitude to death as to the problem of evil and pain, a heroic effort to live up to a human ideal—it is the aspiration to the beauty and holiness of the selfless mind which we found in the *Ode to the Spirit of Earth in Autumn*. Having once accepted the truth, as he sees it, that life and spirit have only immanent existence, Meredith's choice is deliberate and final:

> I raise my head to aspects fair,
> From foul I turn away.[2]

If we confront this attitude with the transcendentalism of Browning, who was otherwise such a kindred spirit, the distance between the two poets grows considerable. Browning (like Tennyson), in the Christian and Platonic tradition, claimed for man a destiny apart from the inferior species out of which he has evolved: he is an entirely new *genus*—a spiritual mutation, so to speak, and thus released from the animal chain, his physical being, in death. Meredith, though he too insists on 'Spirit', refuses to make a distinction between 'here' and 'there', 'we' and 'they'.[3] All existence is one, and to split it is just wishful thinking—'sensual dreams'. There is one law of Life and Death to which all are subject, and Earth, always stern to the self-seeker, gives no promise of eternal life for the individual.[4] Meredith does not allow personal grief to shake this ac-

[1] Cf. *The Test of Manhood*, 26, p. 205.
[2] *Woodland Peace*, 25, p. 235.
[3] See *The Woods of Westermain*, 25, p. 39.
[4] *A Faith on Trial*, 25, pp. 251—52.

235

ceptance of death, though his 'faith' passes through a severe 'trial', and again a comparison with Browning may recall that he similarly tests his faith in *La Saisiaz,* and clings to a transcendental hope in which he finds peace.

It would seem that, so far, Meredith has not discovered any strikingly new meanings in his 'reading' of Life and Earth. The laws of growth are those which Tennyson and Browning also found, as urge, joy, aspiration, love and purgatory, and otherwise he dwells on the struggle for life and the 'divine contraries' accentuated by Swinburne. It is only when we come to his idea of the 'Comic Spirit' that Meredith grasps a formative principle which none of his precursors had exploited—that is, the moral function of satire and comedy applied to biological process.

The Comic Spirit, according to Meredith, works both as a corrective and as a stimulus to evolutionary growth. Above all it has been important in fashioning man into a social being from the predatory animal of the past. In the mental development of man it is the 'Sword of Common Sense', and Meredith, looking back on human history, sees the Comic Spirit as

> the highest, the unwritten Law
> We read upon that building's architrave
> In the mind's firmament, by men upraised
> With sweat of blood when they had quitted cave
> For fellowship, and rearward looked amazed,
> Where the prime motive gapes a lurid jaw ...[1]

In this ode: *To the Comic Spirit,* Meredith describes (at first) the ethical progress as a hunt where the horn of laughter is heard, as a 'fine unaccented scorn'

> At sight of man's old secret brute ...[2]

[1] *Ode to the Comic Spirit,* 26, p. 56.   [2] *Ibid.,* p. 57.

236

Despite his 'mind's firmament' the wild animal is still there, hidden in man's nature, and Meredith stalks him in various shapes: in personal and collective tyranny ('niggard Age'—'ceremonial state'), all 'Creative of their various ape', all striving to sate their unsparing appetite. Then, having detected the game, he appeals to the Comic Spirit to hunt them down:

> Call up thy hounds of laughter to their run.[1]

Wit must conquer greed and folly to wed head and heart, and link men together, for it is 'Victorious laughter'

> Whereat they feel within them weave
> Community its closer threads,
> And are to our fraternal state enlarged;[2]

Thus 'Obstruction'—the self-seeking appetites—is slain and fades into 'Earth's renewing beds'. Yet the Comic Spirit must always remain on guard in 'our civil Fort', which is ever

> By more elusive savages assailed
> On each ascending stage ...

The Comic Spirit kills without malice, for it is fighting in the good cause, for Reason and a better life, and working as part of the providential 'thought' of Mother Earth:

> Thou wouldst but have us be
> Good sons of mother soil, whereby to grow
> Branching on fairer skies, one stately tree;

[1] *Ibid.*, p. 58.
[2] *Ibid.*, pp. 63—4.

Reaching to

> Ambrosial heights of possible acquist,
> Where souls of men with soul of man consort,
> And all look higher to new loveliness
> Begotten of the look: thy mark is there ...[1]

It should be noted that in this Ode the Comic Spirit appears as a more definite teleological conception than it is in Meredith's *Essay on the Idea of Comedy and of the Uses of the Comic Spirit*, which is his fullest discursive treatment of its nature and function. Here too, it is seen as a weapon of common sense:

If you believe that our civilization is founded in common sense (and it is the first condition of sanity to believe it), you will, when contemplating men, discern a spirit overhead ...

Once this spirit had a 'big round satyr's laugh', while now

The laugh will come again, but it will be of the order of the smile, finely tempered ... Its common aspect is one of unsolicitous observation, as if surveying a full field and having leisure to dart on its chosen morsels, without any fluttering eagerness. *Men's future upon earth does not attract it*; their honesty and shapeliness in the present does; and whenever they wax out of proportion, overblown, affected .. the Spirit overhead will look humanely malign and cast an oblique light on them, followed by volleys of silvery laughter. That is the Comic Spirit.[2]

One might suggest that though the Comic Spirit (in the Ode) has a 'mark' in 'new loveliness' and 'Ambrosial heights', it does not consciously or directly stimulate the ascent, but indirectly. The inconsistency remains, however, and it would appear that the Ode,

---

[1] *Ibid.*, p. 65; W. Zeddies points out similar patterns in *A Faith on Trial* and *Ode to the Spirit of Earth in Autumn, op. cit.* pp. 24—5; and G. M. *Trevelyan* in *The Appeasement of Demeter, op. cit.,* p. 194.

[2] Mem. ed. (1910), vol. 23, pp. 46—7; (my italics).

though discursive to a large extent, moves on a different level of perception, with a prophetic awareness lacking in the *Essay*, and soaring with the vision of the world-tree to a higher vantage point, while the *Essay* discusses the Comic Spirit with reference to its actual uses as social criticism. This may partly account for the diverging statements. On the other hand, both the Ode and the *Essay* have an important common stratum in the ethical impulse seen as the essential nature and function of the Comic Spirit, and this means a directive or teleological law.

Though most active as a means of social integration and advance, the Comic Spirit is, as the Ode indicates, a universal principle of growth, like joy, love, struggle, pain and death. It is a safeguard by which Earth maintains balance and proportion, so that the progress of life, which is her chief concern, may go unhampered and in the right direction. Thus, again, Meredith in his idea of the Comic Spirit extends his analogy of human nature to Earth, still on the genetic assumption that whatever is, is out of Earth and an integral part of her life.

All these 'laws of growth', even that of necessity, presuppose a lawgiver or some purposive energy underlying the evolutionary process, but the human analogy on which they are based does not imply that Meredith identifies Mother Earth—the lawgiver—with a man-like intelligence. Though his 'reading' of Earth appears as anthropomorphism—a myth projecting human thought and feeling into Nature and the universe, it is essentially an allegory in which one recognizes something like the Aristotelian concept of potentiality and nisus.

Meredith does not work these laws into a pattern of finalistic axioms or millennial promise, and yet he is convinced that the movement is purposive and ascending, clearly manifested in the heights life has climbed, and we can measure the gain by looking back.[1]

---

[1] See *The Test of Manhood*, 26, p. 202: 'He felt the far advance ...'. *The Woods of Westermain*, 25, p. 45: 'Glance we ...'.

While his leaning towards teleology is obvious in the way he pursues the operation of each individual law, it becomes even more articulate when he surveys the panorama of life, as a whole. This total vision of development often tempts him to look ahead.[1] When reading the 'lines dear Earth designs', his thought takes wing for the future, and then he discovers in Earth 'desires ... For happiness, for lastingness, for light', and a 'thought to speed the race'.[2] Indeed, he finds that Mother Earth is ever looking forwards; for while she sustains her children, her preoccupation is with life yet unborn:

> Earth sits ebon in her gloom,
> Us atomies of life alive
> Unheeding, bent on life to come.
> . . . .
> Earth yields the milk, but all her mind
> Is vowed to thresh for stouter stock.[3]

Again, in the idea of Mother Earth as 'our fate', Meredith implies a directive urge which is teleological without being fatalistic, for Earth leaves it to the individual to work out his destiny, while she is concerned with the universal issues, and with the race.[4] It is possible to deduce her aim from the very course on which life moves, for we are

> Upon an Earth that cannot stop,
> Where upward is the visible aim,

[1] Cf. The Test of Manhood, p. 206.

[2] Quoted in sequence, Outer and Inner, 25, st. iv; Earth and Man, 25, st. xxxi; The Thrush in February, 25, p. 224.

[3] Hard Weather, 25, pp. 213—14.

[4] See Earth and Man, 25, st. ii, Alsace-Lorraine, 26, p. 163, 'Let but the rational prevail ...'; The Empty Purse, 26, p. 52, 'Not thee/She cares for ...'; The Test of Manhood, 26, p. 202, 'As only for the numbers ...'.

> And ever we espy the greater God,
> For simple pointing at a good adored:
> Proof of the closer neighbourhood.[1]

This aim reflects back from the spiritual attainments here on Earth and from the gradual realization of value. It is true that Spirit 'raves not for a goal', but in aspiring and dreaming it 'leads to the Uppermost, link by link'.[2] Through its process of evolving consciousness and reason, life becomes

> A scale still ascending to knit
> The clear to the loftier Clear.[3]

In the symbolism of tree and plant which pervades Meredith's poetry there is a marked emphasis on vertical or spiral movement: the 'crops' of Earth 'climb to light', and the mind is seen as feeding on Earth like 'Rings of clasping parasites',

> Free to wind, and in desire
> Winding, they to her attached
> Feel the trunk a spring of fire,
> And ascend to heights unmatched ...[4]

Allusions to the life-tree are recurrent. In *Meditation under Stars* the poet longs to know that in those distant worlds 'life climbs the

---

[1] *The Comic Spirit*, 26, p. 66.

[2] *The Empty Purse*, 26, p. 52. Cf. similar ideas in *Ode to the Spirit of Earth in Autumn*, 24, p. 259; *Ode to the Comic Spirit*, 26, p. 65; *The Woods of Westermain*, 25, p. 43.

[3] *A Faith on Trial*, 25, p. 257.

[4] In sequence, *The Thrush in February*, 25, p. 224; *The Woods of Westermain*, 25, p. 45.

self-same tree'. The mythological image is later more deliberately fused with that of the genealogical tree of biology: It is a 'blood-tree throbbing' in man, who is 'flower at head and soil at root'; he is the measure of the total growth of life.[1] Or, pointing to the future, it is seen 'Branching on fairer skies, one stately tree..'.[2] The direction, or movement of Earth nourishing the growth of life is stated to be a 'broad rectilinear way'

> Admonishing loftier reaches, the rich adventurous shoots,
> Pushes of tentative curves, embryonic upwreathings in air...

And these 'aërial growths' may be signs of Earth's 'fierier zeal/For entry on Life's upper fields..'.[3]

The 'fate'-motif, as a teleological conception, occurs also associated with two traditional metaphors: that of the 'web' and the 'wheel'. The web of life is a progressive fabric worked out in new and more splendid patterns: Earth has 'wonders in loom;/ Revelations, delights.'[4] Life's creative impulse is 'a shuttle weaving swift', and we, human beings, participate in its effort and are greatly responsible for the outcome. More consciously now we are at work for life in the future, and for our children:

> The young generation! ah, there is the child
> Of our souls down the Ages! to bleed for it, proof
> That souls we have, with our senses filed,
>   Our shuttles at thread of the woof.[5]

---

[1] *The Test of Manhood*, 26, p. 206.
[2] *To the Comic Spirit*, 26, p. 65.
[3] *Alsace-Lorraine*, 26, p. 153.
[4] *The Empty Purse*, 26, p. 54.
[5] Quoted in sequence, *The Woods of Westermain*, 25, p. 42; *The Empty Purse*, p. 45.

The 'wheel'-image is used in *Seed-Time* (quoted *supra*, p. 232) to describe the regenerative process of life—'the springing To-be'—and again in *Youth in Memory*, where Earth is heard 'with her Onward chime, with Winter Spring', and we

> Know in our seasons an integral wheel,
> That rolls us to a mark may yet be willed.[1]

In these various structures concerned with the 'laws of growth' and with their meaning for the future course of life, one may detect a common trend which interrelates them and gives them unity, and it is not necessary to break them up in a thorough semantic analysis to show that they are built around a coherence between the key-words. Such terms as 'thought', 'desires', 'mind.. vowed to', 'aim', 'fate', 'designs', 'leads', 'aspires', 'climbs', 'ascends', —all associated with Earth (or Spirit), point to a force, intelligent, or of a psychic, mind-like nature, engaged in a certain direction. Not all of these words are equally articulate in their teleological implications; yet, whether related to spiritual striving, conscious or unconscious, or simply tracing the historical course of life, they suggest some kind of nisus or urge, increasingly intelligent and purposive, acting upon the evolutionary growth.

Thus, from his basic conception of Earth as 'a thing alive', through the 'laws of growth', to this final phase of purposive 'thought' and 'aim', Meredith intellectualizes the organic process by constantly relating its dynamic to a human analogy, while keeping before our eyes, all the time, the mysterious force—the 'God within' —which is at the root of existence. We have seen his metaphorical 'reading' expand through visions of Earth giving birth to her

---

[1] Vol. 26, p. 74; see also *The Woods of Westermain*, 25, p. 38: 'while the wheel/Speeds the mill and drains the meal.'

children and teaching them—visions where human experience reflects and explains her moods and ways. Mother Earth has 'need', 'thought' and 'aim'—or some form of mental integrity unshaken by her changing and apparently freakish methods and means. Her 'mirth' and love and kindness give way, at times, to indifference, and even cruelty in her dealings with the individual, yet seen in the light of the aim she has set for the race, her attitude is justified. This, in bald outline, is the 'harsh wisdom' Meredith has gained from his reading of Earth. Since he so often returns to this justification of her ways to man, his exegetic message of Earth (and of Life) leaves, in the end, the impression of an Apology, and it might be seen as a successor, in idealistic-positivistic dress, of the rationalist Theodicies of the eighteenth century.

It would seem that Meredith, like Swinburne, conceives of the whole of life as a deterministic current sweeping all individuals to nothingness and moving steadily on, swelled by their blood and tears, until, splendid and majestic, it flows into the promised land of Harmony. To a less robust mind, like Tennyson, and to a fierce individualist like Browning, such a vision would be one of cosmic despotism and human despair, and whenever it occurs to them, the pessimistic response is immediate. It is the very basis of philosophical pessimism, since it generally abstains from a knowledge of first and final causes: the questions 'Whence' and 'Whither', which to Meredith are so futile.[1] In Schopenhauer's idea of the blind 'Will' this pessimism found its most suggestive phrase for the kind of cosmic determinism which Tennyson and Browning could not accept, and which they suspected in Darwin's theory of Natural Selection.

Meredith, who has chosen to cast out all fear and to shed his 'human want' and 'dreams', escapes this pessimism. His act of will

[1] Cf. *The Question Whither*, 25, p. 236; *A Faith on Trial*, 25, pp. 250, 252.

and courage springs from a different temperament, which expresses itself more fully in the pantheistic worship of Earth. As a manifestation of the 'God within', Earth commands his devotion as the highest object of love, and this God, again, gives sanction to his ethical values. Much in the same way as Christian ethics, he accepts the paradox, or *via media,* between free will (in the individual) and necessity (ruling the universal and ultimate issues of life) which places the individual in an active and responsible position. The future of the human race is our immortality, our only one, and we shall answer for our actions. Thus Meredith's pantheism, fusing with the religion of Humanity, takes him safely past Giant Despair on the one side and what to him is the wishful mirage of the Celestial City on the other.[1]

How can Mother Earth—this 'God within'— give man a sense of moral obligation, so that he, the natural egoist, the 'dragon Self', will change into a social, altruistic being who prefers the good of others, and 'Harmony', to his own pleasure? Meredith does not simplify the problem in the manner of Bentham, nor split it into two unrelated processes like Huxley, for he retains in his vitalist cult an object of love and devotion which is superhuman and ultimate. His ethics, like his vision of natural process, has both a mystical and realistic (positivistic) aspect; it links the religious feeling for something adorable and great—greater than ourselves—in Earth (and the universe) with the religion of Humanity, so that both these objects of love and duty stand over against the individual as higher and more compelling realities. On a static view of human nature, this compromise between absolute and pragmatic ethics is meaningless, for clearly its man-God relationship fails to supply a categorical imperative in the accepted sense, or to explain the psychological transition from egoism to altruism. The idea of

---

[1] For informative analyses of Meredith's attitude in this connexion see G. M. Trevelyan,*op. cit.,* pp. 107—13; and J. B. Priestley, *op. cit.,* p. 78 ff.

inevitability is absent in Meredith's world, for although he repeatedly claims that Earth is stern to the self-seeker, he is never fooled into thinking that the aggressive, vicious egoists are all punished in the end, while virtuous altruists are rewarded. Yet he clings to an innocent belief that the 'dragon Self', through reckless egoism, somehow forfeits real happiness and joy and places himself outside the moral order and the harmony which Earth, through all that which is best in her, seeks to establish.[1] Moreover—and this is the most important aspect—in Meredith's world man is not a static, immutable creature, but evolving and gradually awaking to Reason and Spirit and a 'blossom of Good'. Here lies the basis of value as well as of conduct in Meredith's ethics: Through evolution, mankind are moving towards a realization of Good, of values, and a consciousness of Good which creates harmony in them and around them, and in furthering this higher life they have their true moral obligation. Meredith knows that compulsion and duty are cut loose from their very roots if they are not part of devotion and love, and when he exhorts men to love Earth and all her creatures, he frankly bears witness to a personal experience in which there is happiness, joy and a contentment far above that which self-seeking could achieve. Unlike the Utilitarians, Meredith does not promise 'pleasure' or 'happiness', in the ordinary sense of these words, as a reward for such love, since these are the vain pursuits of the Ego. In general, he feels, 'man's lot is not for bliss'.[2] Yet to love Earth and Humanity is to have something greater and more lasting than the mean little happiness of the individual closed on himself, and Meredith finds sanction for this claim in the drift of Earth and Life, where love reveals itself as an increasingly active force:

> Already have my people shown their worth,
> More love they light, which folds the love of Earth.

[1] *The Woods of Westermain*, 25, p. 46.
[2] *A Stave of Roving Tim*, 26, st. viii.

That love to love of labour leads: thence love
Of humankind—earth's incense flung above.[1]

Love is part of that fulfilment of good and of value which is taking
place through the evolutionary process. It is an aspect of the life
of the Spirit, rooted in the 'flesh' and yet rising above it. For 'Life
begets with fair increase/Beyond the flesh, if life be true.'[2]

The 'Triad' of Evolution

We have seen that the 'laws of growth' converge on a teleological
scheme which directs the course of evolution. How does Meredith
conceive of the development as a whole? What is to him the history
of life, and what may be its future?

It is essentially the history of man. Behind man lies an animal
past which has interest mainly in so far as it still haunts the present
with its atavistic features, and serves to explain human nature.
Meredith's exploration begins in that phase of transition where
animal slowly transmutes into man: where his moral and spiritual
nature awakens. Spencer and Darwin have taught him the
importance of environment and adaptation at this stage, and the
nineteenth-century passion for historical interpretation furnishes the
clue to the evolutionary process. For: 'hearing History speak, of
what men were,/And have become. .' one may grasp the secret of
Earth:[3]

Historic be the survey of our kind,
And how their brave Society took shape.
Lion, wolf, vulture, fox, jackal and ape,
The strong of limb, the keen of nose, we find,
Who, with some jars in harmony, combined,

[1] *Foresight and Patience*, 26, p. 95.
[2] *The Thrush in February*, 25, p. 223.
[3] *Earth's Secret*, 25, p. 13.

Their primal instincts taming, to escape
The brawl indecent, and hot passions drape.
Convenience pricked conscience, that the mind.
Thus entered they the field of milder beasts,
Which in some sort of civil order graze,
And do half-homage to the God of Laws.
But are they still for their old ravenous feasts,
Earth gives the edifice they build no base:
They spring another flood of fangs and claws.[1]

Here the view of emotional discipline and of social integration appears to be purely naturalistic and utilitarian: moral instincts evolve through experience of what is most useful. This usefulness is, however, part of the purpose of Earth or the vital force, and in claiming that this purpose runs counter to animal aggression, Meredith avoids Huxley's dilemma of two different processes, one natural and one ethical.

Primeval man was a creature which Meredith contemplates with mingled feelings. From Rousseau's tradition, and from the Romantics, he may have inherited an admiration for the first men, who had 'the beauty of frank animals'.[2] Inconsistently with his evolutionary view he claims in *The Empty Purse* (in the spirit of Rousseau) that there was an age when something like infant innocence reigned: when 'the young chief of the animals' was 'unaware/Of his love of himself..', and therefore, 'Fair was that season'. But it lasted only 'Till entered the craving for more..', till the evil voice of the Ego tempted man: '*Not thou as commoner men!*' That was the Fall, and from that moment the Garden of Eden became a scene of strife, a Hobbesian state. In this world of natural selection—'Woe to the weak!'. Meredith sheds a harsh,

[1] *Society*, 25, p. 271. See also *Progress*, 25, p. 16; *Forest History*, 26, pp. 212—17.
[2] *Foresight and Patience*, 26, p. 91.

satirical light on it, and on this 'Original man ... Carnivorous, cannibal':

> Gross, with the fumes of incense full,
> With parasites tickled, with slaves begirt,
> He strutted, a cock, he bellowed, a bull,
>   He rolled him, a dog, in dirt.
> And dog, bull, cock, was he, fanged, horned, plumed;
>
> . . . . .
> Frightfully living and armed to devour . . .[1]

This is the stage when to be strong and bold and cunning is a condition of survival; here Darwin's law is important. But it is not the only one. Present man, the outcome of the struggle, may seem a 'wanton's choice', emerging through sheer brute force and a mechanical selective process, but if he has managed in the course of his long and turbulent history to transfer 'the battle to his brain/From bloody ground', it is not owing to chance or to his qualities as the fittest fighter. It is due to his purgatory of pain, to common sense, to religion, to love. Meredith never loses sight of 'the internal goad' that spurs man and enables him, at last, to strike 'through crimson mire'.[2]

It was probably from the Hegelian tradition, and from Comte, that Meredith got his idea of the three phases of human evolution, forming a 'Triad' of 'blood'—'brain'—'spirit':

> Each of each in sequent birth,
> Blood and brain and spirit, three
> (Say the deepest gnomes of Earth),
>   Join for true felicity.[3]

---

[1] *Op. cit.* vol. 26, pp. 35, 37, 38.
[2] *The Test of Manhood*, 26, pp. 206, 203.
[3] *The Woods of Westermain*, 25, p. 43.—W. Zeddies's thesis is that Meredith borrowed the *Dynamik* of Comte (*op. cit.*, p. 59), and relates, on the whole convincingly, the 'Triad' to his three stages (p. 65 ff.). However,

Each stage represents a predominant quality in human nature at a certain period, yet the three aspects continue to live side by side, interacting with one another, and gradually modified and refined in the evolutionary growth. Meredith knows the meaning of organic continuity, for: 'All forces that make us are one full stream.'[1] He sees that man retains features 'Of that bestial multiform' which was his ancestry, and that he is 'Made warm by the numbers compact'.[2] It is the glory of evolution to have treasured up the best and most enduring qualities from all three stages and advanced to a point where they are harmoniously balanced. To destroy this balance is fatal:

> Are they parted, then expect
> Some one sailing will be wrecked. .[3]

That is why Meredith describes the first, animal phase—'blood'—in terms of moral condemnation whenever it casts atavistic shadows upon the present. He has a wide range of pejorative names for the creatures and qualities belonging to this stage, such as 'Worm', 'Dragon', 'Monster', 'brute', 'snake', and 'our grim little beast-god'.[4] From these man has inherited the 'blood' or sensual, greedy part of his nature where dwells the 'passion Self'—the 'old devil of a thousand lures' which shatters his own harmony and hides from him that of Earth:

the parallel seems forced as regards the second phase, 'brain'—'metaphysical stage'; (cf. p. 68). 'Brain' and 'Mind' are with Meredith not merely or mainly the instrument of metaphysical speculation ('Whence', 'Whither'), nor are they something of the past. They are man's chief means of knowing reality; cf. *Hard Weather* (25, p. 213): 'Never is Earth misread by brain'.

[1] *The Empty Purse*, 26, p. 50; see also *The Thrush in February*, 25, p. 225, 'a flame, a stream./Flame, stream are we ...'.
[2] *Ibid.* pp. 39, 42.
[3] *The Woods of Westermain*, 25, p. 43.
[4] See *ibid., passim*; the last reference is to *The Empty Purse*, 26, p. 42.

Through terror, through distrust;
The greed to touch, to view, to have, to live:
Through all that makes of him a sensitive
Abhorring dust.

Behold his wormy home!
And he the wind-whipped, anywhither wave
Crazily tumbled on a shingle-grave
To waste in foam.[1]

These are the passions which Meredith in his *Ode to the Spirit of Earth in Autumn* sacrifices on the altar of Mother Earth, to have instead her grace of harmony and joy, and this is a sacrifice demanded of all her children.

In the allegorical Woods of Westermain there are vestiges of the savage rule of the Self:

> that world
> Where the tiger claws the snake,
> Snake her tiger clasps unfurled,
> And the issue of their fight
> Peoples lands in snarling plight.[2]

There we come face to face with hideous embodiments of the 'blood' and the Ego. Yet it is a world of change, in which love and pain are at work to transform the brute: love now leads 'her splendid beast' with 'unfelt constraint'; and the 'scaly Dragon-fowl', once 'growling o'er his bone', is changed and changing, so that his fangs are put to uses, his armour stripped off.[3] Thus he emerges, tamed, but with his old strength uncrippled and made to serve. Then, again, there is the 'Monster'—'flesh', slowly refined in its purgatory of pain.

---

[1] *Earth and Man,* 25, st. xviii, xix.
[2] *Op. cit.,* 25, p. 37.
[3] *Ibid.,* pp. 37, 38, 39, 40.

And, as we look back upon the paths of Westermain, reflecting on what men were and have become, then it is an encouraging and fruitful sight.[1] We see that Earth not only brings forth life, but also the forces which discipline and cure. Yet, the taming may not be final:

> In yourself may lurk the trap:
> . . . . . .
> Doubt you with the monster's fry
> All his orbit may exclude;
> Are you of the stiff, the dry,
> Cursing the not understood;
> Grasp you with the monster's claws;
> Govern with his truncheon-saws;
> Hate, the shadow of a grain;
> You are lost in Westermain . . .[2]

Give in to egoism, submit to the rule of 'blood', allow aggression and hatred to take command, and man is once more back in the 'lair'—'Given to bones and ogre-broods'.[3]

The first stage of human evolution is indeed 'red in tooth and claw', and Meredith is much concerned with its upsurge in civilized man; for, he admits, no matter how far he has advanced, man still, in Darwin's fine phrase, 'bears within his bodily frame the indelible stamp of his lowly origin'.[4] Tennyson, who saw evolution as an aspect of his theistic cosmology, did not brand the 'ape' and 'tiger' in man as a source of 'sin', but as the spring of disharmony and hatred. Similarly, when Meredith in his poetry is at pains to show how urgent is the need of working out the beast (or taming him), and how the beast actually has been worked out in the course of history, he is relating the evolutionary process to an ethical necessity or purpose underlying it all. Though he is more confident in

[1] *Ibid.*, p. 45.   [2] *Ibid.*, p. 46.   [3] *Ibid.*, p. 47.
[4] *The Descent of Man*, 1871, p. 405.

252

his 'forward view' than T. H. Huxley, and sees the organic and ethical processes as merely different aspects of the one creative force, Meredith faces the ethical problems of man in society from the same angle as the author of 'Evolution and Ethics'.[1] The ape and tiger were 'the boon companions of man's hot youth', but now their intrusion into his ordered society is disastrous. This is Meredith's version:

> Then our forefather hoof did its work in the wood,
>> By right of the better in kind.
> But now will it breed yon bestial brood
> Three-fold thrice over, if bent to bind,
>> As the healthy in chains with the sick,
> Unto despot usage our issuing mind.[2]

Huxley's naturalistic interpretation of 'original sin' as our animal, aggressive instincts appears also to have a parallel in Meredith's faith that the 'rules' of Earth bid man 'wash foul sins'.[3]

There is in Meredith, as in his neo-Platonic forbears Tennyson and Browning, a marked conflict between 'flesh' and 'spirit', even though to him these are integral aspects of the one reality—of Earth.[4] Yet, where Tennyson appeals: 'let the ape and tiger die', Meredith advises that they be tamed. For he sees them, both past and present, as valuable instincts or forces created by Mother Earth —her 'essays in being', intensely alive and strong and daring. These are qualities we still need, always need, and they must somehow be preserved and put to use. Meredith, says G. M. Trevelyan,

wages metaphorical war on the 'dragon of self'; but it is not a war to the knife. He has a sympathetic acquaintance with the creature

---

[1] Cf. *supra*, p. 48.   [2] *The Empty Purse*, 26, p. 46.
[3] *Earth and Man*, 25, st. xxx. Also *The Comic Spirit*, 26, p. 66.
[4] Cf. W. Zeddies, who lists a number of contrasting terms which illustrate this dualism or *Polarität* through which his view of evolution moves, *op. cit.*, p. 63.

and his ways, and shows him a wise, fatherly tenderness, paring his claws, taming, civilizing, and ennobling his qualities. But any attempt to kill him, Mr. Meredith considers an attempt at murder which is invariably unsuccessful.[1]

Through the purgatory of pain, through inner urge and love and pleasure, the first stage—'blood'—gradually gives way to a new kind of life. There comes a time when the human animal—*homo erectus*—projects his selfish cravings into dreams and myths. This new departure might be claimed as a parallel to Comte's theological stage.[2] Now man is 'catching at comfort near' in his 'Revelations in legends'; these are 'Desired of the flesh in affright', and Meredith denounces them as 'our sensual dreams'.[3] In this phase man 'drank of fictions, till celestial aid/Might seem accorded when he fawned and prayed', and all the time he was bent on satisfying the Ego.[4] For this, however, he was punished, and is still punished, for while he is 'Crying loud for an opiate boon/To comfort the human want', he alienates himself from reality, and suffers frustration in return.[5] It was in similar terms that George Eliot, pioneering Comte in England and otherwise instructed by Feuerbach and Strauss, explained the religious need of 'opium'. The faith which Meredith tries out in the ordeal of his personal grief is, in fact, the Positivistic creed in a somewhat unusual pantheistic setting. And therefore, after this exposure of the 'Legends' and 'Questions' (Whence-Whither?) follows, as one might expect, a tolerant retrospect of History, in which Mother Earth contemplates these errors of the past (and present), and

---

[1] *Op. cit.*, p. 161: see also this author's discussion of Meredith's attitude to asceticism, p. 174, and J. B. Priestley's treatment of the same subject, *op. cit.*, p. 75.

[2] Cf. Zeddies, *op. cit.*, p. 67.

[3] *A Faith on Trial*, 25, pp. 251—2.

[4] *The Test of Manhood*, 26, p. 201.

[5] *A Faith on Trial*, 25, p. 256.

> smiles on, marking their source:
> They read her with infant eyes.
> Good ships of morality they,
> For our crude developing force ...[1]

Or, in Comte's own words, if 'Humanity definitely occupies the place of God ... she does not forget the services which the idea of God provisionally rendered'.[2]

The religious legends and myths are natural projections of the Self at a primitive, pre-rational stage of evolution, and admittedly they have been useful in developing man's emotional and moral nature. Through them man was first 'Celestially released' from his Ego.[3] Moreover, Earth was first 'religiously divined' by man, and thus religion marks a first step towards truth.[4]

As a poet-thinker, however, Meredith is not at pains to build a rigid geometrical system, such as the *Lois des Trois États,* and though he has no doubt learned a great deal from Comte, his own evolutionary 'Triad' is less clear and definite than the development-structure of the *Philosophie Positive.* There is a great deal of vagueness in his vision of man's ascent from the animal level to the next, where 'blood' gives birth to 'brain' (or 'Mind', 'Reason'). He knows that the transition has been endlessly slow and complex, like all organic growth, and determined by the 'internal goad' as well as by environment. What was the nature of this 'brain'-birth, this intellectual awakening in man, when 'Animal-infant' his 'mind began'? As an evolutionary event it is certainly previous in time to the vaguely corresponding metaphysical stage which in Comte's system destroyed the theological one. Part of the answer is given in another

---

[1] *Ibid.,* p. 256.
[2] *The Catechism of Positive Religion,* Congreve's trans. (1858), concl.
[3] *The Empty Purse,* 26, p. 40.
[4] *The Test of Manhood,* 26, p. 203.

version of Meredith's recurrent theme: 'Historic be the survey of our kind':

> Like a flood river whirled at rocky banks,
> An army issues out of wilderness,
> With battle plucking round its ragged flanks;
> Obstruction in the van; insane excess
> Oft at the heart; yet hard the onward stress
> Unto more spacious, where move ordered ranks,
> And rise hushed temples built of shapely stone,
> The work of hands not pledged to grind or slay.
> They gave our earth a dress of flesh on bone;
> A tongue to speak with answering heaven gave they.
> Then was the gracious birth of man's new day;
> Divided from the haunted night it shone.

> That quiet dawn was Reverence . . .[1]

This was the age when brute Force was 'fast conjoined' with Love to create peace and harmony. The 'Reverence' is an awakening to religious consciousness and practice within a 'brotherhood', and Meredith distinguishes between the Reverence thus born of fellowship and the religious motives of the individual Ego. These latter are hungers and dreams closed on the Self, and these 'Ascend no sacred Mounts'.[2] Meredith, still hunting the 'Self' and concerned throughout with the 'soul of brotherhood', makes here a curious and arbitrary distinction between the sources of religious feeling. In the spirit of Comte, he oversimplifies the psychological and social

---

[1] *The Test of Manhood*, 26, p. 200.—Cf. the 'flood' and 'stream' symbolism in *The Thrush in February*, 25, p. 225; *Foresight and Patience*, 26, p. 89. For Meredith's use of 'Reverence' see *Forest History*, 26, st. xxix; Cf. also W. Zeddies' comment, *op. cit.*, p. 69. G. M. Trevelyan discusses the significance of 'Dawn' as a symbol of man's spiritual growth, *op. cit.*, pp. 84—5.

[2] *Ibid.*, p. 201.

basis of worship, and this contrasts starkly with his otherwise complex intuition of human development. It would appear that the distinction he is making between egoistic, transcendental ('celestial') cult and communal religion is related to Stuart Mill's apology of the Religion of Humanity in his essay *Theism*.[1]

Even if Meredith sees 'brain' as a 'flower' of organic growth from animal nature, and one with it, he, no less than Tennyson and Browning, celebrates it as the attainment which places man apart from the rest of creatures. Man is a new and significant event in the growth of Earth through her children: 'Earth was not Earth before her sons appeared'.[2] In him she has grown 'conscient' and 'sensitive'; he is her 'great venture' and her 'chief expression':[3]

> Him she owes
> For half her loveliness a love well won
> By work that lights the shapeless and the dun,
> Their common foes.
>
> He builds the soaring spires,
> That sing his soul in stone: of her he draws,
> Though blind to her, by spelling at her laws,
> Her purest fires.
>
> Through him hath she exchanged,
> For the gold harvest-robes, the mural crown,
> Her haggard quarry-features and thick frown
> Where monsters ranged.
>
> And order, high discourse,
> And decency, than which is life less dear,
> She has of him: the lyre of language clear,
> Love's tongue and source.[4]

[1] See *supra*. p. 62.   [2] *Appreciation*, 25, p. 15.
[3] *Earth and Man*, 25, i, xliv.   [4] *Ibid.*, xxiv—xxvii.

Among these glories which mark the otherness of man are the 'soaring spires'—expressions of his soul, monuments over his 'Reverence'. The stanzas are a hymn to the beauty of mind, and to the intellectual, material and ethical achievements of the human being.

'Reverence' then, is the dawn of religion and culture and appears to be a transitional stage leading to the birth of 'brain'. When brain emerges within the evolutionary 'Triad', religion is slowly superseded by metaphysical speculation—the questions 'Whence and Whither?'. Again, Comte might be perceived in the background.[1] But these questions are not characteristic of Meredith's conception of brain-activity; they are still seen as part of 'our sensual dreams' and 'Legends'.[2] Brain, to Meredith, is above all the faculty which enables man to read Earth more correctly: 'Never is Earth misread by brain.'[3] Thus he hails the 'warriors of the sighting brain' who lead Humanity from the 'bestial to the higher breed'; who have gained wisdom and harmony of Earth, because: 'The sighting brain her good decree/Accepts.'[4] Brain, therefore, is not chiefly concerned with metaphysics; it is intellect, understanding, empirical exploration of reality.[5] And, as J. B. Priestley points out, 'brain' in Meredith's vague terminology often means 'the universal rationalising power that gives man true insight and enables him to bring harmony into his life.'[6]

Owing to this intellectual, realistic function, it would seem futile to force the analogy of 'brain' with Comte's metaphysical stage.

[1] Cf. W. Zeddies, *op. cit.*, p. 68.
[2] See *A Faith on Trial*, 25, pp. 250, 252.
[3] *Hard Weather*, 25, p. 213.
[4] *The Thrush in February*, 25, pp. 223, 225.
[5] Cf. *A Faith on Trial*, p. 252; *The Empty Purse*, 26, pp. 41, 45.
[6] *Op. cit.*, p. 78.—Yet it can hardly be claimed, as Priestley does, that 'brain' is 'Reason' in the Coleridgean sense, for to Coleridge Reason is 'the organ of the supersensuous'. Meredith's brain-concept is more directly related to Coleridge's 'Understanding'.

When Meredith places 'brain' second in his 'Triad' and claims that it comes from 'blood' in 'sequent birth', he simply means that human history reveals an increasing presence of intellectual activity, of thoughtful and inductive observation of reality. With brain came a wider conquest and understanding of the natural and social environment, and, more important still, a firmer discipline of the self. The men who have earned their title to 'read Earth' are those who have 'mastered sensation'—the 'blood'—

> And out of the sensual hive
> Grown to the flower of brain;
> To know her a thing alive,
> Whose aspects mutably swerve,
> Whose laws immutably reign.[1]

Brain is the Earth's 'prize of gifts,/Sky of the senses!'[2] There is a close interaction between intellectual growth and moral discipline, on this Meredith agrees with Spencer.[3] Greater harmony, a more complete social integration is achieved through the 'brain-rule' (Reason, Common Sense) over the senses. Human nature remains a discord until 'The rebel, the heart, yields place/To brain'.[4] When Meredith asserts that the 'Real' is 'the root of the growth of man', he is thinking of the double stimulus to human development, intellectual and moral, which the challenge of Earth provides.[5] Hence his appeal to Antaeus—'young giant'—to 'strike Earth', for in thus coming to grips with Reality, he will find 'a saving fact', and the 'poisonous' in him will be 'purged'; for then his 'roots have grasp in the stern-exact'.[6]

[1] *A Faith on Trial*, 25, pp. 255—6.
[2] *Hard Weather*, 25, p. 213.
[3] Cf. *supra*, p. 37.
[4] *A Faith on Trial*, 25, p. 250; cf. also *The Woods of Westermain*, 25, pp. 42—3.
[5] Cf. *A Faith on Trial*, p. 252.
[6] *The Empty Purse*, 26, pp. 41—2.

Life and Death, we remember, were basic forces or laws in the creative process. Meredith describes them as 'Reality's flower', for

> Of them, and the contact with them,
> Issues Earth's dearest daughter, the firm
> In footing, the stately of stem;
> Unshaken though elements lour;
> A warrior heart unquelled;
> Mirror of Earth, and guide
> To the Holies from sense withheld:
> Reason, man's germinant fruit.
> She wrestles with our old worm
> Self in the narrow and wide:
> Relentless quencher of lies,
> With laughter she pierces the brute; ..[1]

Reason, synonymous with brain, is celebrated as a means of intellectual advance and moral discipline; it is increased understanding followed by greater self-control. Along with the emotional purgatory, and with Reverence, Reason has been the most active force in the taming process, hunting primitive man out of his 'dens' and 'monstrous bed' and hounding him 'to harrow and plough'.[2] Brain-rule, Common Sense, as Meredith asserted in his *Essay on Comedy,* is the foundation of social life. Yet, the process of social integration derives from a complexity of causes, like that of the evolution of human nature, which it reflects, and Meredith keeps steadily before our eyes the many laws of growth which have made man and his society.[3] Thus suffering was ever conducive to the

---

[1] *A Faith on Trial,* p. 253.

[2] *Ibid.* p. 254; see also *Ode to the Comic Spirit,* 26, *passim,* and *The Empty Purse,* p. 40; for 'taming' idea cf. *Foresight and Patience,* 26, pp. 97—8.

[3] The process, with reference to social integration, is outlined in the *Ode to Youth in Memory,* but emphasis is here more on the effect of love.

growth of human qualities, and so of brain: The 'races' begin in 'barbarous force' and inherit from their forbears self-seeking and bellicosity, and not until they clash in battle and bleed and suffer do they realize the need of controlled strength:

> Then may sharp suffering their nature grind;
> Of rabble passions grow the chieftain Mind.[1]

Here recurs the idea that 'Convenience pricked conscience, that the mind', expressed in *Society:* through painful experience mankind learned to reflect upon its condition and destiny, and to solve by reason problems earlier solved by force.[2]

Or, again, it was Love which guided man out of his animal past to a deeper understanding of existence:

> This way have men come out of brutishness
> To spell the letters of the sky and read
> A reflex upon earth else meaningless..[3]

And all along there was this interaction between growing reason and moral consciousness which leads on to harmony, individual and universal. Meredith worships Reason, or Brain, not for giving us knowledge, as such, but for its power to mould and direct the growth of human nature. Hence his prayer: 'Let but the rational prevail',[4] and his wish for 'The young generation':

> May it be braver than ours,
>
> . . . .
>
> May it know how the mind in expansion revolts
> From a nursery Past with dead letters aloof,

---

[1] *Foresight and Patience,* 26, p. 96.
[2] Cf. *The Comic Spirit,* 26, p. 56.
[3] *Hymn to Colour,* 25, st. xiii.
[4] *Alsace-Lorraine,* 26, p. 163.

261

> And the piping to stupor of Precedents shun,
> In a field where the forefather print of the hoof
> Is not yet overgrassed by the watering hours,
> And should prompt us to Change, as to promise of sun,
>   Till brain-rule splendidly towers.[1]

And:

> May brain democratic be king of the host!

For 'From the head runs the paved firm way for advance.'.[2]

Meredith often dwells on the taming and civilizing process in which the 'blood' or 'senses' are brought under the control of Reason and Love. It is an 'ancient battle', a 'fight' from which Reason mounts 'lordly and a quenchless force'; or a wrestling:

> And long with him was wrestling ere emerged
> A mind to read in him the reflex shade
> Of its fierce torment; ..[3]

Since Meredith places so much importance on 'brain-rule' and reason as a means of moral discipline, his outlook on ethical progress inevitably revives that tenet of eighteenth-century rationalist doctrine which claims that evil is mainly a consequence of error and ignorance. Like the teachers of the age of Enlightenment, he describes moral evolution as an ascent out of night and blindness to clear vision and light: When the mind emerged from its 'animal tangle' and its wrestling with the senses, climbing to a point where it was possible to objectify and understand the nature of its torment, then

[1] *The Empty Purse*, 26, p. 45.
[2] *Ibid.*, pp. 46—7.
[3] Quoted in sequence, *The Woods of Westermain*, 25, pp. 36, 37, 42; *The Test of Manhood*, 26, p. 202.

The man's mind opened under weight of cloud.
To penetrate the dark was it endowed;
Stood day before a vision shooting wide.
Whereat the spectral enemy lost form;
The traversed wilderness exposed its track.
He felt the far advance in looking back;
Thence trust in his foot forward through the storm.[1]

It was then that, seeing himself clearly, he became 'as mirror raised among his kind', gaining understanding of others, and thus 'of brotherhood had sight'. With his mind—like 'a forehead lamp'—exploring this new aspect of existence, man was able to discover the spiritual significance of what had hitherto been a material, 'palpable' world.[2] Now reason is 'the main central light/That gives direction'.[3] Mankind is climbing a 'steep', up the 'fleshly road to beacon-fire of brain', whence 'new light illumes/The dusky web of evil, known as pain.[4] In his 'clear mind' man will see

Evil in a world unread before;
That mystery to simple springs resolved.
His God the Known, diviner to adore,
Shows Nature's savage riddles kindly solved.[5]

Elsewhere Meredith describes our heart ('blood') as a 'force blind-eyed,/On endless rounds of aimless reach', groping in the dark until 'Light of the mind, the mind's discourse,/The rational in graciousness' enthroned reason (or common sense) 'To tame and lead'. It

---

[1] *The Test of Manhood*, p. 202.
[2] *Ibid.* p.203.
[3] *The Comic Spirit*, 26, p. 57.
[4] *Youth in Memory*, 26, p. 72.
[5] *The Test of Manhood*, p. 204.
[6] *The Comic Spirit*, 26, pp. 62—3.

is Reason which directs the 'flame' of life—the life-impulse—upwards through the world-tree:

> the mind that steers,
> By Reason led, her way of tree and flame...[1]

The recurrent tree-image, charged with biological and evolutionary significance, reminds us that this is an organic world—Mother Earth—and Reason is part of its teleological movement.[2] Earth, in her unceasing effort at growth and change

> feels her blood-tree throbbing in her grain,
> Yet skyward branched, with loftier mark and range.
> No miracle the sprout of wheat from clod,
> She knows, nor growth of man in grisly brute;
> But he, the flower at head and soil at root,
> Is miracle, guides he the brute to God.
> And that way seems he bound; that way the road,
> With his dark-lantern mind, unled, alone,
> Wearifully through forest-tracks unsown,
> He travels, urged by some internal goad.[3]

Thus, in the growth from 'blood' to 'brain' Meredith sees two trends, an intellectual and a moral (emotional), interacting, and stimulating the evolutionary process. It is, on the one hand, a movement from wrong (egoism, aggression) to right conduct and value (love, brotherhood), and on the other, from falsehood, self-delusion (error, ignorance) to truth. It follows that Meredith conceives the 'brain'-stage of his 'Triad' as a destructive phase in which 'Obstruction' is slain and the ground cleared for a new seed-time. In this

[1] *Ibid.*, p. 66.
[2] Cf. *supra*, p. 242.
[3] *The Test of Manhood*, 26, p. 206.

264

aspect it conforms to the metaphysical stage of Positivism. Comte praised the metaphysical 'school' for its achievement

> to break up a system which, having directed the early growth of the human mind and society, tended to protract that infantile period: and thus, the political triumph of the metaphysical school was a necessary preparation for the advent of the positive school, for which the task is exclusively reserved of terminating the revolutionary period by the formation of a system uniting Order with Progress.[1]

In his *Ode to the Comic Spirit*, Meredith similarly rejoices in the warfare of Reason against untruth. The 'prized objects' once 'raised for prayer',

> Are sounded by thee, and thou darest probe
> Old institutions and establishments,
> Once fortresses against the floods of sin,
> For what their worth; and questioningly prod
> For why they stand upon a racing globe,
> Impeding blocks, less useful than the clod;
> Their angel out of them, a demon in.[2]

It is the twilight of the gods which Swinburne celebrated in *Hertha*. The passage looks back upon a great deal of what had happened to doctrinal structures since the beginning of the century, through the influence of Feuerbach and Strauss, through Comte and Stuart Mill, through Spencer, Darwin and Huxley.

Browning, it will be recalled, had also seen the temples crumble and fall and rise again serving the 'prime purpose' and dedicated to God, the unchanging truth. In the new Order through which Swinburne and Meredith move, the gods have vanished for ever, but Truth remains—Truth is living and whole, and the human

---

[1] *Positive Philosophy*, transl. by H. Martineau, (1875 ed.), vol. ii, p. 9.
[2] P. 66.

mind has an increasing grasp on it. This is the faith which informs *Foresight and Patience*, a poem from the last decade of the century (1894), and here Meredith faces more directly the intellectual and social predicaments of his age. The dialogue, somewhat in the manner of Browning, has several echoes from the topical controversies and from the *Zeitgeist* in general. Thus Foresight complains to Patience that the age has no care for either of them, for:

> Its learning is through Science to despair.[1]

It is not, however, the despair of Tennyson's and Matthew Arnold's gloomy scenes, but of disharmony, lack of balance in human nature. Still, Patience has faith: 'This Age climbs earth'; Foresight retorts that it is but 'To challenge heaven', and looks out on a landscape of strife and destruction, not unlike that in Browning's *Fifine at the Fair:*

> —But your fierce Yes and No of butting heads
> Now rages to outdo a horny Past.
> Shades of a wild Destroyer on the vast
> Are thrown by every novel light upraised.
> The world's whole round smokes ominously, amazed
> And trembling...[2]

And there are 'other features' in this age:

> Faithless, mean;
> Encased in matter; vowed to Gods obscene;
> Contemptuous of the impalpable, it swells
> On Doubt ...[3]

These accusations appear to be partly Meredith's own grievances, partly those of the anxious sensitive minds of his time. The poem

---

[1] Vol. 26, p. 92.
[2] *Ibid.*   [3] *Ibid.*, p. 95.

moves on through the point-counterpoint of this dialectic analysis until at last, triumphantly, a reconciliation is achieved, in 'Philosophy':

> Philosophy is Life's one match for Fate.[1]

Meredith sees beyond the scene of strife and disruption to where 'the Chieftain Mind mounts over them serene', to guide the world and speed its progress.

Science, despite the warning heard in this poem, is a fruit of the 'brain' and precious indeed. In *The Olive Branch,* Meredith describes it as a 'fair propitious Dove' carrying its message of peace and harmony about the world:

> Let Science, swiftly as she can
> Fly seaward on from shore to shore,
> And bind the links of man to man...[2]

Thus science too is caught into the evolutionary process in a way which reminds us that to Meredith it is not intellectual conquest and knowledge that matter, but the discipline which mind, Reason, imposes upon the 'blood' and the 'senses', to further social integration.

The evolutionary phase of 'brain'—to sum up—is a period of intellectual expansion, with advances in understanding, knowledge, scientific truth, and, above all, an increasing control of Reason over our aggressive Self. It marks a half-way attainment in the 'Triad' and leads directly on to the next stage—'Spirit'.

'Spirit' is a vaguer concept than either 'blood' or 'brain' and its function and range less clearly formulated. Nor is it always distinguished from 'Reason' or 'Mind' which characterize the preceding

---

[1] *Ibid.,* p. 97.
[2] Vol. 24, p. 15.

stage. Indeed Meredith's semantics are those of a poet and prophet, and not of a logical positivist.

How did 'Spirit' emerge and first manifest itself? We are told, dogmatically, in *A Faith on Trial* that 'from flesh unto spirit man grows'.[1] It is the finest fruit of organic growth, and comes with

> Pleasures that through blood run sane,
> Quickening spirit from the brain.[2]

It springs from the harmonious interaction of bodily and mental energies.[3] As 'brain' is the 'sky of the senses' or the highest development of animal instincts and faculties, so 'spirit' comes from this 'in sequent birth' and rises to a higher level still:

> on which height,
> Not disconnected, yet released,
> They see how spirit comes to light,
> Through conquest of the inner beast.[4]

'Brain' is the 'station for the flight of soul', or 'Spirit'.[5]

What is the relationship between 'Brain' (or 'Reason') and 'Spirit' ('Soul') and how does 'Spirit' mark an advance on the faculty from which it is born? When liberated from the senses,

> 'Tis Reason herself, tiptoe
> At the ultimate bound of her wit,
> On the verges of Night and Day.[6]

[1] Vol. 25, p. 255.
[2] *The Woods of Westermain*, 25, p. 43.
[3] Cf. also *A Faith on Trial*, p. 250.
[4] *Hard Weather*, 25, p. 213; see also *The State of Age*, 25, p. 16.
[5] *Ibid.*, p. 214.
[6] *A Faith on Trial*, p. 257.

268

'Spirit' emerges as a higher kind of Reason, no longer merely observing and classifying facts, but with a power to interrelate and unify.[1] It is rational penetration lifted up to a level of intuitive 'embrace', and therefore straining to explore the borderland between the known and the unknown. Does this mean that with 'Spirit' the metaphysical 'Questions'—'Whence and Whither?' have slipped into Meredith's preoccupation by a back door? Has he given up his claim on the 'stern-exact' to follow the quest of the 'Spirit' into the unknowable? It would seem that 'Spirit' expands his temporal vista, and gives him something like a millennial or even transcendent faith, as when he asserts that 'Spirit' points to

> Ambrosial heights of possible acquist,
> Where souls of men with soul of man consort..[2]

But this is transcendence-language simply describing the moral ascent here on earth.[3] Meredith uses 'Spirit' and 'Soul' synonymously, and their ethical significance is throughout predominant:

> 'To my quenchless quick shall speed
> The soul at her wrestle rude
> With devil, with angel more dire;
> With the flesh, with the Fates, enringed.[4]

Like 'brain', the 'soul' harmonizes and disciplines: it is the highest attainment of that striving towards consciousness and order which is unconscious in the plant and in the 'blood', conscious but only partially fulfilled in 'brain' or 'Reason'. It is

---

[1] Cf. *The Test of Manhood*, 26, p. 204; *The Woods of Westermain*, 25, p. 43.
[2] *The Comic Spirit*, 26, p. 65.
[3] Cf. also *Hymn to Colour*, 25, xiv.
[4] *A Faith on Trial*, 25, p. 258.

> sprung of an aim
> Supernal of Reason, to find
> The great Over-Reason we name
> Beneficence: mind seeking Mind.[1]

J. B. Priestley comments on the difficulty in distinguishing between 'brain' and 'spirit' in Meredith's inconsistent use of these terms; 'Sometimes, indeed more often than not, 'brain' simply means the intellect, which, when in harmony with the body, together with it brings forth spirit or soul'.[2] More helpful, perhaps, is the definition given by G. M. Trevelyan: 'The soul is the flushing of the blood, of the cold intellectual by the hot animal. On the spiritual plane, it is passion guided by reason, thought ennobled by emotion.'[3] Thought, that is, spurred by feeling to a heightened awareness of the relations and meanings which exist between beings and things. 'Spirit' (and 'Soul'), then, is something like the gift of the poet: an intuitive power relating man with eternal truth, without slavish reference to empirical knowledge or causal connexions, but which never loses hold of the sensuous and the concrete—Earth. Thus, while Meredith's conception of Spirit is like Coleridge's Imagination-Reason in this power of synthesis, in which 'a more than usual state of emotion' fuses with 'more than usual order',[4] it is unlike it in being always rooted in the sensuous and interacting with the whole of human nature.

'Spirit' or 'Soul' is the outcome of all evolutionary growth and experience; it is, so to speak, a faculty of remembering all things past and seeing them in relationship with all things present. It is a Memory able to

[1] *Ibid.*, p. 259.
[2] *Op. cit.*, p. 77.
[3] *Op. cit.*, p. 178.
[4] *Biographia Literaria*, ch. xiv.

grasp all human truth
Sowed by us down the mazy paths behind.
To feel that heaven must we that hell sound through:
Whence comes a line of continuity,
That brings our middle station into view,
Between those poles; a novel Earth we see,
In likeness of us, made of banned and blest;
The sower's bed, but not the reaper's rest:
An Earth alive with meanings, wherein meet
Buried, and breathing, and to be.
Then of the junction of the three,
Even as a heart in brain, full sweet
May sense of soul, the sum of music, beat.[1]

Again, the purgatory trend of ethical evolution is interwoven with
that of intellectual growth. When conceived as an organic whole,
a product of a continuous process, the human being appears, to
Meredith, to fit into something like the rationalistic scheme of
plenitude: a half-way attainment between animal and God. 'Middle
station' sounds like an echo from eighteenth century speculations
upon the Scale of Life or the Chain of Being, and in particular
from Pope's *Essay*, though the intention could hardly be more different. A similar pattern, associated with the birth of spirit from
blood and brain, occurs in *Foresight and Patience*, where man is
seen both as 'cowering angel' and 'upright beast'.[2] In both poems
the theme is the pilgrimage of man towards harmony—'the sum
of music'.

With this gift of the soul (spirit) to see the fragmentary aspects
of life as one, comes also an understanding of the universal movement of being: it points a direction:

[1] *Youth in Memory*, 26, p. 71.
[2] Vol. 26, p. 89; cf. also the 'mid career' in *The Thrush in February*,
25, p. 225.

Nor sectional will varied Life appear:
Perforce of soul discerned in mind, we hear
Earth with her Onward chime, with Winter Spring.
. . . . .
Know in our seasons an integral wheel,
That rolls us to a mark may yet be willed.[1]

And, finally, with Spirit comes Philosophy (as with Brain Science):

That photosphere of our high fountain One,
Our spirit's Lord and Reason's fostering sun,
Philosophy, shall light us in the shade,
Warm in the frost, make Good our aim and aid.[2]

Spirit, Philosophy—these are our means of integrating knowledge in such a way that it acquires an ethical significance, through these alone we recognize right conduct and value. Therefore, Meredith welcomes Philosophy to supersede the fanaticism of Religion and Science alike, for the one fosters sensualism and egoism, the other cold asceticism—both equally harmful to the 'balanced man' which is his ideal.

A great deal of Meredith's poetry, and notably the *Odes*, is concerned with the harmony of 'blood', 'brain' and 'spirit'—which he marks as the goal of human evolution.[3] It is 'A sober world that walks the balanced mean/Between its tempters',—a world where the mystery of Evil is explained, and Earth—man's 'God the Known,

[1] *Youth in Memory*, p. 74; cf. *The Empty Purse*, 26, p. 54.
[2] *Foresight and Patience*, 26, p. 97.
[3] This is also the main theme of Meredith's novels. See J. B. Priestley: 'It is ... no little part of Meredith's task as a novelist to show us how these three are often parted and how 'some one sailing' is either wrecked or is speeded "between the ascetic rocks and the sensual whirlpools"'; *op. cit.*, p. 77.

diviner to adore,/Shows Nature's savage riddles kindly solved...'.[1] God thus identified with harmony may then also be related to the 'true felicity' which is achieved when the three elements within the 'Triad' are joined: it is the seminal principle of 'the God within' working itself out towards the 'blossom of Good', and man is the 'chief expression' of this principle:

> So moves he forth in faith, if he has made
> His mind God's temple, dedicate to truth.[2]

Meredith admits, however, that there are disconcerting throw-backs to the rule of Self. What hope is there if man 'Be rebel at the core?'

> 'Tis that in each recovery he preserves,
>
> . . .
>
> Sense of his march ahead, more brightly lit ...[3]

It is this 'sense of his march ahead', which is but another aspect of his faith that Earth 'in her children is growing', which informs Meredith's attitude to life. Here, again, is the basis of trust and prophetic optimism where the 'laws of growth' meet with the aim of the 'God within' to point the longer lines of historical and ethical evolution.

In this 'march ahead' towards harmony, Meredith claims, there is full and lasting contentment to be had for the individual who has deadened the Self and found 'a larger Self' in the 'brotherhood' of Humanity, and—

> lasting too,
> For souls not lent in usury,
> The rapture of the forward view.[4]

---

[1] *The Test of Manhood*, 26, pp. 205, 204.
[2] *Ibid.*, p. 206.
[3] *Ibid.*, p. 207.
[4] *The Thrush in February*, 25, p. 222.

Though he is a prophet and a reformer, Meredith has learned patience both from the naturalist's theory of evolution and from Comte's doctrine, and the relapses which so often thwart our march ahead appear to him merely as deviations from a straight course, whose general direction is never lost:

> Judge mildly the tasked world; and disincline
> To brand it, for it bears a heavy pack.[1]

It is like the inebriate's groping homewards from the inn at night —a zigzag—'but he turns not back'. And this analogy suggests to Meredith that the idea of mental progress as 'spiral ascent' might be geometrically projected 'on a flat' to illustrate the world's advance. It is

> the way of worms.
> Cherish the promise of its good intents,
> And warn it, not one instinct to efface
> Ere Reason ripens for the vacant place.[2]

Meredith's attitude, his need to believe that Harmony is the 'goal of goals'[3] makes him, in Trevelyan's celebrated phrase, 'The inspired prophet of sanity', constantly asserting that the 'pinched ascetic' and the 'red sensualist' are wrecked in turn. Against the 'insane excess' of either extreme, Meredith opposes his ideal of the harmonious man—a kind of Attic union of bodily and mental beauty. Such an ideal was achieved, he thinks, in the Garden of Epicurus— 'fenced from passion and mishap'

> Where mind and body, in fair junction free,
> Luted their joyful concord . . .[4]

[1] The World's Advance, 25, p. 17.
[2] Ibid.
[3] The Test of Manhood, p. 206.
[4] The Garden of Epicurus, 25, p. 18.

Translated into terms of political theory, the idea of the Garden of Epicurus means a balance of social interests; it means democracy and some form of socialism. Again, Meredith's evolutionary belief provides the dynamic for his appeal to reform, for his notions of 'brain-rule' and 'brain-democratic' imply progressive, intelligent planning of the human condition.[1] In *Foresight and Patience* he welcomes the signs of spreading democracy and social advance:

> More do your people thrive;
> Your Many are more merrily alive
> Than erewhile when I gloried in the page
> Of radiant singer and anointed sage.
> Greece was my lamp: burnt out for lack of oil;
> Rome, Python Rome, prey of its robber spoil!
> All structures built upon a narrow space
> Must fall, from having not your hosts for base.[2]

Though 'brain-rule' is important in this constructive process, as it is in the evolutionary growth in general, Meredith never ceases to remind us that Love is equally active. In this concern too there is agreement with Comte's plea for the balance of 'Feeling, Reason, Activity'. Now more than ever, Love is a powerful urge in men, towards a great future:

> More gardens will they win than any lost;
> The vile plucked out of them, the unlovely slain.
> Not forfeiting the beast with which they are crossed,
> To stature of the Gods will they attain.
> They shall uplift their Earth to meet her Lord,
> Themselves the attuning chord![3]

---

[1] Cf. the recurrence of this idea in *The Empty Purse, The Test of Manhood, Foresight and Patience.*

[2] Vol. 26, p. 97.

[3] *Hymn to Colour*, 25, xiv.

In his prose-works Meredith sketches a more modest perspective, and there is one which may be included here because it links Meredith's aspiration with the prophecies of Tennyson and Browning. In *Diana of the Crossways*. Redworth in his love of Diana is awakened to a new understanding:

She gave him comprehension of the meaning of love: a word in many mouths, not often explained. With her, wound in his idea of her, he perceived it to signify a new start in our existence, a finer shoot of the tree stoutly planted in good gross earth; the senses running their live sap, and the minds companioned, and the spirits made one by the whole-natured conjunction. In sooth, a happy prospect for the sons and daughters of Earth, divinely indicating more than happiness: the speeding of us, compact of what we are, between the ascetic rocks and the sensual whirlpools, to the creation of certain nobler races, now very dimly imagined.[1]

Here, once more, Meredith foreshadows a time when the 'Triad' of sense, mind and spirit has attained to 'felicity'. But this harmony is not the rewarding happiness of the Utilitarian school, nor the conjugal happiness of woman and man: it marks the human condition from which something new and greater will be born—a nobler race.

Meredith's evolutionary prophecy coincides with that of Tennyson and Browning in this hope for the nobler races, and though with him there is 'no power to interpose', and no leaning to asceticism or worldly renunciation, he agrees whole-heartedly with them that Humanity must strive towards this ideal through self-discipline. Browning's *Paracelsus* describes the tragedy of a man in whom force and love are not 'conjoined', and points, through this warning, to a fusion of these two in 'A temperate and equidistant world'.[2] Similarly Meredith exhorts man to reconcile Artemis and Aphrodite in his nature, to create 'A sober world that walks the balanced

[1] Vol. 16, pp. 420—1.
[2] Cf. *supra*, p. 121.

276

mean'.[1] In him, as in his Platonic forbears, the vision springs from the same fundamental source of idealism and love of life.

Meredith's attitude differs from that of Browning and Tennyson, as well as from Swinburne's, first of all in its astonishing power of assimilation: not of precise or systematic knowledge, but of general creeds and ideas. It might be claimed that, in the end, Meredith's God is strange indeed, and his strangeness derives from the synthesis of varied ideologies which he embraces. Idealism, pantheism, evolution, positivism and the religion of humanity pass with equal ease into the poet's mind and combine in a belief unusually complex for the Victorian age, reflecting the *Zeitgeist* more in general outline than in specific and detailed reference. The unity of attitude and vision which Meredith achieves despite these diverse ingredients is due to their complete subordination to his inner vision—to the energy and persistence of his emotional belief. This process of subordination is best seen in Meredith's oracular reading of Earth, where he passes from a general intellectual acceptance of Darwin's ideas to an intuitive and passionate exploration of the 'laws of growth', an exploration that takes him far away from Darwinian doctrine. In this emotional consistency lies the force of Meredith's evolutionary reading of Earth and Life. It is a deeply original poetry, moving on many levels of awareness, and infinitely varied in its formal qualities. At his best, as in *Hymn to Colour, Earth and Man, The Thrush in February*, Meredith combines imaginative power with simplicity and formal restraint; but at his worst of intricate and verbose meditation, as in some passages of the *Odes*, there is little unity of argument, and the communication is impeded through awkwardness of image and phrase. The subordination of idea to emotion, subject-matter to intuition, does not with Meredith always imply clarity and order, and it would appear that the abstruseness in his poetry is not so much due to a myopic handling of the theme

---

[1] *The Test of Manhood.*

and its sphere of ideas as to his persistent desire to probe deep into all possible ramifications of an idea along different metaphorical tracks.

One might object, both from an intellectual and an emotional point of view, that the unity of Meredith's vision of Earth and Life entails, for all its synthesis, a limited horizon, and that this limitation is self-imposed and involves an aspect of strain. And it would indeed appear, at times, that Meredith's self-effacing and heroic agnosticism, his cult of Earth as the one ultimate reality, 'the God within', is inadequate as an expression of his emotional and intellectual quest. For his aspiration often goes beyond the limiting concepts of both pantheism and positivism, or he would not so persistently have endeavoured to reformulate these and charge them with meanings of transcendence and immortality. And there is, despite his scorn of metaphysics, a constantly felt inability to accept, from an emotional as well as intellectual stance, the full implications of agnosticism. Hence the fusion in Meredith's belief of idealistic and positivistic elements.

Meredith's cult of Earth and Humanity would not have generated important poetry, if it had been based on a particular scientific or epistemological theory, and not on conduct. The integrity of Meredith's attitude and belief, and of his poetry, lies in his moral passion embracing the whole of human destiny. Hence his complete subordination of doctrine and knowledge to life. He, like Comte, sees knowledge merely as a means to fuller and better life, which has value only when translated into activity. Again, in Comte's tenet that Feeling, Reason and Activity can only be balanced through an understanding of man's nature as an evolutionary outcome, there is a conviction closely related to that which informs Meredith's 'Triad'. When, finally, we look back upon Meredith's reading of Earth and Life, and remember Comte's sententious dictum: 'Love, then, is our principle; Order our basis; and Progress our end'—we realize how much Meredith, directly or indirectly, owed to the

278

founder of the Positivist creed. Yet, throughout his poetry, the emotions and attitudes which conditioned his acceptance of these beliefs, were the primary facts, and the pattern he composed from them was his own.

3. Conclusion:
Evolution as a Cult of Life and Man

Tennyson and Browning found in the idea of evolution, as part of their Christian and Platonic cosmology, a promise of the fuller and better existence to which their deepest and most permanent aspiration was directed. It gave them a prophetic vision of life, ascending from its evil and suffering and limitation through purgatory and spiritual growth until, in the 'divine event' and the 'all-reconciling future', God would grant fulfilment to the yearning and struggle which He has made the lot of man.

In Swinburne's and Meredith's attitude—for all their difference in temperament—there is a similar craving for perfection and life everlasting, and their poetic vision reaches out with no less intensity to a goal of complete realization of life and of Good. They, accepting the New Order of agnosticism, are confined with their longing for a life abundant within the space of our planet and the brief moment of our lifetime. Somehow their aspiration must, however, discover for itself some form of permanence, and an absolute object of devotion and worship which might be claimed as identical with the highest scientific and moral truth and point the goal of existence. From this emotional and intellectual dynamic springs their cult of the Man-God and of Humanity, and their belief in racial eternity within time, which look to evolution and positivism for a conceptual framework. In the idea of evolution, empirical truth and prophetic vision meet to disclose undreamt-of glories for mankind. But here their intuition forces their search in its own direction: it is not Darwin's overruling authority which formulates

279

their belief; it is their own need to see evolution as Providence, or at least as intelligent, meaningful process. As poets, they retain their independence, and apparently never troubled to find out whether 'natural selection' was the method by which Hertha (or the One God at Growth) and the 'God within' worked out the destiny of life. Meredith thought that he backed Huxley throughout: the exact scientific theory was unimportant compared to the main miracle which Darwin proved to be a fact—the creative force and persistence of life. If Swinburne and Meredith, in obedience to logical rigour, had come more closely to grips with the epistemological implications of Darwin's theory, they would have discovered something like Hardy's conception of the blind, Immanent Will. Perhaps they did face the possibility, yet their vision moves unhampered in another direction—in the direction first taken by Aristotle and later retraced by neo-Lamarckian theories of evolution.

Swinburne's and Meredith's worship of life reflects, if only in a suggestive parallel, the devotional structure of Christianity, and thus indicates that its underlying impulse or need is of an essentially religious nature. Instead of God, Redemption and Immortality they place Earth, Evolution and Humanity. Hertha—Mother Earth, is the *Creator Spiritus,* the force which sustains and perpetuates Life and directs it to an end, but only as a whole, as a sum total of growth, and only here on earth. Yet, for the greatness and goodness and beauty which this God at growth manifests, he is truly worthy of devotion and self-sacrifice. His nature is unknowable, but by reading Nature and History, by seeing existence *sub specie Humanitatis,* we may discover his providential ways, and then we find, in natural law and above all in evolution, a promise of redemption from the evil which mars existence.

Evolution, the creative method of the God within, explains the destiny of man and how the perennial conflict between good and evil, pleasure and pain, aspiration and limitation—these 'divine contraries'—are gradually being resolved in freedom and harmony.

280

Evolution is the way of salvation, the *via dolorosa et triumphalis* which life must walk to be delivered from evil, from animal aggression, from the 'fleshly sins' of the Self.

Swinburne and Meredith follow the general positivistic and utilitarian doctrines in their subordination of the individual to Humanity. It was a reaction both against social injustice and the Romantic cult of the Self which swung to the other extreme of self-denial and a sacrifice of the individual to the interests of the community. With no Paradise to hope for, with no personal soul to save, Humanity is our life everlasting—the object for which we live and for which we must be prepared to die.

At this level of heroic dedication to the great cause of Humanity, they are also able to accept the fact of inexplicable pain and suffering, and the profuse waste of individual lives which tormented Tennyson. When seen only in relation to the suffering, wasted individual, existence is absurd; but remove the centre of interest from man to men, allow our vision to explore the longer lines of evolution and history, and the general pattern of Progress emerges clearly, to dwarf and shame our petty egoistic desires. Humanity then reveals its true glory: it is 'the live light made of our lives'; it is our 'goal of goals'.

Here, then, is the task towards which the total endeavour of our life should be directed. As we have seen, Swinburne's and Meredith's cult is not passive, mystical contemplation, but a deliberate movement from invocation to exhortation, and each according to his temperamen points mankind to Liberty, Truth, or Order and Harmony. Swinburne, who was obsessed with the evil forces of despotism and the self-delusion of Christian doctrine, tends to place the source of 'obstruction' outside man: man is more sinned against than sinning; but as he gradually comes into his own divine right of Liberty and Truth, as Humanity mounts the throne of the Man-God, the Sunrise will suffuse his world. Meredith, contemplating human destiny within his more complex, monistic world, relates

281

everything good and evil to the organic quality of man's nature, more or less tied to the Self, more or less animal. However, both know that the change of heart does not come easily or naturally to man, and hence their untiring appeal to his highest moral instincts —his love, his desire for truth and harmony. And they know that man needs a sanction and suprahuman encouragement for his effort, and this, again, they find in evolution. Man participates in Creation: he is an ally of those cosmic forces which aspire through the evolutionary process to liberty, truth, and a sober, balanced world.

As an exploration of this moral significance of evolutionary process, the poetry of Swinburne and Meredith is of lasting interest. Yet, in the end one feels that they attempted an impossible task: to gain a vision of the world which had validity not only within their own poetic and emotional experience, but which was exclusively true. Since these two worshippers of life set out to preach the whole truth, not only as beauty but above all as conduct, their message must be judged by the criteria of life and of human experience in a wider ethical and psychological context. The insufficiency of their analysis of human nature, and of their system of values then becomes obvious. At times they appear to have felt this themselves. There are moments of strain when their moral exhortation reveals the inadequacy of their philosophical assumptions. It would seem that they are striving in vain to find adequate realization for their essentially idealistic and transcendent aspiration within a world closed on itself, self-contained and apparently self-explained, but too limited for their search.

282

CHAPTER IV

DARWIN AND HARDY'S UNIVERSE

The 'purblind Doomsters'

AGAINST the chance-directed process of Natural Selection, Tennyson and Browning pitted their Idealistic faith in a divine spiritual energy underlying and informing this world of flux and imperfection. Swinburne and Meredith rejected this transcendental doctrine and were yet able, for two reasons, to retain an optimistic attitude and a bright millennial hope. Firstly, because they continued to read Idealistic and Christian values and ideas into the world process, so that the basis of their belief remained a compromise between the spiritual and moral content of Platonic Christianity on the one side and the naturalistic, biological theory on the other. Secondly, because they accepted the suffering, waste and frustration of the individual as a necessary sacrifice to the larger destiny of Life and Humanity. Hence, the beliefs of Swinburne and Meredith are no more 'objective' than those of Tennyson and Browning: all four poets raise their heads to aspects fair, and reject or reduce the foul ones.

Thomas Hardy was the first great Victorian poet to break away from this optimism, and deny the eclectic assumptions on which it rested. To him, the individual with his struggle and pain became the all-absorbing and tragic spectacle, and it left him with a vision of the universe and of human existence that had no joy and little if any hope.

The present study of evolutionary trends in the work of Hardy does not aim at an exhaustive treatment. Apart from numerous important investigations into Hardy's philosophy as a whole,[1] there is a recent monograph by Mr. H. Curtis Webster, *On A Darkling Plain*, which examines these aspects with admirable scholarship, notably the influence of Darwin's theory upon the nature and growth of Hardy's thought. Our aim is simply to sketch Hardy's evolutionary outlook with a view to its significance within the general framework of this inquiry.

Hardy's intellectual development, and the mature formulation of his thought, offer perhaps the most effective answer to the questions so often asked: How could Darwin's theory of evolution cause such spiritual disturbance in an age that was already familiar with the higher criticism and the positivist challenge? How could a biological hypothesis that merely went counter to the biblical Book of Genesis give such singular impetus to unbelief and affect so powerfully the conditions on which the Christian doctrine is generally accepted? Hardy's answer is not only profoundly moving, and valid within the world of his poetry and novels: it transcends his individual sphere with force and persuasion.

In some ways Hardy's spiritual quest reminds one of Tennyson. There is, deep in their nature, a similar unfulfilled craving for life, and the same preoccupation with inevitable death. One has only to glance at Hardy's *Collected Poems* to notice the recurrence of the death-theme, and the graves and graveyards which form the sinister setting for his meditation upon life and the human lot. What makes Hardy the more tragic—the really tragic character of these two, is not so much the quality of his thought as the fact that, unlike the Laureate, who never quite burnt his bridges, Hardy cuts himself off entirely from intellectual retreat. Even when swept down to his greatest depths of despair Tennyson clings to some slight hope: *The Two Voices* illustrates well the movement of

[1] Cf. those by Brennecke, D'Exideuil, Braybrooke.

his persecuted mind, and its tentative emergence into calm and light. Hardy's *A Meeting with Despair* is a more fatal encounter:

> As evening shaped I found me on a moor
> 　　Sight shunned to entertain:
> The black lean land, of featureless contour,
> 　　Was like a tract in pain.
>
> . . . . .
>
> I glanced aloft and halted, pleasure-caught
> 　　To see the contrast there:
> The ray-lit clouds gleamed glory; and I thought,
> 　　"There's solace everywhere!"
>
> . . . . .
>
> Against the horizon's dim-discernèd wheel
> 　　A form rose, strange of mould:
> That he was hideous, hopeless, I could feel
> 　　Rather than could behold.
>
> " 'Tis a dead spot, where even the light lies spent
> 　　To darkness!" croaked the Thing.
> "Not if you look aloft!" said I, intent
> 　　On my new reasoning.
>
> "Yea—but await awhile!" he cried. "Ho-ho!—
> 　　Now look aloft and see!"
> I looked. There, too, sat night: Heaven's radiant show
> 　　Had gone that heartened me.[1]

Spread out before us is the characteristic Hardy landscape, with its brooding atmosphere and its *vanitas vanitatum.* It had not always

---

[1] *Collected Poems* (1928 ed.), p. 51; in the following, ref. will be to *C. P.*

carried these gloomy features, for to the young Hardy the world was, despite wrong and suffering, suffused with 'Heaven's radiant show' and pointing beyond itself to an existence where earthly injustice would be redressed. Hardy looked back upon this world of Divine Providence as upon a Golden Age of his youth—his paradise lost:

> Show thee as I thought thee
> When I early sought thee,
>   Omen-scouting
>   All undoubting
> Love alone had wrought thee—

If only the 'Glad things that men treasure' might still adorn Nature!

> But such re-adorning
> Time forbids with scorning—
>   Makes me see things
>   Cease to be things
> They were in my morning.[1]

Now the glory of Nature has faded and darkness reigns; and the first sweetness and radiance 'None shall re-awaken'.

Time and again we come upon such laments of his lost faith and joy. Hardy is a spiritual exile—one of the many sorrow-stricken devout of the nineteenth century who have attended God's funeral:

> "So, toward our myth's oblivion,
> Darkling, and languid-lipped, we creep and grope
> Sadlier than those who wept in Babylon,
> Whose Zion was a still abiding hope.

[1] *To Outer Nature, C. P.,* p. 54.

And again Hardy remembers the happy times before this catastrophe darkened his world:

> "How sweet it was in years far hied
> To start the wheels of day with trustful prayer,
> To lie down liegely at the eventide
> And feel a blest assurance he was there!

As for the future, it offers no direction or hope:

> "And who or what shall fill his place?
> Whither will wanderers turn distracted eyes
> For some fixed star to stimulate their pace
> Towards the goal of their enterprise?"...[1]

Hardy never found an answer to these questions, for he could not follow Arnold or Browning any more than Swinburne and Meredith. And thus he remained in exile.

Mr. Curtis Webster has traced, convincingly, Hardy's intellectual development and the main influences which contributed to the growth and formulation of his thought. It is, as Webster has so well shown, a drama whose climax might be said to come at the beginning, when Hardy was just twenty years of age. It was about this time that the orthodox young man, who believed that love alone had wrought Nature, found himself face to face with the world of *Hap:*[2]

> If but some vengeful god would call to me
> From up the sky, and laugh: "Thou suffering thing,
> Know that thy sorrow is my ecstasy,
> That thy love's loss is my hate's profiting!"

[1] *God's Funeral, C. P.,* p. 308.
[2] The poem was written at the age of 26, in 1866.

Then would I bear it, clench myself, and die,
Steeled by the sense of ire unmerited;
Half-eased in that a Powerfuller than I
Had willed and meted me the tears I shed.

But not so. How arrives it joy lies slain,
And why unblooms the best hope ever sown?
—Crass Casualty obstructs the sun and rain,
And dicing Time for gladness casts a moan...
These purblind Doomsters had as readily strown
Blisses about my pilgrimage as pain.[1]

The Swinburne of *Atalanta in Calydon* had challenged a vengeful god and found faith and exultation in this Promethean task, which he was also to carry into *Poems and Ballads* and *Songs before Sunrise*. Here he too, in a mood very different from that of Hardy, celebrated God's funeral and the progress of Truth. The philosophy of *Hap* calls to mind, moreover, that Tennyson had been similarly obsessed by visions of a meaningless cosmos where the stars run blindly and 'brand his nothingness into man'. Swinburne and Tennyson pursued truth in opposite directions, the one into heroic revolt, the other into submission and trust—yet to both the solution was a leap into faith. To Hardy this leap is impossible.

According to Mr. Webster, it was Hardy's temperament—his unusually sensitive response to pain and suffering, which, combined with the particular conditions of family and local background, made him so vulnerably exposed to the intellectual and spiritual disturbance of his time.[2] Born in 1840, and having grown up in a High Church environment which formed the natural setting for his youthful religious fervour, and for his desire to take orders, he met, at this susceptive age, the full flood of positivistic and naturalistic thinking, in the *Essays and Reviews* first, and soon after in the *Origin of Species*. Under the impact of these two works Hardy's orthodox

[1] *C. P.*, p. 7.　　[2] *Op. cit.* Ch. i—iii.

288

faith broke down. Darwin opened his eyes to Natural Selection, or 'Crass Casualty': Nature cares as little for the race as it cares for the individual, and for human value. It cares, in fact, for nothing but the perpetuation of life, and in its very lack of aim and purpose reveals itself a meaningless process. This inevitable conclusion implicit in Darwin's theory denies to Hardy even the philosophical consolation of the religion of Humanity.

During the sixties—the decade when *Hap* was written—Hardy found other exponents of 'Truth for Truth's sake'. There was Stuart Mill's essay *On Liberty*; there was Huxley's crusade for Darwin; there were Spencer and Comte.[1] Hardy knew something of these, and as he was not content to remain in the intellectual impasse to which *Essays and Reviews* and *Origin of Species* had brought him, he continued eagerly to explore natural science and philosophy. He shows, in these early years, an interest in geology and astronomy which recalls Tennyson's similar preoccupation in his youth.[2]

Hardy, then, came to maturity at the most dramatic moment in the intellectual revolution of the nineteenth century, and, like all sensitive minds, he suffered by its ravages—: 'And who or what shall fill his place?'—Because life is made or unmade by crass casualty, because the 'purblind Doomsters' had taken the place of Divine Providence, the whole universe to Hardy, by a simple extension of argument, was an outcome of blind chance. In such a universe ideals and aspirations and happiness have no right and no meaning, for they are, like the rest, produced by accident and unrelated to the general scheme.

---

[1] Webster claims that Hardy's reading from his nineteenth to his twentysixth year, when he wrote *Hap*, was topical and extensive; *op. cit.*, pp. 44—6.

[2] There is also a marked parallelism in Tennyson's and Hardy's poetic treatment of this knowledge, for instance in *Maud* and *Vastness*, and in *Two on a Tower*.

Unlike Darwin himself and unlike men of such various temperaments as Spencer, Stuart Mill, Wallace and even Huxley, Hardy was unable to reconcile the idea of a fortuitous natural process with a faith in purposive existence. These men were as convinced as their eighteenth-century forbears that man had a significant place in Nature, at the top of the animal hierarchy, and pointing to higher forms of life—at least in a moral sense. The survival values which man retains from the struggle for life were to them real values, and history confirmed, on its evidence of cultural and moral progress, their optimistic hopes for the future. In Hardy's world, on the other hand, 'Crass Casualty' obstructs not only the sun and rain, but every event and all beings.

Hardy's early poetry is steeped in this vision of purposeless existence. Instead of the glory he once saw in the things of Nature, he now finds their 'faces dulled, constrained, and worn', as though they were 'cowed' by the 'master's ways'. Now 'field, flock and lonely tree' gaze at him in mute questioning:

> "Has some Vast Imbecility,
>   Mighty to build and blend,
>   But impotent to tend,
> Framed us in jest, and left us now to hazardry?
>
> "Or come we of an Automaton
>   Unconscious of our pains? ...
>   Or are we live remains
> Of Godhead dying downwards, brain and eye now gone?'
>
> "Or is it that some high Plan betides,
>   As yet not understood,
>   Of Evil stormed by Good,
> We the Forlorn Hope over which Achievement strides?"[1]

[1] *Nature's Questioning, C. P.,* pp. 58—9.

290

The young poet knows no answer—none except resignation, for existence has become

> A senseless school, where we must give
> Our lives that we may learn to live![1]

As Mr. Webster has shown, Hardy's early conception of Chance —the 'purblind Doomsters'—is not the metaphysical idea of a First Cause: it denotes the absence of a directive force or principle in the universe. (Cf. *op. cit.*, pp. 64—6.) 'Chance', in the poems and novels, merely symbolizes or personifies the working of natural law, devoid of aim and consciousness, devoid of good and evil, and thus not to be blamed for the disasters and misery of which they are the source. 'Crass Casualty' and 'dicing Time' have woven the web of life blindly, and, by accident, evolved in man a sensitive and intelligent being doomed to suffering, because of his consciousness: because his ideals and aspirations are rarely or never fulfilled in this absurd quandary of existence: 'The emotions have no place in a world of defect, and it is a cruel injustice that they should have developed in it.'[2] Since human emotions and aspirations have emerged, and are a fundamental part of our nature, Hardy contends that they are legitimate, and in a just and rational world-order conditions would have obtained for their fulfilment. Though, in *A Young Man's Epigram on Existence*, Hardy preaches resignation and fatalism, his attitude is, at this time and throughout, stamped by the idealist's lack of acceptance—it is a continued protest against natural as well as social law. Again we notice that Hardy stands directly opposed to Meredith's outlook: the individual remains the centre of his world, and whenever the individual is tormented or destroyed, the calamity spreads outwards to the whole.

[1] *A Young Man's Epigram on Existence*, (1866), *C. P.*, p. 281.
[2] *Op. cit.*, Florence E. Hardy, *The Early Life of Thomas Hardy*, (1928); quoted from Webster, p. 66.

There are, certainly, moments when Hardy experiences a kind of Tennysonian mood of reconciliation and hope. In the poem *1867*, (the year of the Reform Bill), there is a cautious prophecy of happier times ahead, and *Song of Hope* shows an effort to overcome the feeling that 'joy lies slain';

> O sweet To-morrow!—
> After to-day
> There will away
> This sense of sorrow.
> Then let us borrow
> Hope, for a gleaming
> Soon will be streaming,
>   Dimmed by no gray—
>   No gray![1]

On a Fine Morning seems an even more conscious endeavour to reject the vision of *Hap*. Here Hardy, like Tennyson in *In Memoriam*, finds that solace comes only with 'cleaving to the Dream':

> Thus do I this heyday, holding
> Shadows but as lights unfolding,
> As no specious show this moment
> With its iris-hued embowment;
>   But as nothing other than
>   Part of a benignant plan;
>   Proof that earth was made for man.[2]

Yet, on the whole, evidence that 'earth was made for man' is indeed rare in the novels and poems, and Hardy's hope for the better is rather more like the timid flame that flickers in that great poem, *The Darkling Thrush*'. Here, in stark contrast to the cold, dead landscape

[1] *C. P.*, p. 120.   [2] *C. P.*, p. 118.

At once a voice arose among
    The bleak twigs overhead
In a full-hearted evensong
    Of joy illimited;
An aged thrush, frail, gaunt, and small,
    In blast-beruffled plume,
Had chosen thus to fling his soul
    Upon the growing gloom.

So little cause for carollings
    Of such ecstatic sound
Was written on terrestrial things
    Afar or nigh around,
That I could think there trembled through
    His happy good-night air
Some blessed Hope, whereof he knew
    And I was unaware.[1]

Besides these passing and infrequent lighter moods, there is in the novels a more persistent trend of meliorism which at first sight appears to conflict with Hardy's fatalism and his deterministic view of human nature.[2] However, since society, and not natural law, is responsible for a great deal of wrong and suffering, Hardy so far shares in the general faith in progress that he actively strives to change and improve whatever can be improved. Social conditions, he believes, have not their root 'in the heart of things' and can be altered and bettered indefinitely, though not through the facile 'laissez faire' commonly recognized as the quickest mode of advance.

[1] C. P., p. 137.
[2] Webster suggests that Hardy's melioristic intentions were, during the period 1865—70 in particular, stimulated by the Working Class movement and by Shelley's and Swinburne's revolutionary socialism; op. cit., pp. 74—6.

Progress, far from being the law of life, is to Hardy something to be wrenched from fate, in the shape of circumstance and prejudice, and our only hope for the better lies in taking a 'full look at the Worst'.[1]

In the seventies Hardy established his reputation as a novelist with *Under the Greenwood Tree* (1872), *A Pair of Blue Eyes* (1873), *Far From the Madding Crowd* (1874), and *The Return of the Native* (1878). It is probable that, as Mr. Webster thinks, the deepening pessimism which pervades these novels was due to the renewed clash between orthodoxy and scientific determinism. In 1871 Darwin published *The Descent of Man*, and Romanes wrote his *Candid Examinations of Theism*. W. K. Clifford postulated in *Body and Mind* (1874) the determinism and predictability of the human automaton which Tyndall, in his Belfast lecture of the same year, claimed for the universe as a whole. With this deterministic trend was interwoven a darker pattern of philosophical pessimism, the main source of which was Schopenhauer.[2] These combined forces could only emphasize the truth of 'Crass Casualty' and add to the gloom which Darwin's theory of Nature had cast upon Hardy's world. Darwin remains throughout these years a momentous influence, and in *A Pair of Blue Eyes* there is a description which in its masterful blend of concrete observation and thought reveals both the powerful imaginative impact of evolution and the significance which Hardy, as a thinker, distilled from it.

The principal characters of the novel, Knight and Elfride, are out on a walk along the edge of the coastal cliffs, when suddenly the edge gives way and Knight slides down the steep face and barely avoids a fall to certain death. For some agonizing minutes he

[1] *In Tenebris, C. P.*, p. 154.

[2] Though not translated into English till 1883—86, Schopenhauer's philosophy was introduced through periodicals and studies from 1871 onwards; cf. Webster, *op. cit.*, pp. 89—90.

is suspended there, clinging to a tuft of grass, and gazing at the hostile features of the cliff:

He reclined hand in hand with the world in its infancy. Not a blade, not an insect, which spoke of the present, was between him and the past. The inveterate antagonism of these black precipices to all strugglers for life is in no way more forcibly suggested than by the paucity of tufts of grass, lichens, or confervæ on their outermost ledges.[1]

Here, once more, is the scene of strife of Darwin and Huxley, in the sombre colours of Hardy's characteristic nature setting, where even inanimate things, the cliffs, stand forth as destruction personified. Here life was defeated in its youth, and only fossils remain to tell its hopeless story:

By one of those familiar conjunctions of things wherewith the inanimate world baits the mind of man when he pauses in moments of suspense, opposite Knight's eyes was an imbedded fossil, standing forth in low relief from the rock. It was a creature with eyes. The eyes, dead and turned to stone, were even now regarding him. It was one of the early crustaceans called Trilobites. Separated by millions of years in their lives, Knight and this underling seemed to have met in their place of death. It was the single instance within reach of his vision of anything that had ever been alive and had had a body to save, as he himself had now.
The creature represented but a low type of animal existence, for never in their vernal years had the plains indicated by those numberless slaty layers been traversed by an intelligence worthy of the name. Zoophytes. mollusca, shell-fish, were the highest developments of those ancient dates. The immense lapses of time each formation represented had known nothing of the dignity of man. They were grand times, but they were mean times too, and mean were their relics. He was to be with the small in his death.

Trilobite and Man—it is as if the wheel of life had come full circle in this confrontation across millions of years. And at this crucial

[1] *Op. cit.* (Wessex ed. 1912), p. 240.

295

moment Knight sees the history of life unfold like a swift cavalcade of memories:

Time closed up like a fan before him. He saw himself at one extremity of the years, face to face with the beginning and all the intermediate centuries simultaneously. Fierce men, clothed in their hides of beasts, and carrying, for defence and attack, huge clubs and pointed spears, rose from the rock, like the phantoms before the doomed Macbeth. They lived in hollows, woods, and mud huts —perhaps in caves of the neighbouring rocks. Behind them stood an earlier band. No man was there. Huge elephantine forms, the mastodon, the hippopotamus, the tapir, antelopes of monstrous size, the megatherium, and the myledon—all, for a moment, in juxtaposition. Further back, and overlapped by these, were perched huge-billed birds and swinish creatures as large as horses. Still more shadowy were the sinister crocodilian outlines—alligators and other uncouth shapes, culminating in the colossal lizard, the iguanodon. Folded behind were dragon forms and clouds of flying reptiles: still underneath were fishy beings of lower development; and so on, till the lifetime scenes of the fossil confronting him were a present and modern condition of things.

In this large and crowded canvas Hardy gives a striking example of the imaginative scope which natural history may offer to the artist. Darwin's and Lyell's observations are here creative in a very definite sense, but the final unity of the vision is organized through the emotional movement which underlies the pattern and its details. In this pattern the trilobite is the focal point from which Hardy's vision emerges and links its chain of successive forms and images, and it is from the confrontation of fossil insect with man that the poetic significance of the pattern spreads to the varied elements woven into it. Clearly, Hardy's evolutionary epic is not born of any delight in the great pageant of life and the creative power manifested in these spectacular but ephemeral forms. Unlike the poets of the eighteenth century, he does not dwell on the majestic, progressive scale of life ascending to perfection; nor does he share in

296

Browning's joy of seeing all inferior creatures point up to man. The further vista into the future, which so predominates in Swinburne and Meredith, is wholly absent. With Hardy there is a sense of revulsion—a nightmare experience for which he prepares us through the reference to Macbeth; and, at the same time, there is the feeling of *vanitas vanitatum*—of the tremendous surge of vital energy spent to no purpose. It is the same sense of futility, but deeper and more final, which haunted Tennyson at the thought that man too might be for ever 'sealed within the iron hills'. Indifferent, casual Nature pays no heed to human life and value. Therefore, in Hardy's pattern the extremes of life—Man and Trilobite—meet and fuse, to design a futile circle: human being and insect become contemporaries because, in the aimless flux of evolution, the one is of no greater significance than the other.

When man finds himself face to face with an indifferent natural order, exposed at all times to crass casualty and ultimately doomed to death, fatalism is the only possible attitude to adopt towards this 'senseless school' of existence. Knight, Hardy tells us, had not previously been forced to such a resignation, but now he sees the truth in the peasants' outlook:

To those musing weather-beaten West-country folk who pass the greater part of their days and nights out of doors, Nature seems to have moods in other than a poetical sense: predilections for certain deeds at certain times, without any apparent law to govern or season to account for them. She is read as a person with a curious temper; as one who does not scatter kindnesses and cruelties alternately, impartially, and in order, but heartless severities or overwhelming generosities in lawless caprice. Man's case is always that of the prodigal's favourite or the miser's pensioner. In her unfriendly moments there seems a feline fun in her tricks, begotten by a foretaste of her pleasure in swallowing the victim.

This is approaching to something more than a metaphorical personification of Nature, even if Hardy elsewhere points out the

297

pathetic fallacy in Knight's impressions. 'Nature' is here beginning to live as a personified cosmic agency, and in his portrait of her we find, once more, Hardy directly opposed to Meredith, despite their common emphasis on the inexorable severity of natural law. Meredith, rejecting the fate of the individual as unimportant, and placing the human race and its future in the centre of his belief, is convinced that the laws of growth are just and providential. Nature 'prompts her best' to sacrifice, yet the lines she designs through history reveal her plan, and therefore existence has still a meaning, and our conduct an end. Hardy, bent on the tragedy and frustration of the 'miser's pensioner' sees a cosmic scheme, or rather a disorder, where no intelligent force has ever been at work. There are chance kindnesses as well as chance cruelties, but no significant direction.

The influence of Darwin on the world of the Wessex novels has been examined by Mr. Webster so much in detail that for the present only a brief survey is called for. As other critics too have pointed out, the laws of Chance and Circumstance govern almost absolutely the lives of the characters. According to Webster, love and human relationship in these novels are subject to Darwin's deterministic principles of natural and sexual selection; it is physical attraction, and not a deeper sympathy and understanding, which bind human beings to one another, and hence the disillusionment when this ephemeral, idealizing love is shattered against reality. Such is the relationship between men and women in *A Pair of Blue Eyes* (Elfride and Knight), in *Far From the Madding Crowd* (Bathsheba and Troy), in *The Return of the Native* (Clym and Eustacia), in *The Mayor of Casterbridge* (Lucetta and Henchard), in *The Woodlanders* (Fitzpiers, Grace and Suke), in *Tess of the D'Urbervilles* (Tess and Angel), and in *Jude the Obscure* (Sue and Jude).

Interwoven with this theme is that of the struggle for existence. In their unequal battling against fate—against Chance, Circumstance and natural law, nearly all the combatants fall in turn: the Henchards and the Gileses, the Tesses and the Judes are 'predestinate' to defeat, and the survivors from the struggle, with farmer Oak as a notable exception, are rarely the best. At times, as in *The Mayor of Casterbridge* and *The Woodlanders,* Hardy refers explicitly to the 'battle of life', and comments on the hostile circumstances which the persons have to face.[1] In *The Return of the Native* we find one of his darkest visions of existence as determined by natural law. Egdon Heath, the background against which the human beings move, reflects their condition. Egdon is a symbolic presence throughout, not unlike the part played by the stellar spheres in *Two on a Tower,* and measured against its vast expanse men and women appear as mere insects, dwarfed by this indifferent, dispassionate and unchanging waste that 'reduced to insignificance by its seamed and antique features the wildest turmoil of a single man'.[2] Though Hardy does not see Nature, through this symbol, as an evil force planning the destruction of man, he feels, as he did in *A Pair of Blue Eyes,* that the unheeding and casual working of natural law inevitably brings ruin to man, and there is little consolation in knowing that it has not been intended. In Clym's oft-quoted comment on life Hardy expresses an attitude which had not greatly changed since *Hap:*

He did sometimes think he had been ill-used by fortune, so far as to say that to be born is a palpable dilemma, and that instead of men aiming to advance in life with glory they should calculate how to retreat out of it without shame. But that he and his had been sarcastically and pitilessly handled in having such irons thrust into their souls he d'd not maintain long. It is usually so, except with the sternest of men. Human beings, in their generous endeavour to construct a hypothesis that shall not degrade a First Cause, have always hesitated to conceive a dominant power of lower moral quality than their own; and, even while they sit down and weep by the waters of Babylon, invent excuses for the oppression which prompts their tears . . . .

[1] See Webster, *op. cit.,* pp. 114, 129, 148, 167, 186.
[2] *Op. cit.* (Wessex ed.), p. 384.

He frequently walked the heath alone, when the past seized upon him with its shadowy hand, and held him there to listen to its tale. His imagination would then people the spot with its ancient inhabitants: forgotten Celtic tribes trod their tracks about him, and he could almost live among them, look in their faces, and see them standing beside the barrows which swelled around, untouched and perfect as at the time of their erection. Those of the dyed barbarians who had chosen the cultivable tracts were in comparison with those who had left their marks here, as writers on paper beside writers on parchment. Their records had perished long ago by the plough, while the works of these remained. Yet they all had lived and died unconscious of the different fates awaiting their relics. It reminded him that unforeseen factors operate in the evolution of immortality.[1]

Towards the Immanent Will

Hardy's metaphysical concept of the Immanent Will shows a slow and tentative development through the novels and poems of the eighties and nineties. Critics vary as to the importance of Schopenhauer's rôle in forming Hardy's mature idea of the Will. E. Brennecke bases his comparative study on the evident parallelism in Schopenhauer's and Hardy's thought, but points out the anticipations of the Will-concept already in *Far From the Madding Crowd* (1874). Brennecke notes, moreover, that during the decade which followed on this novel, the personifications of Chance and Time give way to the idea of a cosmic force—the Will.[2] The influence of Schopenhauer is disputed by Curtis Webster, though he recognizes that Hardy knew of Schopenhauer's philosophy in the early eighties and refers to him in the poem *The Pedestrian* (1883). Webster concludes that since Hardy does not acknowledge his indebtedness to Schopenhauer, while he does mention Von Hart-

[1] *The Return of the Native*, (Wessex ed.), pp. 455—56.
[2] *Thomas Hardy's Universe*, pp. 42—49.

mann, and, moreover, since there are no traces of Schopenhauer's terminology in his works—apart from the 'Will'—the influence could not be profound.[1] It is difficult to be categorical on this issue, for the fact remains that—as Webster too points out—Hardy owned a first edition of the translation of *Die Welt als Wille und Vorstellung*, (1883—86), and about this time the concept appears to stand forth more clearly, both in Hardy's sketches and notes and in his novels.

Mr. Webster marks *Two on a Tower* (1882) as the first novel in which the workings of an unconscious, co-ordinating power is perceived behind the usual fatalistic vision of Chance and Circumstance, and finds that in *The Mayor of Casterbridge* (1886) this power—the 'iron hand of necessity'—is a more palpable presence still.[2] During the years immediately after this latter work Hardy turned with greater interest to the Idealist philosophers, Plato, Kant, Hegel, and a reorientation in the direction of Idealism becomes evident in his novels. E. Brennecke detects in *The Woodlanders* (1887) a complete change in the expression of Hardy's outlook, and characterizes his attitude as 'Idealistic Monism'.[3] Webster quotes several reflections from *The Early Life of Thomas Hardy* as evidence of a new leaning to transcendental Idealism.[4] Of these, Hardy's comment on Plato's *Cratylus*: that things might be seen as having an 'actual or false name, and an intrinsic or true name', and the one agreeing with Kant's argument that the thing in itself is unknowable, seem to indicate a tentative acceptance of the Idealistic doctrine. This change in outlook does not imply a surrender of Hardy's fatalistic attitude, but it does affect his idea of the nature of the Immanent Will. Whereas previously he had thought of Chance and Circumstance as manifestations of material forces (or

[1] *Op. cit.*, pp. 158—59, 196.
[2] *Op. cit.*, pp. 146—47.
[3] *Op. cit.*, pp. 46, 66.
[4] *Op. cit.*, p. 191.

causes), he gradually comes to perceive an immaterial, monistic agency working through natural law.

In *The Woodlanders* the Will appears as an implacable 'Unfulfilled Intention', or 'Cause', whose laws predestine human beings to suffer in the 'battle of life'. A similar fatalism pervades *Tess of the D'Urbervilles*, where the Power is felt by Tess to be an 'immense sad soul', while Angel Clare sees it as an 'unsympathetic First Cause'. Finally, in *Jude the Obscure* (1895), the concept of the Immanent Will emerges clearly defined in the pantheistic meditations of Sue:

Vague and quaint imaginings had haunted Sue in the days when her intellect scintillated like a star, that the world resembled a stanza or melody composed in a dream; it was wonderfully excellent to the half-aroused intelligence, but hopelessly absurd at the full waking; that the First Cause worked automatically like a somnambulist, and not reflectively like a sage; that at the framing of the terrestrial conditions there seemed never to have been contemplated such a development of emotional perceptiveness among the creatures subject to those conditions as that reached by thinking and educated humanity.[1]

The same idea recurs in a number of undated poems which group themselves fairly closely around *The Dynasts*—the final expression of Hardy's philosophy. In these there is little fluctuation in the treatment of the Will-concept, and they all adhere to a basic structure of pantheistic fatalism. Thus, in *The Lacking Sense*, this question is asked:

"O Time, whence comes the Mother's moody look amid her
　　labours,
　As of one who all unwittingly has wounded where she loves?
　　Why weaves she not her world-webs to according lutes
　　　and tabors,
　With nevermore this too remorseful air upon her face,
　　As of angel fallen from grace?"

[1] *Op. cit.* (Wessex ed.), p. 413.

And this is the answer:

—"Ah! knowest thou not her secret yet, her vainly veiled
    deficience,
Whence it comes that all unwittingly she wounds the lives she
    loves?
That sightless are those orbs of hers?—which bar to her
    omniscience
Brings those fearful unfulfilments, that red ravage through her
    zones
    Whereat all creation groans.[1]

The cosmic force is blind and unconscious, yet urged on by her
'primal doom' to create, and thus, blundering into consciousness,
she has brought forth beings who must perforce suffer by her casual
ways—beings so admirably made that they suggest, at times, that
the Mother is 'nigh to vision' (st. v). In this line, Hardy expresses
the puzzled opinion—a kind of teleological temptation—to which
the Natural Selectionists approached when studying the structure of
complex organs, such as the eye.

Since the 'Mother' is blind, we should 'deal her no scorn', for she
has no malice; and we can, in some small way, assist her and lighten
the burden of her creatures. Similar ideas, again clothed in mythical
garb, inform *Doom and She, God-Forgotten,* and *By the Earth's
Corpse.*[2] A more direct statement, poignant for its clarity and intense realization of cosmic despair, is *The Sleep-Worker:*

When wilt thou wake, O Mother, wake and see—
As one who, held in trance, has laboured long
By vacant rote and prepossession strong—
The coils that thou hast wrought unwittingly;

---

[1] *C. P.,* pp. 106—7.
[2] *C. P.,* pp. 108, 112, 114.

Wherein have place, unrealized by thee,
Fair growths, foul cankers, right enmeshed with wrong,
Strange orchestras of victim-shriek and song,
And curious blends of ache and ecstasy?—

Should that morn come, and show thy opened eyes
All that Life's palpitating tissues feel,
How wilt thou bear thyself in thy surprise?—

Wilt thou destroy, in one wild shock of shame,
Thy whole high heaving firmamental frame,
Or patiently adjust, amend, and heal?[1]

This is a vision of the cosmic 'Mother' very different from Swinburne's and Meredith's 'Fair Mother Earth'. In Hardy's bitter awareness of the predicament of life there are no 'divine contraries', but a web of chance and circumstance holding the sentient being in its coil.

In a poem more closely related to the imaginative and mythical pattern of the *Doom and She*-group, viz. *By the Earth's Corpse*, Hardy visualizes one of the possibilities foreshadowed in the final tercet of *The Sleep-Worker*. Here the cosmic Force—the 'Lord'—has awakened to the ill-conceived world of his making, and, having destroyed it all, is grieving by the Earth's corpse:

"Written indelibly
On my eternal mind
Are all the wrongs endured
By Earth's poor patient kind,
Which my too oft unconscious hand
Let enter undesigned.
No god can cancel deeds foredone,
Or thy old coils unwind!

[1] *C. P.,* pp. 110—11.

"As when, in Noë's days,
I whelmed the plains with sea,
So at this last, when flesh
And herb but fossils be,
And, all extinct, their piteous dust
Revolves obliviously,
That I made Earth, and life, and man,
It still repenteth me!"[1]

The last stanza expresses Hardy's intuition in imagery that recalls similar structures in Tennyson's *Despair* and *Vastness*.[2]

Since the emotions have no place in a world of defect, and since consciousness is a curse, Hardy, like Schopenhauer, repeatedly toys with the idea that nescience is the state to be desired—the only possible form of beatitude. *Before Life and After* looks back upon a Golden Age of unconsciousness:

A time there was—as one may guess
And as, indeed, earth's testimonies tell—
Before the birth of consciousness,
When all went well.

None suffered sickness, love, or loss,
None knew regret, starved hope, or heart-burnings;
None cared whatever crash or cross
Brought wrack to things.[3]

This happy state ended when the 'disease of feeling germed'. Elsewhere the poet conjectures that man's consciousness might have been a 'mistake of God's'.[4]

---

[1] *C. P.*, p. 115.   [2] Cf. *supra*, p. 77.   [3] *C. P.*, p. 260.
[4] *"I Travel as a Phantom Now"*, *C. P.*, p. 429.

The absurdity of human existence is enhanced by the fact that conscious thought and emotion do not imply freedom of will—man is an automaton subject to the inevitable workings of the First Cause. This determinism intensifies the dichotomy of a world where man is all the time exposed to 'Crass Casualty' and to natural law, and unable to achieve fulfilment or shape his destiny. *He Wonders about Himself* expresses a puzzled and uncanny foreboding of what 'I shall find me doing next'; for man is merely acting in a puppet show, 'Tugged by a force above or under'. Yet:

> Part is mine of the general Will,
> Cannot my share in the sum of sources
> Bend a digit the poise of forces,
> And a fair desire fulfil?[1]

We find, at times, also a wavering between hope and despair, free will and necessity, for instance in *The Pedigree,* where the poet rises in protest against the idea of automatism, and claims that *'I am I,/ And what I do I do myself alone'.*[2] However, in the majority of Hardy's poems the feeling prevails that our fates and actions are governed by something not ourselves—we are all, like Jude, 'predestinate'. In *The Unborn,* written about the same time as *The Dynasts* (1904—8), there is a nightmare vision of the 'all-immanent Will' forcing human beings into the exile of life. Thus to Hardy, as to all idealists, birth is 'the eclipsing curse'.

These minor poems illustrate certain fundamental aspects of Hardy's idea of the Immanent Will, and point to its final formulation in *The Dynasts.* But already in the poem *To the Unknown God,* written in 1901, there is a philosophical arrival:

> Long have I framed weak phantasies of Thee,
> O Willer masked and dumb!
> Who makest Life become,—

[1] 1893, *C. P.,* p. 480.   [2] 1916, *C. P.,* p. 432.

306

As though by labouring all-unknowingly,
    Like one whom reveries numb.

How much of consciousness informs Thy will,
    Thy biddings, as if blind,
    Of death-inducing kind,
Nought shows to us ephemeral ones who fill
    But moments in Thy mind.

Perhaps Thy ancient rote-restricted ways
    Thy ripening rule transcends; .
    That listless effort tends
To grow percipient with advance of days,
    And with percipience mends.

For, in unwonted purlieus, far and nigh,
    At whiles or short or long,
    May be discerned a wrong
Dying as of self-slaughter; whereat I
    Would raise my voice in song.[1]

Hardy is here at journey's end, face to face with his truth. It is not a happy discovery, yet now as at the time of *Hap* truth is inevitable, and Hardy's long search across a world governed by Chance, Circumstance and defective natural law could barely have issued in another conclusion. However, in so far as the poem expresses a pantheistic belief it nevertheless marks a significant change of metaphysical (and psychological) emphasis from the atrophy of *Hap*, and in this belief the poet reaches out towards new grounds for hope.

The symmetrical composition of this poem recalls Tennyson's similar juxtapositions, for the despairing vision of the first two

---

[1] *C.P.*, p. 171—2.

stanzas is balanced, or nearly held in counterpoise, by the tentative hope of the final ones. We meet at the outset a familiar figure of the unthinking 'worldweaver'—the 'somnambulist'—whose blind performance invites destruction. The hope, or rather conjecture, emerging in the third stanza seems based on a combination of evolutionary belief and cautious historical optimism. Thus in the idea of 'ripening rule' and of effort that tends to 'grow percipient' Hardy seizes on a dynamic and progressive aspect which was wholly absent in *Hap* and *Jude the Obscure*. Hardy justifies this hope of a growing consciousness in the 'Willer' by evidence drawn from the moral advance which he recognizes has taken place in the history of mankind.

Significantly, then, with the final formulation of the Will-concept there appears also the idea that the First Cause may grow percipient and providential. This is probably a concomitant to Hardy's approach to philosophical Idealism and urged by what E. Brennecke describes as a *horror vacui*.[1] Curtis Webster quotes a letter of the following year (1902) in which Hardy states his belief that

the Unconscious Will of the Universe is growing aware of Itself . . . (for) what has already taken place in a fraction of the whole (i.e. so much of the world as has become conscious) is likely to take place in the mass; and there being no Will outside the mass—that is, the Universe—the whole Will becomes conscious thereby: and ultimately, it is to be hoped, sympathetic.[2]

To the Unknown God is placed directly at the gates of *The Dynasts*, both in time and thought. The present outline will merely

---

[1] *Op. cit.*, p. 135.

[2] See Webster, *op. cit.*, p. 195. Webster, on the authority of W. Rutland, points out that Hardy was mistaken in thinking that his idea of growing consciousness in the Immanent Will was an original one. Von Hartmann had already developed the same theory in *Philosophy of the Unconscious*, translated in 1886. Cf. p. 196.

attempt to trace some of the relevant cosmogonic trends in the drama and their bearing on the maturing concept of the Immanent Will.

In the Fore Scene, where Spirits have gathered in the Overworld, we are at once confronted with the crucial enigma of existence:

What of the Immanent Will and Its designs?

Answer is given by the Spirit of the Years:

> *It works unconsciously, as heretofore,.*
> *Eternal artistries in Circumstance,*
> *Whose patterns, wrought by rapt æsthetic rote,*
> *Seem in themselves Its single listless aim,*
> *And not their consequence.*[1]

We may recall that Tennyson in *In Memoriam* (xxxiv) similarly expressed his fear that the world with its 'Fantastic beauty' might be just like the thing a 'wild Poet' makes 'when he works without a conscience or an aim'. To Hardy, the pattern of existence represents such chaotic, purposeless activity, for the Will, though not unthinking, weighs not '*Its thought*':

> *like a knitter drowsed,*
> *Whose fingers play in skilled unmindfulness,*
> *The Will has woven with an absent heed*
> *Since life first was; and ever will so weave.*

The Spirit of the Pities—the voice of human consciousness—feels that if this be the truth about existence, it were better that '*Such deeds were nulled, and this strange man's career/Wound up . . .*'. Yet the Spirit utters the hope or possibility that consciousness may

---

[1] *Op. cit.*, 1915 ed.

penetrate from the creatures to the Creator, that: *'Sublunar shocks may wake Its watch anon?'*.

In their commentaries—like those of a Greek Chorus—the Spirits meditate upon human destiny and on the nature and workings of the Immanent Will, and it is here that we have Hardy's mature expression of his belief. Early in the drama, (I, i, vi.), an important new metaphysical trend occurs in the idea that the Will cannot be judged by the criteria of human intellection. At first this appears to conflict with Hardy's recurrent statement that if the Will *knew* of the pain It inflicts on human beings, It would mend Its 'rote-restricted ways'. But at the same time, he now claims, the Will is above the activity of the human mind: It is *'scoped above percipience'*.[1] Therefore:

> *Nay, blame not! For what judgment can ye blame?—*
> *In that immense unweeting Mind is shown*
> *One far above forethinking; purposive,*
> *Yet superconscious; a Clairvoyancy*
> *That knows not what It knows, yet works therewith.—*
> *The cognizance ye mourn, Life's doom to feel,*
> *If I report it meetly, came unmeant,*
> *Emerging with blind gropes from impercipience*
> *By listless sequence—luckless, tragic Chance,*
> *In your more human tongue.*[2]

The last lines of this passage show that Hardy still adheres to Darwin's evolutionary doctrine, and imposes upon it, now as at the time of *Hap*, his own sombre interpretation. More relevant in this connexion is the paradoxical movement of the initial lines, where Hardy emerges from the metaphysical impasse of *Hap* and the tragic vision of *Jude the Obscure*. It is not, however, an effort to overcome the burden of determinism, nor a surrender to wishful

---

[1] I, i, vi.   [2] I, v, iv.

thinking, but an inner, more objective transformation of the Will-concept which removes it altogether from the sphere of human analogy. Hardy's intuition, it would seem, is approaching more closely to traditional pantheistic thought, for he now conceives of the will as an immanent, monistic Power which transcends its parts; which must necessarily differ in nature from human thought and activity, and which has 'purposes' though no 'motives'.[1] Hence the contingencies of Chance, Circumstance and defective law, all incomprehensible to the human mind. We cannot *understand* the apparently un-co-ordinated phenomena through which the Will objectifies itself, for they happen outside the causal connexions of human modes of thinking, or they remain beyond our knowledge. The Will—the 'thing in itself'— is for ever unknowable; on this point Hardy agrees with Kant, if not with Schopenhauer.

In adopting this pantheistic concept of the Prime Mover as Immanent Will, superconscious and purposive, though unmotived, Hardy is probing into the mystery of existence in a new way. Unmistakably, his position is related not only to Schopenhauer and the Idealistic tradition, (Kant's agnosticism in particular), but seems to point even further back to the monistic doctrine of Aristotle, with its idea of nisus as a teleological though unfelt urge in Nature. Aristotle too, it will be remembered, held that God—the Prime Mover—had no knowledge of the world. The important thing about the transformation of Hardy's Will-concept is that it offers grounds for hope: in the new elements of superconsciousness and 'purposive' urge which it now embraces, there is a possibility of a union and reconciliation, through evolving consciousness, between the Will and the world.

The poetic intention of *The Dynasts* is to show how the Will objectifies itself in Nature, History and in all human experience, and the

---

[1] Cf. Brennecke's definition of the Will's 'purposes' as different from human 'motives' in having no aim or object; *op cit.,* p. 117.

311

action illustrates its philosophical thesis with magnificent imaginative force. We watch the 'key-scene' of the epic drama—the Europe
of the Napoleonic wars—spread out like 'Will-webs' in which all
human beings, from the common soldier to Napoleon and other
Dynasts, are hopelessly caught. They live in the pathetic illusion of
free will and action, but in reality their existence is a puppet show
where the strings are pulled by '*the Prime Mover of the gear*'.

Thus, the attitude which informs the underlying thought-structure
of the drama is one of consistent pessimism and fatalism: There
are inevitable forces inside and outside man to which he is subject.
All

> *men's passions, virtues, visions, crimes,*
> *Obey resistlessly*
> *The purposive, unmotived, dominant Thing*
> *Which sways in brooding dark their wayfaring.*[1]

It follows that human striving, sacrifice and pain are futile: all this
terrible suffering and waste of war is '*Endured in vain, in vain!*'.
(I, v, iv.) And throughout the drama runs the *leit-motif* that human
tragedy is the '*intolerable antilogy/Of making figments feel!*'.
(I, iv, v.) By choosing an ugly moment of history for his illustration
of the human plight, Hardy intensifies the universal drama of
struggle for existence, or for possession, and when the end comes
to this war, Europe is indeed a 'tract of pain' where 'light lies spent
to darkness'. And therefore, in the After Scene, the Spirit of the
Years rounds off its puppet-show with the conclusion anticipated
at the opening of the performance:

> *Thus doth the Great Foresightless mechanize*
> *In blank entrancement now as evermore*
> *Its ceaseless artistries in Circumstance*
> *Of curious stuff and braid, as just forthshown.*
> *Yet but one flimsy riband of Its web*

[1] II, ii, iii.

312

*Have we here watched in weaving—web **Enorm**,*
Whose furthest hem and selvage may extend
To where the roars and plashings of the flames
Of earth-invisible suns swell noisily,
And onwards into ghastly gulfs of sky,
Where hideous presences churn through the dark—
Monsters of magnitude without a shape,
Hanging amid deep wells of nothingness.
Yet seems this vast and singular confection
Wherein our scenery glints of scantest size,
Inutile all—so far as reasonings tell. ·

Yet, there is the Spirit of the Pities to whom reasonings are not all, and who still speaks for hope, despite the crushing tragedy of the vision just displayed:

Thou arguest still the Inadvertent Mind.—
But, even so, shall blankness be for aye?
Men gained cognition with the flux of time,
And wherefore not the Force informing them,
When far-ranged aions past all fathoming
Shall have swung by, and stand as backward years?

Again the thought-pattern of the Fore Scene is repeated: the world-order may change with the Will growing conscious. As the After Scene comes to a close, the scales of despair and hope are poised, but in the final dialogue between the Spirits of the Years and the Pities the main theme is once more stated, and a significant shift of emphasis is made:

SEMICHORUS I OF THE YEARS (aerial music)

Last as first the question rings
Of the Will's long travailings;
Why the All-mover,
Why the All-prover

313

Ever urges on and measures out the chordless chime of Things.
. . . .

SEMICHORUS I OF THE PITIES

Nay;—shall not Its blindness break?
Yea, must not Its heart awake,
Promptly tending
To Its mending
In a genial germing purpose, and for loving-kindness' sake?
. . . .

CHORUS

But—a stirring thrills the air
Like to sounds of joyance there
That the rages
Of the ages
Shall be cancelled, and deliverance offered from the darts that
were,
Consciousness the Will informing, till It fashion all things fair!

As Brennecke comments, this expression of ultimate hope contrasts starkly with Hardy's philosophy as developed in the minor poems and in the novels. Incidentally, it also breaks with the closely related metaphysical system of Schopenhauer.

If, then, Hardy after his long search out of the human quandary arrives at a hope which almost approaches to the condition of belief, that the Will may grow conscious and providential, what is the metaphysical consequence of this new attitude? It implies a break with the uncompromising agnosticism which informs his earlier novels and poems. Hardy's thought in *The Dynasts* has dared to penetrate 'the material screen' of which he speaks in *The House of Silence*, and resumes the freer movement of the mystic's intuition.

As the philosophy of *Hap* grew into that of *Jude the Obscure*, Hardy moved away from the scientific determinism of Darwin's

314

teaching and gradually adopted a fatalistic outlook in which a mystical trend predominates. Yet, throughout, he continues to see human destiny as a 'palpable dilemma', ruled by inescapable forces, and Nature as a process governed by Chance. Even in *The Dynasts,* published half a century after the *Origin of Species* appeared, the influence of Darwin is still evident, and the world which Hardy deplores to the end, with the Spirit of the Pities, is one of natural selection, of fortuitous variations, and fierce struggle. Darwin, one feels, has given him the truth about natural conditions as they actually are, and our only hope is that they may change. This hope in the despairing poet germinates from an inner need, coinciding with his acceptance of philosophical Idealism and the pantheistic conception of the Immanent Will. It is significant also, that the hope which arises within the maturing idea of the 'superconscious Will' is derived from Hardy's intuition into the dynamic and evolutionary nature of the cosmic process. Thus, in the end, the idea of evolution compensates to some extent for the loss which it had caused, though it could never answer the questions asked in *God's Funeral.*

Among the poets of evolution preceding him in this inquiry, Hardy occupies a unique position in that, even in contrast to the positivists, he begins by making a complete *tabula rasa* of Christian and Idealistic values—with the sole exception of Truth. 'Spirit' and 'God' which all the time remain such momentous evolutionary forces in Swinburne and Meredith, have no significance in the world of *Hap* and *Jude the Obscure.* With the absence of these teleological principles there vanishes also the source of faith and hope which had inspired the worshippers of Life. In the dramatic history of evolutionary belief in poets of the nineteenth century, Hardy creates the tragic peripeteia, and with the sheer force of his art and thought seems to have destroyed once and for all the facile Utopian dreams of idealists and positivists alike.

315

In the end, however, one is tempted to ask whether Hardy did not too readily and uncritically succumb to the deterministic thought of his age, so that, penetrating as is his vision of existence, it defeats itself intellectually through its adherence to a doctrine which has mostly proved a dead end in philosophy. It is true that Hardy met the flood of Darwinistic and Positivistic ideas in his most impressionable years, and that the impact was tremendous. It is true also that scientific determinism was on the offensive and reached its apex of practically uncontested power in the years when Hardy wrote his major works. Even *The Dynasts* was written well before the deterministic myth was exploded in physics as in philosophy. Yet, despite the *Zeitgeist,* Hardy's acceptance of Darwin's theory reveals the limitation of his thought, an emotional as well as intellectual limitation. He does not appear to have asked the obvious and destructive questions: does evolution actually take place in this way? Are chance mutations and natural selection the only or primary causes of new forms of life? Therefore, though he is a profounder thinker than Browning, we miss in Hardy's attitude something of the protest, however fumbling and subjective, with which Browning answered the deterministic challenge.

This intellectual limitation affects, clearly, the value and scope of Hardy's poetic interpretation of existence. Yet it is obvious that whatever doctrinal framework Hardy might have found at hand, the world of his poetic vision would sooner or later have developed into a scene of strife and a puppet-show, where individuals suffer and die to no purpose. It would in all circumstances have been an ill-conceived world in which not to be born would have been best. That he himself in the end should break the boundaries of this limited world is what we might have expected, for the poet and prophet exercised his birthright:

> The visionary powers of souls who dare
> To pierce the material screen.

CHAPTER V

BUTLER'S MORE LIVING FAITH

SAMUEL BUTLER'S writings on evolution are of such a nature, and in part composed under such unusual circumstances, that they involve problems of criticism very different from those which confront us in prophets like Meredith or philosophers like Hardy. The spirit and form in which they are presented make it necessary to ask: is this a confession of faith or a clever joke? Is Butler really in earnest when he preaches his theory of heredity as memory, and is his chief reason for the violent and persistent exposure of Darwin that he had 'banished mind from the universe' or the fact that he had altered the Krause article?

The question of 'sincerity' or 'seriousness' has indeed been a touchstone in Butler criticism since his own day. Among the men of science of Darwin's camp it was reasonable and convenient to dismiss his theories as jokes and himself as a comedian with a persecution mania. His fantastic speculations looked too much like parodies of scientific argument; and as such they have been treated also by later and more sympathetic critics, who have often been tempted to stress the force of Butler's destructive genius, at the cost of considering whatever positive intrinsic values his ideas might have. This over-emphasis is in part due to a revulsion from the fastidious attempts of a few naturalists to vindicate Butler's evolutionary theories, out of their imaginative contexts, in part to the apologetic assumption that the quality and content of Butler's ideas do not matter as long as they are good comedy.

317

Because of their often peculiar environment, and because of the mocking smile which plays about them, it is difficult to accept these ideas at their face value, and even more perilous is the task of seizing the attitude and intention behind them. Perhaps Butler is mainly or merely the 'mischievous clever schoolboy' whose 'mental frivolity' makes him 'play with revered things'.[1] Perhaps, as Mr. Furbank suggests in his admirable recent study, pleasure is the best key to Butler's writings on evolution.[2] Yet most of them were forged as weapons in an embittered controversy, and to the reader they present every shade of transition in mood and expression from what C. E. M. Joad calls the 'bluff' of the machines in *Erewhon* to the passionate appeal for 'a more living faith' in *Life and Habit* and the angry denunciations in *Evolution Old and New*.

It is no doubt true, as Mr. Furbank shows, that an important aspect of Butler's writings on evolution is the way in which he pursues his theories *ad absurdum*, and thus is able to corrode scientific doctrine from the inside.[3] After reading *Life and Habit*, however, it is difficult not to feel that Butler's evolutionary belief has a great deal of positive, original value, and suggests evocative answers to problems which are still with us.[4]

The present chapter will deal mainly with the imaginative impact of the idea of evolution on Butler's writings up to *Erewhon*, and finally with *Life and Habit* as the freshest and least polemical profession of Butler's own evolutionary faith. Our justification for omitting the three books which Butler wrote during his controversy with the Darwinians—*Evolution Old and New* (1879), *Unconscious Memory* (1880), *Luck or Cunning* (1887)—is that, apart from the vibration-theory borrowed from Hering and introduced into the two last works, there is only an elaboration and repetition of ideas already

[1] C. E. M. Joad, *Samuel Butler*, p. 170.
[2] P. N. Furbank, *Samuel Butler*, p. 51.
[3] *Op. cit.*, pp. 56, 61.
[4] This thesis is well argued by C. E. M. Joad in *Samuel Butler*.

contained in *Life and Habit*. Moreover, the controversial elements relevant to our inquiry are clearly set out in that work, in a dramatic confrontation of Lamarck and Darwin, and in a personal charge which was to grow more bitter and stubborn but also more tedious with the years.[1]

Towards the Machines of Erewhon

As a member of the general public, at that time residing eighteen miles from the nearest human habitation, and three days' journey on horseback from a bookseller's shop, I became one of Mr. Darwin's many enthusiastic admirers, and wrote a philosophical dialogue ... upon the "Origin of Species".[2]

It was the sheep-farmer Samuel Butler, then twenty-five years of age and exiled, for economic and religious reasons, who was thus converted to evolution. In his life as well as in his letters he had begun that war of independence the most salient early stages of which are marked by his break with his father and with Christianity. Having decided that he could not take orders, he left for New Zealand, and it was here that Darwin's work on the species found him early in 1860. The 'philosophical dialogue' which Butler wrote on the *Origin of Species* merely stated Darwin's theory in a shrewd, oblique attack on Christianity. His second contribution to *The Press* in New Zealand was 'Darwin among the Machines', (June 1863), and here Butler seized the theme which he later worked into the chapter on the machines in *Erewhon*.[3] This first treatment is an imaginative *tour de force,* and reveals already some of Butler's gift of the humorous twist and surprise. It consists in developing a mock analogy between the vegetable, animal and 'mechanical' kingdoms,

[1] For a detailed objective account of the quarrel see J. B. Fort, *Samuel Butler*, pp. 165—204.

[2] Introduction to *Unconscious Memory*, (1922), p. 11.

[3] Cf. Preface to the 1901 ed. of *Erewhon*, where the genesis of the book is fully related.

and translating the terms of the one into those of the other.—
Compared with the slow progress in the animal and vegetable kingdom, the growth of machinery, from the 'earliest primordial types
of mechanical life; such as the lever and the wedge, has been so
vast and rapid that inevitably we are forced to ask: What will this
progress lead to? Analogy gives us reason to think that

as the vegetable kingdom was slowly developed from the mineral,
and as, in like manner, the animal supervened upon the vegetable,
so now, in these last few ages, an entirely new kingdom has sprung
up of which we as yet have only seen what will one day be considered the antediluvian prototypes of the race.[1]

There follows a passage in which the author regrets that his knowledge of natural history and machinery does not enable him to clas-
sify machines into genera and species nor to trace the connecting
links between machines of different characters, nor to point out the
rudimentary organs occasionally found in them.

Through these preliminary reflections the author approaches 'one
of the greatest and most mysterious questions of the day .. : What
sort of creature man's next successor in the supremacy of the earth
is likely to be.' Clearly, the answer is that we are ourselves making
these creatures, in the machines, constantly increasing their beauty
and power and supplying them with self-regulating devices which
serve them as the intellect serves man. Therefore,

In the course of ages we shall find ourselves the inferior race. Inferior
in power, inferior in that moral quality of self-control, we shall look
up to them as the acme of all that the best and wisest man can ever
dare to aim at. No evil passions, no jealousy, no avarice, no impure
desires will disturb the serene might of those glorious creatures. Sin,
shame and sorrow will have no place among them. Their minds
will be in a state of perpetual calm, the contentment of a spirit that
knows no wants, is disturbed by no regrets.[2]

[1] *Op. cit., The Note-Books*, (1930 ed.), p. 43.
[2] *Ibid.*, p. 44.

What, then, will be man's position in the future, when the machines have become his masters?

He will continue to exist, nay even to improve, and will be probably better off in his state of domestication under the beneficent rule of the machines than he is in his present wild state.[1]

This, however, is the choice now placed before mankind: either to submit to the new superior race which is gradually though kindly enslaving us, or to wage war to the death on them. The author, despite his admiration for the machines, unhesitatingly advocates the latter course, which means a return to the 'primeval conditions of the race'.

'Darwin among the Machines' is an ingenious piece of verbal see-saw, and the analogy from which Butler works gives fine scope to his power of transfiguring, with a few simple strokes of caricature, the humdrum facts of reality. This is no longer the pupil's timid exercise, as in the 'Dialogue', but the clown's expert fun. Yet, though the fun is obvious, and quite innocent, it was resented by Darwin's supporters who suspected a disguised parody of the theory of transmutation, and this illustrates well enough Mr. Furbank's point that Butler already in this slight piece of writing 'had found the proper way to make things awkward for the Darwinians'.[2]

Two years later, in 1865, Butler sent his second article, 'Lucubratio Ebria' to *The Press*. His concern for the fate of this new article is greater, for: 'There is hardly a sentence in it written without deliberation'.[3] Here once more Butler steps forth as the disciple of Darwin, at least in the serious introductory meditation upon the history of life:

The limbs of the lower animals have never been modified by any act of deliberation and forethought on their own part. Recent researches have thrown absolutely no light upon the origin of life—

[1] *Ibid..,* p. 45.   [2] *Op. cit.,* p. 61.   [3] *Note-Books,* pp. 41—42.

upon the initial force which introduced a sense of identity, and a deliberate faculty into the world; but they do certainly appear to show very clearly that each species of the animal and vegetable kingdom has been moulded into its present shape by chances and changes of many millions of years, by chances and changes over which the creature modified had no control whatever, and concerning whose aim it was alike unconscious and indifferent, by forces which seem insensate to the pain which they inflict, but by whose inexorably beneficent cruelty the brave and strong keep coming to the fore, while the weak and bad drop behind and perish. There was a moral government of this world before man came near it—a moral government suited to the capacities of the governed, and which, unperceived by them, has laid fast the foundations of courage, endurance and cunning.[1]

The passage is worth quoting, for it shows that Butler is trying to maintain an impossible logical position between chance variations on the one hand and a moral government, or purposive evolution, on the other. He solves the dilemma in a way characteristic of the most sanguine Darwinian naturalists—by deducing the 'moral government' from the survival values which evolution has preserved in the fittest. Thus, in a sweeping gesture, he compresses into one sentence Hardy's philosophy of *Hap* and Meredith's evolutionary ethics, and forces them to become reconciled. Typical of Meredith is the idea of the 'inexorably beneficent cruelty' of the forces of Nature, selecting the 'brave and the strong'. The identification of the fit and the good and the bad and the weak in this passage is of such intellectual audacity that if it were not for the conclusion and the emphasis on 'courage, endurance and cunning', one would be tempted to suspect here the impish laugh that was soon to be heard in *Erewhon*.

To Butler, however, these postulations are necessary for the ensuing argument. He believes in Darwin without reserve, he believes

[1] *Ibid.*, p. 48.

in progress, in the accumulation of values and qualities, and in their inheritance, until

at last when human intelligence stole like a late spring upon the mimicry of our semi-simious ancestry, the creature learnt how he could, of his own forethought, add extra-corporaneous limbs to the members of his body and become not only a vertebrate mammal, but a vertebrate machinate mammal into the bargain.[1]

There has been a constant interaction between the use of tools and the development of the human brain: 'The mind grew because the body grew'. Animals and insects with no gifts for using tools remain fixed, or change very slowly, while man, whose physical powers are rapidly increasing through his 'mechanical limbs', has become a 'quicksand for the foundation of an unchanging civilization', and there is no limit to his progress. Hence the author of 'Lucubratio Ebria' refutes the argument of 'a previous correspondent'—the author of 'Darwin among the Machines'—who had seen machines as identities, animated them and predicted their final triumph over mankind. This was a mistake, for

They are to be regarded as the mode of development by which human organism is most especially advancing, and every fresh invention is to be considered as an additional member of the resources of the human body. Herein lies the fundamental difference between man and his inferiors.[2]

Thus in the railway train—'that seven-leagued foot which five hundred may own at once'—man has developed a unique 'unity of limbs' which shows that his advance on animals is no longer one in degree, but in kind.

In the following passage, as he meditates upon the effect of environment, Butler again shows his talent of caricaturing an idea.

---

[1] *Ibid.*, pp. 48—49.

[2] *Ibid.*, p. 50. This idea is later to be repeated in connexion with an argument for teleology in *Life and Habit*, p. 243.

Modern man, the argument runs, is the child, not only of his parents, but of his institutions and tools and machines. These 'new limbs were preserved by natural selection...; they descended with modifications, and hence proceeds the difference between our ancestors and ourselves.' Modern man has grown into an exeedingly complex organism, varying with age and season and, above all, with the degree of wealth. He has added umbrella, watch, knife and pencil case to his other limbs, and 'if he be a really well-developed specimen of the race, he will be furnished with a large box upon wheels, two horses, and a coachman.' Consequently, 'we may assert with strictly scientific accuracy that the Rothschilds are the most astonishing organisms that the world has ever yet seen.' However, Butler concludes with a shrewd self-contradictory return to the moral issue of the fittest, 'We do not say that the thousand-horse man is better than a one-horse man, we only say that he is more highly organized...'.[1]

It is obvious that the value of Butler's two first excursions into evolution lies not in any evidence they yield of his attitude to life or of his own personal belief, but in the way they reveal his imaginative preoccupation with the evolutionary idea: despite comedy and caricature, it is to Butler a new and fascinating instrument of thought.

'Darwin among the Machines' reappeared in a slightly altered form in 'The Book of the Machines' in *Erewhon* (1872), and into a later edition of that same work 'Lucubratio Ebria' also found its way.[2] 'The Book of the Machines' is a mock treatise by an Erewhonian professor, and the theme and its implications fit neatly into the satirical environment of the 'Colleges of Unreason' preceding it, and the chapters on the 'Rights of Animals' and the 'Rights of Vegetables' which succeed it in the final edition.

[1] *Ibid.*, p. 52.
[2] Cf. Preface of 1901 ed., pp. xi—xii.

There is little development in the body of ideas from the press article to *Erewhon*, but the man-machine analogy is carried further *ad absurdum*—and with ingenious skill. Moreover, there is a significant change of emphasis to mainly two aspects, i.e. an all-pervading consciousness in the universe, and determinism.

Once more Butler sets out from the idea that we can clearly observe the emergence of a new superior race in the machine evolution, and a large part of his treatise is devoted to a refutation of the argument that machines have no consciousness, and consequently will never supersede the human race. After all,

who can say that the vapour engine has not a kind of consciousness? Where does consciousness begin, and where end? Who can draw the line? Who can draw any line? Is not everything interwoven with everything? Is not machinery linked with animal life in an infinite variety of ways?[1]

Consciousness emerged on our globe, though at the time when it was a hot round ball there was no sign that anything like mind could ever evolve from its matter. And just as animal consciousness superseded that of vegetables we have reason to fear that a new phase of mind will arise, growing from its 'primordial cell'—the higher machine, which is already here.

The writer goes on to develop the point that machinery is linked with animal life in an infinite variety of ways, and conversely, that consciousness is manifest in what we see as the mechanical action of, for instance, plants. In this sense every action, in plant as in man, is mechanical, that it will continue as long as the plant or man is 'wound up'. Yet if the action of the growing potato or growing boy does not reveal consciousness, what is the use of this term?

As the argument on the theme of 'Who can draw the line?' proceeds, it incorporates a trend of materialistic determinism, in a subtle blend of cunning analogy and naïveté:

[1] 1872 ed., p. 190.

If it be urged that the action of the potato is chemical and mechanical only, and that it is due to the chemical and mechanical effects of light and heat, the answer would seem to lie in an inquiry whether every sensation is not chemical and mechanical in its operation? whether those things which we deem most purely spiritual are anything but disturbances of equilibrium in an infinite series of levers, beginning with those that are too small for microscopic detection, and going up to the human arm and the appliances which it makes use of? whether there be not a molecular action of thought, whence a dynamical theory of the passions shall be deducible? Whether, strictly speaking, we should not ask what kind of levers a man is made of rather than what is his temperament?[1]

Thus, since 'everything is interwoven with everything', since man is a piece of chemical and mechanical machinery whose mind grew from unconscious matter, we may legitimately assume that the machines will one day become conscious. That day will mean either extinction or slavery for the human race.

There follows in the machine 'Book' a demonstration of the thesis that 'everything is interwoven with everything'. At present the mutual dependence of man and the machine has become such that they can hardly exist without one another. The machines depend upon man for feeding and reproduction while man would be practically helpless without their service. Indeed, one day he may become 'a sort of parasite' upon the machines—'An affectionate machine-tickling aphid'.[2]

Whatever can be conjectured about the future, it is certain that the machines evolve at great speed, and there are now even 'many which have got stomachs of their own', in contrast to more primitive species like the spade and the plough:

This is a great step towards their becoming, if not animate, yet something so near akin to it, as not to differ more widely from our own life than animals do from vegetables. And though man should

[1] *Ibid.*, pp. 192—3.   [2] P. 197.

326

remain, in some respects, the higher creature, is not this in accordance with the practice of nature, which allows superiority in some things to animals which have, on the whole, been long surpassed?

Against this idea of machines becoming animate it has been objected that they have no reproductive system:

If this be taken to mean that they cannot marry, and that we are never likely to see a fertile union between two vapour-engines with the young ones playing about the door of the shed, however greatly we might desire to do so, I will readily grant it. But the objection is not a very profound one.[1]

In the conclusion Butler resumes the trend of mechanistic determinism. It is true that the present machines may have no will of their own, but this is no weighty argument against their being 'the germs of a new phase of life'. For 'What is there in this whole world, or in the worlds beyond it, which has a will of its own? The Unknown and Unknowable only!' On this point man differs but little from the machine, for though he is infinitely more complex and therefore less predictable in his actions, he behaves as regularly 'as though he were a machine'. 'And this', Butler adds with a very obvious chuckle, 'is a great blessing; for it is the foundation on which morality and science are built'.[2]

In the earlier editions of *Erewhon* (1872, 1880), this mock treatise ends on the exhortation to destroy all machinery, lest man should come under its despotic rule.[3] Later, in 1901, Butler incorporated 'Lucubratio Ebria', in a shortened form, as a counter-argument.

'The Book of the Machines' adds effectively to the main stream of satire in *Erewhon,* and its merits of style, of verbal contortion and finely controlled burlesque, are those of a master of imaginative prose. If, however, we ask for any personal underlying motives or

[1] Pp. 202—3.   [2] Pp.209—10.
[3] Cf. 'Darwin among the Machines', conclusion.

327

ideas, these elude us in the mazes of farcical analogy and twisted argument. And it is in this subtle technique that we see Butler's destructive genius most powerfully at work. In its *bona fide* naïve claims of 'who can draw the line', of determinism, and of 'everything is interwoven with everything', 'The Book of the Machines' in the end reveals itself as an oblique attack, a caricature, not of Darwin's theory, but of scientific hypothesis in general, and of the pristine smugness of men of science. Butler's parody strikes home to the excessive enthusiasm of materialistic determinism which reached its apex in the decade when *Erewhon* appeared. The pulpit tones of this new orthodoxy had begun to jar on Butler's ears, and his response is a *reductio ad absurdum* of scientific theory. But this is not the whole truth about the 'Book of the Machines', for, as critics have pointed out, there is, underneath the humour and fun, a real fear of spiritual slavery in a machine age, and the fact that Butler laughs while he warns does not invalidate this view. It is characteristic of him to make fun of the persons and things he most dislikes, and here, in the image of man as 'an affectionate machine-tickling aphid' he blends humour and horror to an effect which is the more powerful for its ambiguous and apparently careless tone.[1]

Evolution is Memory: Life and Habit

Life and Habit, Butler's biographer tells us, descended 'with modifications from the machines in *Erewhon*'.[2] It would be more correct to say that the book descended from the tools and machines in 'Lucubratio Ebria', and it was some time after 1873 *(The Fair*

[1] It is this warning against machine domination which makes C. E. M. Joad characterize *Erewhon* as an allegory or prophecy which 'stands out as one of the most remarkable pieces of insight of the last century', *Samuel Butler*, p. 182.

[2] *A Memoir*, I, p. 232; see also Butler's own account in *Unconscious Memory*, p. 16.

Haven) that Butler, while absorbed in the writing of *Life and Habit,* reversed in a typical see-saw movement his idea of machines as limbs into the idea of limbs as machines. This new line of thought inevitably leads to the question: 'How did we come to make them without knowing anything about it?'[1] Is it possible that we have made them unconsciously, by 'habit', because we have made them so often and learnt to make them so well that we no longer reflect on the process nor remember how we came to learn it? If so, *when* did we acquire this expert knowledge? Surely not as a foetus before birth. The answer must be that we practised it in our ancestors, and remember it in our pre-natal growth as well as after birth. Heredity and habit are, in other words, unconscious memory. It is the bearing of this hypothesis upon the evolution of life which is Butler's main task in *Life and Habit.* His method of approach is already indicated: he proceeds through a series of analogies to apply our mental (mnemic) experience to physical growth and development.

Actions, Butler observes, which once required great attention and practice, like playing the piano, walking and talking, may be learnt so thoroughly that they no longer involve a conscious effort—they have become habits. If all acquired actions and habits have to be learnt by thorough practice before they become automatic and perfect, then it is legitimate to assume that such actions as we perform with no trace of consciousness—actions which we could not have learnt in our life-time, have also been acquired through long practice and 'upon a balance of considerations'.[2] The term 'hereditary instinct' has been coined to explain such unconscious actions as the oxygenisation of the blood, which the infant knows how to perform ten minutes after birth. Yet, Butler claims, on closer scrutiny the term proves absurd, unless we may show that the same law of learning and of fading consciousness holds good throughout all phases of life. And surely it would be illogical to think that the

---

[1] *Unconscious Memory,* p. 16.
[2] *Life and Habit* (1877), p. 49.

conditions of experience differed essentially at the various stages of growth, before birth and after. If 'hereditary instinct'—'the experience of the race'—has a meaning, it must be a closer 'continuity of life and sameness between living beings, whether plants or animals, and their descendants... than we have hitherto believed'.[1] How can this instinct or experience be shared? Because the individual is one with and part of his progenitor, 'imbued with all his memories, profiting by all his experiences—which are, in fact, his own—'.

Man then, is the outcome of infinite learning and practice, and every individual repeats unconsciously his ancient lore:

His past selves are living in him at this moment with the accumulated life of centuries. "Do this, this, this, which we too have done, and found our profit in it", cry the souls of his forefathers within him. Faint are the far ones, coming and going as the sound of bells wafted on to a high mountain; loud and clear are the near ones, urgent as an alarm of fire.[2]

If we see man thus belonging to one vast being, continuous in time, and immortal, all the habits—like seeing, breathing, digesting—which a baby one day old masters perfectly—can be explained. Conversely, to assert that it is capable of these actions without ever having done them before, and learnt through infinite repetition to do them so well that the memory of the how and where and when has faded, would be to contradict the 'whole experience of mankind.'[3]

A corollary of this is that 'Birth has been made too much of'—it is an artificial barrier thrown across the unbroken current of heredity, or memory, and Butler sets out to re-examine 'the whole history and development of the embryo in all its stages'.[4] He finds that birth is not so much the point at which we begin to live as the

[1] *Ibid.*, p. 50.   [2] *Ibid.*, p. 52.   [3] *Ibid.*, p. 54.   [4] P. 59.

330

point at which we leave off knowing *how* to live. This is true of all creatures:

A chicken, for example, is never so full of consciousness, activity, reasoning faculty, and volition, as when it is an embryo in the egg-shell, making bones, and flesh, and feathers, and eyes, and claws, with nothing but a little warmth and white of egg to make them from.[1]

The conclusion forces itself upon us that the chicken has existed before, in an infinite number of lives. And it follows that

To shear the thread of life, and hence of memory, between one generation and its successor, is, so to speak, a brutal measure, an act of intellectual butchery...[2]

The chicken growing in the shell has little or no perception of what it is doing or what it wants, but the certainty with which it works proves that it has done the same thing a vast number of times, and consequently, it must be '*the same chicken which makes itself over and over again*'.[3] Butler arrives now at one of the main obstacles to his thesis: the problem of how to reconcile 'personal identity' with this idea of unbroken memory. His approach is characteristic, for in one bold sweep—in the name of common sense—he reduces the term to a *façon de parler,* and hence deceptive, since 'The least reflection will show that personal identity in any sort of strictness is an impossibility'.[4] Butler's argument is based, mainly, on the claim that there is a higher degree of identity between the foetus one hour before birth and the new-born baby than between the baby and the octogenarian into which it may grow. Yet if we say that there is personal identity between the old man and the baby, we have also to admit sameness between him and the foetus. Again, the identity of the foetus must be extended, not only to the impregnate ovum from

[1] P. 60.   [2] P. 61.   [3] P. 74.   [4] P. 84.

which it grows, but to the germ cells, and further still, to the parents.[1] Each impregnate ovum 'should be considered not as descended from its ancestors, but as being a continuation of the personality of every ovum in the chain of its ancestry, which every ovum *it actually is* . .'[2]

In this way, linking parent and germ-cell in a continuous chain of sameness, Butler traces personal identity back to the primordial cell, and even beyond. For

This process cannot stop short of the primordial cell, which again will probably turn out to be but a brief resting-place. We therefore prove each one of us to *be actually* the primordial cell which never died nor dies, but has differentiated itself into the life of the world, all living beings whatever, being one with it, and members one of another.[3]

Butler here expresses an idea closely related to Schopenhauer's notion of the indestructibility of the Will, i. e. life, and brings to its extreme consequence the monistic and evolutionary doctrine of Swinburne and Meredith.

Personal identity, Butler goes on arguing, is not conditioned by sameness of matter (Cf. octogenarian and baby), nor by a perception of continuity, but by this fusion of the various phases of growth, which 'have flowed the one out of the other in what we see as a continuous, though it may be at times, a troubled stream.' This is the point at which Butler's key-stone is to be placed into position; for this stream of life, he claims, is 'the very essence of personality,

[1] P. 85.

[2] P. 86. — M. Hartog, in 'Samuel Butler and Recent Mnemic Biological Theories', *Scientia* 1914, notes that William Bateson gives Butler credit for having formulated in *Life and Habit* the theory of the continuity of the germ-plasm. Ref. to 'Heredity and Variation in Modern Lights', *Darwin and Modern Science*, 1909.

[3] P. 86.

but it involves the probable unity of all animal and vegetable life, as being, in reality, nothing but one single creature ...'[1] And if this unity be granted, there should be no logical (though there is an emotional) difficulty in admitting personal identity between parents and their offspring and thus in supposing that an organism, whether plant or animal, remembers, 'in a profound but unselfconscious way' all the experience accumulated from its long life's history.[2]

It remains for Butler to show that the process of growth is actually identical with, or of the same nature as the process of memory, and it remains to show *how* this process operates. The latter task, however, is not attempted in *Life and Habit*.[3] Butler's approach to the former is again that of bold analogy, and his method consists in transferring what he sees as the principal mnemic laws—about six in number, to corresponding phases or phenomena of organic development. First among these he places the tendency to remember and repeat the set of impressions or actions in which we have most recently been engaged; in terms of biology: the closest family likeness is to be found between offspring and their immediate forbears.[4] Secondly, an action repeated so often as to become a habit, will normally be performed in the same manner or sequence, and similarly: offspring adopt the same order of development as their parents, and pass through the same successive phases, before birth and after, with only slight deviations.[5] Thirdly, a habitual set of actions (or memories) may be changed through new ideas which, if they are useful and not too novel to disturb the habitual perform-

[1] P. 97.

[2] P. 102.—In the ensuing chapter (vii) on 'Our Subordinate Personalities', Butler attempts to demonstrate the same theory of identity from physiological evidence, and quotes profusely from Darwin, Ribot and Carpenter.

[3] In *Unconscious Memory*, 1880, Butler offers the 'vibration'-theory as an explanation.

[4] Pp. 156, 168.   [5] Pp. 158, 170.

ance, may be adopted as part of the action. Butler finds that this tendency is manifest in the 'predominance of sexual over asexual generation', and in the way 'intelligent embryos' sometimes alter the ordinary course of growth.[1] From now on, however, Butler appears to be somewhat out of step with his laws and corollaries, for the real genetic parallel occurs in the fact that 'Species ... are occasionally benefited by a cross' ... if it be not too wide.[2] As a fourth law, Butler claims the tendency to forget the process of learning once the performance has become perfect and automatic: This explains the instinctive actions and habits of offspring.[3] Next comes the law of associations, the biological corollary of which is found in the way in which offspring deal with problems or aspects of growth with which their progenitors have dealt at corresponding stages, each stage or situation calling up a definite set of memories.[4] Finally, as a sixth law, which is mainly an adjunct to the one preceding it, Butler points out the sudden recurrence of a memory which breaks a chain of associations. This accounts for the genetic tendency to reversion to discontinued types or structures.[5]

If it be accepted, then, that all creatures are really one continuous being, rooted in the same origin, and living over and over again until they become millions of years old; if it be granted, moreover, that growth and reproduction is a process of memory, then the total history of life appears in a new light. It reveals how organisms have been able to vary, how, in fact, evolution has been a creative and advancing process; for without this force of memory and accumulated experience, a variation, a new habit, could not persist and be integrated as a permanent structure.[6] We are here approaching the point at which Butler breaks with his great master, Darwin, and forms a new alliance with Lamarck.

[1] Pp. 158—60, 173.   [2] Pp. 173—4, IV.
[3] Pp. 161—2, 183—6, 189—90,—V, VI.
[4] Pp. 162, 191.   [5] Pp. 164, 192—7.   [6] Pp. 198 ff.

Evolution is Faith and Desire

In 1877, when Butler was preparing *Life and Habit* for the press, a friend advised him to read Mivart's *Genesis of Species*.

> When I had finished the "Genesis of Species", I felt that something was certainly wanted which should give a definite aim to the variations whose accumulation was to amount ultimately to specific and generic differences, and that without this there could have been no progress in organic development. I got the latest edition of the "Origin of Species" in order to see how Mr. Darwin met Professor Mivart, and found his answers in many respects unsatisfactory.[1]

From this edition, moreover, Butler learnt that there was a struggle for survival also in the field of biological theory, where Darwin for the moment proved by far the fittest, and, worst of all, Butler found that Darwin had anticipated his own theory and refuted it.[2] Warned of this danger, and with his own survival instincts now thoroughly roused, Butler made his own way to Lamarck—'this long-since exploded charlatan'—while all the time the necessity to choose between Natural Selection and teleology became increasingly urgent. The spirit in which Butler makes his choice is significant: Lamarck's doctrine has long since been exploded, yet still Darwin attacks it 'to slay the slain, and pass on'[3]. Apart from his own personal interest in the matter it is this ponderous march of authority which provokes Butler and makes him a champion of Lamarck already in *Life and Habit*, before the Krause controversy broke out.

Clearly, however, the underlying need which decides Butler's choice is not dictated by *amour-propre*, nor by defiance, and it is

---

[1] *Unconscious Memory*, pp. 22—3; see also letter from Butler to Francis Darwin in *A Memoir*, I, p. 257.

[2] *Origin of Species*, 6th ed. (1876), p. 206. Darwin states that it would be a 'serious error' to suppose that instincts have been acquired by habit, and then transmitted.

[3] *Life and Habit*, p. 242.

implicit in his meditation upon growth and memory before Mivart forced him to recognize that 'the numerous slight spontaneous variations' of which Darwin speaks, as the material on which Natural Selection is to work, must have some creative or purposive cause. Butler's conclusion, that this cause can only be defined as a sense of need, and experience, is an emotional as well as intellectual arrival: 'But if sense of need and experience are denied, I see no escape from the view that machines are new species of life'.[1] Darwin's theory is beginning to take on the absurd, mechanical aspect of the mock scientific theory of 'Darwin among the Machines'; it deprives life and its evolution of all significance. There is only one alternative to this dead end, namely the conviction forced upon us by living organisms, that 'there seems hardly any limit to what long-continued faith and desire, aided by intelligence, may be able to effect'.[2]

Before Butler read Mivart, he had hoped that his book 'was going to be an adjunct to Darwinism'.[3] The pages of the first draft 'teemed with allusions to "natural selection"'. Mivart's influence, and after him Lamarck, changed the genesis of the book in a dramatic manner, for Butler proceeded to cut out all expressions which were 'inconsistent with a teleological view', and then wrote the four concluding chapters in which the confrontation of Lamarck and Darwin (xiii), and Mivart and Darwin (xiv) enables him to clarify his own view of evolutionary causes.

Mivart's name is mentioned for the first time in chapter xi, and significantly in connexion with a broader scrutiny of causation. Quoting Mivart on the force and effect of mimicry, Butler contends that, while creatures have never sufficient faith or desire to become something widely different from what they are, they nevertheless strive to imitate 'creatures or objects which it was to their advantage or pleasure to resemble'.[4] This effort is 'doubtless often one of the

[1] *Ibid.*, p. 241.　　[2] P. 241.
[3] *Unconscious Memory*, p. 21.
[4] Pp. 202—3.

336

first steps towards varying in any given direction', and it is sustained by faith and desire:

> Against faith, then, and desire, all the "natural selection" in the world will not stop an amœba from becoming an elephant, if a reasonable time be granted; without the faith and the desire, neither "natural selection" nor artificial breeding will be able to do much in the way of modifying any structure.[1]

Throughout the book there are arguments in favour of teleology breaking to the surface, and at times, as in the discussion of the chicken's effort to get out of the shell, Butler's polemic reaches a formidable pitch of caustic eloquence. (Cf. *supra*, p. 331). The science that ascribes the activity of the chicken to chance or promiscuous action is 'mere horse science, akin to the theories of the convulsionists in the geological kingdom':

> Curious, such a uniformity of promiscuous action among so many eggs for so many generations. If we see a man knock a hole in a wall on finding that he cannot get out of a place by any other means, and if we see him knock this hole in a very workmanlike way, with an implement which he has been at great pains to make for a long time past, but which he throws away as soon as he has no longer use for it, thus showing that he had made it expressly for the purpose of escape, do we say that this person made the implement and broke the wall of his prison promiscuously? No jury would acquit a burglar on these grounds.[2]

Humour and irony are already in *Life and Habit* Butler's most ready weapons of controversy.

It is no accident, and no surprise, to find that Butler is reminded of Aristotle during his observation of the growth and efforts of the chicken, for the creature is 'attempting to better itself, doing (as Aristotle says all creatures do all things upon all occasions) what it considers most for its advantage under the existing circumstances.'[3]

[1] P. 203.   [2] P. 62.   [3] P. 65.

The chicken makes feathers instead of hair, because it thinks feathers more useful. And we,

during the more intense and active part of our existence, in the earliest stages, that is to say, of our embryological life, we could probably have turned our protoplasm into feathers instead of hair if we had cared about doing so.[1]

Reflecting on the observations made by Dr. Carpenter of one-celled organisms and their adaptability to environment and need, Butler again concludes: 'This is what protoplasm can do when it has the talisman of faith—of faith which worketh all wonders ...'.[2] Butler takes Carpenter to task for his failure to draw the obvious common-sense corollaries from his facts, namely that the amœba is 'highly reasonable and intelligent'.[3] To Ribot's puzzled statement: "All seems directed by thought" Butler answers: 'Yes; because all *has been* in earlier existences directed by thought.'[4]

Thus, it would seem, Butler intellectualizes the evolutionary growth to an extent unknown even in Meredith's belief. On the other hand, his theory of heredity as unconscious memory reverses Swinburne's and Meredith's development perspective, in which life is seen to grope from its unconscious levels to the 'beacon-fire of brain'. Butler presupposes some kind of intelligence or cunning inventing or choosing, throughout, new habits and structures, and losing consciousness of its effort once the habit is learnt to perfection and the new structure achieved. In a biological sense, Butler agrees with Schopenhauer and Hardy that consciousness is a curse:

When we were yet unborn, our thoughts kept the roadway decently enough; then we were blessed; we thought as every man thinks, and held the same opinions as our fathers and mothers had done upon nearly every subject. Life was not an art—and a very difficult art—much too difficult to be acquired in a lifetime; it was a science of which we were consummate masters.[5]

[1] *Ibid.*   [2] P. 68.   [3] P. 71.   [4] P. 206.   [5] P. 60.

In its ultimate logical consequence, Butler's theory would seem to point to a state of universal unconsciousness—a Nirvana of perfect organic process. Yet, being a prophet of common sense, he has no hankering after such possibilities, and besides, he shares Browning's faith that 'progress is the law of life'. And 'progress', Butler agrees with Meredith, 'must have an internal current setting in a definite direction'.[1] It is this attitude which steers his gospel clear of the fatalism and longing for nothingness which we find in Schopenhauer, whose Will-to-live and Will-to-make are otherwise closely related to Butler's insight.

Despite his bold defence of teleology, Butler does not return all the way to the long-range conjectures of Lamarck, for while he insists on faith, intelligence and cunning, he allows these factors only a very limited scope of forethought.[2] Butler's position is characteristic of the neo-Lamarckian whose claim for teleology has been modified by Darwin's overwhelming evidence bearing upon the slow and tentative nature of the evolutionary process, and upon the inability of too wide crosses to survive. Hence we find Butler asserting, again with the aid of a machine analogy, that,

> I have already sufficiently guarded against being supposed to maintain that very long before an instinct or structure was developed, the creature descried it in the far future, and made towards it. We do not observe this to be the manner of human progress. Our mechanical inventions, which, as I ventured to say in "Erewhon", ... are really nothing but extra-corporaneous limbs ... have almost invariably grown up from small beginnings, and without any very distant foresight on the part of the inventors.[3]

Butler's teleological belief, in common with the neo-Lamarckian outlook in general, is based upon what he sees as the purposive organization of structure.[4] Against Darwin's theory of Natural Selection Butler adduces two arguments well-known in biological

---

[1] P. 248.   [2] Cf. p. 73.   [3] P. 243; cf. also pp. 199—200.
[4] P. 247: 'but I can no more believe ...'

339

discussion since 1860, and which he found in Mivart's *Genesis of Species*.[1] The first of these has been called 'the swamping effect of inter-crossing'.[2] It means that indefinite, fortuitous variations would tend to disappear in later generations owing to crossing with types where these variations had not occurred.[3] The second objection is that, even if some progress could be made along these chance lines, there has not been sufficient time for the indefinite variations to evolve into the highly complex structures we find to-day.[4]

Yet, for all his effort of his later chapters to prove that Darwin 'made us see evolution ... in an exceedingly mistaken way', Butler admits that Darwin's achievement was not a small one, for 'to the end of time, if the question be asked, "Who taught people to believe in evolution?" there can only be one answer—that it was Mr. Darwin.'[5] And he further concedes that

Given the motive power which Lamarck suggested, and Mr. Darwin's mechanism would appear (with the help of memory, as bearing upon reproduction, of continued personality, and hence of inherited habit, and of the vanishing tendency of consciousness) to work with perfect ease.[6]

It is the world of chance and blindness emerging from the sole agency of Natural Selection that Butler rejects, and in its place he offers 'the more living faith' of *Life and Habit*.

By what criteria should one judge this curious essay in natural philosophy? It is not science, nor philosophy, and neither is it poetry. And yet it has something of all these categories. As a layman's think-

[1] Pp. 64 ff, 155.

[2] The term was invented by W. Bateson, according to D. Dampier-Whetham, *A History of Science*, p. 347.

[3] *Life and Habit*, pp. 277 ff.

[4] *Ibid.*, pp. 282—4. Since Butler's time, however, research on the age of the earth has shown that the first known fossils are about 600,000,000 years old, and the first life on earth probably twice that age. This period is thought to suffice for Darwin's theory—according to J. B. S. Haldane, *Possible Worlds and Other Essays*, p. 44.

[5] Pp. 275—6, 277.   [6] P. 261.

ing about biology it is original and even ingenious; as an effort to solve some of the fundamental problems of existence it introduces vitalistic concepts and works towards conclusions which philosophers have used since. And as for Butler's main doctrine of heredity as memory, and of evolution as faith and desire, what is it but the great poetic vision of life?

Butler advanced his mnemic theory of heredity at a time when this field was still relatively unexplored and open to conjecture.[1] Mendel's laws had not yet revolutionized the study of genetics, and even if Butler had known of these laws they would not have made much difference either way. The main objection to Butler's theory was, however, raised from the beginning and is still valid. It is that the germ-cells, which according to Butler form the continuous identity of a being with all his progenitors, are not part of the tissue-cells or soma where the mnemic experience is lodged. While these tissue-cells grow into the complex organs of brain and nervous system, the germ-cells remain simple and isolated, and there appears to be nothing to indicate that these cells are capable of receiving or transmitting impressions or experience in the way Butler suggests. Thus the weakness of Butler's theory, M. Hartog notes, is his failure to account for the mechanism underlying memory in evolution.[2] Mr. Furbank raises a similar objection: 'however ingeniously and amusingly Butler elaborates his theory of memory, he cannot convince us of more than that something rather *like* memory explains the processes of growth.'[3]

[1] It had been anticipated, without Butler's knowledge, by Professor Hering of Vienna in 1870, in his lecture on 'Das Gedächtnis als allgemeine Funktion der organisierten Materie'. Haeckel developed the theory, and in England Ray Lankaster was for some time an enthusiastic supporter, but he later abandoned it. The relationship of Butler's ideas to later biological theory is outlined by M. Hartog in 'Samuel Butler and Recent Mnemic Biological Theories', *Scientia*, 1914.

[2] Introduction to *Unconscious Memory* (1922 ed.)

[3] *Samuel Butler*, p. 55.

It would seem, however, that the serious flaw in Butler's 'more living faith' is not this inability to prove, in terms of biology or psychology, that we grow because we remember, but the fact that this growth leads nowhere—it has no significant goal. All that results of a million lives a being has lived, and of its tremendous effort to 'better itself', is unconscious perfect action. Thought, intelligence and conscious endeavour belong to the realm of uncertain knowledge, doubt and 'trouble'. Hence the awkwardness of Butler's attitude to the human intellect which, since he believes in progress, must be something more than a negative aspect—hence also the lack of direction in Butler's meditations upon life. Whence does it flow, and whither? His attempts to answer these questions are feeble, and he fails to persuade us, moreover, that the perfection of which he so often speaks has any vital relationship with human value. Perhaps for this reason one would prefer the inspired and searching faith of Swinburne and Meredith to the more cogent and ingenious thought of Butler. Though he should not be judged by the things he has left undone, it is nevertheless unfortunate that his evolutionary concepts of 'faith and desire' are such barren soil for prophecy and of value. When we look for prophecy outside the machines in *Erewhon*, we find merely the vague anticipation of a 'super-organic kingdom' in the *Note-Books*:

As the solid inorganic kingdom supervened upon the gaseous ... and as the organic kingdom supervened upon the inorganic ... so a third kingdom is now in process of development, the super-organic, of which we see the germs in the less practical and more emotional side of our nature.

Man, for example, is the only creature that interests himself in his own past, or forecasts his future to any considerable extent. This tendency I would see as the monad of a new regime—a regime that will be no more governed by the ideas and habits now prevailing among ourselves than we are by those still obtaining among stones or water.[1]

[1] P. 78.

342

This is drab and unimaginative, and it has that air of indecision which characterizes Butler whenever he approaches metaphysical issues without having, at the same time, a more definite polemic task. As Butler formulates his prophecy of the 'super-organic kingdom' it looks like an ontological reduction of Coleridge's great idea of the 'state of pure intellect', and though it is clearly rooted in the idealistic tradition with its predominant notion of evolving consciousness, it has none of the constructive enthusiasm of Meredith's related belief.

It would be unfair however, to leave Butler without remembering his essential achievement—the gallant stand he made for faith and aspiration as evolutionary forces, at a time when the materialistic and deterministic theories of selection and environment flooded the minds of men. Darwin did not banish mind from the universe, but his disciples were quite prepared to do so. And though Butler offered instead a theory which was less attractive to the scientific mind, it contained at least one energetic and valuable element that was to influence the thought of the coming generation. Butler added to Lamarck's doctrine the conception of life as an autonomous power which takes possession of matter and, even rising above the tyranny of environment, works out its own destiny and creates itself according to its will and faith. Meredith, it is true, preached the same gospel, yet his ideas were less accessible. Nor did he forge them in the heat of public controversy and in close association with a reviving biological theory. Butler's appeal was, perhaps, never very wide. But to some of those who could not accept Darwin's blind agency of Natural Selection, nor Mivart's return to Divine Providence, Butler's vitalistic message had a healthy and invigorating air, which saved them from the pessimistic dead end of Hardy's *Hap*. It is for this achievement that Butler's disciple Bernard Shaw salutes him, and remembers him as 'the prophet who tried to head us back when we were gaily dancing to our damnation across the rainbow bridge which Darwinism had thrown over the gulf which separates life and hope from death and despair'.

343

CHAPTER VI

TWO EVOLUTIONARY UTOPIAS

> The use, however haltingly, of our imagination
> upon the possibilities of the future is a valu-
> able spiritual exercise.
>
> J. B. S. Haldane, *Possible Worlds.*

THE WORKS of the Victorian poets included in our study have
shown time and again that the idea of evolution, when firmly rooted
in a teleological belief, may give rise to millennial dreams and anticipations. Idealists and positivists, poets of divine discontent and
prophets of progress share this hope that human nature shall be
transformed in the evolutionary catharsis and give birth to the
crowning race of the future. And they trust, moreover, that once
this regeneration is achieved, our world of suffering, fear and crime
shall know lasting peace, harmony, brain-rule, a brotherhood, a
federation of the world.

This prophetic impulse was evident already in the heretical reflections about the 'crowning race' in *Vestiges of Creation,* and it
gathered momentum, in particular among the 'healthy and wealthy',
throughout the century. It became an integral part of the Victorian
belief in material progress, but survived long after this belief had
perished. Quite naturally, we find it as a creative impetus in the
literary Utopia.

From about 1870 the Utopia, long neglected and at low ebb,
begins to assert itself once more in English literature. It is, to repeat
a commonplace, a *genre* that thrives on bad times and divine discontent; it expresses, according to Lewis Mumford, either a desire to
escape or a will to reconstruct.[1] And this was an age, or rather the

[1] *The Story of Utopias,* p. 11.

344

beginning of an age, from which sensitive minds, like William Morris, took flight, and in which the more robust ones, like H. G. Wells, found much to demolish and rebuild on their own ideal pattern. Now, as the century drew to a close, the facile, utilitarian belief in progress was being rapidly corroded by the all too obvious results of industrial expansion. An ugly and sordid life, toil, poverty and crime for the large masses, and not the greatest happiness for the greatest number, was the outcome of the capitalist system and machine civilization. Inevitably, the social revolt, long provoked and unwisely handled, was adding to the disturbance and to the consciousness of something rotten in the state.

In this troubled climate, the Utopia again came into its own, both as a means of criticism and planning, and as a way of escape. Lord Lytton's popular work, *The Coming Race* (1871), might be seen as the first in a long series of Utopias and anti-Utopias which culminated in the novels of H. G. Wells.[1] In some of these, the idea of evolution is a recurrent and at times a dominant feature, so dominant that one may legitimately speak of an evolutionary Utopia. This is true in particular of the works proposed for study in the following chapter—the plays and Utopian fantasies of Bernard Shaw and H. G. Wells.[2]

Students of this ancient *genre* have pointed out that, strictly speaking, there can be no such thing as an evolutionary Utopia; for the Utopia is, *sui generis,* an apocalyptic vision of an ideal state, perfect once and for all, or a place of lasting happiness.[3] Thus, for

---

[1] As V. Dupont has pointed out, the Utopia and anti-Utopia must, formally, obey the same rules, and for this reason no distinction will be made between them in this survey. Cf. *L'Utopie et le roman utopique dans la littérature anglaise,* p. 404.

[2] P. Bloomfield has used the term 'Utopia of evolution' of Shaw's drama *Back to Methuselah* in his study *Imaginary Worlds,* p. 220.

[3] *A New English Dictionary* gives these definitions: (1) 'An imaginary island, depicted by Sir Thomas More as enjoying a perfect social, legal and political system'. (2) 'A place, state or condition ideally perfect in respect

two reasons, it would seem, the idea of evolutionary development is incompatible with the traditional Utopian pattern. First, because on an evolutionary view there can be no static, final and perfect condition, or any ultimate goal of biological or historical development; secondly, because evolution as a naturalistic theory tends to encourage, in speculations about the future, deductions or inferences from factors and causes more or less known. Instead of apocalypse, we get probability calculus.[1]

Yet, since the Utopia still persists as a dream of the ideal, and since evolution has become part of its dream, it must have adapted itself somehow to the new Darwinian and Lamarckian environment. What modifications has this wrought in the Utopian structure? According to H. G. Wells,

the Modern Utopia must be not static but kinetic, must shape not as a permanent state but as a hopeful stage, leading to a long ascent of stages.[2]

In More's and Bacon's times the ideal state could be built on rock, as a tremendous final postulate, firmly rooted in a system of absolute value and safe against temporal decay, since in fact, it was

of politics, laws, customs and conditions'.—For a more detailed discussion of formal and historical aspects, cf. V. Dupont, op. cit., pp. 10—14.

[1] Cf. J. Hertzler's pioneer study, The History of Utopian Thought: 'With the reign of the evolutionary principle, and of the conception of controllable forces, with the human productive power magnified a thousand-fold by machines, ... the hard-and-fast conception of a perfect state of society of Utopian philosophy has disappeared'; p. 313.

[2] A Modern Utopia, (Tauchnitz ed. 1905), p. 15. Cf. also V. Dupont: Et aussi l'idée de l'avenir s'impose avec les théories de l'évolution et les sombres pronostics de Malthus, et partant, l'idée de l'espèce qui crée des devoirs nouveaux à l'individu. L'Utopie ... cherche désormais la formule qui permettra à tous moments à l'homme d'agir sur son propre sort et de coopérer avec les lois naturelles pour transformer son milieu physique et sa propre personne dans un mouvement collectif, raisonné et continu. De statique elle se fait dynamique'; op. cit., p. 703.

a kingdom not intended to be realized in this world. In the nineteenth century much happened, besides the *Origin of Species,* which undermined this solid rock. Values, the one fundamental link between reality and Utopia, had become relative and like shifting sands, and the growing consciousness of historical process, of flux and change, made it impossible to meditate upon the human condition or upon the future without paying heed to the forces which are continually active in shaping it. Both these aspects are important in the change from a static to a 'kinetic' Utopian form. It is true that, without values, however relative and individual, no Utopia could be written, but its claim to static, ultimate perfection can only be made if, and to the extent that, the values are recognized as static and absolute.

For the nineteenth century Utopist, whether he was influenced directly by Hegel or Comte, Spencer, Darwin or the Utilitarians, or more indirectly taught by any or all of these, it was not possible to conceive of a Utopia isolated in time at either end, nor was it necessary to dream of it any more as an unattainable state. Owing to the idea of progress, Utopia became an event within history, a condition in the future. Consequently it was no longer enough to describe the Utopian present: almost equally important was to give an account of its past. This account, for the dreamer of the ideal state was the bridge thrown between reality and Utopia, and it served him both as approach and as justification. For thus Utopia would emerge as the outcome of a historical development in which the social and material forces were ideally controlled and directed.

In the individual Utopias, this 'kinetic' or 'dynamic' vision is often simply linked with a theme of historical retrospect which 'explains' the ideal state.[1] Sometimes, the idea of evolution adds a vivid movement to this background, as when Lord Lytton, who did so much to influence the thematic renewal of the *genre,* sees his 'Coming

---

[1] Cf. Wells' *A Modern Utopia.* pp. 222—24.

Race' as descendants from a giant frog. They had passed through phases of evolution which roughly correspond to our own, and achieved that serene and disciplined nobility of character which ranked so high among Victorian virtues. Yet to Lord Lytton this social and evolutionary development has stifled genius and made existence unbearably dull, and his object is to warn against a way of life—ideal in appearance—in which all' creative struggle and tension has ceased.

Both Lord Lytton, to whom his perfect 'Vrilya' were a menace, and Edward Maitland, who wrote to contradict him, thought and dreamed within an evolutionary and historical perspective and gave to this the widest possible scope.[1] Maitland's work, *By and By, a Historical Romance of the Future* (1873), describes a future civilization in which the individuals, owing to the very factors that Lord Lytton denounced, have attained to a rich and varied development of personality.[2] The Victorians were, obviously, on the horns of a dilemma when facing the possibilities of human nature in its evolution. It was the problem of human eugenics in its wider social and moral context: What sort of a human being do we want for the future, provided we can control and direct the development? Lord Lytton's 'Coming Race' was a negative formulation of the same problem: How can we avoid a degenerate future race? To give a positive answer it was not sufficient for the Utopist to project and enlarge the virtues of the human ideal, however widely recognized by the age, upon the screen of the future, and make them universal. It was necessary to ask at the same time what consequences this attainment would have for the whole of human nature, and what changes, favourable or not, might be wrought by social conditions

[1] On Maitland versus Lytton see V. Dupont, *op. cit.,* pp. 430, 435.

[2] Maitland's work disproves the claim made by W. Simon that the Utopia of H. G. Wells was the first to give expression to the evolutionary tendencies of the time and to bring positive Utopian structures derived from these; cf. *Die englische Utopie im Lichte der Entwicklungslehre,* p. 9.

and new ways of life. It was generally agreed that evolution ought to bring about the death or taming of the ape and tiger in man, and make him a rational, harmonious being. But some of those who tried to imagine what an age without evil instinct or animal passion would look like, felt that the price for peace and harmony might be too high. For in an age without the incentive of struggle, competition and the effort of sublimation and self-control there would be no emotional drama necessary for the growth of art and of greatness.

We see this dilemma haunting several Utopias of the later half century, and, in the more or less explicit discussion they contain of moral and eugenic issues, there is a shifting pendulum movement from one attitude to its opposite. After the pioneers, Lytton and Maitland, W. H. Hudson published about 1886 *A Crystal Age,* which, despite great differences in treatment of value, adopts a view of future psychological and moral evolution similar to that of *The Coming Race.* Though Hudson loves the ideal depicted, he nevertheless rejects it as unrealizable, for, as he states (in the preface to the second edition, 1906): 'now I remember another thing which Nature said—that earthly excellence can come in no way but one, and the ending of passion and strife is the beginning of decay'. This characteristic Meredithian axiom continues to influence a great deal of Utopian speculation, as a testimony to Darwin's lasting effect upon contemporary and modern thought. Yet this was not the final word, and Maitland too had his followers, even more sanguine and radical in their belief, as for instance the author of *Meda, a Tale of the Future,*[1] though he is not anxious to maintain the all-round perfection which was Maitland's ideal. As for the dilemma of human perfectibility, its various difficulties are nowhere better illustrated than in the inconclusive struggle of Bernard Shaw and H. G. Wells.

[1] 1892, pseudonym Kenneth Folingsby.

349

Whatever the human ideal dreamed of in the modern Utopia, evolution and the idea of progress provide the general scheme on which its history moves, along with a theory of racial and psychological development which is invoked or exploited to justify the Utopian theme of reform. It is this scheme which H. G. Wells describes as 'kinetic'.

Apart from the structural change in the Utopia since Darwin, there are other traces of the evolutionary principle. Sometimes a traditional Utopian theme revives and is active in a new direction, sometimes an entirely new phenomenon occurs, such as new characteristics, new species even, unknown within the human demarcations of Plato and More. After Darwin it became easier to believe that man was, however slowly, working out the beast, and that he would not remain for ever in the 'middle state' which Pope found so pathetic. Before long the prophet of the ideal future being could claim with Swinburne and Meredith that man was growing up to be a god, and indeed, 'Men like Gods' is an ideal that haunts the Utopia recurrently, long before H. G. Wells gave it a name, and for this ideal the theory of evolution is largely responsible.

An old theme to which evolution gives fresh interest is that of eugenics. Plato in *The Republic* offered a State programme of race hygiene and improvement which More, Campanella and Bacon later accepted in its main outline.[1] With Darwin's researches the idea of selective breeding of animals found a more precise biological formulation, while Francis Galton, applying Darwin's theory of heredity to the inheritance of mental characters (in *Hereditary Genius*, 1869), coined the term 'eugenics', and pointed out that, as environment can only favour the development of qualities already latent in the organism, but not create them, good breeding is most

---

[1] Cf. J. Hertzler, *op. cit.*, p. 288, and H. Ross, *Utopias Old and New*, p. 64.

important.[1] At the same time Malthus in his gloomy analysis of overpopulation forced the writers of Utopias to ask whether Plato was not right and charitable after all when he advocated preventive eugenics: In the ideal state the ailing and deformed could have no place. In the ideal state, moreover, it was urgent to keep the population balanced so that there would be space, work and food for all.[2]

A Thousand Years Hence, 1882, (pseudonym 'Nunsowe Green') gives eugenics a task to perform which points back to Plato as well as forward to Bernard Shaw. Here the State selects *élite* individuals for 'State marriages', and the children of these are given special public care. Thus a 'natural aristocracy' is established which multiplies and in time will become universal.

Longevity, another traditional theme associated with legends and dreams of the Golden Age, now recurs within an evolutionary context. Longevity means the same thing to the modern writer of Utopia as to the ancient: it is a transcendence quest seeking lasting happiness and life. Though Bernard Shaw uses the idea as a moral challenge, this underlying motive is clearly active in his mystical prophecy of the future expansion of life. In Campanella's *City of the Sun (Civitas Solis)* it is already science that rejuvenates people and enables them to live for two hundred years; and Lord Lytton's 'Coming Race' are still in their prime at the age of a hundred, thanks to the climate, their habits and a wholesome diet. *The Case of the Fox* (1903), by William Stanley, might be noted for the way in which it links longevity with evolutionary characteristics, such as decreased size, reduced muscle-power, and great expansion of brain —all due to an ideal environment.[3] It is with such phenomena that

---

[1] Cf. Dampier Dampier-Whetham, *The History of Science*, pp. 306—8.
[2] Among the Utopias which deal with preventive eugenics are the obscure works *Pyrna, A Commune under the Ice*, anon., 1875; and *Etymonia*, anon. 1875; cf. V. Dupont, *op. cit.*, pp. 444, 451.
[3] Cf. Dupont, *op. cit.*, p. 551.

the modern writer sometimes introduces a new set of themes on human variability and perfectibility, which, as in the fantasias of H. G. Wells, tend to dominate the pattern completely.

An early forecast of this type is *Meda, a Tale of the Future* (*supra*, p. 349), which anticipates, in the year 5575, something like a transmutation of the human species: Man in that distant age has become small and light, his body wholly dwarfed by his large head. This evolution was due mainly to a change in diet which spiritualized the body and gave man infinitely greater moral and intellectual power. By his will he now controls the forces of Nature, and determines his own development to such an extent that objectionable or cumbersome organs have been disused or discarded and his lungs trained to such perfection that he lives on nothing but air.[1] In this last aspect, comical though it seems, evolution revives an ancient millennial hope inherent in certain idealistic and puritanical attitudes, and also in the prophets of Pure Reason. Robinet's conjecture, that intelligence shall become wholly freed from matter, has allied itself with evolution, and we meet once more the strange offspring of this union in Bernard Shaw's *Back to Methuselah*.

1. *George Bernard Shaw*

Though Bernard Shaw claimed to be 'by profession what is called an original thinker', he nevertheless borrowed, with generous acknowledgements, his most important and cherished ideas from others. It has often been observed that in his composite 'new religion'—Creative Evolution—Schopenhauer's conception of the World as Will is juxtaposed to Nietzsche's Superman. From Wagner he learned to believe in Life as a tireless power driving onward and upward, and by Butler he was converted from the Darwinian

---

[1] V. Dupont points out several aspects by which this author anticipates the fantasies of Wells, *op. cit.*, p. 490.

heresy of his youth to a lasting faith in Evolution as a purposive, intelligent and voluntary process.

Yet, to repeat a commonplace of criticism, Shaw *is* an original thinker in the sense that he transforms his borrowed material in the heat of moral passion—in his furious and impatient desire to chastise and better the world—and makes of the various and often discrepant ideas a new and disturbing pattern, vivid in colour, boldly impressionistic and subjective, and frankly theatrical, yet a composition alive with tremendous energy and complex human interest. The pattern does not settle into a consistent and carefully organized system, or philosophy, nor does Shaw attempt, despite C. E. M. Joad's assertion, 'to present a coherent and comprehensive view of the universe as a whole, of the status of human life within it..'.[1] As so many of his admirers and even antagonists have emphasized, Shaw is a mystic and a prophet, perhaps misled and misleading, but a passionate soul who sees in flashes and sweeping vistas, without much concern for the gaps that are left so often in so many places. At times, no doubt, the force and penetration of his intellect bent on analysis or exposure give him a deceptive air of systematic logician, but when we come to his essential and positive gospel—the religion of the Life Force, it is abundantly clear that Chesterton's 'wild logician' cares little about logic and a great deal about the intuitive, passionate truth. Hence Joad's admitted failure to fit his thought into the rigid scheme of formal philosophy.[2] Hence also the easy but unprofitable triumphs of those who set out to denounce the 'paralogisms' in the Shavian doctrine.[3] On the whole it would appear that the wisest things about Shaw have been spoken by those who, like Archibald Henderson, have accepted him as a mystic and

[1] *Shaw*, p. 172.
[2] *Op. cit.*, pp. 199—203.
[3] See for instance M. Belgion, *Our Present Philosophy of Life*, pp. 102—3.

prophet, or like Chesterton, as an untiring champion of faith and hope.[1]

Shaw's 'new religion' of Creative Evolution has been often analysed and explained, and the only justification for including it here is that in a survey of the idea of evolution in English literature, though it aims at no inclusive picture, Bernard Shaw has an undisputed place. It is the object of this brief inquiry to determine what significance Shaw's nineteenth century heritage acquires in his religion for the twentieth, and in particular what prophecy evolution engenders in his 'Metabiological Pentateuch'—*Back to Methuselah.* Despite the changing expressions of his faith, despite his shift from one 'desperate remedy' to another in his moral and reformatory zest, an attempt will be made to indicate what seems to be an indestructible unity of his evolutionary vision, and of his programme for human regeneration.

The Life Force Creed

From a vague and general knowledge of Schopenhauer, from his enthusiasm for Butler still fighting the Darwinians, and finally from a study of Wagner's *Ring,* Shaw had arrived, by 1890, at the faith which later informed *Man and Superman.*[2] In his essay of that year, *The Perfect Wagnerite,* Shaw contends that

The only faith which any reasonable disciple can gain from *The Ring* is not in love, but in life itself as a tireless power which is continually driving onward and upward... growing from within by its own inexplicable energy, into ever higher and higher forms of organization...[3]

---

[1] Cf. A. Henderson's authorized biography, *Bernard Shaw, Play-boy and Prophet,* pp. 516, 519; G. K. Chesterton, *Bernard Shaw,* conclusion.

[2] Cf. M. Belgion, *op. cit.,* p. 55; E. Bentley, *The Cult of the Superman,* p. 166.

[3] *Major Critical Essays,* Standard ed. 1948, p. 221.

In the Wagner essay Shaw is already consciously drawing upon his spiritual heritage: it is as if the soul of Carlyle were reborn and rushes into a new crusade against the infidel century. Much is rotten in the modern state, and in civilization, but there may be more than one remedy, and there is, it seems, at the heart of the world's disease, the problem of free will and necessity on which the method of salvation depends. Shaw here, to use an apt phrase by Chesterton, to some extent talks in order to find out what he thinks: Is human nature really degenerating? Or is the tireless power, life, still active in man, despite the chaos and corruption of his society? In the first case, he reflects, we must, like Prometheus, set about making new and better men; in the second, anarchist revolt will best serve the purpose of life, by removing obstacles.—But, Shaw's critics have objected, if human nature is degenerating, how can man *will* his regeneration to the extent of making new men, even if he knew how to go about it? And, on the other hand, if 'the energy of life is still carrying human nature to higher and higher levels', why should he trouble himself to will anything at all? How, finally, can anarchism, even the anarchism of thought which is the only form Shaw permits, be conducive to progress, since it implies disintegration and a scattering of effort? Shaw's self-contradiction in this essay is more apparent than real, for though he is entangled in the dilemma of how to reconcile the tireless power of life with man who so miserably fails in his appointed evolutionary task, it is not a choice for him between free will and necessity, nor does he surrender his implicit trust that man, at his best, is capable of carrying life to higher forms of organization. It is precisely this faith, as the quoted passage shows, that Shaw distils from Wagner's *Ring*. What brings him almost to despair of human nature is the selfishness, corruption and inefficiency of the large democratic masses in contemporary Europe. Throughout the essay there runs a note of impatient pessimism, and a disgust with democracy which, here as elsewhere, so curiously blends with Shaw's socialism and republican fervour. Even if we allow for the calculated outrage, this statement is still a verdict:

The majority of men at present in Europe have no business to be alive; and no serious progress will be made until we address ourselves earnestly and scientifically to the task of producing trustworthy human material for society. In short, it is necessary to breed a race of men in whom the life-giving impulses predominate...[1]

Man, Shaw agrees with Nietzsche, is something that must be overcome and superseded.[2] But how?—Through eugenics; through selective breeding, which had been recognized and practised as a necessity already in the days of aristocratic rule.

Thus, in 1890, Shaw had the main material which was eleven years later to go to the making of *Man and Superman*. Owing to the peculiarly incoherent structure of this drama, which claims to be at the same time a philosophy, we may limit our attention to the third act—the dialogue in hell—and to the appendix, 'The Revolutionist's Handbook', for it is here that we find what Shaw later described as 'the new religion at the centre of the intellectual whirlpool'.[3]

In *Man and Superman* Shaw's idea of the Life Force is still a slender conception, and its development from the Wagner essay is seen to lie mainly in one direction—towards a formulation of the aims and causes which are active in the evolutionary ascent. Life is driving onward and upward because it 'strives to attain greater power of contemplating itself'.[4] From the beginning, 'Life was driving at brains—at its darling object: an organ by which it can attain not only self-consciousness but self-understanding.'—'Are we agreed', asks Don Juan,

[1] *Ibid.*, p. 215.

[2] Cf. E. Bentley: 'It is out of a deep sense of contemporary political failure that the philosophy of heroism arose in Carlyle, Wagner, Nietzsche and Bernard Shaw'; *The Cult of the Superman*, p. 167.

[3] Preface to *Back to Methuselah*, p. lxxxvi.   [4] *Op. cit.*, p. 100.

that Life is a force which has made innumerable experiments in organizing itself; that the mammoth and the man, the mouse and the megatherium, the flies and the fleas and the Fathers of the Church, are all more or less successful attempts to build up that raw force into higher and higher individuals, the ideal individual being omnipotent, omniscient, infallible, and withal completely, unilludedly selfconscious: in short, a god?[1]

The seminal principle was not love, and neither was it beauty, but intelligence. In Shaw's gospel there is an emphasis on creative intelligence wholly absent in the 'Will'-concepts of Schopenhauer and Nietzsche, and different from Samuel Butler's idea of cunning that grows unconscious, though it has a similar teleological significance. For with Shaw intelligence is both the end and the means, the final as well as efficient cause of the progress of life. Thus, in his overriding cult of intellect Shaw moves more directly into line with positivistic life-worshippers like Meredith, who look to 'brain' and 'philosophy', as Shaw looks to the 'philosophic man', for carrying life to higher levels.[2]

Life, Shaw agrees with Spencer and Darwin, has been an incessant, unrelenting struggle.[3] It tries and often fails, and fails most fatally where intelligence is weak:

Things immeasurably greater than man in every respect but brain have existed and perished. The megatherium, the icthyosaurus have paced the earth with seven-league steps and hidden the day with cloud vast wings. Where are they now? ... These things lived and wanted to live; but for lack of brains they did not know how to carry out their purpose, and so destroyed themselves.[4]

In his own manner Shaw faces both the palpable dilemma of Hardy and the cruel indifference in Nature which saddened Tennyson: In

---

[1] *Ibid.*, p. 109.
[2] See other references to 'brain' and evolutionary purpose, *ibid.*, pp. 110, 113, 123, 127—8. [3] *Ibid.*, p. 110. [4] *Ibid.*, p. 102.

its trial and error, life 'wastes and scatters itself,.. it raises up obstacles to itself and destroys itself in its ignorance and blindness'. — This irresistible creative force needs a brain to guide it, and even with this guidance, the effort of life towards higher organization and greater self-understanding 'is only, at best, a doubtful campaign between its forces and those of Death and Degeneration'.[1] Even man, Life's masterpiece, is an ignorant blunderer, yet he has been chosen for a great task:

Just as Life, after ages of struggle, evolved that wonderful bodily organ the eye, so that the living organism could see where it was going and what was coming to help or threaten it, and thus avoid a thousand dangers that formerly slew it, so it is evolving today a mind's eye that shall see, not the physical world, but the purpose of Life, and thereby enable the individual to work for that purpose instead of thwarting and baffling it by setting up shortsighted personal aims as at present.[2]

Only one sort of man has ever been happy, Shaw claims—the man who consciously strives to fulfil this purpose of life: the 'philosophic man':

he who seeks in contemplation to discover the inner will of the world, in invention to discover the means of fulfilling that will, and in action to do that will by the so-discovered means.[3]

This plea for teleology springs from the very centre of Shaw's Life Force belief, and like Samuel Butler he feels the need of defending it against the demon of fatalism. It is in his refutation of the Devil's advocacy of *Vanitas vanitatum* that Shaw (*alias* Don Juan) most furiously comes to grips with the ultimate worst temptation—Giant Despair. In his reflections on politics and civilizations he has come near to yielding to it, both here

[1] *Ibid.*, pp. 101, 108.   [2] *Ibid.*, p. 110.   [3] *Ibid.*

and in the Wagner essay, but the Devil's mockery covers the whole of existence:

Where you now see reform, progress, fulfilment of upward tendency, continual ascent by Man on the stepping stones of his dead selves to higher things, you will see nothing but an infinite comedy of illusion.[1]

And this may indeed be true of politics and social reform. But the history of Life , which is Evolution, proves it to be a damnable heresy as regards the movement of Life itself. From Evolution Shaw takes his argument: 'is man no better than a worm, or a dog than a wolf? ... has the colossal mechanism no purpose?' None, the Devil replies, and uses the pathetic fallacy as counterpoint: 'You might as well expect it to have fingers and toes because you have them.' The neo-Lamarckian answer comes promptly: 'But I should not have them if they served no purpose.'[2] From this field of Butlerian crusade Shaw rushes directly into his own: Just as my finger is the instrument of my purpose, and made by it, so my brain 'is the organ by which Nature strives to understand itself'. The brain therefore—the philosopher's brain—has a function and aim beyond its own: it is 'in the grip of the Life Force'. Shaw admits, like Butler, that environment and chance (or luck) have played their part in the early stages of evolution, when Life did 'a thousand wonderful things unconsciously by merely willing to live and following the line of least resistance'. But this line would, ultimately, lead to a dead end—to self-destruction, and therefore, in the brain of the philosopher—'Nature's Pilot'—the Life Force has made an instrument that will enable it to 'choose the line of greatest advantage'.[3] Throughout this teleological argument two aspects are noteworthy for the link they establish between Shaw and the positivistic life-worshippers, Swinburne and Meredith:—the purpose beyond one's own, and the philosopher's brain as the means by which life rises to higher existence. Their emphasis is expressive of dominant traits in Shaw's

[1] *Ibid.*, p. 126. [2] *Ibid.*, p. 127. [3] *Ibid.*, pp. 127—8.

attitude, where the passion to serve and the passion to think are for ever joining forces to defend the cause of life, which to Shaw is the cause of man, in the teeth of selfishness, indolence and disillusionment.

Brain has changed the course of life from the line of least resistance to the line of greatest advantage, yet this shift, as Shaw sees it, is not from determinism to free will, but from lesser to greater freedom.[1] It means, however, that a different ethical condition has arisen in the world, for intelligence is the key, the only one, to the good life. With this tremendous claim Shaw appears to emerge directly out of the eighteenth century, sweeping aside not only Christian and Idealistic ethics, but Utilitarianism as well, and also the synthesis preached by Meredith. Yet as with Meredith, it is the ethical significance of 'brain rule' that commands Shaw's attention, and his teleology is all the time a moral fervour directed towards the problem of how to make better men, how to persuade or change man to deaden his ego and accept the great task for which life has chosen him. And the reason why Shaw puts his sole trust in the philosopher's brain is that all other means of advance have, in his eyes, miserably failed. Progress to him is no longer 'the law of life', and, as far as man the 'political animal' is concerned, it is an illusion.[2]

[1] For a discussion of the will-concept in Shaw see E. Bentley, *Bernard Shaw*, pp. 84—5; C. E. M. Joad, *op. cit.*, p. 202; A. Henderson, *op. cit.*, p. 686.

[2] Cf. 'A Revolutionist's Handbook', pp. 188—93.—A. Henderson notes this break with the optimism of the worshippers of life and Humanity, *op. cit.*, pp. 686—87.—According to Chesterton, Shaw's loss of faith in progress was one of the chief events leading to *Man and Superman,* and it coincided with his discovery of Nietzsche and his reading of Plato; *op. cit.*, pp. 207—8.—As we have seen, this loss of faith was already felt in *The Perfect Wagnerite.* E. Bentley states that as Shaw's belief in quick, revolutionary progress faded, his faith in slow, evolutionary progress gathered force; *Bernard Shaw*, p. 70.

360

Life, according to the central postulate of the third act, has made innumerable experiments towards higher and higher individuals, the ideal individual being omnipotent, omniscient and completely self-conscious:—a god. While the inner will of the world thus reveals its purpose to us, it is obvious that man, or rather the majority of men, fail to make it theirs. The majority of men pursue their petty selfish aims that thwart life in its growth, and remain in their hell of unreality, sensuous pleasure, and idleness. Will the human species, then, turn out to be an utter failure, blundering into death like so many species before it? The signs of degeneration, as Shaw denounced them in the Wagner essay, are already patent—even to the extent that the procreative instinct is overpowered by a desire for comfort.[1] Yet, before the danger of self-destruction becomes real and imminent, all that is sound in man, in the best men, will wake to the great purpose of life—'The great central purpose of breeding the race: ay, breeding it to heights now deemed superhuman'.[2]

In these three dominant themes of the third act—the Life Force, the danger of human failure, and the demand for eugenics, Shaw transposes the slight and hesitant suggestions of the Wagner essay into a more definite evolutionary context. The unity of attitude and argument is obvious, despite the change, at the same time, from a minor key to major, from the essay to the gusto, speed and exuberance of Shavian comedy. In the appendix, 'The Revolutionist's Handbook', we are back again in the more reflective treatment of the essay, though here too the hyperbolic style persists. The 'Handbook' functions as a Shavian preface, and it is chiefly a discussion of the great central purpose of breeding the race, why it is urgent, and how it could be done. A mere outline suffices to indicate Shaw's approach to the problem. He sets out with the Comtean proposition that the God of dogmatic religion, the *deus ex machina* who 'helped those who could not help themselves' is now an exploded myth. Now

[1] *Ibid.*, p. 117.   [2] *Ibid.*, p. 119.

Man must take in hand all the work that he used to shirk with an idle prayer. He must, in effect, change himself into the political Providence which he formerly conceived as god ...[1]

This is the only real and effective change, in contrast to the changes in political and social institutions, which give merely the illusion of progress: 'Man, as he is, never will nor can add a cubit to his stature by any of its quackeries, political, scientific, educational, religious, or artistic.'[2] But he can be changed, as the crab apple has been changed into the pippin and the wolf into the dog, by the providential effort of man, 'subduing Nature to his intention, and ennobling or debasing Life for a set purpose.'[3]

The need of such change has been felt and expressed in the higher religions, and it was stated, long before Nietzsche, in the cry for the Superman. Yet, granted that we can change man into the Superman, what kind of Superman do we want? This, Shaw realizes, is the crux of the problem, and the speed and certainty of his thought flags as he faces the choice of possible superhuman qualities. Having remarked shrewdly that 'Unfortunately you do not know what sort of man you want', he suggests 'Some sort of goodlooking philosopher-athlete, with a handsome healthy woman for his mate, perhaps.'[4] And he further begs the question by expressing a trust that 'The proof of the Superman will be in the living; and we shall find out how to produce him by the old method of trial and error, and not by waiting for a completely convincing prescription of his ingredients.' The only quality which Shaw prescribes, and on which he feels there is general agreement, is a 'superior mind'. As for the realization of the new man, Shaw falls back on the mystical hope that 'What is really important in Man is the part of him that we

[1] *Ibid.*, p. 171.—Cf. Comte: 'we must look to our own unremitting activity for the only providence by which the rigour of our destiny can be alleviated, *The Catechism of Positive Religion.*
[2] *Ibid.*, p. 202. [3] *Ibid.*, p. 171. [4] *Ibid.*, p. 172.

do not yet understand.' And for all the Shavian cult of the philosophic man as 'Nature's pilot' he is not so far given any obvious part in the effort of breeding the race:

We are therefore driven to the conclusion that when we have carried selection as far as we can by rejecting from the list of eligible parents all persons who are uninteresting, unpromising, or blemished without any set-off, we shall still have to trust to the guidance of fancy (*alias* Voice of Nature), both in the breeders and the parents, for that superiority in the unconscious self which will be the true characteristic of the Superman.[1]

In the end, however, it is this very caution which constitutes the virtue of Shaw's plea for eugenics, and reveals it to be, not a practical plan so much as a mystical prophecy and a moral challenge. To temper his impatient zest for regeneration comes his great wisdom, and it should be noted that from the beginning Shaw rejects the idea of breeding for special qualities or purposes.[2] Equally he denounces the folly, recurrent in totalitarian politics as well as in the evolutionary Utopia, of segregating humanity into groups for eugenic, political or social ends.[3] And those who have accused Shaw of latent fascism appear to ignore both his insistence on 'superior mind' and the universality of his ideal. He repeatedly asserts that it is a Democracy of Supermen we want and not the isolated Shakespeares, Goethes and Shelleys.[4]

---

[1] *Ibid.*, p. 174.   [2] Cf. 'That they must cross ...'; p. 174.

[3] Cf. 'To cut humanity...'; *Ibid.*, p. 174.

[4] Cf. Shaw's statement, quoted by E. Bentley without reference: 'It is assumed on the strength of the single word Superman (Übermensch), borrowed by me from Nietzsche, that I look for the salvation of society to the despotism of a single Napoleonic Superman, in spite of my careful demonstration of the folly of that outworn infatuation'; *op. cit., The Cult of the Superman*, p. 174.—Shaw's ridicule of Napoleon in *Back to Methuselah*, Part IV, illustrates this point. Shaw lived long enough to see and mock State eugenics as practised by Hitler; cf. 'The Genetic State', *Everybody's Political What's What?*; pp. 248—49.

In a final chapter on 'The Method', we find the same deliberate evasion of practical suggestions as in the meditation upon super-human traits: 'As to the method, what can be said as yet except that where there is a will, there is a way? If there be no will, we are lost.'[1] The counterpoise of the last phrase is more significant than the hopeful assertion of the first. Yet, Shaw goes on, we must avoid the way of despair; we must assume and believe that we 'have still energy enough to not only will to live, but to will to live better'. And once more we notice the mystical trust that man, despite his laziness and aversion, will do the bidding of the Life Force: there will be 'a general secret pushing of the human will in the repudiated direction; so that all sorts of institutions and public authorities will under some pretext or other feel their way furtively towards the Superman.'[2] In passing, Shaw toys with the idea of a 'joint stock human stud farm', that might 'produce better results than our present reliance on promiscuous marriage', and comes finally to the Platonic conclusion that 'The matter must be taken up either by the State or by some organization strong enough to impose respect upon the State.'[3]

If we ask how much of all this Shaw *means* literally—how serious his plea for Superman eugenics is in 'The Revolutionist's Handbook', the answer must clearly depend upon the fact that the pretended author, John Tanner, the Don Juan of the third act, is not only a mouthpiece but an intellectual clown, who makes it possible to keep the discussion all the time within 'the intellectual whirlpool' of the comedy. Shaw does not yet know the solution to the problem of how to improve the race, and so, through Tanner he avails himself of the clown's licence to shock and outrage and pose the problem in a jocular tone. 'All very serious propositions',he wrote in *The Quintessence of Ibsenism,* 'begin as huge jokes'. Yet it is obvious that the Superman here, as a serious proposition, is no more than a moral challenge and an expression of the hope that something,

[1] *Ibid.,* p. 204.   [2] *Ibid.*   [3] *Ibid.,* pp. 205—6.

perhaps eugenics, might be discovered as a radical and effective means of changing the human heart. On the other hand, it is easy to see why Shaw chose this idea of breeding the race as a vehicle for his appeal, for eugenics was 'in the air', and, notably in the first two decades of the century, appeared to give promise of a more complete control over racial development. The geneticists, who alone knew of the difficult and complex problems involved, and of the unyielding riddles of heredity and transmutation, were not responsible for the growing enthusiasm, but the temptation was great for intellectual radicals and social reformers to read a practical and hopeful meaning into Sir Francis Galton's final definition: 'Eugenics is the study of agencies under social control which may improve or impair the racial qualities of future generations either physically or mentally.'[1]

But even if accepted in this sense of moral persuasion, there remains something ineffectual about Shaw's prophecy of the Superman, because, when his holy war against man the political animal is over, the constructive effort implied in the alternative—in the ideal being—fails. And it fails mainly because Shaw is unable to fabricate out of his righteous indignation something sacred and permanent, something of absolute value. From its double source of Platonic love of man and intellectual contempt for the majority of men there rushes up in his mind this idea that refuses to enter a solid form, for the reason that to Shaw, having gathered up and practised the critical destructiveness of a century, such forms do not exist. The message which Shaw distilled from Ibsen's work: 'there is no formula', applies, of course, more aptly to his own attitude. Therefore, Shaw's Superman, ultimately to be 'omnipotent, omni-

---

[1] Quoted from an article on 'Eugenics' in the *Encyclopaedia Britannica*, which also notes that Karl Pearson was the first professor appointed to the chair of Eugenics established at University College, London, by a legacy from Galton after his death in 1911. Among the literature in this field there is *The Need of Eugenic Reform* (1926), by Leonard Darwin.

scient ... a god', is less energetic and attractive than Meredith's more warmly sculptured ideal and the evolutionary anticipations of the 'crowning race' in Tennyson and Browning, which derive their force from the intelligent and idealistic desire in the liberal Victorian to integrate religious and secular values.[1]

It has been observed that Shaw did not solve in *Man and Superman* the dilemma of free will or determinism which is inherent in his moral analysis of civilization and in his religion of the Life Force already from the Wagner essay.[2] On the one hand there is the Life Force driving onward and upward, on the other there is the majority of men who apparently decline and fail to will their own regeneration—on which the destiny of our species depends. How, then, is this regeneration to be achieved? Is it determined, or voluntary? Shaw's outlook appears to have something of the paradox of Christian doctrine in its reconciliation of necessity and free will. Man, according to Shaw, is free to will his extinction or his rebirth: the Life Force imposes no constraint upon him. Human will becomes identical with the Life Force will only at its highest and intensest levels of faith and selfless devotion, in the men with a clear head and a wide purpose, in the philosophic man, Nature's pilot, who is capable of vision as well as action. And in the end, Shaw views the destiny of mankind, not as determined by its lowest levels, its selfish pleasure-seeking masses, but by these few men in whom Life works the salvation of the race, because they dedicate their power to the future and gain their soul by losing it. But for these,

[1] Chesterton characterizes Shaw's and Nietzsche's idea of the Superman as a 'superstition'; *op. cit.*, p. 206; G. M. Trevelyan as 'a reaction from self culture that mistakes means for ends and neglects human love and charity'; *George Meredith*, p. 158. E. Bentley describes Shaw's idea of eugenic breeding of the Superman as a desperate remedy which he embraced when he found that men did not really will democracy; *Bernard Shaw*, p. 81.

[2] For a discussion of the dilemma and the 'self-contradictions' relating to Shaw's will-concept, see E. Bentley, *Bernard Shaw*, p. 81, C. E. M. Joad, *op. cit.*, p. 202—3, and M. Belgion, *op. cit.*, p. 94.

Life would scrap the human species and make new attempts at higher organization and intenser self-consciousness. And from these few, Shaw implies, some solution to the problem of human rebirth will come.

With *Man and Superman* Bernard Shaw had taken a position which was to remain unchanged in its basic features throughout his life. His furious disgust with prevailing democracy, with utilitarian materialism, progress-worship, with the fatalism and indolence dominant in the thought and life of his times, and, on the other hand, his mystical, fervent belief in the Life Force, his desire to awaken man to a sense of his great responsibility to Life—these persist in unabated strength. But nearly twenty years were to pass between this first sermon on Creative Evolution and the 'Metabiological Pentateuch'—*Back to Methuselah*.

In the meantime, Creative Evolution had transcended the field of biological theory and built cosmologies in the grand philosophical manner. It became, in fact, the most fruitful principle for a reinterpretation of cosmic process. Henri Bergson published his *L'Évolution Créatrice* in 1907, Alexander his Gifford Lectures of 1916—18, *Space, Time and Deity,* in 1920, and within the next ten years Lloyd Morgan wrote *Emergent Evolution* (1923), General Smuts *Holism and Evolution* (1926), and Whitehead *Process and Reality* (1929). On the whole, the tide was moving with Shaw's 'new religion', though, needless to say, not quite in the same direction. Yet his gospel of *Man and Superman* fell on stony ground, not only because, as he himself thought, it had been presented as a joke, but chiefly because the evolutionary ideal on which Shaw insisted had so little suggestive value.[1] And indeed Shaw must have felt this lack of appeal when he took up work with his dramatic cycle of *Methuselah,* for though the idea of the Superman is inherent in his new prophecy, it has singularly changed in form.

[1] C. E. M. Joad contended that Bergson and Alexander 'eclipsed' Shaw's work; *op. cit.,* 197.

Back to Methuselah and forward to Utopia

Creative Evolution is already a religion, and is indeed now unmistakably the religion of the twentieth century, newly arisen from the ashes of pseudo-Christianity, of mere scepticism, and of the soulless affirmations and blind negations of the Mechanists and Neo-Darwinians. But it cannot become a popular religion until it has its legends, its parables, its miracles.[1]

For a study of the Utopian trends in *Back to Methuselah* it is not necessary to pause for long over the Preface, which here swells to a lengthy treatise (87 pages) and is intended to provide an extensive panorama of the 'infidel century' of Darwin. This preface is more than ever a machine of war, and Shaw now charges in two directions at once: against the despicable Western democracy that had gone from corruption to crime until it produced the catastrophe of the World War; and against Darwinism, that had banished mind and purpose from the universe. To Shaw these curses are but different symptoms of the one world-wide malady—despair—the Devil's *Vanitas vanitatum*; for in both there is the same lack of active faith and will, of purposive effort, of moral responsibility.

The case against democracy resumes the main themes from *Man and Superman,* and this time with the tragic evidence of the war to substantiate its charges. It inevitably leads to the condemnation of man as a 'political animal'. What, then, is wrong with man and his society?

At the root of the world's ills Shaw finds everywhere the spirit of Darwinism. It was Neo-Darwinism in politics that made war unavoidable; it is Neo-Darwinism—the immoral and fatalistic doctrine of 'natural selection'—which gives justification to all the greed, aggression and disorder in the world. Consequently, the main task for Shaw in this preface is to demonstrate the basic falsity of Darwin's, or rather, the Neo-Darwinians' theory of evolution. One

---

[1] *Back to Methuselah* (1921 ed.), Preface, p. lxxviii.

must not expect, however, that Shaw's analysis of Darwinism in this historical context should be chiefly concerned with biological or scientific 'fact', though he claims the only sound science as a foundation of his views. It is as a moral fact, as a basis of choice and action, that 'natural selection' is the most damnable heresy. Thus Shaw, like Carlyle and Matthew Arnold, tests the truth of religion above all by its effect upon conduct.

In his crusade against Darwinism Shaw has learned a great deal, both in technique and argument, from Butler's *Evolution Old and New*, and his aim is similarly to dethrone Darwin from his unique position among biologists and thus undermine his authority. Shaw's thesis, chiefly, is that Darwin rose to greatness because he pleased his times, in many fields and in many ways. He courted an intellectual and spiritual milieu starved on uncomfortable agnosticism and ineffectual dogma; he explained the problem of evil and dispensed with God. And, not knowing the horrid void to which this pointed, 'we all', Shaw remembers, 'began going to the Devil with the utmost cheerfulness'. Again, Darwin pleased the Socialists, the Marxists, the economic exploiters, the political opportunists, because his theory of natural selection offered a law of Nature as sanction and excuse for their animal selfishness and appetite. In the end, the universal application and practice of Darwin's theory brought Europe to chaos, war and ruin.

Yet—and in these ostentatious, dramatic encounters of good and evil Shaw is very conscious of the heritage he holds from Bunyan and Carlyle—

throughout all the godless welter of the infidel half-century, Darwinism has been acting not only directly but homeopathically, its poison rallying our vital forces not only to resist it and cast it out, but to achieve a new Reformation and put a credible and healthy religion in its place.[1]

[1] P. lxx.

To turn back was impossible, and Shaw's illustration of this fact is another patent comment upon his heritage: it would mean to do 'what Pliable did in The Pilgrim's Progress when Christian landed him in the Slough of Despond: that is, run back in terror to our old superstitions.[1] No—the salvation from this very hell of despair lies in our new religion—Creative Evolution—'the religion of metaphysical Vitalism', which has been gaining in 'definiteness and concreteness' ever since 'the discovery of Evolution as the method of the Life Force'.[2] Yet a religion needs imaginative interpretation in order to move the many, and since Shaw is out to move the many he sets himself the task of providing, in Back to Methuselah, the poetic legend and parable that shall make the truth of metaphysical Vitalism energetic and attractive.

As for the idea of longevity which underlies this legend, Shaw took his clue, he tells us, from the biologist Weismann, who 'pointed out that death is not an eternal condition of life, but an expedient introduced to provide for continual renewal without overcrowding.'[3] Death, therefore, may be postponed, and in Shaw's mind this notion quite naturally becomes a matter of will: It meets his old axiom that 'Where there is a will there is a way', and hence emerges the postulate that man could live as long as he is capable of willing. Next, inevitably, Shaw makes one move further and claims that man *must* live longer, in order to think better, live better and govern better.[4] Experience, and, above all, the responsibility attendant upon the expectancy of long life, bring wisdom, thoughtfulness and self-discipline. Therefore, longevity becomes a condition, urgent and ineluctable, of moral consciousness, of intelligence and indeed of survival.

Back to Methuselah, we may already anticipate, springs from the

---

[1] P. lxxiv.   [2] P. lxxi.   [3] P. xvii.
[4] Cf. *Man and Superman*: "I would think more, therefore I must be more"; p. 113.

370

same intention, and the same attitudes and idiosyncrasies as *Man and Superman*. We meet again Shaw's moral zest, his contempt for democracy, his loathing of fatalism. And the only sacred and lasting fact is Life, whose force is once more invoked, with Evolution, to save mankind from extinction. Here too, underneath the destructive criticism, we find Shaw's passionate though not very tender care for man, or rather for the divine image, the man-idea, which to his exasperation remains undeveloped behind the twisted, savage features of the present political animal. And just as Shaw in *Man and Superman* explored the possible Life Force direction onward and upward in human nature, so here he embarks on a journey even more fantastic, and, it would seem, even less hopeful of practical discoveries than his Superman eugenics.

The Legend and the Miracle

Back to Methuselah, as the Preface indicates, is an ambitious work, the work of one who claims to be an Artist-Prophet, and within its vast time-scheme it contains both an epic of Evolution and a Utopia, a doctrine of 'metaphysical Vitalism', and, above all, a moral analysis of the human condition.

The drama is a cycle of five plays, of which the first takes place in the Garden of Eden, the second in contemporary (1920) England, the third in the Britain of 2170, A. D., the fourth in Ireland in the year 3000, and the fifth in a nameless land in 31,920 A. D. Obviously, within such a structure there can be little or no unity of character and action, nor a psychological development in any ordinary sense. Instead of this, Shaw aims at a picture of the intellectual and moral evolution of the human species, and moreover, by his trick of reincarnation of type he achieves also something like a unity and development of character, essential to his purpose of satire and moral challenge. More important to the structural unity, however, is the inner coherence of directive attitude and vision, expressed in

371

the *leit-motif* of the 'metabiological' theme. Like Hardy's *Dynasts,* this 'Metabiological Pentateuch' has the unity of the underlying idea. Yet while the idea in Hardy, which is similarly an idea of cosmic destiny and its fatal forces, generates an ever-widening pano-rama—a large cross section of history at one significant moment, the corresponding idea in Shaw's drama forces the vision swiftly through a narrow temporal perspective, virtually without end.

Methuselah is not a historical drama, but it might be called a moral sermon upon the text of human history. As such Shaw never-theless provides it with a symbolical and temporal framework—a legend, which has interest in so far as it illuminates the inner growth of the moral and prophetic theme. What is this legend?

'In the Beginning' Adam and Eve are growing conscious of the meaning of eternal life—of having to exist for ever in the unchang-ing monotony of the Garden of Eden. Adam is obsessed by the hor-ror of 'having to be here for ever', while to Eve a thought comes 'from within' that 'we must not cease to be'. Then death is revealed to them, and between the fear of death and of unending boredom Adam and Eve are tormented, until the subtle Serpent confides to Eve the secret of birth: the regeneration by which death is conquered and the individual has eternal life in the race.[1] But how is this miracle to be performed? Through will and imagination. The Ser-pent whispers in the ear of Eve: 'You imagine what you desire; you will what you imagine; and at last you create what you will.'[2]

Thus Cain and Abel are born. Unhappily, however, in Cain the principle of death, from being a necessary condition of renewal, becomes a self-destructive force, and human history in its early stages, we anticipate at the close of the first play, will be a contest between life and death, the mother and the murderer.

Shaw does not give a historical illustration of this contest, nor bridge the gap between 'the Beginning' and the present, for in the

[1] Cf. the later moral comment upon this event, pp. 75—7.   [2] P. 8.

second play—'The Gospel of the Brothers Barnabas'—we are in the England of our times. Cain, it would seem, is on the winning side, for death has recently taken a heavy toll again in the World War. Yet this global catastrophe leaves the statesmen, the 'typical' liberal politicians Burge and Lubin, cynically confident and cheerful, unconscious of their share in the disaster, and wholly irresponsible within their petty party schemes. However, the need of racial and moral regeneration—the necessity of conquering death again and in a new way—is beginning to urge itself upon men of 'a clear head and a wide purpose', and such men are the brothers Barnabas. In the confrontation between these and the politicians, Shaw illustrates through sermon and satire the lack of responsibility and competence in the average statesman who, now more than ever, is entrusted with the destiny of our race. To save mankind from extinction at the hand of these, the brothers Barnabas (who are, significantly, a biologist and a defrocked priest) launch their programme of 'Back to Methuselah':—'that the term of human life shall be extended to three hundred years.'[1] Only by accepting the burden of long life and responsibility which the first human beings—in the Fall—rejected, can man grow wiser, more disciplined and capable. Again, how is this miracle to be achieved? Through the imagination and will of those who know, deep down in their unconscious, that they *must* live longer 'if the world is to be saved.'[2]

'The Thing Happens' in the year 2170 A.D.—We are still in Britain, and Shaw sustains his satire on the play-boy politician both through a perpetuation of type—Burge-Lubin now rolled into one —and through his whimsical and wholly irrelevant idea of importing civil servants from China.[3] The significant confrontation, however, is this time between the child-statesman and the two

---

[1] P. 68.   [2] P. 85.

[3] Cf. p. 97: 'Ever since the public services...', which, on logical exigencies, gives his case for longevity away. See also 'We extricated ourselves..'; p. 99.

individuals, (both minor characters in Part II), who have performed the 'miracle' and lived for nearly three hundred years. Longevity has worked the changes in them which the brothers Barnabas predicted: they are indeed austerely thoughtful, self-disciplined, forward-looking, and intensely conscious of the meaning of their lives and actions for the future. In fact they decide to breed a race of longlivers in order to save mankind from self-destruction.

From these two pioneers descend the long-lived people of the fourth play. These have established a colony in Ireland, and here, in the year 3000, takes place the 'tragedy of an Elderly Gentleman'. Already the gulf has grown almost insuperable between the two human varieties, for the longlivers not only think differently—they still look young, but are unyouthful in 'their severity and determination'; they commune with one another through some kind of telepathy, and have the power to kill at a glance. Discipline, order and aloofness characterize them and their society, though of their social life we learn little except that there is perfect co-operation, and that the education of reason is the only training. Their sole controversial issue is whether the pernicious, stupid race of short-livers should be still tolerated or destroyed.

The confrontation between shortlivers and longlivers takes on a new aspect in this play, owing to the evolutionary characteristics gained through longevity. It is not only that ordinary man is help-less, intellectually and physically, against the new race which is actually threatening him with annihilation. The nature of this help-lessness derives from a significant Shavian insight: the shortlived man dies through 'discouragement' in contact with these ancient supermen. For the effort needed at the intellectual and moral level of these people, who have accepted the burden of long life, is beyond the reach of man—or the majority of men who have no business to be alive.

Part IV, then, represents a middle stage in the evolution of Shaw's Utopia, and in the numeric expansion of the longlivers, as well as in their superior powers, there is already more than a hint that the days of man—the 'political animal'—are numbered. In the fifth play this has actually happened, and here Shaw goes 'As Far as Thought Can Reach'—to the year 31,920 A.D.

It would appear, at first sight, that Shaw, like so many exiles from reality, has gone back to the Golden Age for his vision of the ideal land:

Summer afternoon...A sunlit glade at the southern foot of a thickly wooded hill. On the west side of it, the steps and columned porch of a dainty little classic temple. Between it and the hill, a rising path to the wooded heights begins with rough steps of stones in the moss. On the opposite side, a grove. In the middle of the glade, an altar in the form of a low marble table as long as a man, set parallel to the temple steps and pointing to the hill. Curved marble benches radiate from it into the foreground . . . .

A dance of youths and maidens is in progress. The music is provided by a few fluteplayers seated carelessly on the steps of the temple. There are no children; and none of the dancers seems younger than eighteen. Some of the youths have beards. Their dress, like the architecture of the theatre and the design of the altar and curved seats, resembles Grecian of the fourth century B.C., freely handled. They move with perfect balance and remarkable grace, racing through a figure like a farandole...[1]

Yet this scene of classical beauty and Arcadian delight is a deceptive prelude, for soon

a strange figure appears on the path beyond the temple. He is deep in thought, with his eyes closed and his feet feeling automatically for the rough irregular steps as he slowly descends them. Except for a sort of linen kilt consisting mainly of a girdle carrying a sporran and a few minor pockets, he is naked. In physical hardihood and uprightness he seems to be in the prime of life; and his eyes and mouth shew no signs of age; but his face, though fully and firmly fleshed, bears a network of lines, varying from furrows to hairbreadth reticulations, as if Time had worked over every inch of it

[1] P. 209.

incessantly through whole geologic periods. His head is finely domed and utterly bald. Except for his eyelashes he is quite hairless. He is unconscious of his surroundings, and walks right into one of the dancing couples, separating them. He wakes up and stares about him...[1]

In Shaw's ideal land—as far as it can be seen within earthly existence—there are only these ancients, and the potential ones, the youth, and human evolution has worked drastic and curious changes. Babies are no longer born, but hatched from eggs, and during their incubation period, which lasts for two years, they pass through a development 'that once cost human beings twenty years of awkward stumbling immaturity after they were born'.[2] Indeed, the newly born 'knows by instinct many things that their [the shortlivers'] greatest physicists could hardly arrive at by forty years of strenuous study'.[3] During the first four years of their lives the youth pursue their innocent Arcadian pleasures, sing and dance, cultivate the arts, perform miracles of science (Pygmalion and the human dolls), and love one another. There is no education, no training for professions, and no moral indoctrination: the newly born are told to do what they like. But in these years they attain to the same degree of maturity as human beings formerly took a lifetime to acquire, and in the fourth year, very rapidly, they tire of their games, love and human relationships and grow into ancients who live indefinitely, or until their 'accident' comes.[4]

Shaw's description of the ancients dwells emphatically on their utter independence of material need and comfort. They hardly

[1] Pp. 209—10.

[2] P. 221;—Shaw here exploits Butler's idea of embryonic memory and 'learning'.

[3] P. 234.

[4] While Shaw in the fourth play introduces the idea of selective breeding, cf. 'successful mothers' (p. 154), he here indicates that preventive eugenics is practised: 'Children with anything wrong do not live here'; p. 221.

dress, never feed, never sleep, and only rarely, as in their meetings with the young people, become conscious of their environment. Life to them is solitary thought and all-absorbing contemplation—an unceasing effort to gain deeper understanding and intenser self-consciousness. The drastic reductions of their material requirements imply a general simplification in the economic, social and political structure of their community. For here the necessity of work has vanished and along with it all problems of State economy. Indeed, the State as such is implicitly discarded, there being no longer any need of government, education, police or social care. Human nature has long since evolved beyond evil and rid itself of social and moral conflict.

Thus Shaw's Utopian pattern is a very simple design indeed—so simple that it does not, strictly speaking, fulfil the formal exigencies of a Utopia in the traditional sense.[1] Shaw, having long since lost faith in the efficiency of political institutions, takes no interest in whatever systems may flourish and fade in the future. His sole pre-occupation is with Utopia as an ideal condition of life, that is, of thought. Hence the slender formal elaboration of the legend and the miracle through which he seeks to illustrate his new religion of Creative Evolution.

The Life Force and Longevity

In *Back to Methuselah* as in *Man and Superman* the Life Force is the central and basic concept, and from 'The Beginning' it manifests itself as will and aspiration: in woman as will to live and beget life, and in both man and woman as urge to greater perfection.[2] And this will becomes creative through the knowledge imparted to

[1] Cf. H. Ross: 'A Utopia must comprehend the whole of the social structure..', *Utopias Old and New*, p. 13.

[2] Cf. Eve: 'We must not cease to be'.—Adam: 'I want to be different; to be better': p. 3. This is something like the juxtaposition of man and woman in *Man and Superman*, p. 107. Gradually Shaw tends to invest Eve with

Eve by the Serpent: 'You imagine what you desire; you will what you imagine; and at last you create what you will'.[1] Thus Shaw rejects emphatically the classical metaphysical axiom *Ex nihilo nihil fit*, and claims instead: 'Everything must have been created out of nothing'.[2] Moreover, he contends, 'there is no such thing as nothing, only things we cannot see'.[3]

If one may take this first part of Shaw's legend as an evaluation of human nature in its fundamental goodness and soundness— despite the 'Fall', despite the inability of the first human beings to face the responsibility of eternal life—the succeeding plays of the Pentateuch are concerned with the decadence resulting from this 'Fall' and with the problem of a drastic regeneration of mankind. Shaw is still puzzled by the fact that, for all their will to live and to be better, human beings have made chaos and wars and crimes innumerable. And the disturbing questions remain these: Is human nature really degenerating? Will man be scrapped as useless by the Life Force, and replaced by something superior? This last question echoes again and again, and makes it abundantly clear that to Shaw, despite his contempt for the majority of men, the human being matters more than anything.[4] Behind his explicit postulate: 'Life must not cease. That comes before everything', there is an implicit claim that man, as mind or soul, must live for ever, live better and more fully. It is significant that, as the problem of degeneration is posed here once more, the moral and metaphysical aspects become, as in *Man and Superman*, inseparably one.

Throughout the second, third and fourth play runs the theme of *irresponsibility*, expressed in the politicians, since these to Shaw are

both these instincts, in contrast to Adam whose lack of creative desire and imagination serves as a foil to Eve, cf. pp. 32—3; 265—6.

[1] P. 8.   [2] P. 8. — Cf. also Preface, pp. xvi—xvii.

[3] P. 10. This may be regarded as Shaw's laconic answer to Joad's criticism of the difficulty of 'origin' in his philosophy; cf. *Shaw*, pp. 197—200.

[4] Cf. pp. 82, 125, 266.

the people who can do most harm, but with general implications. The men who make deaths and ruins, the incapable and inefficient men who humbug the masses and lead the world from bad to worse, are merely thoughtless play-boys never grown up from their games and pleasures. They *play* at politics instead of facing their tremendous tasks seriously. And why? Because 'Life is too short for men to take it seriously';—so short that it is not worth while 'to do anything well'.[1] Their failure inheres in the common lot, and as individuals the statesmen are not to be blamed for their inability to handle and control the forces, almost too great for gods, which thrust the nations into war and calamity. The World War was only a portent of what is to come, for our civilization is rushing to its decline and fall; indeed the very existence of our species is threatened, and 'We shall go to smash within the lifetime of men now living unless we recognize that we must live longer'.[2]—'It is now absolutely certain', Conrad Barnabas contends,

that the political and social problems raised by our civilization cannot be solved by mere human mushrooms who decay and die when they are just beginning to have a glimmer of the wisdom and knowledge needed for their own government.[3]

The striking and significant aspect in Shaw's new idea of human rebirth is not so much its quality of intellectual shock—of outrage to common sense, as its insistence on what appears to be a moral paradox. For on the one hand Shaw finds man as immoral and undisciplined as he did in *Man and Superman,* on the other hand he excuses the human being his most serious shortcomings: Man is irresponsible but he is not to be blamed. He is bad and reckless, but mainly because he is stupid and inexperienced. Thus, it would seem, Shaw has changed the direction of his attack since the Wagner essay and *Man and Superman,* for the emphasis is now not at all on the devouring, anarchistic egoism of the political animal, but on the frivolity of the political child. The formula of

[1] Pp. 39, 77.   [2] P. 73.   [3] P. 69.

his moral analysis has changed because Shaw aims at a different prophetic message, and to justify and develop his theme he needs some such postulate as this: man is evil, that is, irresponsible, because life is too short for him to know the meaning of wisdom, or good. Longevity, which is the central trend in Shaw's new prophecy, is indeed an outrage to common sense; it is such a towering piece of nonsense that only by following up its moral implications can we hope to find in it the core of truth which Shaw intended to lay bare.

We shall first consider how, in Shaw's 'legend', longevity is to be achieved. The main difficulty to be overcome, we are reminded at once, is lack of *will*, and at this crucial point Shaw invokes, here as in *Man and Superman*, the providential working of the Life Force. Thus in the second play the brothers Barnabas (the appointed spokesmen) prepare the ground for the longevity programme in a solemn comment upon the Eternal Life—Life which persists through new bodies and minds in Its eternal pursuit:

The pursuit of omnipotence and omniscience. Greater power and greater knowledge: these are what we are all pursuing even at the risk of our lives and the sacrifice of our pleasures. Evolution is that pursuit and nothing else. It is the path to godhead.[1]

And through this pursuit the change will come, not by imperceptible degrees, but suddenly and in great strides:

The notion that Nature does not proceed by jumps is only of the budget of plausible lies that we call classical education. Nature always proceeds by jumps. She may spend twenty thousand years making up her mind to jump; but when she makes it up at last, the jump is big enough to take us into a new age.[2]

What part will man's voluntary effort play in this 'jump' to longevity? So far Shaw has implied that human will matters greatly, for 'you create what you will'. Yet, on the other hand,

[1] P. 76.   [2] P. 81.

We shall not be let alone. The force behind evolution, call it what you will, is determined to solve the problem of civilization; and if it cannot do it through us, it will produce some more capable agents. Man is not God's last word: God can still create. If you cannot do His work He will produce some being who can.[1]

The Life Force is still driving onward and upward, but in its ceaseless effort to attain higher levels of life it may find man a recalcitrant and useless tool and scrap him. The majority of men are useless tools, no doubt, now as before. But there are the best men, and to these we must look for the miracle that shall revive our species and take us into a new age.[2] Shaw, however, no longer insists on the best men being the philosophic men—they are merely individuals with an unusual capacity for *willing*.

In the way Shaw forecasts *how* longevity is to be achieved, it is obvious that the process from the beginning is cut loose from any practical programme or method—it is indeed miraculous; and the idea thus presents itself, more clearly than the prophecy of the Superman, as a metaphor of mystical belief and of moral exhortation. Its genetic path is easily retraced, from Shaw's disgust with the majority of men into his passionate cult of Life—Life that worketh all wonders, and thence into the potential ramifications of the Life Force in human will. The path is one familiar to us from *Man and Superman,* though here, it would seem, there is a new and in Shaw unexpected touch of necessity. For longevity, he simply states, 'is a thing that is going to happen', almost, one feels, despite man or at least without his conscious, voluntary participation.[3] What, then, of the best men and their creative will? The thing is going to happen because the Life Force is working through the subconscious will of these men—a will that is different from our petty intentions and efforts directed upon egoistic motives. These are merely idle fancies:

[1] P. 82.   [2] P. 83.   [3] P. 84.

Do not mistake mere idle fancies for the tremendous miracle-working force of Will nerved to creation by a conviction of Necessity. I tell you men capable of such willing, and realizing its necessity, will do it reluctantly, under inner compulsion, as all great efforts are made. They will hide what they are doing from themselves: they will take care not to know what they are doing. They will live three hundred years, not because they would like to, but because the soul deep down in them will know that they must, if the world is to be saved.[1]

Necessity, then, in Shaw's belief, is not fatalism nor determinism, but an identification, at a level deeper and more intense than conscious thought, of the Life Force intention with human will. One seeks in vain, in this statement, for the 'wild logician', and in common-sense semantics it would be difficult to reconcile the notion that men 'realize' the necessity of willing and yet endeavour 'not to know what they are doing'. The passage expresses a mystic's faith, something like a translation into 'metabiological' terms of the paradox of freedom and necessity involved in the Christian conception of man as a moral being and a soul, free to will the will of God, free also to be damned. Already in *Man and Superman* there are indications that this is the way in which Shaw is trying to solve the dilemma of human degeneration and creative will.[2] The Life Force is working, like Divine Grace, secretly and steadily in human nature, until the miracle of rebirth may take place.[3]

[1] P. 85.

[2] Cf. 'a general secret pushing of the human will in the repudiated direction': 'The Revolutionist's Handbook', p. 204.

[3] Cf. H. Bergson's comment on the surprise of finalists and mechanists at the realization of complex structures: '*Au fond de notre étonnement il y a toujours cette idée qu'une partie seulement de cet ordre aurait pu être réalisée, que sa réalisation complète est une espèce de grâce. Cette grâce les finalistes se la font dispenser en une seule fois par la cause finale; les mécanistes prétendent l'obtenir petit à petit par l'effet de la sélection naturelle ...*': *L'Évolution Créatrice*, p. 96.

382

Shaw has come a long way from his Promethean programme of making new men—as proposed in the Wagner essay—to this mystical conviction that deep down in the human soul there is a miracle-working will nerved to creation. It is, apparently, a retreat along the whole line of practical suggestion and of reformatory method, and a surrender even of the hope that man's conscious striving might add a cubit to his stature—the hope that lived in *Man and Superman*. Indeed it would seem that Shaw is here clutching at the last straw, after a complete disillusionment with man, the political animal. Yet, the opposite thing is taking place, and what Shaw expresses in this passage is, above all, his trust in man, and his certainty that Life—the tireless power—is still driving onward and upward in human nature.

It follows, however, that the idea of longevity is less concerned with active planning or effort than the corresponding advocacy of eugenics in *Man and Superman*. Is it, therefore, less significant as a moral challenge? If it is a thing that is going to happen, if the most one can do is to convince men 'that there is nothing to prevent its happening', one might argue that its value as a moral incentive is slight. But to Shaw this removal of mental obstruction is of the utmost importance, for it means the rejection of the spirit of despair, of *Vanitas vanitatum,* and already in the first scene its far-reaching, creative function is revealed through the Serpent's question: 'Why not?' To the Life Force nothing is impossible, nor are there any difficulties too great for the creative will of man: the energy through which the Life Force works its miracle.

If this conviction be granted, the significance of longevity as a moral message and a mystical goal,—as something devoutly and persistently to be desired—must lie in its ethical content and value. And after having professed his faith that the miracle will happen, because it must, Shaw's main task throughout the dramatic cycle is to formulate and define its ethical implications. Ultimately, since longevity means a radical transcendence of human nature, it would

383

seem to point forward to a Utopian consummation of all the values which it might comprehend or symbolize. But in the meantime the 'thing' is going to be tested dramatically, in Part III and IV, through a confrontation between shortlivers and longlivers. It is, one might expect from such an intention, a pathetic and unequal battle, neither fair nor conclusive, yet it illustrates clearly enough, partly through satire, partly by sermon, the moral meaning of Shaw's concept of longevity.

In various ways, but mainly in matters of sex and intelligence Shaw's longlivers are wholly different from ordinary shortlived beings. In their attitude to sex the longlivers of the third play are already as severe as the ancients of the fifth:

Can you shortlived people not understand that as the confusion and immaturity and primitive animalism in which we live for the first hundred years of our life is worse in this matter of sex than in any other, you are intolerable to us in that relation?[1]

Longevity means self-discipline, detachment from animal instincts, and public concern and earnestness, in contrast to the egoism and childish pursuit of pleasure that waste the ordinary life.

Responsibility and experience, we were told from the outset, are to be the chief gains from longevity, for it implies a long prospect as well as retrospect. While in his satire on the reckless politicians Shaw tends to stress the latter aspect, in the fourth play he throws all emphasis on the former. This is how the longlived Zoo lectures the elderly gentleman on the subject:

it is not the number of years we have behind us, but the number we have before us, that makes us careful and responsible and deter-mined to find out the truth about everything. What does it matter to you whether anything is true or not? your flesh is as grass: you

[1] P. 125; cf. also: 'to outlive the childish passions ...', p. 167, and Part V, *passim*.

come up like a flower, and wither in your second childhood. A lie
will last your time: it will not last mine. If I knew I had to die in
twenty years it would not be worth my while to educate myself:
I should not bother about anything but having a little pleasure
while I lasted.[1]

Not the accumulation of memory and experience so much as the
greatness of his task urges man to think and act with more intensity
and care:

How often must I tell you that we are made wise not by the recollections of our past, but by the responsibilities of our future.[2]

For 'to a longliver every extra year is a prospect which forces him
to stretch his faculties to the utmost to face it'.[3] Therefore, Shaw
concludes, 'It is a law of Nature that there is a fixed relation between conduct and length of life'.[4]

Having thus defined the significance of longevity as chiefly greater
seriousness in thought and action, and keener awareness of responsibility, Shaw in the final play presents a society in which the values
gained from this human condition have accumulated and become
almost universal. We should expect to find in this future society
something of penultimate though not static perfection. This at any
rate is the formal development implied in the total scheme of
the cycle.

As Far as Thought can Reach

In going as far as his thought can reach Shaw has not left behind
his divine discontent, for this is always a condition of Utopian dream.
He still needs a confrontation between the ideal and reality, the good
life and the bad or useless, between value and waste. In the dramatic
structure this is achieved by contrasting a group of immature, pleasure-seeking youth with the formidable lonely figures of the ancients.

[1] Pp. 164—65.   [2] P. 167.   [3] P. 174.   [4] *Ibid.*

And by the peculiar device of the human automata the shadow of primitive evil, stupidity and aggression still falls into this world of innocent joys and grave contemplation: It is the traditional Utopian encounter of the citizens of reality with those of the ideal state, and reality is represented by the youth at its possible best and by the automata at its very worst.[1] These ghastly and fantastic apparitions from a species long extinct carry on the Cain-theme of stupid destructiveness from the first play and the mock-heroic satire on Napoleon from the fourth.[2] The synthetic couple provides a foil both to the ancients and the youth and enables Shaw to continue his exposure of human nature. Their relationship with man is continually stressed, as in Pygmalion's remark that 'there really is some evidence that we are descended from creatures quite as limited and absurd as these'. Thus Shaw condemns men in retrospect as creatures who were 'all reflexes and nothing else'; creatures who were swayed by their hungers and vanities, lusts and greeds. Yet, again with a significant comment, and one which corresponds to Shaw's pardon to the politicians, these creatures are excused, while they cannot be allowed to live: Life has not yet entered fully into them and evolved them. They are immoral because they lack vitality, and as the ancient, in the moment of execution, proposes to 'put a little more life into them', they lose their brutal selfishness.[3] Again, 'discouragement'—the spirit of despair and of *Vanitas vanitatum*—is the mortal power that strikes ordinary man: he dies because the will to live fails him.

In Shaw's general confrontation in this play between two modes of life and thought (or activity), these human dolls offer a pretext for one of his lengthy debates upon art for life's sake or art for art's sake. Here we are reminded of *Man and Superman* and Don

[1] G. Whitehead suggests that the figures made by Pygmalion are Darwinian automata; *Bernard Shaw Explained*, p. 120.

[2] Cf. p. 178.

[3] P. 246, cf. p. 251, 'If your Automata ...'.

386

Juan's loathing of hell as the home of the unreal and of the seekers of happiness.[1] Thus when the maiden Ecrasia claims that 'I have found a happiness in art that real life has never given me', the She-Ancient snubs her with a moral lesson:

Yes, child: art is the magic mirror you make to reflect your invisible dreams in visible pictures. You use a glass mirror to see your face: you use works of art to see your soul. But we who are older use neither glass mirrors nor works of art. We have a direct sense of life. When you gain that you will put aside your mirrors and statues, your toys and your dolls.[2]

This clash between life and art, reality and unreality, value and waste, ancients and youth, takes us back to the very beginning of the play, where Shaw first brings his Utopians together. At once Shaw makes the two sides come to grips on the issue of value and the good life. A youth challenges the ancient:

Come! own up: arnt you very unhappy? It's dreadful to see you ancients going about by yourselves, never noticing anything, never dancing, never laughing, never singing, never getting anything out of life. None of us are going to be like that when we grow up. It's a dog's life.[3]

And the ancient replies: 'It is you, my children, who are living the dog's life'. Real happiness is as yet unknown to them, for: 'one moment of the ecstasy of life as we live it would strike you dead'. These children are in the hell of unreality, but soon they will mature and give up their 'toys and games and sweets'.[4]

Shaw next gives us a scene in which we observe the growing up of these youths and maidens—from idle pleasure, from art for art's sake, from love and human relationship, and from all the material comforts of life, like sleep and clothing. The Arcadian values are

[1] *Op. cit.*, p. 99.   [2] P. 254.   [3] P. 210.   [4] P. 212.

defended in vain against this ripening process. In vain Strephon protests:

What is the use of being born if we have to decay into unnatural, heartless, loveless, joyless monsters in four short years? What use are the artists if they cannot bring their beautiful creations to life? I have a great mind to die and have done with it all.[1]

For the She-Ancient knows better: 'Infant: you are only at the beginning of it all'. It is the 'imitation of happiness', not the genuine thing, which these undeveloped young people pursue like a mirage, just as in art they cultivate the imitation—and in Shaw's opinion it is no more than that—of reality. And these works of art, these imitations, may even, as in Pygmalion's human dolls, have a disastrous effect. They can be 'amusing and lovable' to a certain irresponsible young age, but they must not attempt to replace the true, the real object of human interest—Life. If they do, it means destruction of one's 'direct sense of life'. Thus in Shaw's ideal human condition, as in Plato's *Republic*, the arts have a precarious place indeed. The only artist who is useful and worthy of esteem is, according to Shaw, the artist-prophet, who is engaged upon the interpretation of life, instead of the imitation of life which is the fallacy of 'pure art'. To grow up, to embrace and understand the real object of our minds, it is necessary to discard not only these counterfeits, but all sensual pursuits—happiness, pleasure, friendship, love and Nature. It is a formidable list of renunciations Shaw sets up for his ideal man, but one justified, he claims, by the truth gained from experience with men, art and Nature: 'you can create nothing but yourself'.[2]

Shaw thus concludes—though the Arcadian protest is heard to the end—the argument between the seekers of happiness and the masters of reality, between the old life and the new. Yet these masters—these ancients—for all their ecstasy of thought, for all

[1] P. 217.   [2] P. 253.

their creative will and supreme detachment from material things, are still not in complete possession of their power. They too have their 'trouble'. And now another battle is revealed, more fierce and lasting: the perennial battle, in fact, between mind and body, spirit and matter, with issues more fatal to the realization of the purpose of the Life Force. Through the body the ancients are still chained to matter and racked with its limitation. In their struggle for complete mastery and freedom they had exercised their creative will in vain—made themselves into 'all sorts of fantastic monsters, with many heads, arms and legs'. In an amusing dialogue Shaw describes their dilemma and points to their destination:

THE SHE-ANCIENT. One day, when I was tired of learning to walk forward with some of my feet and backwards with others and sideways with the rest all at once, I sat on a rock with my four chins resting on four of my palms, and four of my elbows resting on four of my knees. And suddenly it came into my mind that this monstrous machinery of heads and limbs was no more me than my statues had been me, and that it was only an automaton that I had enslaved.

MARTELLUS. Enslaved? What does that mean?

THE SHE-ANCIENT. A thing that must do what you command it is a slave; and its commander is its master. These are words you will learn when your turn comes.

THE HE-ANCIENT. You will also learn that when the master has come to do everything through the slave, the slave becomes his master, since he cannot live without him.

THE SHE-ANCIENT. And so I perceived that I had made myself the slave of a slave.

THE HE-ANCIENT. When we discovered that, we shed our superfluous heads and legs and arms until we had our old shapes again, and no longer startled the children.

THE SHE-ANCIENT. But still I am the slave of this slave, my body. How am I to be delivered from it?

THE HE-ANCIENT. That, children, is the trouble of the ancients. For whilst we are tied to this tyrannous body we are subject to its death, and our destiny is not achieved.

389

THE NEWLY BORN. What is your destiny?
THE HE-ANCIENT. To be immortal.
THE SHE-ANCIENT. The day will come when there will be no people, only thought.
THE HE-ANCIENT. And that will be life eternal.[1]

The mind cannot yet exist without the body—it is wholly immanent, since it does 'everything through the slave'. At the same time Shaw postulates the 'master', the mind, as, originally perhaps, and finally at least, free from and transcending matter. Despite its burlesque and humour, the passage is expressive of one important aspect of Shaw's belief: he cannot conceive of mind as both immanent and transcendent at the same time.

As the play draws to a close, it develops into something like a dualistic treatise on the necessity of freeing mind from matter. To the ancients, as to the Romantics, the body is a 'prison' that forbids them to 'range through the stars'.—'The body', Shaw agrees with the Schoolmen, 'always ends by being a bore. Nothing remains beautiful and interesting except thought, because the thought is the life.' And the philosophical consolation of Shaw's ancients is that 'None of us now believe that all this machinery of flesh and blood is necessary. It dies.'[2] And as it dies and becomes superfluous, the mind, wholly freed from its trammels, becomes a vortex of pure intellect. This, since thought is life, is the life eternal. How shall it be achieved? The ancients give no answer, except that to evolution nothing is impossible; and the way of 'creation', as the Serpent told Eve, lies through desire, imagination and will. Ultimately, the fancy will be father to the fact. Through this mystical belief Shaw endeavours to reconcile his mutually exclusive postulates—that the mind cannot exist without the body, and yet all this machinery of flesh and blood is not necessary—for the mind is only now, at this phase of evolution, immanent in matter, exiled into it, destined to

[1] P. 257. [2] Pp. 259—60.

390

fight and conquer it, and finally to rise out of it—omniscient and omnipotent. The solution, however, tells us nothing about the meta-physical problem of this mind-matter relationship, or how, from a state of pure immanence the intellect can enter a state of pure transcendence. But then Shaw is not a philosopher, and the drift of his aspiration is clear: it is towards a life abundant of thought.

Before Shaw comes to the climax and conclusion of his evolu-tionary prophecy—the final speech of Lilith—there is a brief inter-mezzo in which Lilith, the Serpent, Adam, Eve and Cain are con-jured up to review the history of man and its outcome: the drama is coming full circle. This history is seen as an incessant effort on the part of life, or thought, to overcome matter in all its manifesta-tions of pain, evil, toil, ignorance, from the moment Lilith—the Life Force—created the first parents until now the ancients have freed themselves almost entirely from material need. It is also, at first, the history of natural selection, of Cain who 'invented killing and conquest and mastery and the winnowing out of the weak by the strong.'[1] But now this animal instinct is dead and intelligence —the 'clever ones'—has inherited the earth. And this happened because to direct the whole evolutionary effort there was the Serpent principle of cunning and moral consciousness: 'the knowledge of good and evil'. It is not the least evolutionary attainment that now, in the ancients, evil is outgrown, and 'wisdom and good are one.'[2]

In the concluding speech Shaw adds a lengthy and splendid com-ment on the achievement of his ancients and on their destiny. It is Shaw officiating with prophetic and ritual solemnity at the altar of the Life Force, and as an apex of his Utopian vision, finely sustained by a masterly cadenced prose, this speech deserves to be quoted at some length:

They have accepted the burden of eternal life. They have taken the agony from birth; and their life does not fail them even in the hour

[1] P. 264.   [2] P. 265.

of their destruction... Is this enough; or shall I labor again? Shall I bring forth something that will sweep them away and make an end of them as they have swept away the beasts of the garden and made an end of the crawling things and the flying things and of all them that refuse to live for ever? I had patience with them for many ages: they tried me very sorely. They did terrible things: they embraced death, and said that eternal life was a fable. I stood amazed at the malice and destructiveness of the things I had made ... The pangs of another birth were already upon me when one man repented and lived three hundred years; and I waited to see what would come of that. And so much came of it that the horrors of that time seem now but an evil dream. They have redeemed themselves from their vileness, and turned away from their sins. Best of all, they are still not satisfied: the impulse I gave them ... still urges them: after passing a million goals they press on to the goal of redemption from the flesh, to the vortex freed from matter, to the whirlpool in pure intelligence that, when the world began, was a whirlpool in pure force ... I say, let them dread, of all things, stagnation; for from the moment I, Lilith, lose hope and faith in them, they are doomed. In that hope and faith I have let them live for a moment; and in that moment I have spared them many times. But mightier creatures than they have killed hope and faith, and perished from the earth; and I may not spare them for ever. I am Lilith: I brought life into the whirlpool of force, and compelled my enemy, Matter, to obey a living soul. But in enslaving Life's enemy I made him Life's master; for that is the end of all slavery; and now I shall see the slave set free and the enemy reconciled, the whirlpool become all life and no matter. And because these infants that call themselves ancients are reaching out towards that, I will have patience with them still; though I know well that when they attain it they shall become one with me and supersede me, and Lilith will be only a legend and a lay that has lost its meaning. Of Life only is there no end; and though of its million starry mansions many are empty and many still unbuilt, and though its vast domain is as yet unbearably desert, my seed shall one day fill it and master its matter to its uttermost confines. And for what may be beyond, the eyesight of Lilith is too short. It is enough that there is a beyond.

This, then, is Shaw's ultimate anticipation—the attainment, within his imaginative range, of the ideal human being and of the good life. But the speech is something more than a fantastic prophecy: it is an epitome of Shaw's Religion of the Life Force, in which we recognize the elements of a genesis and an ethics, a gospel of redemption, and a confession of faith in the life abundant to come. Above all, it is a sermon on the necessity of tireless effort in the cause of life, with a significant emphasis on atonement as something which can be achieved by man alone, through an acceptance of his duty: his 'Fall', we remember, was his failure to do so, in the beginning.

In this final pronouncement upon the nature and purpose of the Life Force, the mystical and religious quality of Shaw's faith is deliberately underlined through a verbal and conceptual parallel with Christianity and philosophical Idealism, and the most striking thing about this faith is perhaps its neo-Platonic dualism of spirit, here identical with life, and matter, its 'enemy'—the principle of recalcitrance, imperfection and evil. Again, despite the triumphant and optimistic note in which the victory of life is celebrated, despite the implicit conviction that man will fulfil the purpose of life, we still hear the anxious note of warning: against stagnation, against a failing will to live and create. And so persistent is this theme that the main content of the speech remains its moral challenge, though both the basic trends in Shaw's vitalistic religion become particularly distinct in this—his evolutionary valediction. There is on the one hand his passionate, mystical belief in the purposive creative power of life, and there is his anxiety for man with its mingled feelings of devotion and disgust.

Shaw's 'metabiological Pentateuch' begins with the first people and ends in Utopia. Three of its plays are concerned with the genesis of the promised land, but only the last one approaches to a genuinely Utopian pattern, and even this, the land of the ancients, does not present a rounded and comprehensive picture of a society in its life and works. It is not 'A place, state or condition ideally perfect in respect of politics, laws, customs and conditions'. For this reason, probably, historians of Utopia pass it by without comment.[1] Yet, since the idea of evolution has altered so radically the Utopian structure—channelled into it a current of inexhaustible speculation and opened up fields of unlimited imaginative scope, *Back to Methuselah* may legitimately be ranked with the dreams of the ideal life, though this dream is no longer determined by aspirations to political or social perfection, but wholly by an evolutionary faith in the ideal human being. Shaw, whose disillusionment with political and social systems is particularly embittered, represents this shift of interest very clearly. Man will not add a cubit to his stature by any of his political quackeries;—the Hill Difficulty will never be climbed by Man as we know him, so all we can hope for is that man shall be born again and born better—that he shall save his soul. For if he does, Shaw preaches both in *Man and Superman* and *Back to Methuselah*, all the rest shall be given unto him—or rather, all the rest does not matter. It is in this light that one must view Shaw's ancients, and the particular form and condition of their rebirth.

Since Utopia is always concerned with *value*, it is to the ancients we must turn in order to find out what Shaw aspires to as the most worth-while things in the future. And, to begin with, we suggest that the values which are at the core of Shaw's fantasy depend for their validity and acceptance, not upon the specific method—longevity—by which Shaw forecasts their realization, but upon the conviction they carry in terms of the human ideal and the good life.

The ancients, says Duffin, 'are loftily conceived and attractively presented'.[2] If they reject ordinary human values, like art, love, friendship, it is because they have something better—a 'direct sense of life', and the ecstasy of thought. One of the beauties of *Back to Methuselah*, according to P. Bloomfield, is that it looks for Utopia

[1] Only P. Bloomfield, to my knowledge, has included 'As Far as Thought Can Reach', in his study *Imaginary Worlds*, p. 220 ff. It is not dealt with in the works of Hertzler, Mumford, Ross, Dupont or Simon.

[2] *Op. cit.*, p. 198.

in 'man's living sense of values'; and nevertheless, he concludes, Shaw's ideal is unacceptable, because it has nothing left to think about—it is 'the silent and invisible brooding of thought over a world it has no more use for'.[1] C. E. M. Joad deplores not only this absence of an object of thought, but the very absence of value: 'Shaw might have said that life evolves in matter, through matter and beyond matter to a knowledge of value. He hints as much, but never explicitly says it'.[2] From the beginning, reviewers announced this absence of an absolute object of contemplation as the chief defect in Shaw's message. *The Times Literary Supplement* wrote: 'Mr. Shaw, having stated his thesis of creative evolution and the omnipotence and supreme reality of the will, is at a loss for something worth willing, for something good enough; he cannot charge his truth, if truth it be, with human values and feelings'.[3]

These comments might exemplify the main critical reactions to Shaw's gospel in *Methuselah,* and it would appear that even his admirers are not quite at ease in the Shavian world of pure thought. The objections remain pertinent and valid, and yet they do not invalidate the inmost core of the drama, which is a faith in the creativeness and moral meaning of life. Shaw has failed, partially at least, to formulate an adequate goal of living and striving, and nevertheless this goal or object is implicit in his prophecy, for without it the drama would never have been written.

In Shaw's campaign for longevity there is a hierarchy of values and virtues, some concerned with nearer tasks, others pointing to the ultimate ideal. Where Shaw's intention is to show that an evolutionary 'jump' is necessary to regenerate man as a social being, he does, in passages of witty and searching satire, effectively express his zest for moral awareness, self-discipline, earnestness and sense

---

[1] *Imaginary Worlds,* pp. 222, 234—5.

[2] *Op. cit.,* p. 201; to Joad Shaw's thought seems to 'demand the inclusion in the universe of an element of static and immutable perfection'—something like the Forms of Plato; cf. p. 193.

[3] *Op. cit. The Fiftieth Anniversary Number,* Jan. 1952, p. 60.

of responsibility. Yet these are means rather than ends, virtues rather than values, all bound up with human conduct in society and directed upon activity and collective effort. And apart from these few austere features Shaw's ideal human being remains undefined—a mere mouthpiece. It would appear that Shaw's ethical challenge is most evocative and vivid in the middle plays, the satirical comedies, and fades away as the ancients take over. These, it has often been observed, are neither lovable nor charitable, but cold and authoritative teachers of a doctrine of asceticism whose justification is no longer to be sought in moral obligation in any real sense. It is unprofitable to insist too much on the inconsistencies in Shaw, but it seems nevertheless unfortunate that, having said that wisdom and good are one, and wisdom comes with longevity, he should almost condemn his ideal ancients out of his own mouth in the remark: 'Child, child, how much enthusiasm will you have for man when you have endured eight centuries of him, as I have ...?'[1] If longevity means growing tired of or indifferent to man, and if, on the other hand, it is expectancy of long life rather than experience that fosters moral earnestness, then youth and not old age would have most kindness and love, and the keenest awareness of truth.[2] For this reason also, one would seem justified in turning away from Shaw's ideal ancients to join in the art and love and friendship of the Arcadian youth.

The chief value which the ancients derive from longevity—from having practised contemplation and will-power beyond any conceivable human limits—is a 'direct sense of life', and an 'ecstasy' that, one may assume, must spring from an experience of truth and approach to the man-god condition of omniscience and omnipotence. While in this world, the ancients think about numbers and contemplate the universe; and when here it is still possible to accept

---

[1] P. 256.   [2] Cf. Zoo: 'I shall be more reckless when I am a tertiary than I am today'; Part IV, p. 167.

396

them as symbols of an intellectual and mystical aspiration, it is even possible to accept—in terms of Shavian intuition—the 'ecstasy' as a condition charged with emotional and intellectual values without a name. It might be read as a phrase—to use Matthew Arnold's definition of biblical language—'thrown out, so to speak, at a not fully grasped object of the speaker's consciousness'. As for Shaw's transcendent dream—'no people, only thought'—it has little or no evocative force. With the emotional values of love and friendship gone, with nothing left but a 'Whirlpool in pure intelligence' unrelated to any object of value or veneration, Shaw fails to suggest that this is a life eternal in which all the best qualities in human nature shall come to flower. Shaw's apotheosis of man, for it is no less he aimed at since *Man and Superman*, represents an ideal which is not so much a fulfilment of human nature as a liberation from it. For this reason Shaw can tell us little about the ideal life except that it is a condition gained when food, sleep, child-birth, love, the body itself—have all become superfluous. Shaw rejects man and his nature except for that flickering light of intelligence which to him is the divine presence, caged and hampered by matter, yet ultimately to be set free. Thus, in his Promethean struggle, Shaw craves no other goal but freedom: freedom of the intellect—omnipotence through omniscience—is the truth and beauty of the Shavian heaven.

Shaw's failure to express a satisfactory Utopian ideal in *Back to Methuselah* inheres partly in his puritanical, ascetic and intellectual attitudes, partly in the spiritual climate in which these attitudes came to maturity. Shaw could not return to any dogmatic Christian or Idealistic conceptions of the life abundant and of value; like Carlyle he scorned the 'hollow Shapes or Masks' of the church, but, unlike Carlyle, he was unable to make for himself a composite heroic god. Besides, Shaw came too late to be saved by the positivistic and humanitarian gospel with which Swinburne and Meredith mingled their idealism in order to bring heaven down to earth. What Shaw nevertheless retains from these traditions, is a dream of the life eternal as a state freed absolutely from material imperfection, and he retains, moreover, the cult of the man-god. God—the Life Force —is immanent in man and evolving through him to omniscience and omnipotence.[1] Shaw's particular brand of heresy is, however, less attractive than that of the positivistic life-worshippers, like Meredith, and mainly for two reasons. In their world the creative and conservative force of love is fully recognized and integrated with reason in the future ideal. And though their gospel of pure immanence is inadequate as a metaphysical doctrine, they achieve an adequate formulation of their human ideal through their love of man and mankind. Secondly, however confined they remain in their Mother Earth, they at least choose consistently (despite verbal ambiguities) to stay in this world. Shaw, in contrast, has no use for love as a creative force; and with his superb contempt for logic and first principles he looks forward to an evolutionary 'jump' from people to thought, from matter to disembodied vital energy, which means a jump from a doctrine of pure immanence to one of pure transcendence. But then Shaw is a mystic who often defies, in the name of Life, both logic and first principles. His intention in *Back to Methuselah* is, above all, to set forth an outrageous intellectual heresy, in order to emphasize his credo all the more: I believe in Life, and in the Life to come.

Shaw would have been most offended if one were to smoothe over this heresy and excuse his prophetic vagaries on the ground that, of course, he did not literally *mean* his ideal—'no people, only thought'. Yet, though nothing is gained by explaining away this barren ideal, there is one sense in which it may stand as something more than a failure to conceive of value, or a hatred of the human animal. If Shaw abstains from defining the 'direct sense of life', the 'ecstasy' of thought, and the 'life eternal' to which the ancients aspire, it is not solely because of his agnostic and nihilistic training

---

[1] Cf. Shaw's Swinburnian answer to the question of how he conceived of God: 'God is I'; A. Henderson *op. cit.*, p. 521.

and outlook, but because he knows, with the mystic's insight, that this ideal life cannot be described in terms of earthly categories, and neither can the object of contemplation which must necessarily inhere in it. Shaw, the living paradox, the agnostic mystic, the Puritan pagan, the earthbound idealist, agrees implicitly with Shelley that Life—on earth—'Stains the white radiance of Eternity'. It would be futile to define that for which there are no words or concepts. This is the perennial claim of mystical Idealism. Shaw's French contemporary, Paul Valéry, restated it in his story *La Soirée avec M. Teste,* and in his celebrated dictum: *Il n'y a rien de plus beau que ce qui n'existe pas.* It is something like this claim which underlies Shaw's beatific dream of the world of pure thought, unstained by matter.

What remains in the end of lasting value in this evolutionary prophecy is Shaw's indestructible faith in life—the faith we have followed in its growth from the Wagner essay, through *Man and Superman* until here it attains its climax of strength and conviction. *Back to Methuselah* communicates very forcibly Shaw's devotion to this, the highest value he can conceive of, and his feeling of sanctity in the contemplation of life—the creative power, in which, like all Idealists, he recognizes the divine though to him unknowable presence. And for this reason Shaw's vision of the ideal life has yet its greatness and nobility. It is a searching movement in which we perceive the idealistic dedication to spiritual beauty and value—a quest for something lasting and absolute that as yet has no name and no situation on the map of the human mind. Life, in this quest, is the first and last thing, and Shaw remains its champion against death and despair. Therefore, Chesterton's magnificent valediction to the younger Shaw still applies—and even more aptly—to the author of *Back to Methuselah:*

But this shall be written of our time: that when the spirit who denies besieged the last citadel, blaspheming life itself, there were some, there was one especially, whose voice was heard and whose spear was never broken.[1]

Even without the idea of evolution Shaw would have fought for life and hope, with whatever arms contemporary thought or religion might have forged for him. Yet evolution was an idea that not only explained, but suggested and promised, and hence it released in him an energy of faith and prophecy which perhaps no other doctrine or creed could have done. It made him an 'Artist-Prophet'; it rescued from the ashes of burnt idols the 'new religion' which, despite its errors and fantastic assumptions enabled him to fight despair and to formulate his answers to the fundamental questions: What is life? What is the moral meaning of existence? What is our destination? Like all great souls, Shaw placed these questions uppermost in the hierarchy of human knowledge. He found the conceptual framework of his answers in Butler, Nietzsche and Lamarck, but it was no more than that—a slight perspective pointing nowhere in particular. Shaw, by asking: What is the purpose? forced the perspective in his own direction and thus widened the horizon of vitalistic faith. It is in this way that Shaw imposes upon the inherited evolutionary framework an energetic pattern alive with effort, conflict, moral and spiritual struggle, will and purpose, and, despite its vagueness—a goal. In so doing, he adds something of inestimable value to the answers of Schopenhauer, Nietzsche and Butler—for in their universe the central idea, the creative will, is an empty gesture. Shaw conceives of will and intelligence as the universal creative energy, the inner will of the world, the Life Force, driving onward and upward through matter, driving at brains, the means by which life attains to moral consciousness and to deeper understanding of itself and of its destiny, and, finally, as the crowning achievement, urging man to identify his will with the cosmic will in an effort to free mind from matter. For Shaw, being like all

[1] *G. B. Shaw*, p. 257.

idealists an exile from a world of perfection, is not content to stay confined in his earthly prison. He desires to range through the stars and experience the ecstasy of absolute freedom and knowledge. Here again he seizes on evolution to break the boundaries of matter and set the spirit free. In evolution Life ascends to intenser self-consciousness, ascends to the ideal human being, omnipotent and omniscient: the man-god. Thus, evolution is the path to godhead.

The unity which underlies Shaw's varying formulation of his vitalistic belief, from the Wagner essay to *Back to Methuselah*, is manifest in these central trends of his thought and aspiration. It is a mystical and passionate intuition, and it remained thus to the end. After the age of ninety, Shaw was still in armour against the fatalism of Darwinian selection, and for this cause he rushed gallantly to the aid of Lysenko, asserting, in what was perhaps his last words on the matter, that

Fatalism is now dropped or certified as materialism gone mad. Creative Evolution is basically vitalist, and, as such, mystical, intuitive, irrational, poetic, passionate, religious, and catholic; for neither Lamarck nor Butler nor I nor Bergson nor Lysenko nor anyone else can account rationally for the life force, the evolutionary appetite, the *élan vital*, the Divine Providence (alias will of God), or the martyrdoms that are the seed of Communism. It has just to be accepted as a so far inexplicable natural fact.[1]

Much has been written about Shaw the fierce nihilist who set out, posing in various roles—sometimes as Bunyan, sometimes as Carlyle—to make himself the prophet of the twentieth century; dramatizing himself, transfiguring himself and the world in a wild intellectual pantomime. And there is some truth in this. But Shaw's vitalistic faith was always and increasingly a serious and genuine thing. It was, perhaps, at a deeper subconscious level, the fact through which Shaw strove to integrate himself and his universe, which had

[1] 'Behind the Lysenko Controversy', *The Saturday Review of Literature*, April 16, 1949.

suffered such ravages from his own dissecting intellect and from a century of accumulated doubt—the 'infidel century' that, for all his rebellion against it, had trained him. There may be histrionic pose in Shaw's reference to Bunyan's *Pilgrim's Progress*, but he none the less saw life as a pilgrimage, through Creative Evolution—a sustained tremendous effort, intellectual and moral, to raise mind out of its material bondage to an abundant life. Yet, though Shaw participates in this effort with all his untiring energy, he remains imprisoned within the intellectual horizon of his time. For this reason there is in Shaw's evolutionary belief the same tension and the same conflict between means of formulation and emotional and intellectual pressure, as that which we noted in Swinburne and Meredith. Shaw's answers are not deep and large enough for his questions.

2. *Homo Sapiens in a Modern Utopia: H. G. Wells*

> I've been living in Utopia ...
> I wish I could *smash* the world
> of everyday ...
>
> *A Modern Utopia*

Wells, Darwin and the Utopian Quest

It is in his talent for the Utopian vision that critics increasingly find the greatest imaginative achievement of Herbert George Wells. Georges Connes noted it already twenty years before Wells himself laid down his pen:

C'est dans l'élaboration et la présentation des Utopies que Wells a trouvé les plus belles jouissances de sa vie et le couronnement de son œuvre: son rêve final est, en somme, une Utopie ...[1]

And Mr. Vincent Brome, in his biography, concludes that, though Wells made many mistakes in his favourite role as a prophet;

[1] G. Connes, *Étude sur la pensée de Wells,* p. 441.

402

His brilliant imaginative powers had unlocked new ways of life hidden in dull, scientific data until we were self-conscious at a profound level of emotional understanding of the greatness within our grasp, and in his own ineffable fashion he had left a glorious sense of expectancy on the air, which remains to-day. We knew now that life need not be like this ... He prepared us for communion with the creative society to come.[1]

Hertzler makes reference to Well's' *A Modern Utopia* as 'the work of a great imaginative writer ... A masterful grappling with the Herculean problem of human advance'.[2] Lewis Mumford describes Wells' work as the 'quintessential Utopia'.[3]

There is, of course, no critical consensus on Wells as a writer of Utopias, and the negative responses are mainly of two kinds. On the one hand there are those who dislike Wells because they find in him an intolerable mixture of naïveté and conceit—an implicit claim that he, and he almost alone, knew how to build a better world.[4] On the other hand there is the accusation that Wells (and other English authors) brought Utopia so close to reality that he destroyed it.[5]

---

[1] H. G. Wells, *A Biography*, p 239.

[2] *The History of Utopian Thought*, pp. 244—5.

[3] *The Story of Utopias*, p. 184. V. Dupont, in agreement with Connes, characterizes Wells as *un génie spécifiquement anticipateur, op. cit.*, p. 620.

[4] Cf. Odette Keun's articles in *Time and Tide*, 1934, and H. Ross, *Utopias Old and New*, pp. 176, 182.

[5] Cf. W. Simon, *Die Englische Utopie im Lichte der Entwicklungslehre*, pp. 4, 51, 53.—Simon takes his thesis from a widely generalizing statement by K. Mannheim in *Ideologie und Utopie* to the effect that the Utopia, by approaching closer to reality, has become dependent upon the exigencies of historical and social process. Its *Näherücken an den historisch-sozialen Prozess* leads to a *Senkung der utopischen Intensität;* p. 234. Therefore, now, *Wir gehen einem Stadium entgegen, in dem das Utopische sich durch seine verschiedenen Gestalten völlig (zumindest im Politischen völlig) destruirt;* p. 236. This claim may be valid as far as the *Utopia of Reconstruction* is concerned, but it is highly improbable that it applies to

403

The present inquiry is on the side of those who see in Wells a warmhearted and ingenious dreamer of a better future for mankind. Assuming this, and taking for granted that Well's new worlds for old grow from one or other of the two dominant Utopian motives —the desire to reconstruct or the wish to escape—our next step is towards the stuff of his dreams. Broadly speaking, two main impulses inform the Wellsian Utopia, one socialism, the other evolution. The first aspect will not be immediately relevant to our study, though it is not possible to disentangle the theme of social progress quite from that of evolution in Wells' dream of the ideal life.

Voici, en Wells, says Connes, *un écrivain qui a édifié toute sa pensée autour de l'idée d'évolution.*[1] More recently, Otto Barber has made out a good case for his claim that Darwin's ideas pervade not only Wells' biological theses, fantasies and Utopias, but the works of history, social planning and religion.[2]

It was obvious already from the imaginative search of *The Time Machine* (1895) that Wells aspired to be the literary champion of Darwin, just as his revered teacher in biology, T. H. Huxley, had been his champion in the field of science. Wells never had any disturbing doubt about the validity of Darwin's theory, and he

the general development of the genre. It ignores the indestructible imaginative force of the *Utopia of Escape*—the pure dream—, in which the millennial fervour or 'Utopian intensity' has always been greater than in that of 'reconstruction'.

[1] *Op. cit.,* p. 11. The author notes that Wells was uncritical in his attitude to the various problems of knowledge involved, and lacked interest in the controversies provoked by Darwin's and Huxley's theories.

[2] *H. G. Wells' Verhältnis zum Darwinismus.* The author distinguishes between two 'Problemkomplexe' in Wells' purely fantastic or imaginative speculations: 1. What, considering that evolution means flux and change, would be the fate of man if the conditions of life suddenly and drastically changed? 2. What new forms will the human species develop into in the future? Can we, in the light of Darwinian theory, anticipate the effect of change in environment, regimen, etc.? Cf. p. 35.

almost pities Shaw for his erratic devotion to Lamarck,[1] while Shaw in his turn, one might conjecture, had Wells in mind when he wrote (in the preface of *Back to Methuselah*) that Darwin pleased the socialists because he gave them a congenial clue to historical process. For as Wells saw history, and society at the present—with capitalist exploitation and the beginning of class war—it was a fierce and cruel struggle for life, for power, and for freedom. Darwin's theory stimulated his dramatic sense of existentialist conflict, of man's effort to survive and adapt himself, and natural selection—to this sense—was a principle as valid in sociology and politics as in biology. This did not mean, of course, that Wells accepted it as a moral principle: on the contrary, here too he followed Huxley (and Stuart Mill) in proclaiming that the natural process must be replaced and controlled by an ethical force. This is a central motive in his Utopian planning.

Throughout Wells' work there is abundant reference to Darwin and also enthusiastic praise.[2] Significantly, he begins his *Modern Utopia* by stating that:

The Utopia of a modern dreamer must needs differ in one fundamental aspect from the Nowheres and Utopias men planned before Darwin quickened the thought of the world ... the Modern Utopia must be not static but kinetic ...[3]

It was Darwin who dissolved the static pattern of the classical ideal and released a current of fructifying ideas upon the imagination. Moreover, the optimistic conclusion of the *Origin of Species* was not wasted on the author of *A Modern Utopia:* 'all corporeal and mental endowments will tend to progress towards perfection'. But Darwin did something more than justify Wells' inborn passion for human progress and for Utopian exploration, he suggested to Wells one of the most energetic and permanent conceptions of his thought: the

[1] *The Science of Life* (1931), p. 263.
[2] Cf. Barber, *op. cit.*, p. 3.   [3] P. 15.

uniqueness of things and creatures.[1] In an article to the *Fortnightly Review* in 1891 about 'The Rediscovery of the Unique' Wells first sketched this idea which he later elaborated in a paper, 'Scepticism of the Instrument' (1903), and finally included as an appendix to *A Modern Utopia*. The idea of uniqueness and individuality, he states here, comes naturally to a mind preoccupied with the study of anatomy and biology: 'A biological species is quite obviously a great number of unique individuals ...'[2] And so, also, are the component atoms of any element. Hence his claim that this idea of uniqueness 'matters profoundly' in philosophy. As we shall see, it matters greatly also in his Utopian dream.

It would be impossible within the scope of this study to attempt an exhaustive account of the fantasies, anticipations and stories of a Utopian nature that Wells has written, and we propose, therefore, to trace, however sketchily, the human ideal in his dream. This line of inquiry will enable us to see Wells together with Shaw in a more definite human context, and provide material for a comparison of the two. We suggest, further, that one may do this most conveniently by selecting for a basis or centre mainly one work—*A Modern Utopia*. The choice is somewhat arbitrary, it would appear, and what makes it particularly difficult to single out one specimen from Wells' abundance is that he has created Utopias at so many various distances from reality—some quite close, others infinitely removed in space and time. Which of these is the most representative— the vision in which his most universal and passionate hope finds its most adequate expression? The answer is *A Modern Utopia*, though it by no means gives the whole range of Wells' prophetic force. Rather it is a modest dream and the most realizable, perhaps, of all his discoveries. Within the more limited and sober orbit of this work, however, where reconstruction and escape are still combined motives, the quality and condition of Wells' ideal, and his

[1] Cf. Connes, *op. cit.*, pp. 35, 40.
[2] *A Modern Utopia*, Tauchnitz ed. (1905), p. 326.

values, are most clearly defined in human terms. The book is expressive of his faith at a time of mental exuberance and vigour, before the catastrophes of the world wars had shaken his conviction and forced him into more distant exiles, and before old age and illness had come to torture his mind at the end of its tether. Finally, *A Modern Utopia* is Wells' most carefully thought-out anticipation, which makes it, if not the most fascinating imaginative flight, at least a structure of great solidity and of steady vision.

Around this Utopia it will be necessary to group a few others, in an extension of the perspective of desirable human development. Wells ranges from his *samurai* to *men like gods* along a vertiginous scale of biological and progressive conjecture, and these remote visions also bear evidence, and in some respects the most interesting evidence, to the imaginative energy he drew from the idea of evolution. On the other hand, one may leave out the purely biological fantasies, like *The First Men in the Moon, The Valley of the Spiders,* and *The Sea Raiders,* for these are irrelevant to the delineation of Wells' human ideal. In these Wells plays with evolutionary hypotheses—goes back to the 'grisly folk' and the Beast Men, or explores the possible directions of vital development into the Selenites, the Spiders or the Morlocks. Wells' obsessive search into the ramifications of the evolutionary idea is evocative and strange to watch, but it stems from a different intuitive source, and its emotional basis—apart from curiosity—is not aspiration but fear, anxiety—a kind of cosmic shiver at the thought of 'what might have happened' and what may still come to pass.

Man in the Early Utopian Fantasies

In the decade that preceded *A Modern Utopia* Wells rose to fame as the genius of science fiction, and most of his early works—*The Time Machine* (1895), *The Island of Dr. Moreau* (1896), *Anticipations* (1901)—have something of the cosmic shiver: the dizzy look

407

down into the past, or a nausea at the thought of a far-off de-humanized future. Where Homo Sapiens appears in a more realistic context, for instance in *When the Sleeper Awakes* (1898), the main interest for Wells is the effect of a changing environment upon the human species, or rather, upon the individual. For the condition of individuality is already his main concern, though as yet it is seen only in its negative aspects—the weakness of the individual swamped by a uniform, mechanical and strictly regimented community.

Perhaps the most revealing feature of this early negative approach to the condition of Homo Sapiens is Wells' preoccupation with mechanical and scientific development, and its bearing on human evolution. He—the prince of Progress, the champion of the Machine: 'Strangest of Saviours', whose 'glittering angular promise' he saw rising above the misery of mankind—Wells inherited also something of the anxiety of Bulwer Lytton, W. H. Hudson and William Morris. Thus *The Time Machine* presents two versions of human degeneration through mechanical progress— the 'little people' and the Morlocks, the first reduced to infantile and uncreative existence, the second to cannibalism. At first sight these beautiful 'little people' appear as remnants of the Golden Age: 'They spent all their time in playing gently, in bathing in the river, in making love in a half-playful fashion, in eating fruit and sleeping'.[1] Life has been too easy for them; there has been no struggle or 'grindstone' to sharpen their intellect, and in consequence they have lost not only their creative energy, but their will to survive.[2] Their ghastly subterranean masters, the Morlocks, have undergone a different kind of adaptation—towards an antlike society of what Samuel Butler called 'machine-tickling aphids'. In both cases the swamping of the individual is the

[1] *Op. cit.*, p. 70.
[2] Cf. also 'A Story of Days to Come' in *Tales of Space and Time*, (1899), where Wells, like Meredith, sees struggle as a necessary stimulus for intelligence, creative energy and will to live.

predominant fact; but Wells in this book goes far beyond the loss of individuality, beyond the twilight of mankind in some infinitely distant future to watch the last grotesque vestiges of life defy the sun-death by the water's edge. It is a young man's fantasia, yet underneath the excitement of evolutionary discovery grows the nausea and horror of an earth from which feeling, thinking and acting mankind has vanished.[1]

Wells' fear that a uniform mass, made by a uniform environment, may destroy the individual, involves another aspect of machine progress: the growth of power, mechanical power dwarfing man and leaving him, like the sorcerer's apprentice, in the grip of forces beyond his moral control. Perhaps this new kind of slavery would prove more fatal to the toiling breed of Adam than hard, underpaid work. Perhaps man, like the Sleeper, would soon awake to a 'world of base servitude in hypertrophied cities'.[2]

Barber finds in many of these early works the theme of 'the insecurity of existence'.[3] And it is obvious that Darwin, and Huxley more directly, have given Wells an insight which has strong affinity with the fatalism of Hardy's 'Hap', without its underlying tragic sense. Anything might have happened to mankind in the past, owing to accidental changes in the environment; anything may happen in the future—unless man imposes a stronger force: an ethical process, upon the blind and wanton play of natural selection. This is the concern which runs through Wells' biological fantasy into his Utopia, and urges him to search, not first of all for the ideal condition that may favour the growth of the ideal human being, but for the spring of intellectual and moral energy in man by which he may conquer Nature, chance, himself, and preserve and develop that most precious thing he owns: his individuality. Here is the theme and creative idea of *A Modern Utopia*.

[1] Wells' anxiety for the destiny of Homo Sapiens is traced by Connes to the teaching of T. H. Huxley, *op. cit.*, p. 78.

[2] *When the Sleeper Awakes*, preface to 1921 ed.   [3] *Op. cit.*, p. 35.

The Ethical Process

A Modern Utopia is pre-eminently an attempt at reconstruction, and Wells therefore builds it as close as possible to reality.[1] Through constant reference and analogy he keeps the earthly parallel steadily before our eyes, and reminds us that his dream is composed 'in the key of mortal imperfection'.[2] Though much space is given to discussion and planning of laws, economics, social security, way of life, it is clear that the focus of interest is the ideal man, the *samurai,* whose work the modern Utopia will be. But Wells, true to his doctrine of individuality, takes great pains to emphasize that his dream world will be one of ample diversity and variety. He is following up the 'rediscovery of the unique' in one of the main trends of the book: 'the insistence upon individuality and the individual difference as the significance of life'.[3] His modern Utopia 'finds the final hope of the world in the evolving inter-play of unique individualities'.[4]

Wells' *Utopia* is modern in this sense too that it is not laid out in descriptive detail as an ideal land or island, it is a knowledge of a new world gradually unfolding to a speculative mind—'the Owner of the Voice': a pure and conscious product of the imagination, a day-dream justified by the implicit assumption that it is through similar intuitive quests and aspirations that Utopia ultimately will be realized: the ideal future world will emerge from our 'best selves', our boldest fancies, our most generous instincts, and our most powerful will. However, from the point of view of method and presentation, this inward and discursive growth of knowledge makes the Utopian panorama less distinct in concrete detail, and 'story', than it was in the classical prophecy. For our purpose a broad outline will suffice to indicate what kind of world it is.

Wells' Utopians are living in a World State, speaking one language, obeying just and humane laws which allow for a maximum

[1] P. 31.   [2] P. 224.   [3] P. 27.   [4] P. 38.

of individual freedom and private initiative.[1] The State exists for the individuals and as a means to growing individualism: thus for the Utopians there are many prohibitions but no positive compulsions.[2] There is work for all and few working hours, an intimate and easy social life, abundant opportunity for learning, free education, swift and comfortable means of global travel to encourage understanding and sympathy between races. All institutions and human relationships are permeated by these principles of freedom, tolerance, consideration. Science has been the chief instrument in the hands of those who organized the World State, and in this prophecy Wells consciously takes up his Baconian heritage: 'Bacon's visionary House of Solomon will be a thing realised, and it will be humming with this business'.[3] Humming with scientific and mechanical business is almost the whole of this world, with its club-trains and pneumatic tubes for parcel delivery: indeed—'There appears no limit to the invasion of life by the machine'.[4]

Wells dreams of a kind and happy world; a place without unemployment, capitalist exploitation, social aggression, waste and inefficiency; without toil and poverty and slums and ugliness. He insists throughout on the ease and beauty of this world, on its tremendous and well organized activity, on the healthy life of the people, and on their stimulating relationships.

How was this modern Utopia realized? What is the idea underlying its creative faith, and what sources of energy have been channelled into it? Soon Wells makes it clear that his Utopia has grown from a process different from that of Nature and also from that of our world of everyday. It is the outcome not of a natural but an ethical process. And as we watch this exploration into a generous and humane dream it becomes increasingly evident that Wells has been taught by Darwin and Huxley, and long remains faithful to his

[1] P. 83.   [2] Pp. 37—9, 63.   [3] P. 60; cf. also p. 236.   [4] P. 91.

revered masters, though they complicate his transposition from the real to the ideal:

The real world is a vast disorder of accidents and incalculable forces in which men survive or fail. A Modern Utopia, unlike its predecessors, dare not pretend to change the last condition; it may order and humanise the conflict, but men must still survive or fail.[1]

Utopia must be founded in human nature as we know it here and now, and take shape, partly at least, as an outcome of environment and adaptation. Natural selection will always play its part in the human condition and in the descent of man. But it must not—and here Huxley takes over—be the blind and cruel law it has been in the past:

The way of Nature in this process is to kill the weaker and the sillier, to crush them, to starve them, to overwhelm them, using the stronger and more cunning as her weapon. But man is the unnatural animal, the rebel child of nature, and more and more does he turn himself against the harsh and fitful hand that reared him. He sees with a growing resentment the multitude of suffering ineffectual lives over which his species tramples in its ascent. In the Modern Utopia he will have set himself to change the ancient law.[2]

It is necessary to control and direct Nature through an ethical process of voluntary, intelligent and compassionate effort. And though man will never be completely saved from struggle and suffering— though he will 'remain a competitive creature'—it is yet possible to make him healthy and happy to an extent now unknown.

The planning of Wells' Utopia hence develops as a moral campaign—a pioneer invasion of savage territories, to cultivate and pacify these, and guard them against the upsurge of wild and pernicious growths. Like Huxley, he is acutely aware of the 'scene of strife' on which we live, and sensitive to the pain and tragedy inherent in the human drama. But he is far more optimistic, and he

[1] P. 121.   [2] P. 122.

412

believes, with Meredith, that it is possible to tame the tiger and yet retain some of its primitive vital energy. We should not forget, in bringing Nature under ethical control, that 'the root of all evil in the world, and the root of all good too, is the Will to Live'.[1] The problem of building Utopia is, then, above all 'a moral and an intellectual problem'.[2] Mankind will never know a harmonious and secure life if things are allowed to drift:

We of the twentieth century are not going to accept the sweetish, faintly nasty slops of Rousseauism that so gratified our great-great-grandparents in the eighteenth. We know that order and justice do not come by nature ... These things mean intention, will, carried to a scale that our poor vacillating, hot and cold earth has never known. What I am really seeing more and more clearly is the will beneath this visible Utopia. Convenient houses, admirable engineering that is no offence amidst natural beauties, beautiful bodies, and a universally gracious carriage, these are only the outward and visible signs of an inward and spiritual grace. Such an order means discipline. It means triumph over the petty egotisms and vanities that keep men on our earth apart; it means devotion and a nobler hope; it cannot exist without a gigantic process of inquiry, trial, forethought and patience in an atmosphere of mutual trust and concession. Such a world as this Utopia is not made by the chance occasional co-operations of self-indulgent men, by autocratic rulers or by the bawling wisdom of the democratic leader.[3]

Thus, in the same sweep of moral indignation, Wells rejects the unethical and romantic idea of the 'natural man' as well as the biological principle of natural selection and struggle for life applied to human society. Man, the rational as well as compassionate creature —man the 'rebel child of nature' must build Utopia through the rule of ethical will, discipline and purpose.

In what way can the ethical process change and direct that of Nature? How can reason and will humanize the conflict? First of

[1] P. 132.   [2] P. 152.   [3] P. 151.

all by checking the cruel play of natural selection. For Wells the approaches to this problem are lit by Malthus as well as Huxley: Without a control of the increase of population, 'no Utopia is possible'.[1] In civilized society we can no longer pay the ancient price for progress which was death and frustration for the unfit. Even if 'Progress depends essentially on competitive selection', it is possible to reduce suffering and still encourage mental and physical improvement—'by preventing the birth of those who would in the unrestricted interplay of natural forces be born to suffer and fail'.[2] In preventive eugenics, as Wells translates its meaning and function into terms of the ethical process, we achieve the double goal of bettering our race and eliminating misery. This eugenics programme is determined by a wish to remain close to reality and proceed with scientific caution:

Let us set aside at once all nonsense of the sort one hears in certain quarters about the human stud farm. State breeding of the population was a reasonable proposal for Plato to make, in view of the biological knowledge of his time and the purely tentative nature of his metaphysics; but from anyone in the days after Darwin, it is preposterous.[3]

Therefore, all we can do is to prevent procreation by the vicious and ailing, so as to keep the population sound and balanced, and as for the positive improvement of the human species— 'In the initiative of the individual above the average, lies the reality of the future'.

[1] Pp. 134—5; cf. also p. 158.
[2] P. 159; cf. also p. 122: 'These people ...' and p. 126: 'social surgery...'
[3] P. 160;—the 'certain quarters' is probably a reference to the enthusiastic disciples of Francis Galton, cf. the direct mention, p. 183 and: 'a premature attempt at "stirpiculture"'; cf. also p. 227: there is no attempt in a modern Utopia to breed a special class—'simply because the intricate interplay of heredity is untraceable and incalculable'; and p. 237: 'The order is not hereditary ...'.

And the 'cardinal will, the supreme and significant expression of individuality, should lie in the selection of a partner for procreation'.[1] All the State can do—apart from denying children to the inferior and thus eliminate the 'base' strain in the population—is to demand of the parents a certain standard of living, and health, mental and physical. For the rest its role is to support and educate the children and give them the widest possible scope for physical and intellectual growth. Moreover, in the modern Utopia it will be recognized that 'motherhood is a service to the State and a legitimate claim to a living ..'.[2] There will be flexible marriage laws, unhampered by convention, with the aim to 'secure good births'.[3]

Like Plato, Wells insists that the State must care for the children and educate them in a manner which will benefit the community; but unlike Plato he claims that the State must not attempt to replace the home. For the growth of individuality, of healthy emotions and moral consciousness, the home and parental love are essential.[4]

The ethical process, then, must aim at a healthier and happier race, and operate through the control of birth-rate, the elimination of inferior qualities, the encouragement of good motherhood and good homes, and through a check on social evils inherent in the struggle for life.[5]

The Average Utopian and the Samurai

Granted that a Modern Utopia will have achieved these things, what effects does Wells anticipate in the future men and women? Again he differs from the classical Utopia in which a universal human ideal (apart from the classification into rulers and slaves) was the ultimate goal. For having pledged himself to his fundamental concept of individuality, he recognizes a future world com-

[1] P. 161. [2] P. 164. [3] P. 167. [4] P. 173.
[5] The economic policy of Utopia is also, needless to say, an important aspect of the ethical process, but to the present inquiry this programme is not relevant. Cf. pp. 124, 125, 246.

munity in which the differences in intellectual, physical and emotional qualities are as great as on earth, and even greater.[1] However, his effort to transpose the variety of our world on to the higher Utopian level aims clearly at a general improvement. In what sense are the average modern Utopians superior to their earthly 'doubles'? What qualities does Wells aspire to as a common boon? It is significant that he begins his delineation by a negative portrait, for the first Utopian we meet is an archaic creature, somebody out of the romantic caves of Rousseau; and this child of Nature, who deplores the artificial civilization of his world, appears to the earthly explorer (*alias* Wells) as 'a most consummate ass', and an 'incurably egotistical dissentient'.[2] The average Utopians are not like this at all, and they bear witness to the soundness and wisdom of their society:

You have only to mark the beauty, the simple cleanliness and balance of this world, you have only to see the free carriage, the unaffected graciousness of even the common people, to understand how fine and complete the arrangements of this world must be.[3]

And, Wells reminds us with a Meredithian concern for the perfect harmony of the ideal human being, the 'beautiful bodies, and a universally gracious carriage, these are only the outward and visible signs of an inward and spiritual grace'. These Utopians have grown out of the conflicts that disfigure the minds and manners of the earthling—this 'emotional fool', this egoist, this 'introspective carcass'. Even the Utopian women whose faces strike the explorer as 'a little unintelligent' and affected, would on earth be admired as women of 'exceptional refinement'.[4] Here is the Utopian crowd on a broader canvas:

The general effect of a Utopian population is vigour. Everyone one meets seems to be not only in good health but in training; one

[1] Cf. 'The trend of evolutionary forces ... has been towards differentiation, p. 175.

[2] Pp. 105, 115.   [3] P. 151.   [4] P. 194.

416

rarely meets fat people, bald people, or bent or grey. People who would be obese or bent and obviously aged on earth are here in good repair, and as a consequence the whole effect of a crowd is livelier and more invigorating than on earth. The dress is varied and graceful; that of the women reminds one most of the Italian fifteenth century ... There is little difference in deportment between one class and another; they all are graceful and bear themselves with quiet dignity, and among a group of them a European woman of fashion in her lace and feathers, her hat and metal ornaments, her mixed accumulations of "trimmings", would look like a barbarian tricked out with the miscellaneous plunder of a museum.

Yet, Wells insists, let us bear in mind that this is a not very distant transposition of people on earth, and variety will express itself here too not only in refinement, but also in foppishness, bad taste, and untidiness.

But these will be but transient flashes in a general flow of harmonious graciousness; dress will have scarcely any of that effect of disorderly conflict, of self-assertion qualified by the fear of ridicule, that it has in the crudely competitive civilisations of earth.[2]

Wells is much preoccupied with Utopian costume as an expression of psychological qualities. But above all else he delights in the vitality of these modern Utopians. Size is important: 'here I feel small and meanlooking'. A sound regimen and efficient medical science have checked the physical and mental ailments common on earth. There are few old people about, but 'a greater proportion of men and women at or near the prime of life': regimen has helped them to postpone the years of decay.[3]

The feverish hurry of our earth, the decay that begins before growth has ceased, is replaced by a ripe prolonged maturity. This modern Utopia is an adult world. The flushed romance, the predominant eroticisms, the adventurous uncertainty of a world in which youth prevails, gives place here to a grave deliberation, to a fuller and more powerful emotion, to a broader handling of life.[4]

[1] P. 195.   [2] P. 196.   [3] P. 267.   [4] P. 268.

Here, it would seem, we have the Utopian theme of Shaw's *Back to Methuselah,* and Shaw had reason to say that Wells' teaching had not been wasted on him.[1] Wells' ideal is, if not asceticism, a high degree of moral and intellectual discipline. But in Utopia too there is an age of romance and adventure:

Amidst the men whose faces have been made fine by thought and steadfast living, among the serene-eyed women, comes youth, gaily-coloured, buoyantly healthy, with challenging eyes, with fresh and eager face ...[2]

And there is, throughout, variety and individuality: hence race prejudice has completely vanished, and the explorer notices that a black man, whom he chances to meet, 'walks, as most Utopians walk, as though he had reason to be proud of something'.[3]

Despite the naïve tenderness which informs Wells' portrait of the Utopian people, it is clear that he is not primarily interested in the average man, and he makes no secret of his undemocratic propensities. He brings the crowd on to the backstage to enhance the action of the real protagonists—the Samurai. We first hear of the Samurai from the 'natural' man—the 'consummate ass', who disclaims them: 'I'm not one of your *samurai,* your voluntary noblemen who have taken the world in hand ... voluntary Gods I fancy they think themselves'.[4] Next we approach these men through conjectural reference to the wisdom, order and competence to which this world bears witness:

Somewhere in the Modern Utopia there must be adequate men, men the very antithesis of our friend [the 'natural' man], capable of self-devotion, of intentional courage, of honest thought, and steady endeavour.[5]

[1] *Op. cit.,* Part III, p. 118.   [2] *Ibid.*   [3] P. 289.   [4] P. 109
[5] Pp. 115—16.

418

And then the first encounter, which reveals to the Utopian explorer something entirely new, something apart from the 'common-place type' of people he has met so far:

But suddenly there looks out from this man's pose and regard a different quality, a quality altogether nearer that of the beautiful tramway and of the gracious order of the mountain houses. He is a well-built man of perhaps five-and-thirty, with the easy movement that comes with perfect physical condition, his face is clean shaven and shows the firm mouth of a disciplined man, and his grey eyes are clear and steady ... His general effect reminds me somehow of the Knights Templars.[1]

Throughout, Wells' technique of presentation continues in this see-saw manner: from the Utopian achievement to the men behind it, and thence back to the greatness of their victorious task. Thus gradually a mutual illustration is effected. Having left his first Samurai with the culminating impression of the nobility and dedication of the Knight Templar, Wells reverts to the beauty, order and grace of this world—expressive of 'intention', 'will', and 'inward spiritual grace'; of 'discipline', 'devotion and a nobler hope'; of human attainment that is inconceivable without intellectual curiosity, scientific spirit, patience, and 'an atmosphere of mutual trust and concession'. Conversely, it means the triumph over egoism and anarchy, political and social muddle, and the ousting of 'autocratic rulers' as well as the 'bawling wisdom of the democratic leader'.[2]

This method of mutual presentation finally involves an element of contrast; for Wells, in order to thrust home his message the more energetically, requires the traditional confrontation between the real and the ideal, between our world of everyday and Utopia. Certainly, the comparison has been going on all the time, in the passages of discursive planning as well as in the imaginative episodes and glimpses of people and places. But in the end it has

[1] Pp. 140—41.   [2] P. 151.

to be a confrontation between men—the men who make our world and those who build Utopia. For this confrontation Wells is served, in an original manner, by his idea that Utopia must be a direct and realistic projection—an evolution of existing things. Thus he places the explorers from our world over against their Utopian 'doubles' or 'selves'. Already before the encounter the assumption underlying this hypothetical treatment is clear, for the confrontation, we are told, will mean to 'measure something of what we might have been?'.[1] And Wells, always anxious to keep his ideal within sight of reality, underlines its moral and practical significance: 'My Utopian self is, of course, my better self—according to my best endeavours.'[2] The Owner of the Voice finds himself face to face with his Utopian duplicate—a Samurai:

He is a little taller than I, younger looking and sounder looking; he has missed an illness or so, and there is no scar over his eye. His training has been subtly finer than mine; he has made himself a better face than mine ... I can fancy he winces with a twinge of sympathetic understanding at my manifest inferiority. Indeed, I come, trailing clouds of earthly confusion and weakness; I bear upon me all the defects of my world.[3]

Suddenly, however, Wells abandons this unique opportunity of individual psychological revelation: he avoids the 'personal' and 'emotional' incidents to show us the *samurai* as an order and as builders of Utopia. The planner for a better future is in evidence in his explicit statement that it is the organization of the *samurai* which commands his curiosity.[4]

The order, we are told, is 'open to every physically and mentally healthy adult in the Utopian state who will observe its prescribed austere rule of living ...'[5] In Wells' mind this voluntary nobility approaches near to the guardians of Plato's *Republic*, and indeed

[1] P. 203.   [2] P. 212.   [3] P. 212.   [4] P. 222.   [5] P. 221.

Plato is given as one source of the Samurai idea, while Comte is another.[1] They combine the philosopher-king with the positivistic leader-scientist. In his account of their social and political function, Wells pursues a more specific progress-theme irrelevant to our inquiry, but in order to justify this vision of progress, he has to show us the men behind it. It is owing to the psychological and moral growth of the *samurai* that there is, between Utopia and earth, 'the profoundest differences in the mental content of life'.[2] This order of men and women, whose faces are 'strengthened by discipline and touched with devotion, is the Utopian reality; but ... for them, the whole fabric of these fair appearances would crumble and tarnish ...' They hold all the key positions in Utopia:

Typically, the *samurai* are engaged in administrative work. Practically the whole of the responsible rule of the world is in their hands; all our head teachers and disciplinary heads of colleges, our judges, barristers, employers of labour beyond a certain limit, practising medical men, legislators, must be *samurai,* and all the executive committees, and so forth, that play so large a part in our affairs are drawn by lot exclusively from them.[3]

Wells, faithful to his conception of the Utopia as a 'kinetic' structure, tells us something of *samurai* history. The organization was 'a quite deliberate invention', urged by the force of 'enthusiasm and self-sacrifice in men' to save the world from democratic chaos.[4] It was struck out from the 'clash of social forces and political systems as a revolutionary organisation'. But it was not a precipitous and rash movement, and it had prepared for the Utopian task through research and planning before the inevitable moment came when the *samurai* as a militant body fought and conquered and 'assimilated the pre-existing political organisations'. And since the world must remain imperfect, the *samurai* are still crusaders, though 'no longer

[1] Cf. ref. to Plato, p. 222; to Comte, p. 233.   [2] P. 222.
[3] Pp. 236—37.   [4] P. 223.

421

against specific disorders, but against universal human weaknesses, and the inanimate forces that trouble man ..'.[1] How—and the question is relevant because their methods must express their superior qualities—how did the *samurai* achieve their political renaissance? They found a new principle of combined creativeness and order, of progress and preservation, in the classification of people into the Poietic (or creative), the Kinetic (or practical), the Dull (or incompetent), and the Base (or criminal). In Utopia only the first two classes count—they are 'the living tissue of the State'—and through a perfect co-operation of these the crucial problem of 'combining progress with political stability' was solved.[2] Wells here follows up Comte's idea that '"spiritual" must precede political reconstruction'.[3] For while the Poietic with their exceptional artistic and scientific talents provide the impulses for advance in all fields of human activity, the Kinetic, or more 'normal' men and women apply these poietic ideas and discoveries and with their high sense of discipline maintain a stable line of development. Thus imagination unites with efficiency and practical method in a persistent effort to realize the ideals of Utopia. The *samurai* themselves combine poietic and kinetic qualities: they are the creative minds, but above all they are disciplinarians, teachers and rulers. In his emphasis on the latter function Wells points to the basic flaw in earthly society: order and discipline are the things most urgently needed. It is with this recognition that Wells formulates the meaning of *samurai* conduct in the 'Rule' or ethical code by which these voluntary noblemen live, and it is here that we find the core of his conception of the new human ideal:

The Rule aims to exclude the dull and base altogether, to discipline the impulses and emotions, to develop a moral habit and sustain a

[1] Pp. 224—25.
[2] P. 231.—Cf. Comte's *Positive Philosophy* (1875), vol. ii, p. 9.
[3] P. 233.

man in periods of stress, fatigue, and temptation, to produce the maximum co-operation of all men of good intent, and, in fact, to keep all the *samurai* in a state of moral and bodily health and efficiency.[1]

To achieve this, and to prepare the *samurai* for their task, the Rule lays down certain laws, some preventive, some compulsive, and besides it requires an adequate standard of education. Furthermore, the order must know the 'Canon'—a compilation of the best poems, articles and essays written to express the *samurai* idea. Again, there are health regulations which demand that members should be fit and well exercised, and 'free from certain foul, avoidable, and demoralising diseases'. Only adults are admitted to the order, for the *samurai*, before they volunteer, must have 'experience' and a 'settled mature conviction'.[2]

In the list of things Wells rejects from the order he reveals a blend of personal phobias and traditional Utopian ideals. He excludes stupid people and those who are fat; forbids usury, personal trade, undignified services and games which might detract from the *samurai* honour. The traditional Utopian pattern emerges in the idea that 'Our hygiene and regimen are rapidly pushing back old age and death, and keeping men hale and hearty to eighty and more'.[3] This regimen implies a specific diet, almost exclusively vegetarian; forbids tobacco, alcohol and drugs. In the matter of vegetarianism, Wells' belief in the civilizing effect of education is again patent, for, as he anticipates, 'in a population that is all educated, and at about the same level of physical refinement, it is practically impossible to find anyone who will hew a dead ox or pig'.

The *samurai* 'Rule' is, in its bare outline, a codification of moral and intellectual virtues, stated in definite reaction to the excesses and indulgences of a 'barbaric past'. However, the *samurai* discipline is not ascetic in its view of sexual relations, and of art, property, and the general enjoyment of the good things of life.

[1] P. 238.   [2] Pp. 242—43.   [3] P. 243.

One psychological factor is emphatically singled out for its importance in the formation of the order. The *samurai* virtues, we are told, had emerged from many and various sources, but the cardinal virtue—self-control, came from 'Pride': 'Pride may not be the noblest thing in the soul, but it is the best King there, for all that'. Pride, in the first days of *samurai* rallying, kept men 'clean and sound and sane'.[1]

In his detailed description of the positive qualities and duties of his human ideal, Wells has something like a classical balance in mind. The 'Rule' 'would aim at once at health and that constant exercise of will that makes life good'.[2] Bodily strength and well-being is achieved by a practice of almost Spartan rigour. With this comes a monastic alternation of solitude and communal life, and a daily reading from the Book of the Samurai which also reminds one of monastic spiritual discipline. Thus, through self-cultivation and through the stimulating intercourse between individuals, the *samurai* character is developed and sustained.

Wells (like Spencer and Huxley) believes that this interaction between internal and external factors, between moral will and environment, is the way in which the 'ethical process' prevails upon the 'natural man'. He accepts the paradox of naturalistic ethics, that man is fundamentally good, and yet, as an heir of so much animal aggression and appetite, a dangerous being to let loose upon society. The paradox resolves itself, implicitly, on the evolutionary view that man has largely outgrown the animal, has acquired new mental and spiritual characteristics, like reason, conscience, compassion and religion. In the *samurai* ideal of the good life, human reason plays a part analogous to grace in that of Christian doctrine, and this again is in the rationalistic and positivistic tradition. Yet in his reinstatement of religion Wells stands for a second generation of English Positivism, which (partly at least) recognized that a doctrine of agnosticism, and Humanity as the sole object of worship, were

[1] P. 250.   [2] P. 252.

424

ineffectual in their appeal to man as a moral being and a mind desirous of certainty and faith. We watch on these pages of *A Modern Utopia* a mellowing of the radical movement—a tentative fusion of naturalistic Humanitarianism with Idealism and even religion:

The leading principle of the Utopian religion is the repudiation of the doctrine of original sin; the Utopians hold that man, on the whole, is good. That is their cardinal belief. Man has pride and conscience, they hold, that you may refine by training as you refine his eye and ear; he has remorse and sorrow in his being ... How can one think of him as bad? He is religious; religion is as natural to him as lust and anger, less intense, indeed, but coming with a wide-sweeping inevitableness as peace comes after all tumults and noises. And in Utopia they understand this, or, at least, the *samurai* do, clearly. They accept Religion as they accept Thirst, as something inseparable in the mysterious rhythms of life.[1]

It would seem significant that religion enters into Wells' anticipation of the ideal life at the moment when he is about to face the most 'difficult' aspects of its realization: 'the will and motives at the centre that made men and women ready to undergo discipline ... to master emotions and control impulses, to keep in the key of effort ...' Wells approaches with uncertain steps this mysterious source of moral energy which is religion, for here he is on unfamiliar ground. Tacitly he implies that reason, pride and will-power are not, after all, sufficient to ennoble human nature; but how is this religious 'Thirst' to be defined and utilized? For Wells, as for the early Positivists, the central problem is how to enlist the religious sentiment as a moral force. Yet religion, he knows, means a suprahuman object of worship, and Wells reinstates God—a complex and 'synthetic' God, disengaged from dogma, and nevertheless a 'transcendental and mystical God'.[2] We are told nothing, however, of the relationship of God to *samurai*, neither are we made to feel

[1] P. 254—55. [2] P. 257.

425

that this relationship has any definite bearing on their ethical code and conduct, or on their values. Wells, in fact, does not know what it is or how to interpret its mystical and ethical significance. We see this most clearly in the cultic practices: the *samurai* God is to be worshipped in solitude, while there are temples and priests for the common man. The order are 'forbidden the religion of dramatically lit altars, organ music, and incense ...', and their attitude to 'creeds and formulæ, to catechisms and easy explanations ... will be distrust'. For the *samurai* 'will have emerged above these things'.[1] Thus, despite his concession to mysticism and religion, Wells still hears the warning voice of George Eliot to whom these things were opium. And he remains loyal to the early Positivists, moreover, in his claim that the communal religious service of the *samurai* consists in 'maintaining the state, and the order and progress of the world'.[2]

In the final and most important *samurai* rule Wells returns with new emphasis to his doctrine of individuality: in the individual life lies the 'fount of motives' for all creative thought and effort, and this source can be released only through 'silent and deliberate reflections'. Hence Wells ordains for his voluntary noblemen a retirement, for at least 'seven consecutive days in the year ... into some wild and solitary place ...', in order to 'be alone with Nature, necessity, and their own thoughts'.[3] It is the idea of a hermit life of contemplation combined with the Spartan concern for strength, endurance and courage. 'We civilised men', the *samurai* tells us in Meredithian terms, 'go back to the stark Mother that so many of us would have forgotten were it not for this Rule'.[4] Thus, in his lonely return to a primitive, strenuous way of life the individual wears off the less fortunate effect of an urban, mechanized civilization and finds new moral and physical stamina. What does the *samurai* contemplate in his solitude? Wells' 'double' thinks a good deal about the 'Night of this World'—as Wells himself has done so often in his fantasies

[1] Pp. 255—56. [2] P. 257. [3] Pp. 257—58. [4] Pp. 258—59.

426

—when our sun has cooled and all life is extinct on this planet.[1] And he meditates on the destiny of man and 'whether it is indeed God's purpose that our kind should end, and ... all that we have given substance and a form, should lie dead beneath the snows'. And from this anxiety springs an idea of rescue—a prophetic idea and perhaps a creative one—thrown out towards the stars, in the hope that these 'should not escape us in the end'. Before the sun passes into twilight and earth ceases to harbour its life, other homes will have opened up for man in the universe.[2]

This, then, is the outline of Wells' ideal human being; and in the working out of this portrait the means as well as the end of his prophetic faith become equally distinct. He sets out with a conscious acceptance of Darwin's theory of selection and environment, but instead of following this into its logical corollaries of determinism and fatalism, Wells, like Meredith, is led by his indomitable optimism and under the influence of Huxley's concept of the 'Ethical Process' in the opposite direction, to an evolutionary belief in intelligence, will, a selfless purpose which combine to change the ancient law of chance and cruelty. And in this purposive moral effort, rooted in the highest human qualities, we have, according to Wells, the unfailing promise that man will build at last a modern Utopia.

Wells, therefore, applies to the evolution of his human ideal and his society an unambiguous teleological principle, and indeed without such a principle no Utopia would be conceivable. Nevertheless the aspect of environment retains its importance, and he never ceases to remind us that social improvement is an ineluctable condition of human progress. Along with the development of his evo-

---

[1] P. 261.

[2] In this idea of human emigration, occurring also in *Men Like Gods,* Wells has anticipated J. B. S. Haldane's fantasy, *Possible Worlds,* 1927. The idea in Shaw's *Back to Methuselah* of filling the universe with life 'and master its matter to its uttermost confines' (P. 267.) has a different mystical and vitalist genesis.

lutionary theme, there goes the planning for security, justice, and above all, for education. Wells' Utopia is basically a challenge, and a yardstick to 'measure something of what we might have been'— if the moral effort of the *samurai* had changed the 'mental content' and the conditions of life on earth.

Wells' *samurai* is no distant departure: it is essential to the message he embodies that he should remain within reach of man— as his 'better self'. His evolutionary advance on man lies, therefore, solely in his more highly developed moral consciousness and will, in his better trained intellect and imagination.

Critics have objected to the *samurai* order that it is based on an antidemocratic contempt for ordinary man, the dull and stupid average, and a belief in the intelligent few as the only source of progress. This belief, according to H. Ross, 'is an indication of the astounding simplicity of Wells'.[1] If carried to its logical conclusion, the argument runs, it would mean a heartless discrimination and even extermination of ordinary man by the *samurai*, and indeed, but for their precarious religion of Social Purpose, they would have destroyed the stupid creatures of whom they are appointed guardians. The first of these objections certainly holds, for Wells, like Shaw, has no hope of regeneration and progress from the majority of men. Yet it would seem to be the very strength of Wells' ideal that he insists on the *samurai* as 'our best selves' and the best individuals, for surely any advance, whether intellectual, moral or political, can only come from these. And within the humane and altruistic framework of this Utopian world, and the moral awareness which is the very core of Wells' human ideal, the second objection is irrelevant. On the other hand, while Wells is wholly against any cruel or drastic eugenic measures, his dream is, ultimately, directed to a time when the *samurai,* in contrast to 'all the privileged castes the world has seen', will increase 'relatively to the total population, and ... at

[1] *Utopias Old and New,* p. 182.

428

last assimilate almost the whole population of the earth'.[1] But this is a sublimation of humanity, not an extermination.

It would appear that, as Brome points out, the *samurai* ideal is the greatest achievement of the book—great in the underlying idea and in its development—despite a summary and at times naïve treatment of psychological and moral aspects. The weakness of *A Modern Utopia,* as he also shows, lies elsewhere, mainly in the technical and imaginative qualities of the presentation of the whole Utopian picture.[2]

One of the most remarkable features of Wells' Utopian dream is that he effects a synthesis of Plato and Darwin, idealism and naturalism: Natural selection ruled in the past, and it is active in present day society, but its fierce play is being checked and controlled. With man it is no longer chance and struggle for life that determines evolution, it is the ethical and intellectual growth watched over by guardians of unusual intelligence and moral will. These are not the 'fittest' according to the ancient law, they are the new ethical force, the teleological law bent on combating the animal ego and raising life to higher levels, urging humanity on towards a realization of its highest conceivable good. In *A Modern Utopia* very little is left to fortuitous variations and chance; instead, there is a pervasive sense of human value, of purpose, and of all things moving to such splendour as may be attained within mortal existence.[3]

What happened later to the inspiring faith of *A Modern Utopia?* Brome indicates that the public response to the book brought

---

[1] P. 254.   [2] Cf. *op. cit.,* pp. 94—95.

[3] For a comment on Wells' attitude at the time of *Anticipations* and *A Modern Utopia,* see *Experiment in Autobiography,* 1934, p. 653: Despite his theoretical adherence to 'the fatalistic optimistic fashion of the time', there were doubts in his mind 'whether it might not prove necessary to *assist* the process of emergence [of the 'New Republic']'. In practice, however, the *samurai* idea which underlies the whole work is a purposive and teleological conception.

disillusionment to its author, for Wells wrote later in his *Experiment in Autobiography:*

I realized that an Order of the Samurai was not a thing that comes about of itself, and that if ever it were to exist, it must be realized as the result of very deliberate effort.[1]

Yet unless we mistake the meaning of 'deliberate effort', it would appear that such a purposive and teleological idea is implicit throughout in the ethics and the organization of the order, and once, at least, even explicitly stated: 'This organisation of the *samurai* was a quite deliberate invention'.—'It must have set before itself the attainment of some such Utopian ideal as this Utopia does, in the key of mortal imperfection, realise'.[2]

No doubt the reaction to the book made Wells aware that the world is not teeming with potential *samurai,* and forced him to accept the necessity of planned action. Disillusionment came, and it seemed for a time that the 'Theory of Revolution by Samurai hung in the air and I could not discover any way of bringing it down to the level of reality'.[3] Yet now as before there was the way of imaginative exploration which he had used so often. Even before *A Modern Utopia* Wells had been struggling with the problem of how to *assist* the evolution of moral will and world government, and trying to think out the solution under 'fantastic forms'.[4] And after *Utopia* there is an increasing tendency to imagine a drastic change of human nature—a moral transmutation—effected from without through some *Deus ex Machina,* through science perhaps, or perhaps through some higher form of intelligence.[5] As the years went by, Wells' faith in man lost its note of jubilant conviction; he grew weary of com-

---

[1] P. 660.   [2] Pp. 223, 224.

[3] *Experiment in Autobiography,* p. 662.

[4] *Ibid.,* p. 654; ref. to *The Food of the Gods,* 1903.

[5] *In the Days of the Comet* (1906) is a fantasia of moral regeneration through the effect of a comet.

mon humanity whom he had so confidently set out to guide and educate, and more and more he was drawn towards the perfect ideal of the dream-world. Nevertheless, he did not lose sight of Homo Sapiens, never, until the last year of his life, abandoned him, nor did he give up his more realistic ideal of the *samurai*. In the *Autobiography* of 1934 he still claims it: 'The device of the order of the Samurai, as I worked it out in this book {*A Modern Utopia*}, does I think solve this problem better than any other method that has ever been suggested.'[1]

Disillusionment came most bitterly with the Great war, which for Wells too meant the final collapse of the nineteenth-century cult of Progress. For some time Wells experienced the horror of the dead end, and then his indestructible faith reasserted itself again, in the hope that 'After this collapse there was to be a wave of sanity'.[2] But the immediate effect of the war on Wells' Utopian dream was, as Connes pointed out, a desire to escape from man and his world.[3]

From Homo Sapiens to Men Like Gods

In *Men Like Gods* (1923) there is a departure towards a human ideal so remote, and so freely conceived within the omnipotence of the pure dream, that at first sight it looks quite unrelated to the *samurai*. In this Utopia there is no attempt at flying close to earth, and Wells, with the aid of Einstein, 'swings' in an imaginative *tour de force* into another dimension and another world, as different from our ugly, woebegone world as he can make it. And yet, despite this 'irruption' through which all contact, spatial and temporal, with our own reality is cut off, Wells does not wholly escape, and a constructive underlying impulse is increasingly felt, both in the con-

[1] P. 659.   [2] *Ibid.*, p. 666.
[3] *Après la guerre, la veine utopique s'est réveillée chez Wells; mais maintenant il ne conçoit plus que des utopies d'évasion ou de refuge. Op. cit.*, p. 463.

frontation between earthlings and the god-like Utopians, and in his 'History' of Utopia. This historical sketch traces a development very similar to that of *A Modern Utopia,* only much longer, from the anarchy and wars of the 'Last Age of Confusion' up to the wonderful present when the world is not only one, but a loving and beautiful brotherhood. Through this 'kinetic' perspective *Men Like Gods* is, however distantly, rooted in reality and intended to suggest a possible future development on earth.[1] The pattern of moral and political renaissance is also, in the main, a repetition of that in *A Modern Utopia*: From the fierce struggle, not for life but for possession, which threatened this Utopian world with disaster, the best and ablest men turned to 'the idea of creative service'.[2] There was no sudden revolution—Wells has given up that hope—but through a slow endeavour

the foundations of the new state were laid by a growing multitude of inquirers and workers, having no set plan or preconceived method, but brought into unconscious co-operation by a common impulse to service and a common lucidity and veracity of mind.[3]

To begin with, then, the development appears to have something of Darwinian casualness about it, but in the individual mind there is a purposive urge. To the aid of this idea of service came the new 'psychological science' which enabled its pioneers to investigate 'the processes of human association', and gradually the new insight spread through books, psychological laboratories, and above all, in the schools and colleges. This civilizing process grew throughout from the generous, unselfish effort in brilliant men and women who had set themselves the task of shaping 'the world anew in the minds of

[1] Cf. Chapter Five.
[2] *Op. cit. The Sleeper Awakes and Men Like Gods,* (The Lit. Press ed., undated.), p. 230.
[3] P. 233.

the young'.[1] In the end the new constructive consciousness had taken action against greed and class-war, and for five centuries there had been incessant fighting to establish 'the universal scientific state, the educational state'. Slowly, at the price of self-sacrifice and martyrdom, Utopia dawned on the old-world chaos.

In all this we recognize some permanent and characteristic Wellsian beliefs: belief in moral and intellectual evolution as the spring of action, belief in education as the chief means of stimulating this growth, belief in a final complete overthrow of prevalent political, economic and social systems. What has changed is his youthful conviction that a small minority, an intellectual and moral *élite*, is adequate for this tremendous task. The war has taught him that the growth must be slow and inward and reach deep and wide into society, until there is a majority of superior men and women prepared to act.

Through his retrospect of Utopian history, with its obvious analogy and constant reference to earthly conditions, Wells even in this unhampered day-dream stands forth again as the incurable optimist and idealistic teacher. In a very real sense *Men Like Gods* (though an inferior work) is *A Modern Utopia* more highly evolved and perfect, and it is mainly by the distance between them, which is a divergence in the human ideal, that one may measure its emotional direction and the nature of its 'escape'. The revulsion from Homo Sapiens takes Wells to men like gods as it took Shaw to his ancients, and it is this mood, however transient, which in the present fantasy denies a place to 'dull' and 'base' classes: there are a few scattered 'failures', but they do not affect the general vision, and only one of them is allowed to speak.

This more perfectly evolved human being—the god-like man— is a soaring consummation of qualities half-formed or latent in the

[1] P. 234; cf. *A Modern Utopia*: 'so on his higher plane of educability the social reference of the civilised man undergoes the most remarkable transformations'; p. 272.

samurai, with certain superhuman traits which are justified by a longer process of evolution, and by the freely unrealistic setting of this remote world. Stately and statuesque in appearance, with the beauty of Greek gods and goddesses, they live serenely aloof from the turmoil of the human mind, and no evil or conflict detracts from their dignity. From their world all ugliness, crime and misery have vanished, and they have conquered all ailments and contagious diseases. Above all, their brains have reached a power unknown on earth—they are indeed approaching to Shaw's ideal of omnipotence and omniscience. With their heightened gifts of intellection, speech has become an outgrown habit: they *think* to one another in a direct process of communication, which is largely beyond the reach of ordinary human beings. Their thought and science are developing at a rate inconceivable to the mind of man.

Yet—does not this very perfection, and its absence of struggle and pain, carry with it the seed of degeneration? In a confrontation between Utopians and earthlings (Chapter Five) Wells returns to this familiar and long-debated problem.[1] As a representative of the old order, Mr. Catskill with vulgar and aggressive rhetoric pits the ancient law of natural selection against the incipient decadence of this seemingly perfect world. In answer to him a Utopian sits quietly 'thinking audibly about him'—tearing to pieces his contention that struggle and pain and misery are ineluctable springs of vitality. Look at this world! All the 'devouring forces' of life have been banished from it, but nothing worth having has gone with them. This is still a world of effort and competition: 'Every one here works to his or her utmost—for service and distinction'.[2] In this world, moreover, 'the indolent and inferior do not procreate'; —how, then, can there be a threat of decay? Racial deterioration expresses itself in drift and inactivity, but these Utopians are engaged upon an intense mental activity: incessant research, countless

[1] Cf. *The Time Machine* and the discussion of the *samurai* 'Rule'.
[2] P. 249.

discoveries, the stimulating challenge and urge of unlimited knowledge opening up before them, and now even new worlds within
their reach.

These earthlings, the Utopian finds, are not just ugly and aggressive—they are primitive, ignorant and superstitious savages, steeped
in the old fatalism and romantic view that Nature is wise, and
keeps balance:

They do not see that except for our eyes and wills, she is purposeless
and blind. She is not awful, she is horrible ... She made us by accident; all her children are bastards—undesired; she will cherish or
expose them, pet or starve or torment without rhyme or reason.
She does not heed, she does not care ...
With Man came Logos, the Word and the Will into our universe,
to watch it and fear it, to learn it and cease to fear it, to know it
and comprehend it and master it. So that we of Utopia are no longer
the beaten and starved children of Nature, but her free and adoles-
cent sons ... Every day we learn a little better how to master this
planet. Every day our thoughts go out more surely to our inheritance,
the stars.[1]

Here as in *A Modern Utopia* Wells preaches the ethical process and
education as the only way to order, power and beauty, and this
sermon is another important comment upon the values, conduct and
activity of his ideal man.

Among the earthlings, only Mr. Barnstaple falls in love with
Utopia, and through him Wells explores its splendour and perfection. He is entranced at having escaped our own world with the
'dust and disorder and noise of its indiscipline, out of limitation,
cruelties and distresses, out of a weariness in which hope dies ...'.[2]
After the great epidemic (caused by the earthlings), by which Wells
tests Utopian endurance and vitality and puts Mr. Catskill to shame,
Mr. Barnstaple alone deserves to become a 'neophyte in Utopia'.

---

[1] P. 250.   [2] P. 261.

Through him we see 'how boldly and dreadfully the mind of man had taken hold, soul and body and destiny, of the life and destiny of the race'.[1] Underneath the tranquil and effortless appearance of this world there flows the tremendous surge of creative energy, in science as in art:

And how did it feel to be living in Utopia? The lives of the people must be like the lives of very successful artists or scientific workers in this world, a continual refreshing discovery of new things, a constant adventure into the unknown and untried. For recreation they went about their planet, and there was much love and laughter and friendship in Utopia and an abundant easy informal social life.[2]

Later, having grown to know Utopia better, Mr. Barnstaple elaborates the canvas:

"It is a life of demigods, very free, strongly individualised, each following an individual bent, each contributing to great racial ends. It is not only cleanly naked and sweet and lovely but full of personal dignity. It is, I see, a practical communism, planned and led up to through long centuries of education and discipline and collectivist preparation. I had never thought before that socialism could exalt and ennoble the individual and individualism degrade him, but now I see plainly that here the thing is proved. In this fortunate world—it is indeed the crown of all its health and happiness—there is no Crowd. The Old World, the world to which I belong, was and in my universe alas still is, the world of the Crowd, the world of that detestable crawling mass of unfeatured, infected human beings."[3]

The desire to escape is, clearly, a dominant impulse: Wells from his weariness of man and our world of every day fabricates a daydream of ideal existence. But even here the reformatory attack is sustained, and *pari passu* with this there is the incessant criticism of the romantic conception of life, corresponding to the denunciation of the egotism and stupidity of the botanist and the 'natural

[1] P. 286.   [2] P. 287.   [3] P. 353.

man' in *A Modern Utopia*. Here Mr. Catskill and the Utopian 'failure', Lychnis, speak for the ancient law against evolution and progress. While to the neophyte Barnstaple Utopia is 'Loveliness, order, health, energy, and wonder; it has all the good things for which my world groans and travails', Lychnis is lost in a nostalgic backward view and deplores this restless, avtive world: 'Every day men and women awake and say: What new thing shall we do to-day? What shall we change?'.—'And research never rests, and curiosity and the desire for more power and still more power consumes all our world.'[1] Barnstaple, however, finds this a 'healthy appetite' and indeed Wells through Lychnis answers Mr. Catskill's argument that order, peace and the absence of pain and misery mean mental stagnation. And to emphasize this retort Wells contrasts Lychnis with Crystal, a typical Utopian youth of thirteen who intellectually and physically already dwarfs the more than average earthling.[2] In his portrayal of Crystal, however, Wells contradicts his claim, dictated by his reconstructive fervour, that the Utopians are not fundamentally different from their stone age ancestors: that the Utopia may be for us, in fact, close at hand. Crystal, whose name bespeaks his intellect as well as his moral attitude; who is already mastering scientific and mathematical problems beyond the gifted earthling's comprehension, is an evolutionary product not to be explained in terms of education or the influence of environment: he is the fruit of a slow cumulative mental and organic process.[3]

In this world of brotherhood and instinctive co-operation there is no need of compulsive laws or a strict public code of conduct: crime and evil are outgrown habits. Being more highly evolved than the *samurai*, these demigods have no 'Rule' or 'Canon' to form and

[1] P. 337.   [2] Pp. 340 ff.
[3] Crystal corresponds to the idea of precocious intellect through inheritance of Shaw's youth in 'As Far As Thought Can Reach'.

sustain them, but instead they learn in youth the Five Principles of Liberty on which all civilization rests: The Principle of Privacy, of Free Movement, of Unlimited Knowledge, of Lying as the Blackest Crime, of Free discussion and Criticism.[1] Here again Wells' concern for the individual is in evidence, and while he places the government of Utopia in the hands of specialists (as in *A Modern Utopia*) this government remains subject to free and democratic criticism.

Wells had returned from his excursion into *A Modern Utopia* with a promise to humanity, and a hope for the future is what he brings this time too. *Men Like Gods*, despite its hatred of the Crowd and of earthly ugliness and discord, ends on a note of reconciliation: 'Life is still only a promise, still waits to be born, out of such poor stirrings in the dust as we ..'.[2] From his Pisgah sight Wells has gathered new faith:

"Three thousand years ago this was a world like ours .. Think of it—in a hundred generations ... In three thousand years we might make our poor waste of an Earth, jungle and desert, slag-heap and slum, into another such heaven of beauty and power ..".[3]

Barnstaple, reluctantly taking leave of Utopia, trusts that Earth too would see the 'Great Revolution', to which he now belongs with all the hundreds of thousands whose 'minds are set towards Utopia':

Earth too would grow rich with loveliness and fair as this great land was fair. The sons of Earth also, purified from disease, sweet-minded and strong and beautiful, would go proudly about their conquered planet and lift their daring to the stars.
"Given the will", said Mr. Barnstaple. "Given only the will." ...[4]

Fundamentally, there is no change in attitude from *A Modern Utopia* to *Men Lige Gods*, though the human ideal is more remote and unattainable. As for formal qualities, the latter work has more

[1] Cf., pp. 346—48.   [2] P. 363.   [3] P. 365.   [4] P. 369.

438

evocative scenes and descriptions, but these, particularly towards the end, are spoilt by a sentimental note and an elaboration of the sweetness and light of Utopian culture that grows too dense, artificial and repetitive. The argument, moreover, is less solid and consecutive than in the earlier prophecy, and mainly for the reason that Wells cannot fully reconcile his desire to escape, which is probably the stronger impulse, with his reformatory zeal. Hence the vacillation between a human being of god-like qualities, a being that is clearly the outcome of a long evolutionary process and not of three thousand years of teaching—and his idea that this man has not essentially changed since the stone age, or the Last Age of Confusion: Homo Sapiens may still assert his better self and learn to be a demigod—given the will. Yet for all this *Men Like Gods* is a noble dream with a high purpose, and the abiding impression it leaves is the faith that the intellectual energy in man is inexhaustible, and that he will rise to higher things.

What happened eventually to Wells' dream of the ideal man? *Star Begotten* (1937) is one of his final excursions, and one which falls more directly into this Utopian line than the discursive works on the 'Fate' and the 'Outlook' of Homo Sapiens. The development in this late fantasia is significant, for it marks the growing certainty in Wells' mind that man as we know him, will not, indeed cannot, improve his world: He must, therefore, be born anew, must transmute into a new genus, if he is to survive at all. It is the certainty which culminated in the sinister message of *Mind at the End of Its Tether*.

The Transmutation of Homo Sapiens

Wells was 71 when he wrote *Star Begotten* and still his mind was moving with youthful curiosity among the scientific enigmas of his time. Einstein's cotemporal 'dimensions' had provided the trick of *Men Like Gods*, and now the cosmic rays give him the clue to another, and more genuinely evolutionary fantasy. *Star Begotten* is not a Utopia, but, something in the manner of the middle plays of *Back to Methuselah,* a prophetic speculation in which a Utopian dream seeks outlet: we do not this time explore the ideal land and its people so much as we watch the growing awareness in a few minds of how a new kind of man is emerging—the heir of our earth.

Significantly, Wells no longer appeals to *samurai* will and discipline, neither does he plead for 'the idea of creative service'; he postulates a *Deus ex Machina*—the cosmic rays—acting upon the human genes. As this idea first takes shape in the protagonists' fantasy, it comes as an answer to two disturbing problems in the present human condition. For one thing:

Biologists...say that when a species comes to a difficult phase in its struggle for existence—and I suppose no one can say that is not fairly true of the human situation nowadays—there is an increased disposition to vary.[1]

Secondly, there are unmistakable indications that this disposition to vary is now more manifest than before: something new is taking hold of human nature, as if trying to change it. From these speculations grows the hypothesis that somewhere in the universe there are

beings like ourselves...but far wiser, more intelligent, much more highly developed [the Martians, for instance, are an older species than man]..able to influence human life...that for the last few thousand years they have been experimenting in human genetics.. firing away with increasing accuracy and effectiveness at our chromosomes...planning human mutations.[2]

At first these mutations—these *Martianized* men, are felt with characteristic human prejudice to be evil and inhuman and revolting

[1] P. 60.   [2] Pp. 62, 64, 67.

in appearance. But to the more optimistic minds it seems certain that the Martian who is trying to change man is 'humanity's big brother' and not only a superman, but good and benevolent—a sane and mature guardian of human destiny.[1] The hypothesis finally to be tested, then, is whether there is an increase of high-grade intellectual types, and in what respects these differ from ordinary men. The inquirer finds, in fact, that, whatever the cause,

A new sort of mind *is* coming into the world, with a new, simpler, clearer and more powerful way of thinking...a hard, clear, insistent mind. It used to appear at uncertain intervals. Rarely. It said 'Why not?' and it made discoveries. Now apparently it is becoming— frequent.[2]

These new minds have been particularly active in science and mechanical inventions, and over the last hundred years have produced a technical revolution beyond the moral control of ordinary man. Hence the dilemma of modern civilization.[3] While material progress rushes onward with gathering speed, humanity is drifting 'on a raft of rotting ideas...customs, moral codes, loyalties ...'.[4] The crucial question is: What part will these new minds play in our shipwreck?—'Are they going to salvage us?' They do indeed promise rescue, since they are all that which man ought to be and is not.—Man is half born, blundering about...his mind lost in a confusing dualism; he shirks responsibility; he is the boy who won't grow up; he is obsessed by infantile cravings for protection and direction.[5]

In this unsparing Shavian verdict Wells sums up the human weaknesses that particularly provoke his disgust, and this revulsion changes his method of man-making: it would seem that he no longer aims at a retouching of the negative human portrait—he wants something entirely new.

[1] Pp. 84—85.   [2] Pp. 139, 143.   [3] P. 141.   [4] P. 154.
[5] Pp. 155—57.

The star begotten men differ from the *samurai* ideal not only in the quality of their brain, but in their moral and emotional disposition. They are beyond good and evil in a human sense, and no longer share the burden of heredity and environment of Homo Sapiens. Goodness, moral consciousness, self-control in them are no longer matters of will or training—they are inherent, exclusive instincts. Therefore, Wells ceases to insist on ethical effort—on *samurai* revolution as the dynamism in social and general progress. On the other hand—the argument runs—this new being will not be lacking in tenderness and sympathy:

A hard, clear mind does not mean what we call a hard individual. What we call a hard man is a stupid man, who specializes in inflexibility to escape perplexity. But a hard, clear mind is a clear crystalline mind; it turns about like a lens, revealing and scrutinizing one aspect after another, one possibility after another, and this and that necessary correlation.[1]

Inevitably, for Wells there comes the moment when his biological fantasia, with its ambiguous symbolic 'Martian' disguise, has to be translated into terms of social process, and of rescue from the rotten raft of our civilization: 'How will sanity ever gain any sort of control of the world?' The answer is not, as in *A Modern Utopia*, the consorted endeavour of a militant *élite*, but a slow organic growth, more like the intellectual and moral evolution in *Men Like Gods*—a 'constant seeping of clearer intelligences into our world. .'; and a spreading of these minds which, without deliberate organization, will think and act in concord, because 'for the human brain, properly working, there is one wisdom and not many'.[2] Since these minds are, as Wells naturally holds they will be, more highly individualized and independent, they are going to resist Crowd mentality and mass prejudices.[3] Equally they will reject and sabo-

[1] P. 160.   [2] P.162.   [3] P. 163.

442

tage the compulsion of Bosses and Dictators. In consequence there will be many martyrs among them before the world goes sane, but nevertheless the number of these 'cool-brained gentlemen' will increase:

Trust those cosmic rays now they have begun. Trust the undying intelligence behind our minds...One sane man will follow another; one sane man will understand another, more and more clearly. A sort of etiquette of the sane will come into operation. They will stand by each other. In spite of bad laws, in spite of foolish authority.[1]

What they will have achieved in the end is something better than a revolution, for 'A revolution changes nothing essential'—it will be a fundamentally new kind of behaviour, determined exclusively by rational thinking. For rational minds 'have to follow definite laws'. And gradually—Wells pursues his dream—these star-men will 'spread a network of sanity about the world and stop what you call the Common Fool—Demos, *Homo pseudo-sapiens*—from ravening, grabbing and destroying—just by barring his way, refusing to implement his silly impulses..'.[2] Thus, eventually, these new men, like the *samurai*, will act as guardians; and Wells reverts to his *samurai* idea, moreover, in the prophecy that at one stage in the 'mental treatment of our world' there will be fighting and killing and police hunts for 'would-be dictators'.[3] But as intelligence gains power to control the human genes there will be no need to purge humanity by means of force: 'Sanity will ride this planet with fine hands'.

What great future are these men going to build? What may a world 'gone sane' look like? In Wells' tentative answer the qualities of the ideal man are inextricably interwoven with those of his ideal society; the new man *is* the new world.

[1] P. 166.   [2] P. 169.   [3] P. 173.

Order and individuality are again the corner-stones of Wells' anticipation. It will be a state of permanent peace, and its citizens will 'make a sort of garden of the planet'. They will eliminate the struggle for life, and suffering and ugliness; they will master Nature and create a richer and more beautiful home for mankind. And Wells, still anxious that his ideal should be the *complete* man, is certain that 'These masterful people with their control over materials, over all the forces of the world and over their own nervous reactions are not going to starve their aesthetic impulses.[1] As their sensibility is more refined than ours, their artistic achievements will be more subtle and varied. To their greater individuality; to their mental and physical vigour and beauty will correspond a harmonious and richly individualized expression in works of art.

The finest observation Wells makes of these new human beings is that owing to their more highly individualized personalities, they will care more for one another;[2] 'they will want and find satisfactions in companionship, friendship, partnership and caresses'. And with a characteristic and inconsistent reversion to man Wells establishes, after all, their human identity, by applying to their growth the phylogenetic evolutionary law:

Maybe they will pass through an emotional adolescence and have their storms of individual possessiveness, inflamed egotism, intense physical desire. The individual will repeat something of the romantic experiences of the race.[3]

Despite the genetic miracle through which the clearer mind will emerge; despite Wells' persistent tendency to scrap the human material altogether for a radically new departure, he keeps the link with Homo Sapiens, and once more the conflict of loyalties is manifest in his self-contradictory effort to bridge the real and the ideal. The effect of education and environment, we are told, is even for

[1] P. 176   [2] Pp. 176—77.   [3] P. 177.

these crystalline minds of great importance, though previously, to make his hypothesis plausible, Wells contended that these people are independent of such external conditions, independent of heredity even. Now, meditating upon the emotional development of the future men and women, he emphasizes, as he did in *A Modern Utopia* and *Men Like Gods*, that they will come to maturity in an atmosphere of understanding and freedom—'with a better morale about them, a lovelier poetry to guide them, a pervasive, penetrating contempt for ugliness, vanity and mere mean competitiveness and self-assertion'.[1]

Can we imagine, in general terms, what these people will be doing and how they will live? For Wells it is not enough to make sketches of the ideal man, he desires to participate in his life—his passion is, more than ever, to *live* in Utopia. We have, he suggests, in our mental urge a clue to the life and activities of these new 'incessant minds'. They will be constantly bent on new discovery and greater control of things and forces; they will be engaged in changing and experimenting in a great drive of intellectual and scientific enthusiasm; and they will 'be much more *alive to things*'.[2] And with this tantalizing glimpse of the promised land, Wells—a handicapped mere Homo Sapiens—admits that it is not possible for us to share in their life and world: 'They will be capable of knowledge I cannot even dream about, they will gain powers over space, time, existence, such as we cannot conceive'.[3]

In the end, then, *Star Begotten* adds up to a dream of the ideal man very like that already pictured in *Men Like Gods*. The predominant qualities: individuality, a profounder instinct for love and sympathy, and first and last an all-conquering intellect, these are the traits which have persisted from *A Modern Utopia*, become more marked and articulate with the greater prophetic freedom in the later works, until the whole portrait looks like a frank rejection

[1] *Ibid.*   [2] P. 180.   [3] P. 181.

445

of the human being, despite the fact that it represents—in Wells' purpose—a sublimation of 'our best selves'.

As for the cosmic rays, this symbol of unknown or unexploited evolutionary forces may mean different things, and it appears to have no clear definition in the prophet's mind. It is the next thing to eugenics, as it may be applied with greater knowledge and wisdom in the future. Indeed, one of the most remarkable statements in the whole fantasy is the mystical and oracular promise, characteristic of Shaw but not of Wells, the disciple of Darwin and Huxley: 'Trust the undying intelligence behind our minds'.[1] It would appear that we are here watching a development parallel to that of Shaw, from the belief in *Man and Superman* that man must be his own Political Providence, must shape his own destiny, to the realization of moral impotence from which springs the mystical hope in *Back to Methuselah*. From his confident faith in reason and the moral consciousness of man, and in its creative power, Wells gradually—driven by disillusionment—retreats to a vague, mystical hope that some force, inside or outside man but not dependent on his moral will, may take hold of his destiny, may act as an evolutionary grace and save him from doom.

For this reason, *Star Begotten* is far inferior to *A Modern Utopia*, and to its closer relative *Men Like Gods*, in its moral and human appeal. Wells' idea of the *samurai* was, for all its psychological shallowness, a great vision, rooted in the liberal Victorian tradition: a being of sweetness and light, of moral will and awareness, an individual, a beautiful mind in a beautiful body, a sublime intellect. In *Star Begotten* the revulsion from man amounts almost to a denial of his right to exist. The world has become to Wells, at least in this despairing mood, a madhouse ready for 'mental treatment'. Despite the faint optimistic note on which the book ends, it is a dark and hopeless vision, and it already announces the final collapse

---

[1] See *supra*, p. 443.

446

of his faith. Wells even during the second world war continued to dream and plan, and explore the outlook for Homo Sapiens, but in the last year of his life the old and suffering prophet recanted his entire Utopian creed in *Mind at the End of Its Tether*. A tragic end to come to for the most sanguine of champions in the cause of human progress, but an inevitable end for one who had set out with such impatient zest, who had struggled to realize Victorian idealism in the harsh and cruel world of the twentieth century. Wells' task had begun, in that era, as a triumphant Promethean effort and seemed, as the second world war repeated and dwarfed the horror of the first, to issue in a pointless Sisyphus' ambition. The end was inevitable also, perhaps, in view of Wells' psychological and moral reference. His view of human nature has the shallowness of all predominantly rationalistic and naturalistic doctrines: it ignores the deeper nature and reality of evil.

And yet, these final pronouncements upon the fate of Homo Sapiens cannot obliterate the greatness and splendour of his earlier —and most satisfactory—Utopian visions, nor the range of his Pisgah sight. For Wells had this sight, and though he suffered the more for it in the end, he gave it powerful voice in *A Modern Utopia*. Measured against the massive structure of this work, or even seen against the evocative fairy-tale projection of *Men Like Gods*, it is not probable that posterity will accept Wells' resignation from his Utopian office. As far as life on earth is concerned, he will continue to preside over and direct our hopes.

3. *Shaw and Wells—* *Summary and Comparison*

Between Wells and Shaw there is a great deal of unconscious communication as well as direct mutual influence, and for all their temperamental differences, they shared essential beliefs. Both remained socialists at heart and both had the same anti-democratic

447

contempt for the crowd and the mass; both embraced evolution as the way to a greater future life; and both, even the Shaw of *Methuselah*, saw in human reason and will the principle of grace that works salvation. Very similar, too, are the values and virtues which go to the making of their human ideal.

It is only when we come to their adherence to a specific evolutionary doctrine that they differ in outlook, and from this divergence stems also the contrast between their ultimate Utopian goals: In his final vision of the good life Shaw leaves Wells behind, on earth, as it were, to dwell in a vortex of pure thought. For to Shaw evolution is a mystic's faith, something approaching to the condition of cult and rite, while to Wells it remains a moral and social concern.

Perhaps the most interesting aspect yielded by a comparison of the two contemporary prophets is that their evolutionary Utopias set out from such different points and yet manage to steer almost parallel courses and arrive at approximately the same earthly destination. To Shaw the clues were Lamarck and Creative Evolution; to Wells it was Darwin; to the one an unknowable, providential force bound for higher and still higher forms of life; to the other, mainly environment and education. Of the two Shaw alone preaches a consistently teleological message: to him life is for ever purpose, will, effort. Wells vacillates between Darwinian selection or fatalism and teleology, and finally, in his conception of the creative will, found himself very close to Shaw. In his discursive educationist work, *The Science of Life* (1931), Wells describes the Shavian Life Force as a 'pantomime giant', and as 'Lamarckism in caricature'.[1] Here he feels confidently secure on Darwin's side— the only truly scientific side—which sees 'Evolution as a response of life to its environment'. And to explain this process in its *modus operandi*, natural selection and the struggle for life are adequate

---

[1] *Op. cit.*, pp. 384—85.

means. Like the Devil in *Man and Superman* Wells holds that the 'apparent purpose' is an illusion: 'Life...is not the arbiter of its own destiny'.[1] Yet the whole imaginative and moral effort of *A Modern Utopia* and *Men Like Gods* (among others) boldly and nobly contradicts this view: with man there *is* purpose, and will, and power to work towards a greater and more beautiful life. With man a teleological force has taken hold of life—a force bent on changing the ancient law. Man is no longer a slave of fatalism and determinism; he may, if his will be strong, become a god. The 'undying intelligence behind our minds' in *Star Begotten* may be a whimsical idea, in the 'Martian' key, or it may be a rhetorical apotheosis of human reason, but it nevertheless coincides with Wells' trust in intelligence as a kind of grace, and the notion expresses something of the Shavian belief that 'We shall not be let alone. The force behind evolution, call it what you will, is determined to solve the problem of civilization'.[2]

It is in their moral attitude and challenge, and to some extent in their conception of the human ideal, that Shaw and Wells fight abreast, and with strikingly identical aims and means. There is a similar appeal to *will* and *reason,* set against a background of positivistic man-cult. There is throughout an idealistic emphasis on sacrifice and self-discipline. *Man and Superman* proclaims that nothing can save civilization except 'a clear head and a wide purpose', and *A Modern Utopia* anticipates an ideal future world built by a 'clear common purpose'. Shaw 'sings' the philosophic man who discovers the inner will of the world and its direction, and whose will is active in the same course. Though Wells wrote in *A Modern Utopia:* 'This world has still to discover its will', he also contended that Utopia is the outcome of 'a great and steadfast movement of will'.[3] And: 'Will is stronger than Fact, it can mould and overcome Fact'. The conceptions of creative purposive will are,

---

[1] *Ibid.,* p. 386.   [2] *Back to Methuselah,* p. 82.   [3] Pp. 314—15.

particularly in their later works, *Back to Methuselah, Men Like Gods* and *Star Begotten,* closely related. Despite their rationalism, more consistent in Wells than in Shaw, their view of the evolutionary or creative will contains increasingly an element of the mystical and the miraculous, and even in *Man and Superman* and *A Modern Utopia* this will, almost in the function of a *Deus ex Machina,* is felt to be secretly at work in man, guiding and exploring, and causing the new ideal qualities to emerge. This element of mysticism is expressive in both Wells and Shaw of the realization, perhaps unconscious to begin with, that reason—a 'clear head'—is not adequate, nor is a wide social purpose, for the survival and renaissance of our civilization.

In their verdict on civilization and on historical process there is again considerable agreement. *A Modern Utopia* first and *Back to Methuselah* later review history as waves of civilizations moving and mounting until, inevitably, decadence sets in through egotism and self-destructive anarchy.[1] The decline and fall of civilizations is a moral disease, and accordingly there is in the message of Shaw and Wells something hard and ascetic and even puritanical: Wells deplores man as a being 'disposed to excess', and Shaw denounces his cigars and champagne and games. Both condemn him for his lack of responsibility, for his puerile pleasure-seeking habits which make of him such an asocial being and a dangerous politician. Man is the boy who never grows up, we read in *Back to Methuselah* and in *Star Begotten.* Therefore, the ideal which they both anticipate when man has grown out of these weaknesses, is a Samurai or an ancient, guardians of an adult, sober and ordered world in which the sensuous fevers of youth hold no sway. Their ideal man is a

---

[1] Cf. *A Modern Utopia,* 'The past history ... social collapses due to demoralisation by indulgences ...'; p. 249; and *Back to Methuselah:* 'Flinders Petrie has counted nine attempts at civilization ... They failed because the citizens and statesmen died of old age or overeating ...'; p. 73.

serious, thinking man, a being whose features are made fine by thought and steadfast living.

It is very obvious also that their dream of the ideal State has a similar emotional and intellectual basis: it grows from a disgust with existing things, and this was marked in Shaw already in 1890 while in Wells it increased with the years. Their individualism has a strong leaning to intellectual pride—even arrogance—and in their anti-democratic socialism the element of love and sympathy is, in Shaw at least, a relatively unimportant impulse. Dedicated to an all-absorbing idealism, they worship the divine image in man, the great individual and the powerful mind, while the majority of men remain objectionable failures. Yet, Shaw who is the more fierce hater of the crowd is not at pains to stress the evolution of individuality, which is one of Wells' main concerns. In 1890 Shaw sentenced Demos—the many-headed monster—to death, and in 1921 his ancients are living in solitude, avoiding human relationship. In Wells' early Utopias there are still gay and pleasant crowds; but they have vanished from the beautiful and happy world of *Men Like Gods,* and in *Star Begotten* one of the spokesmen of the new race turns on common humanity with Shavian fury: 'I am tired of humanity—beyond measure. Take it away ... Clear the earth of them!'.[1] It is not surprising, then, to find that Shaw and Wells base their Utopian State entirely on the emergence of an intellectual and moral *élite*—a modern select aristocracy whose brains and wills are powerful enough to keep the crowd at bay and educate it. To both of them the crowd is a die-hard dragon that has to be fought and conquered, and Shaw in *Back to Methuselah* salutes Wells for the insight he has given him into the ineluctable conflict between the great few and the base many.[2] Yet the *élite* stage is, they realize, untenable and must be only a transition to a universal spreading of 'reason' and 'sanity' and the good life—

[1] P. 184.   [2] Cf. p. 118.

451

which is scientific exploration and thought. Hence, to solve the problem—insoluble in terms of politics and education alone—of how to populate the future world with exclusively ideal human beings, they both invoke the potent magic of evolution. Evolution is the path to godhead, to the ultimate goal which is the object of their dream: omniscience and omnipotence. For Shaw the idealist, who from the beginning soars above common humanity, this goal lies in a transcendent (or at least disembodied) life of pure thought —a mystic's paradise. Wells stands more squarely in the humanitarian and positivistic tradition, and his dream never leaves the immanent plane, though to all practical intents it leaves man so far behind as to prophesy a kind of divine life on earth.

Shaw's ideal man has a beautiful and omnipotent mind, but no body, or one that is unimportant and therefore unattractive. Wells takes up Meredith's heritage and dwells on the harmonious development of his Utopians. Yet with him too thought is the quintessence of the new life, and significantly there is a statement in a *A Modern Utopia* which looks like a seed of Shaw's ancients: 'thought itself is only a finer sort of feeling (than his)—good hock to the mixed gin, porter and treacle of (his) emotions ...'[1] The distinctive quality of the ancients, and the *samurai*, is intelligence and self-discipline, and they are most happy in solitary meditation. The god-like men and the 'martianized men' bring Wells' ideal even closer to that of Shaw, and it is probably no accident that a chief characteristic of the star begotten is that they invariably ask the question: 'Why not?'—the question which lifted man from Adam to ancient in *Back to Methuselah*. To the human brain—the darling object of life in evolution, and Nature's pilot—there can be no insuperable barrier. It is this faith which in Shaw releases man finally from all material bondage, enables him to range through the stars and carry life to the uttermost confines of the universe. Wells dreams of a

[1] P. 155.

similar conquest, but not with a mystic's yearning for the life abundant: to him the emigration from earth is a practical necessity —a condition of survival when the sun has died down. Thanks to our brain, thanks to Science our saviour, the race shall not perish, for as the old sage in *Men Like Gods* puts it: 'We have hardly begun!' ... 'Life is still only a promise'.[1]

Finally, it might be noted that Wells, in defining the inevitable myopia of his vision in *Star Begotten*, at the same time brings theoretical support to Shaw's reticence in *Back to Methuselah*—for which he has been so much criticized—of what his ideal ancients are contemplating, and what their object of pure thought might be:

"Let us admit ... that this is attempting the most impossible of tasks. The hypothesis is that these coming supermen are stronger-witted, better-balanced and altogether wiser than we are. How can we begin to put our imaginations into their minds and figure out what they will think or do? If our intelligences were as tall as theirs, we should be making their world now."[2]

We have 'no material in our minds out of which we can build a concrete vision of things to come', and it is only in general terms that we can conceive of future life and thought.—This reads almost like a direct sympathetic comment upon 'As Far As Thought Can Reach'.

For all these points of similarity in attitude and prophetic intention, there are, as one might expect, also fundamental differences between their human ideals. And it would appear that, both for emotional and moral appeal, and in the matter of imaginative delineation, it is Wells, the more naïve and genuine dreamer, who has achieved the most satisfactory and evocative vision, the most attractive in its sensitivity and social reference, because it is a sub-

[1] P. 363.   [2] P. 170.

limation of human nature and not—at least not in *A Modern Utopia*—mainly a liberation from it, as it appears to be in Shaw.

The essential achievement of the Utopias of Shaw and Wells was to make of evolution a moral challenge and a source of creative faith. It was inevitable that they should fail in translating this faith into terms of practical methods of human regeneration, nor could they be called upon to explain exactly *how* the evolutionary process will operate—granted that it is taking place. The creative will of the ancients and the *samurai* eludes rational analysis; it is a poetic conception—an object of trust and aspiration, and can only be accepted in terms of its own medium. Its basis is a teleological interpretation, for Shaw of the whole of life, for Wells of human mind and history.

It was inevitable too, that these highly temperamental visions, struck out from political and intellectual idiosyncrasies that excluded them from the Christian as well as the democratic tradition, should be repellent to many, should be branded in turn as heresies and superstitions and grotesque experiments in human destiny. Orthodoxy was outraged, since what they preached was in fact a religious substitute. Humanitarian intellectuals were against them, since they threatened to tamper with the natural evolution of the human being, and make of him a hideous test-tube product: a docile, predestinate instrument in the hands of an all-powerful State. Though Shaw and Wells had taken precautions against this kind of misrepresentation, their message was suspect, and it seemed to keep the new poison hidden in readiness—eugenics.

Of the various counter-attacks and anti-Utopias concerned with the threat of eugenics the best known is Aldous Huxley's *Brave New World* (1932). Huxley belongs to that group of intellectuals who, as Berdiaeff hopes and suggests, will dream of avoiding Utopia and return to a freer and less 'perfect' society. Shaw's mystical vision is wholly outside the range of Huxley's charge, but it strikes home to Wells' later Utopia, *Star Begotten*. In *A Modern Utopia*

454

the individual has far greater freedom than any man has had in past or present society. Wells throughout sees individuality as not only a means of intellectual and moral growth, but as an end in itself, and individuality, he rightly maintains, will not be lost or thwarted in a co-operative and well organized World State.[1] Wells does not need to defend his Modern Utopia against the accusations of *Brave New World*, for to him as to Huxley man and the individual remains the measure. The pathos of the Savage in a functionalistic, supra-rational future world appears at first sight to be an apt indication of the latent tragedy of a great many individuals in the increasingly scientific civilization of Wells' dream. The 'natural man' in *A Modern Utopia*, Mr. Barnstaple and Lychnis in *Men Like Gods*, might be taken as inadvertent admissions that for some, Utopia will be a cold and unsympathetic world, very like the ant-society to which the Sleeper awakes. But Wells' dream grows from a desire to see the good life as a universal condition, and he bases his hope on a belief in intellectual and moral evolution raising the whole of mankind, except for a few 'failures', to beauty and dignity, and to a more complete mastery of the mind and moral will of itself and of its surroundings. Moral evolution, he claims, will control scientific progress, and human relationship and sympathy will grow through the free interplay of individualities, stimulated by a harmonious environment. This, within the limitations of Wells' medium, is not an empty formula. The Savage would not have committed suicide in *A Modern Utopia*, but conversely, Mr. Barnstaple and Lychnis would not have been tolerated in *Brave New World*.

Against the threat of human decadence manifest, as they thought, in their times, Shaw and Wells pit their faith that this moral and intellectual evolution of man is all the time going on, though the process can only vaguely be described in terms of increasing intel-

[1] See Wells' answer to Huxley's *Brave New World* in *The Outlook for Homo Sapiens* (1942), p. 166.

ligence and an unreleased creative will—in the best men. Of course, they could *prove* nothing—they could only bear witness to their prophetic experience. Apart from Huxley, other powerful voices have risen in protest against their idea of the superman. In the great liberal Meredithian tradition, G. M. Trevelyan blames Shaw for mistaking means for ends and neglecting human love and charity. Chesterton and T. S. Eliot have in turn denounced the superman as a gross superstition. Indeed, to the religious conception of man as essentially a soul and an immortal being created in the image of God, any idea of *interference* must be repellent, particularly if this idea comes as near to eugenics as it does in *Man and Superman* and *Star Begotten*. To this view of man, eugenics—even the denial of children to 'inferior parents'—is not only sinful, but the ultimate excess of human *hubris*.

We do not believe, however, that eugenics, either in this sense or in the crude test-tube caricature, is the real core of Shaw's and Wells' message. It is not a forcing of issues to claim that their Utopia, with its human ideal, is above all a challenge to moral and creative effort, an appeal to selfless dedication. Their evolutionary belief may or may not be legitimate from a scientific or orthodox point of view, but it is certainly so from a moral stance. It is rooted ultimately in the abiding values on which our civilization rests, though this fact is often concealed by their reformatory zest. And they continue a great and noble tradition. For if one shares the mystical faith of Shelley or Browning in the everlasting minute of Creation: if one accepts the general scientific data of evolution and the possibility that this process is going on; if one embraces the moral faith of Tennyson and Meredith in the ascent of man to a fuller and better life, to beauty, love and harmony, then the messages of Shaw and Wells are important. Their ethical challenge cannot easily be put aside or reduced to absurdity, for there is something permanently great in their exhortation to creative faith and purposive, generous effort, and in their crusade against 'the spirit

456

that denies'. Apathy and fatalism will not help man to rise on the stepping stones of his dead selves to higher things, and it is by restating the moral meaning of existence—by identifying human will at its best with the cosmic will, that Shaw and Wells have reasserted the moral obligation of man, and his dignity here on earth. And for what may be beyond, their eyesight, as they admit, is too short.

SUMMARY AND CONCLUSION

THE LITERATURE we have examined in these pages is a poetic interpretation of existence. It is a characteristic trait in our poets and authors that the idea of evolution, as a mere scientific concept, as the most important and fascinating component of the modern theory of Nature, offers only the pretext—the point of departure—of an imaginative and prophetic exploration of the destiny of life. It may have challenged them at first as an object of discursive thinking, but when it emerges from the alchemy of their minds we find that it has transcended its theoretical context, and, even in the frankly moralizing sermons of Wells and Shaw, has undergone a symbolical transformation in their vision and belief. The idea of evolution does not, even in Hardy and Wells, impose upon the writer a rigid formula: it is for the poets to make their choice, to impose upon the specific theory their own visionary pattern. Thus the scientific data remain to them merely framework concepts, a bridge towards significance, value, duty and the ultimate mysteries of existence.

In the early, hypothetical stage of evolutionary theory, Tennyson and Browning exercised this poetic autonomy, and their attitude, choice and method are fairly representative of most of our writers —of those who believe that 'life is not as idle ore'. We have said that they were able, owing to Coleridge and the liberal idealistic tradition, to adapt themselves to the changing intellectual climate, and even to the unattractive idea of 'man from ape'. Within the compass of their vision Darwin's account of transmutation and selection occupied a minor place—a brief episode in the 'everlasting minute of creation'. But since this account involved the problem of man's place in Nature, since Darwin's fanatical pupils ruled out categorically the transcendental meaning which to them was essential—since, finally, a choice had to be made between theory and belief, Tennyson and Browning chose as poets. Hence their rejection of the agnostic and fatalistic implications of the theory. For these implications brought them face to face with a world in which the law of natural selection, or blind, unmeaning chance, went beyond its biological field and became a cosmogenetic principle. Science, they then claimed, had begun at the wrong end: with Nature, instead of beginning with the fact which gives significance to the whole process—man. From this anthropomorphic centre they explore the evolutionary genesis and find, everywhere, as Coleridge and Shelley had found, a divine spiritual force at work.

In the choice of Swinburne and Meredith there is the same poetic freedom and essentially the same idealistic fervour, though they are born into the age of positivistic agnosticism and find their world reduced to space and time. Swinburne in his ecstasy of revolt, Meredith bent on his evolutionary 'Triad' and the moral, purposive growth of life: both take from Darwin merely the concept of evolution as struggle and progress. But while the fittest to Darwin are products of chance, and fittest only in a biological sense, they are to Swinburne and Meredith the best, in a moral and teleological sense. Through these the 'one God at growth' realizes his purpose. Thus it is mainly in their emphasis on immanence and pantheism that they deviate from the course of transcendental idealism. This shift of emphasis involves a new object of worship and a new goal of evolutionary aspiration—Man. Man epitomizes the effort of all Nature to become God, he is the highest step towards a reconciliation and identification of matter and spirit. To this end, then, man must exercise his entire power and sacrifice his ego, for this is the moral

459

significance of life, the value and obligation that should rule our conduct. Within the range of this agnostic and humanitarian creed, the vision of Swinburne and Meredith is saturated with aspiration towards freedom, beauty, harmony and love.

This teleological and poetic interpretation of evolutionary process is borne on an unabated current of philosophical idealism throughout the century and into our own day. From generation to generation the tradition is handed down, reformulated, changing in accent and direction according to the individual poet's attitude. But always there is an intimate correspondence between the writer and his intellectual milieu, and this at times may, as in the case of Hardy and Butler, give a capricious turn to the poet's choice. Samuel Butler wrote in the times of Meredith, but already then the scientific protest against Darwin was gathering force in well-reasoned arguments. The neo-Lamarckians offered an alternative congenial to the poet's inherent thirst for more and fuller life, for significant existence, for value and moral purpose. Butler chose the world of Lamarck instead of that of Darwin, as Meredith did in a more compromising and peaceful spirit. For Hardy there was, after 1871 at least, the same theoretical alternative, yet the choice which 'Hap' represents—(provoked by *Origin of Species*)—was too deeply rooted in his attitude and in his emotional awareness of frustration and pain. Therefore, with an obsessive coherence of argument, he derived from Natural Selection a profoundly tragic vision of existence. But he chose as a poet, and on the slight theme which Darwin provided, developed a mystical cosmology transcending the epistemological framework of the theory, and in the end, from a growing inner need, arrived at a tentative belief in the evolving consciousness and providence of the creative Will.

After Meredith and Butler come, in a direct line of descent, Wel's and Shaw. In Wells' grasp of the idea there is again the overruling poetic liberty of incoherence and paradox. Wells chose Darwin's formula, but only on condition that it could be infused with an

460

ethical significance, and interpreted in terms of Homo Sapiens, not in terms of the 'devouring forces of Nature'. In theory Wells, who had more scientific schooling than any of our writers, comes near to fatalism; in his Utopian dream he excels in the art of pathetic fallacy and teleological projection. Without this intuitive adherence to a teleological belief, he could not have brought Meredith's ideals of 'brain-rule' and 'brotherhood' to their apex of Utopian perfection in his vision of men like gods. There is no strain in his vision (apart from its moral fervour)—no stoical effort to reconcile the absurdity of a chance-ridden existence with our aspirations and moral consciousness, as one might expect if he were to establish a logical coherence between his theoretical outlook and his imaginative practice. Wells' anticipation is a happy and confident dream, tinged with the naïveté and ardour of the inspired preacher and prophet, inspired in fact by the implicit trust that there is a moral significance in human life. This meaning does not to him, as to Tennyson and Browning, extend below man to all life, but it extends beyond him in a vista of idealistic quest as unlimited as that of Swinburne.

Bernard Shaw, this rebel sage who met all creeds, new and traditional, with equal destructiveness, came nearer than any of our poets—Meredith apart—to a synthesis of these creeds. All except the theory of Darwin, which he permanently detested as a reincarnation of Giant Despair. And he continued to preach his changing heresies, all on the same text: the ethical significance of human life, and its bearing on the future. In these sermons too, the mystic and rationalist often contradict and defeat one another, but in his vitalistic plays it is the mystic and poet who rules, and the final prophecy achieved is a poetical exhortation to a better and fuller life.

It would seem that the poetical choice here referred to involves our writers in a conflict with empirical truth, since Natural Selection, amplified by Mendelian genetics, is held by the leading naturalists of our time (like Sir Ronald Fisher) to be the only verifiable

461

and adequate theory. Yet, as long as no one can claim to know the *causes* of variations, there is a field open to free interpretation in which no direct conflict between 'truth' and 'belief' can arise. Moreover, as we have seen, our writers do not base their interpretation on detailed theoretical reference, whether they adhere to Darwin or to Lamarck. Their evolutionary visions are largely independent of particular scientific data, and there is in their meditation, as we have observed in Browning as well as in Meredith, that 'subordination of reference to attitude' which I. A. Richards sees as a criterion of poetical, *emotive* language.

The validity, or 'truth'-value of this evolutionary poetry lies, not mainly in its metaphysical or epistemological search, but in its translation of a belief in creative and purposive evolution into terms of moral aspiration and prophetic dream. In this predominant aspect our writers are very representative of their times and country. They experienced the waves of materialism, scepticism and German philosophical pessimism which in turn broke over England in the nineteenth century; their minds were open to the despair of Schopenhauer and the fierce nihilism of Nietzsche, as Coleridge's mind had been open to Hegel and Kant. Yet these were, by and large, uncongenial to their poetic intuition and to the spiritual and moral climate which stimulated their thought. It was the heritage of Coleridge which decided on their Christian and idealistic choice, and, even in the positivists, fired their moral and spiritual earnestness. It is not the least achievement in our later poets that they combine and reconcile the two strongest conflicting ideological currents of their age—Idealism and Positivism.

Since the idealistic tradition, however, is so closely bound up with Christianity and to a large extent dependent on its doctrine, it is inevitable that those of our writers who deliberately and aggressively reject this doctrine, should impair the general experience and framework of their belief. Swinburne, Meredith, Butler and Shaw often worship God, truth and value in something like Christian terms,

462

and emphasize the spirit as a creative evolutionary force. But since the object and content of their belief are changed, these concepts lose their accepted meanings and are reduced to vaguer and less effective symbols. We feel this most clearly in their interpretation of value and in their strenuous exhortation to the good life.

It is not possible, of course, to draw a general conclusion from the belief of our writers. Yet on the whole it would seem that—the early Hardy apart—they see existence as expansion, fulfilment and meaningful direction. It is characteristic of their greater awareness of value, and their poetic sensitivity to the importance and joy of living, that they crave and assert more and fuller life. From this fundamental need, no less strong in Hardy than in the others—grow their aspirations and prophecies—of the future, of Utopia, or of the life hereafter. Faith in life and its significance is their deepest instinct, hence their choice (germinating also in Hardy) of teleology for a principle of chance. From the protozoa to man life has climbed through the ages: How could this movement be fortuitous and blind? And humanity has, despite vicissitudes, despite the rise and fall of civilizations, been advancing; the human mind has steadily though slowly gained control of itself and its environment; the ethical law has superseded the brutality of Nature. Human greatness and nobility is the centre of their interpretation: it is at the root of Browning's and Tennyson's 'crowning race' as well as of the man-god of Swinburne and Meredith, of the Shavian ancient and the *samurai* élite. This vision of human dignity and nobility is the abiding impression left by their evolutionary faith.

Though it may seem to involve an element of tiresome and unattractive metaphysical pleading, it has been necessary and relevant to our study to emphasize the teleological aspect in our writers' belief—if only because it obviously was of the utmost importance to themselves. But their effort to discover a meaning and a direction in life transcends this one aspect, as it transcends their individual spheres altogether, and actualizes a much more comprehensive and urgent situation—the general loss of faith and of value, the whole complex of questions left by the great schism in modern consciousness. Their answers, needless to say, were neither final nor adequate, yet, though they often appear to stress the distinction rather than resolve it, we may venture to think that they have suggested intuitive ways by which the split between knowledge and feeling, science and faith, could be healed.

464

BIBLIOGRAPHY

(The dates given refer to the editions consulted here.)

Background and General

Matthew Arnold, *Culture and Anarchy*, 1909.

J. Warren Beach, *The Concept of Nature in Nineteenth-Century English Poetry*, 1936.

Henri Bergson, *L'Évolution Créatrice*, 1948.

J. B. Bury, *The Idea of Progress*, 1920.

D. Bush, *Science and English Poetry*, 1950.

Thomas Carlyle, *The Life of John Sterling*, 1897.

— *Sartor Resartus*, Everyman 1948.

E. Clodd, *Pioneers of Evolution from Thales to Huxley*, 1907.

R. G. Collingwood, *The Idea of Nature*, 1949.

Auguste Comte, *Positive Philosophy*, (Harriet Martineau's translation) 2 vols. 1875. *The Catechism of Positive Religion*, (R. Congreve's translation) 1858.

Charles Darwin, *The Origin of Species*, 1860, 1872, and Corrected copyright ed. 1910.

— *The Descent of Man*, i—ii, 1871.

Francis Darwin, *Life of Charles Darwin*, 1902.

D. Dampier-Whetham, *The History of Science*, 1929.

Benjamin Disraeli, Earl of Beaconsfield, *Coningsby*, 1849.

— *Tancred*, 1871.

The Life of the Earl of Beaconsfield, by J. A. Froude, Everyman 1931.

George Eliot, *The Mill on the Floss*, 2 vols., *Works*, 1878—85.

The Life of George Eliot, by J. W. Cross, 1885.

Ralph Waldo Emerson, *Essays*, 1883.

Evolution in the Light of Modern Knowledge, (A Collective Work), 1925.

P. G. Fothergill, *Historical Aspects of Organic Evolution*, 1952.

William Ewart Gladstone, 'Authority in Matters of Opinion', *The Nineteenth Century*, March 1877.

John Herschel, *Preliminary Discourse on the Study of Natural Philosophy*, 1831.

T. H. Huxley, *Man's Place in Nature*, 1863.
— 'Evolution and Ethics', Romanes Lecture, 1893.
— *Collected Essays*, 2 vols. 1894.
— 'The Interpreters of Genesis and the Interpreters of Nature', *The Nineteenth Century*, December 1885.
— 'Agnosticism', *The Nineteenth Century*, February 1889.
The Life and Letters of Thomas Henry Huxley, by Leonard Huxley, 1900.

J. Huxley, *Evolution: the Modern Synthesis*, 1943.

W. R. Inge, *The Platonic Tradition in English Religious Thought*, 1926.

Jean Baptiste Lamarck, *Philosophie Zoologique*, 1809.

John Locke, *Essay concerning Human Understanding*, 1894.

A. Lovejoy, *The Great Chain of Being*, 1942.

Charles Lyell, *The Geological Evidence of the Antiquity of Man*, 1863.

J. Th. Merz, *The History of European Thought in the Nineteenth Century*, 4 vols., 1896—1914.

Hugh Miller, *The Testimony of the Rocks*, 1890.

John Stuart Mill, *Utilitarianism*, 1863.
— *Three Essays on Religion*, 1874.

G. Mivart, *The Genesis of Species*, 1871.

John Henry Newman, *Apologia Pro Vita Sua*, 1913.

H. Fairfield Osborn, *From the Greeks to Darwin*, 1924.

C. Raven, *Natural Religion and Christian Theology*, 1953.

G. Santayana, *Platonism and the Spiritual Life*, 1927.

A. Sedgwick, *Discourse on the Studies of the University of Cambridge*, 5th ed., 1850.

Herbert Spencer, 'The Development Hypothesis', *The Leader*, 1851.
— 'Progress: Its Law and Cause', *Westminster Review*, 1857.
— *First Principles*, 1863.
— *An Epitome of the Synthetic Philosophy*, by H. Collins, 1901.

John Sterling, *Essays and Tales*, 1848.

L. Stevenson, *Darwin Among the Poets*, 1932.

John Tyndall, *Fragments of Science*, 1883.

Vestiges of the Natural History of Creation, (anon.) 1844.

Alfred Russel Wallace, *The Wonderful Century*, 1903.

A. N. Whitehead, *Science and the Modern World*, 1927.

Basil Willey, *Nineteenth Century Studies*, 1950.

466

Chapter II

Alfred Tennyson, *Poetical Works*, Globe ed., Macmillan and Co., 1911.
— *The Early Poems of Alfred Tennyson*, ed. by J. C. Collins, Methuen, 1901.
— *In Memoriam, The Princess and Maud*, by Alfred, Lord Tennyson, ed. by J. C. Collins, Methuen, 1902.
Alfred, Lord Tennyson, A Memoir, by his son, vols. i—ii, 1897.
A. C. Bradley, *A Commentary on Tennyson's In Memoriam*, 1929.
A. Stopford Brooke, *Tennyson, His Art and Relation to Modern Life*, 1895.
T. S. Eliot, 'Tennyson's *In Memoriam*', *Selected Prose*, Penguin 1953.
S. Gwynn, *Tennyson*, 1899.
G. Hough, 'The Natural Theology of *In Memoriam*', *Review of English Studies*, 1947—48.
Th. Lounsbury, *The Life and Times of Tennyson*, 1915.
Sir Harold Nicolson, *Tennyson*, 1923.
G. R. Potter, 'Tennyson and the Biological Theory of Mutability of Species', *Philological Quarterly*, 1937.
W. Rutland, 'Tennyson and the Theory of Evolution', *Essays and Studies* (publ. by the English Association); vol. xxvi, 1940.

*

Robert Browning, *The Poetical Works*, vols. i—vi, London: Smith, Elder & Co., 1868.
— *The Works*, vols. vii, ix, (Cent. ed.), London: Smith, Elder & Co., 1912.
— *Parleyings With Certain People of Importance in their Day*, London: Smith, Elder & Co., 1887.
— *Letters of Robert Browning*, (coll. by T. J. Wise, ed. by T. L. Hood) John Murray, London, 1933.
G. K. Chesterton, *Robert Browning*, (English Men of Letters Series) 1903.
J. M. Cohen, *Robert Browning*, 1952.
Stuart Holmes, 'Browning, Semantic Stutterer', *Publications of the Modern Language Association of America*, vol. lx, 1954.
H. L. Hovelaque, *La jeunesse de Robert Browning*, 1932.
W. De Vane, *Browning's Parleyings. The Autobiography of a Mind*, 1927.
S. T. Coleridge, *Aids to Reflection*, 1913; *Poetical Works*, 1889.
P. B. Shelley, *The Poetical Works*, 1871.
W. Wordsworth, *The Poetical Works*, vols. i—vii, 1892—93.

467

Chapter III

Algernon Charles Swinburne, *Songs Before Sunrise*, F. S. Ellis, London, 1871.

G. Lafourcade, *La jeunesse de Swinburne*, 2 vols., 1928.

Sir Harold Nicolson, *Swinburne*, English Men of Letters Series, 1926.

E. M. W. Tillyard, *Five Poems*, 1948.

*

George Meredith, *Poems*, Memorial ed. vols. 24—26, Constable, London, 1910.

— *Diana of the Crossways*, Memorial ed. vol. 16, Constable, London, 1910.

— *Miscellaneous Prose*, Memorial ed. vol. 23, Constable, London, 1910.

— *Letters*, vols. i—ii, Constable, London, 1912.

E. Clodd, 'Some Recollections', *Fortnightly Review*, 1909.

J. H. E. Crees, *George Meredith*, 1918.

J. W. Cunliffe, 'Modern Thought in Meredith's Poems', *Publications of the Modern Language Association of America*, 1912.

B. Fehr, 'George Meredith. Der Dichter der Evolution', *Die Neueren Sprachen*, xviii, 1910.

C. Photiadès, *George Meredith*, 1910.

J. B. Priestley, *George Meredith*, English Men of Letters Series, 1926.

G. M. Trevelyan, *The Poetry and Philosophy of George Meredith*, 1913.

W. Zeddies, *George Merediths Naturauffassung in seinen Gedichten*, 1934.

Chapter IV

Thomas Hardy, *Collected Poems*, Macmillan and Co., London, 1928.

— *The Works of Thomas Hardy in Prose and Verse*, Wessex ed., Macmillan and Co,. London, 1912.

— *The Dynasts*, Macmillan and Co., London, 1915.

P. Braybrooke, *Thomas Hardy and His Philosophy*, 1928.

E. Brennecke, *Thomas Hardy's Universe*, 1924.

H. Curtis Webster, *On a Darkling Plain*, 1947.

Chapter V

Samuel Butler, 'Darwin Among the Machines', *The Note-Books*, Jonathan Cape, London, 1930.

— 'Lucubratio Ebria', *The Note-Books*, 1930.

468

Samuel Butler, *Erewhon*, Trübner and Co., London, 1872.
— *Life and Habit*, A. C. Fifield, London, 1877.
— *Unconscious Memory*, Jonathan Cape, London, 1922.
J. B. Fort, *Samuel Butler*, 1935.
P. N. Furbank, *Samuel Butler*, 1948.
M.Hartog, 'Samuel Butler and Recent Mnemic Biological Theories', Reprint from *Scientia*, 1914.
C. E. M. Joad, *Samuel Butler*, 1924.
H. F. Jones, *A Memoir*, 2 vols., 1920.
M. Sinclair, *A Defence of Idealism*, 1917.

Chapter VI

P. Bloomfield, *Imaginary Worlds*, 1932.
V. Dupont, *L'Utopie et le roman utopique dans la littérature ·· ·laise*, 1941.
J. B. S. Haldane, *Possible Worlds*, 1927.
J. Hertzler, *The History of Utopian Thought*, 1922.
Aldous Huxley, *Brave New World*, 1932.
K. Mannheim, *Ideologie und Utopie*, 1930.
Lewis Mumford, *The Story of Utopias*, 1923.
H. Ross, *Utopias Old and New*, 1938.
W. Simon, *Die Englische Utopie im Lichte der Entwicklungslehre*, 1937.

*

George Bernard Shaw, *Major Critical Essays*, Standard ed., Constable and Company, London, 1948.
— *Man and Superman*, Standard ed., Constable and Company, London, 1947.
— *Back to Methuselah*, Constable and Company, London, 1921.
— *Everybody's Political What's What?* Standard ed., Constable and Company, London, 1944.
— 'Behind the Lysenko Controversy', *The Saturday Review of Literature*, April 1949.
M. Belgion, *Our Present Philosophy of Life*, 1924.
E. Bentley, *Bernard Shaw*, 1950.
— *The Cult of the Superman*, 1947.
J. D. Bernal, 'Shaw the Scientist', in *G. B. S. 90*, 1946.
G. K. Chesterton, *George Bernard Shaw*, 1909.
H. C. Duffin, *The Quintessence of Bernard Shaw*, 1939.
A. Henderson, *Bernard Shaw, Playboy and Prophet*, 1932.
C. E. M. Joad, *Shaw*, 1949.

G. Whitehead, *Bernard Shaw Explained*, 1925.
'Shaw and Creative Evolution', *The Times Literary Supplement*, The Fiftieth Anniversary Number, January 1952.

*

Herbert George Wells, *The Time Machine*, Heinemann, 1895.
— *Tales of Space and Time*, Harper, 1899.
— *Mankind in the Making*, Chapman & Hall, 1904.
— *A Modern Utopia*, Tauchnitz, 1905.
— *The Sleeper Awakes* and *Men Like Gods*, The Literary Press, 1921.
— *The Outline of History*, Cassel, 1920.
— *The Science of Life*, (in collaboration with J.Huxley and G.P.Wells), Cassel, 1931.
— *Experiment in Autobiography*, 2 vols., Victor Gollancz and Cresset Press, 1934.
— *Star Begotten*, Chatto and Windus, London 1937.
— *The Outlook for Homo Sapiens*, R. U. and Secker & Warburg, 1942.
— *Mind at the End of its Tether*, Heinemann, 1945.
Otto Barber, *H. G. Wells' Verhältnis zum Darwinismus*, 1934.
V. Brome, *H. G. Wells, A Biography*, 1950.
G. Connes, *Étude sur la pensée de Wells*, 1926.

INDEX

474